Saudi Arabia and the Gulf Arab States Today

Library of Congress Cataloging-in-Publication Data

Maisel, Sebastian, 1970–
    Saudi Arabia and the Gulf Arab States today: an encyclopedia of life
in the Arab States / Edited by Sebastian Maisel and John A. Shoup.
        p. cm.
    Includes bibliographical references and index.
    ISBN 978-0-313-34442-8 ((set) : alk. paper) – ISBN 978-0-313-34444-2 ((vol. 1):
alk. paper) – ISBN 978-0-313-34446-6 ((vol. 2) : alk. paper)
    1. Saudi Arabia—Encyclopedias. 2. Saudi Arabia—Social life and customs.
3. Persian Gulf States—Encyclopedias. 4. Persian Gulf States—Social life and customs.
I. Shoup, John A. II. Title.
DS202.2.M35 2009
953.003—dc22   2008040737

British Library Cataloguing in Publication Data is available.

Library of Congress Catalog Card Number: 2008040737
ISBN: 978-0-313-34442-8 (set)
       978-0-313-34444-2 (Vol. 1)
       978-0-313-34446-6 (Vol. 2)

First published in 2009

Greenwood Press, 88 Post Road West, Westport, CT 06881
An imprint of Greenwood Publishing Group, Inc.
www.greenwood.com

Printed in the United States of America

∞™

The paper used in this book complies with the
Permanent Paper Standard issued by the National
Information Standards Organization (Z39.48-1984).

10 9 8 7 6 5 4 3 2 1

Contents

Alphabetical List of Entries

Alphabetical List of Entries

Topical List of Entries

CULTURE AND TRADITIONS

Arabian Horses
Arabic Language
Archaeological and Historical Sites and
    Museums
Architecture
Calendar, Islamic
Camels
Coffee: Arabic and Turkish
Coffeehouses
Cuisine
Cultural Heritage
Dance, Traditional
Death Rites
Dress
Education
Festivals in the United Arab Emirates
Film Industry
Fine Arts
Folklore
Handicrafts
Holidays and Festivals: Islamic
Holidays and Festivals: National
Incense
Janadiriyah Heritage Festival
Jewelry
Leisure
Literature: Classical and Contemporary

Material Culture
Music: Traditional and Contemporary
Religions, Non-Islamic
Sports
Universities and Higher Education

ECONOMY

Agriculture: Traditional and Commercial
Aramco
Banking and Finance
Banking, Islamic
Companies
Dates
Dhows
Economic Structures
Economies, Traditional
Hijaz Railway
Incense
Markets, Traditional
Oil
Oil Industry
Pastoralism, Nomadism, and
    Transhumance
Pearling
Saudization
Tourism

Organization of Petroleum Exporting Countries
Al Qa'idah

PEOPLE AND TRIBES

'Abd al-'Aziz b. Muhammad b. Sa'ud
'Abd al-'Aziz bin 'Abd al-Rahman Al Sa'ud
'Ajman
'Ali bin Hussein bin 'Ali
'Anazah
'Awamir
Bani Khalid
Bani Tamim
Bani Yas
Bayt Kathir
Bedouin Culture
Al Bu Sa'idi
Al Bu Shams
Dhafir
Duru'
Emir
Ethnic Groups
Ethnicity
Fahd bin 'Abd al-'Aziz
Faysal bin Abd al-Aziz
Harasis
Hashemites
Huwaytat
Intellectuals, Secular
'Isa bin Salman Al Khalifah
Jannabah
Lawrence of Arabia
Mubarak al-Sabah al-Sabah
Muhammad
Muhammad ibn 'Abd al-Wahhab
Muntafiq
Mutayr
Nabateans
Philby, Harry St. John
Qabus bin Sa'id
Qahtan
Qasimi Empire
Quraysh
Al Rashid
Sabah Al-Salim Al-Sabah
Sa'id bin Taymur Al Bu Sa'idi
Shammar
Sharif and Sayyid
Sharif Hussein bin 'Ali

Shi'ah
Social Organization, Tribal and Non-Tribal
Sulubba
Travelers and Explorers
Usamah bin Ladin
'Utaybah
Wahibah
Yamani, Ahmad Zaki
Yemen, Tribal Confederations in
Zayid bin Sultan al-Nahayan

PLACES

Abha
Abu Dhabi (City)
Abu Dhabi (Emirate)
'Ajman and Umm al-Quwayn
Arabian Gulf
Arabian Peninsula
Asir
Bahla
Bahrain
Al-Batinah
Buraydah
Dammam
Al-Dawhah
Dhahirah
Dhahran
Dhufar
Dubai
Fujayrah
Ha'il
Al-Hasa
Hijaz
Ikhwan
Jiddah
Jubayl
Kuwait
Kuwait City
Madinah
Makkah
Al-Manamah
Masqat and Suburbs
Al-Muharraq
Al Murrah
Musandam
Najd
Najran (City)
Najran (Region)
Nizwa

Topical List of Entries

Preface
John A. Shoup

Saudi Arabia and the Gulf Arab States Today: An Encyclopedia of Life in the Arab States contributes to our knowledge of the Arabian Peninsula. The main goal is to provide a reliable resource for those interested in going beyond the sensationalist headlines and who want to know more about the people, culture, traditions, and religions of the region. A team of thirteen academics and researchers from several countries in the Middle East, North Africa, and North America has written entries on a wide range of key topics.

Entries are on the countries, peoples, religions, traditions, customs, and events that have shaped the modern map of the Arabian Peninsula. Greater emphasis has been placed on the complexity of the cultures of the region, putting political and economic issues within a cultural context. Histories of the countries that make up the Gulf States (Bahrain, Kuwait, Oman, Qatar, and the United Arab Emirates) and Saudi Arabia are included in specific country entries with emphasis on the events of the last 100–150 years. For the United Arab Emirates (UAE), each of the seven individual emirates that make up the federation has its own entry in addition to the main country entry for the UAE. Although the region's history stretches back to the origins of civilization, most of the countries that now occupy the Arabian Peninsula are modern creations. Only Oman has an unbroken historical/ political identity that extends back to the early Islamic period. Saudi Arabia's oil wealth and regional strength often overshadow its smaller neighbors; thus, the country entries on the Gulf States are more detailed. Countries such as Bahrain have been important centers for trade, agriculture, and pearling for centuries.

Entries on several important people have been included. The selection of whom to include was difficult, but in the end we decided to include those who have played a significant role in the region or beyond. Furthermore, any work on the Arabian Peninsula has to include an article on the Prophet Muhammad. His legacy dictates daily life not only for the people of the Peninsula but also for all Muslims.

Most of the entries included in this encyclopedia focus on the rich cultures of the Arabian Peninsula. Too often works on the region focus on the economics (oil, investments, banking, or real estate schemes) or on the politics without much reference to the culture and traditions that influence the way the region works. Cultural content entries cover such topics as architecture, cuisine, dress, dance, and music, and the authors have attempted to include regional differences as well as note general similarities in all of them. Other entries deal with the geography and environment of the Peninsula, which have greatly influenced many of the traditional cultural expressions and regional economics.

Social organization and gender issues are covered, noting the rapid changes since the discovery and exploitation of oil. The Arabian Peninsula is often seen as a region where the tribe is the main form of sociopolitical organization. Several entries discuss individual tribal groups that are or have been significant players in the region's history. "Tribe" is a controversial concept in social science because the label has been overused to include non-tribal people. The term is used here in its strictly anthropological meaning and where the people refer to themselves in Arabic as a *qabilah* or *'ashirah*. "Tribe" is a convenience for researchers giving a framework to understand the complex and sometimes bewildering kinship connections between lineages and their perceived obligations to each other. Leadership is usually weak and most tribal "leaders" are unable to give orders but can suggest and lead by example or use the power of rhetoric to convince others to agree with their point of view. A "powerful" tribal leader is one who is seen to be just in his decisions and who puts the welfare of the people before himself and his immediate family. Traditional concepts such as honor have their own entries in this encyclopedia. The authors have attempted to explain gender and gender issues (not only as they pertain to women) through local culture. No attempt is made to excuse attitudes or customs that seem prejudicial to an outsider, but to give a better understanding of local perspectives. Travelers to the region are often confused by the different attitudes encountered between those of Saudis and others in the Gulf, although they may spring from the same forms of Islam.

The Gulf Arab States discussed include Saudi Arabia, Bahrain, Qatar, the UAE, Kuwait, Oman, and to some degree Yemen. Yemen is part of the Arabian Peninsula, but it can be argued that it has its own special history and culture. Yemen has been as much a part of the Horn of Africa as it has the Arabian Peninsula. Yemen developed a form of Southern Arabic and Southern Arabian script that has been replaced by the Northern Arabian script with the emergence of Islam, although there are still isolated pockets where Southern Arabic is spoken. In a work on the Arabian Peninsula, something about Yemen must be included, but the focus of this volume is on Saudi Arabia and the Gulf States. It can be argued that Oman is also not really a Gulf State because it does not border the Arabian/Persian Gulf, but it does share a history and culture with the UAE, which used to be included in the general area referred to as Oman, and it is a member of the Gulf Cooperation Council, unlike Yemen.

Readers can find entries of interest quickly in the front matter alphabetical list of entries and topical list of entries. Text that appears in **bold** type within the entries indicates another entry in the encyclopedia. The entries typically conclude with further reading. We have limited these sources to English-language materials, although some are published outside of the United Kingdom and the United States and the contributors certainly consulted non-English sources at times. The selected bibliography is also largely limited to English-language sources for this audience. A note on transliteration from Arabic and a chronology of Arab Gulf history are also found in the front matter.

Acknowledgments

Without team effort this book would not be possible. I would like to express my greatest thanks and gratitude to the many people who helped shape this book and helped shape me in writing it with their support, knowledge, and criticism. While extending my appreciation to all of them, I would like to thank a few of those in particular. First, I would like to thank Wendi Schnaufer of Greenwood Press for her constant, patient, and cheerful assistance. I wish to thank my colleagues and friends, Professors Majd al-Mallah, Grand Valley State University, and Eckehard Schulz, Leipzig University, for the advice and support they extended to me. David Long, a great friend and mentor, himself a distinguished author and teacher on the Middle East, deserves my sincere thanks for his continuous encouragement and help in numerous ways that significantly influenced my understanding of the people of Arabia. I would like to thank my co-editor John A. Shoup for being a fabulous person to work with on this book. And finally, special thanks go to my wife, Shannon, who has been my unwavering supporter, inspiration, and critic. Without her consistent love and help, and that of my daughters Fiona and Sophia, this project would have been impossible to finish.

Sebastian Maisel
Grand Valley State University
Allendale, Michigan

Acknowledgments

It is difficult to know where to begin in thanking the many people who have contributed to this work. I would like to begin with thanking Wendi Schnaufer of Greenwood Publishing Group, who has been an excellent working partner for the third time, although we have never met except by e-mail. I would also like to thank the other major contributor to this work, Sebastian Maisel, who took on the major share of the writing. I would like to thank all of the people who have contributed articles and shared their expertise, but I would like to add a special word of thanks to Carla Higgins, who has hosted me numerous times in the UAE and Egypt. Carla introduced me to much of the Gulf culture while traveling with me in the UAE and Oman.

I would like to thank several of my professors from when I was a student studying Arabic and Middle Eastern courses: the late Dr. 'Aziz 'Atiyah, who was a great historian; Dr. Philip Hammond, who is an archeologist and enthusiast of Bedouin culture; and Dr. John Bennett, who is, in my opinion, *the* expert on development issues. I would like to thank Dr. Donald Cole, whose book *Bedouin of the Bedouin* greatly influenced my research interests in the Bedouin. I would also like to mention Dr. Soraya Alturki, the first Saudi woman to earn a PhD in anthropology. I assign many of her writings in my classes. I had the great pleasure of knowing them both while at the American University in Cairo.

I would like to make special mention of several good friends from Saudi Arabia and the Gulf who shared much of their culture with me while we were all students. I would like to begin by thanking 'Abd al-Muhsin al-Dughaither and Ibrahim 'Awamir, who introduced me to Saudi music and food. Khalid al-Dughaither forced me to speak Arabic, and I owe my abilities in the language to him. Muhammad al-Bukhari gave me a better insight into the intellectual life of the region. Dawud Khamis, as a friend, helped sponsor my visa for my first visit to a Gulf country (Kuwait) in 1979, shortly after the fall of the Shah of Iran. At that time, many Iranians were trying to escape the Islamic Revolution via Kuwait, and the place had the feel of a spy novel. I would also like to thank 'Abbas Bafikih, Balqis al-Najjar, 'Abdallah al-Ghazali, Muhammad Aba Husayn, Khalid Tarrah, Talal al-Fatayhi, and all of the others who invited me into their homes and lives when they were students in the United States. The list is long, and if I have not mentioned a name specifically it is only because I do not have the space here to list you all. I want to thank you all for your kindness—and letting me as a non-Arab be a member of the University of Utah Arab Students' Association.

Special mention must be made of my former student at the American University in Cairo and now good friend *Shaykh* Ma'an al Baroudy Al Khalifah. *Shaykh* Ma'an took the time to show me around the major sites of modern Bahraini history, including historic homes of the Al Khalifah family. His generosity during my visits to Bahrain is always overwhelming. *Shaykh* Ma'an introduced me to Dr. 'Abdallah Yateem, one of the first anthropologists from the region; Dr. Yateem and I maintain good contact. I invited him to contribute to this encyclopedia, but he was unable to do so because of other commitments.

There are many more people I would like to thank for many experiences I have had over the years in the Arab world. Some of the smaller incidents have stuck in my mind, such as the two Bedouin from Saudi Arabia who, seeing me walking in the August heat of Kuwait, refused to let me walk and insisted they take me wherever I wanted to go—even to museums. They stopped by the hotel where I was staying every evening to ask if my Kuwaiti friends were coming to pick me up and, if not, I was to spend the evening with them because no one should be alone in a foreign country.

Finally, I would like to thank my parents, Mr. and Mrs. John A. Shoup. My mother's love for Arabian horses began while she was a teenager, and as a result, our house had several books about them. Growing up with Arabian horses was a major influence on my desire to visit the Middle East and to learn Arabic. Both of my parents are now gone. I would also like to thank my youngest sister, Heather, for her constant and unwavering support.

John A. Shoup
Al Akhawayn University
Ifrane, Morocco

Introduction
John A. Shoup

The peoples, cultures, religions, and history of the Arabian Peninsula remain greatly unknown to most people in the West despite the long history of interaction between these two parts of the world. Stereotypes of suppressed and veiled women living in secluded *harim*s (harems); religious fundamentalists who want to wage holy war to destroy Western democracy; greedy and corrupt "oil *shaykh*" (shiekhs) living decadent lives underneath the cover of religious piety; or romanticized images of Bedouin tents and camels are the usual mental images that immediately come to mind when hearing such words as Arabs, Saudi Arabia, or the Persian Gulf. These stereotypes are supported by sensationalist news coverage and by Hollywood films. Conditions in Saudi Arabia are too frequently generalized to not only the other Gulf countries, but also the entire Arab or even Muslim world. Although there sometimes may be some basis for the stereotypes, they are only that, stereotypes, and far from the full picture of the Gulf countries and Saudi Arabia.

ARABIA AND THE BEDOUIN

There is a Western fascination with the Bedouin of Arabia, a complex in fact often called the "Lawrence Complex" after the World War I British agent, T. E. Lawrence, the famous Lawrence of Arabia. The romantic image of Bedouin in graceful flowing robes, tents, and camels is hard to dispel, even among some who have actually had the chance to do fieldwork among Bedouin. Part of the appeal is that nomadic pastoralism has gone through massive changes since 1918, including the introduction of trucks, and there is nostalgia for the way it used to be. For many in the West, the Hollywood film *Lawrence of Arabia* (1962) has had a greater impact than the written work by Lawrence himself, *Seven Pillars of Wisdom* (first printed in 1935—the year of his death). *Lawrence of Arabia* was at least filmed in Jordan and Morocco and used authentic Bedouin equipment and

Bedouin as extras, but other ethnographic as well as historical detail is far from accurate. The anthropologist Steven Caton's 1999 publication *Lawrence of Arabia: A Film's Anthropology* delves into the appeal of the David Lean epic as well as the lure of the Lawrence Complex. A more recent film, *Hidalgo* (2004), also filmed in Morocco and supposedly depicting the Arabian Peninsula, continues the same images of the Arab Bedouin: tents, flowing robes, and sand dunes. *Hidalgo* provides dialog in Arabic (classical) and develops the character of at least one Arab woman even if most of the cultural/ethnographic/historical detail is fictional. The Lawrence Complex is greatly influential and is often cited as the reason why many students became interested in Middle Eastern studies.

THE UNITED STATES AND THE PENINSULA

Americans have been deeply involved in the Arabian Peninsula since the first explorations for oil in Saudi Arabia in the 1930s. The United States has been an important political player in the region since the end of World War II and the creation of Israel in 1948. American presidents since Franklin Delano Roosevelt have needed to have Middle Eastern foreign policies that balance good relations with the Arab states with what the United States said was its moral obligation to Israel. Arab leaders such as King 'Abd al-'Aziz ibn Sa'ud of Saudi Arabia were confused by the Americans when it seemed to them that the expulsion of Palestinians from their homeland was a moral injustice no different from the moral injustices Jews suffered in Europe. King 'Abd al-'Aziz's confusion about America's "moral" responsibilities in the region best characterize the position of Arab Gulf leaders still today. Although the United States seemed to be a "natural" ally against the spread of communism in the 1950s and 1960s, its unconditional support for Israel was difficult to understand.

Confusion and misunderstanding seem to continue to characterize the relationships between the Gulf States and the West, especially with the United States. Although American academic institutions have excellent programs in Middle Eastern, Islamic, and Arabic language studies, they have not dispelled the "mystery" of the region or been able to diminish the stereotypes held by the general public. The U.S. government has responded to certain periods of crisis by encouraging Middle Eastern studies, such as immediately after the 1973 oil embargo, the 1979 Islamic Revolution in Iran, and more recently after 9/11, but it has not sustained its interest and properly funded positions in Middle Eastern studies and Arabic language in U.S. universities. More importantly, materials prepared for high school and junior high school instruction contain very little about the region and its people.

It is of supreme importance that Americans in particular, but people in the West in general, better understand both Arabs and Islam. Greenwood's series *Culture and Customs of the Middle East*, written by experts, is helping to fill the information void with well-rounded texts on specific countries of the region. This encyclopedia helps in a similar way, providing a quick reference not only for the general readership but also for experts in Middle Eastern studies.

LAND, ENVIRONMENT, AND TRADITIONAL ECONOMICS

The Arabian Peninsula is called *Jazirat al-'Arab*, or the Island of the Arabs, because the Nafud Desert and Wadi Sirhan effectively separate it from the Syrian Desert and make it an "island." It is a huge region about half the size of the continental United States, and the Rub' al-Khali Desert alone, which occupies about one-third of Saudi Arabia's southeast, is the size of France. It is often difficult to imagine the immense size of the Peninsula and the fact that there are no permanent streams or lakes even in the high mountains of Yemen. The Peninsula's arid climate is subject to cold fronts from the Mediterranean and from the Caspian Sea and Central Asia in the winter that bring rain and occasional snow to the northern part, whereas the southern part receives rain in the summer, catching the monsoons as they move across the Indian Ocean from the Ethiopian Highlands to India. Although generally speaking the overall climate is arid, certain coastal regions have high humidity. People have adjusted to the climate by adopting several distinct architectural styles to best deal with specific problems.

Water is a major issue for the people living in the Arabian Peninsula. Arabs from the Peninsula often joke that water costs more than gasoline. Water has dictated the traditional economics as well as greatly limited the areas that can be utilized; more than 80% of the Peninsula is desert. Permanent sources of water such as springs have long been owned either by lineages or by individuals, and no settlements are possible without permanent water. Oases have been developed using sophisticated irrigation systems such as underground water channels called *aflaj*. Until the discovery of oil, date production formed one of the four important economic activities in the Arabian Peninsula, because dates can grow in salty water and high temperatures.

The arid nature of the Arabian Peninsula has given rise to the second major economic activity, pastoral nomadism. Domestication of the camel around 1500 BC allowed a greater part of the desert to be used. Camels can go up to twenty-one days without water, whereas other livestock raised in the Peninsula such as sheep, goats, and cattle need water on a daily basis. The camel serves not only as the economic base but also is one of the cultural bases for the Bedouin. Bedouin divide themselves into the "noble, great" tribes who raise camels and "lesser" tribes whose economies have traditionally been based on sheep, goats, and cattle. Bedouins came to dominate much of the region politically and culturally, although they have rarely been more than 10% of the total population of the Peninsula. Cultural ideals of generosity and hospitality are thought of in the context of the sixth-century Bedouin poet Hatim al-Tayy, who as a boy sacrificed his father's entire herd of camels to feed guests. Hatim's generosity has become legendary for all Arabs, not only for those in the Arabian Peninsula. Other cultural ideals of proper behavior for both men and women are judged against the Bedouin hero and pre-Islamic poet 'Antar bin Shadad and his beloved cousin 'Ablah bint Malik. Even the idea of "proper Arabic" is judged against the "purity" of Bedouin speech, and poetry as an art is still thought of as a Bedouin art.

The desert gave rise to two of the main pre-oil types of living in the Peninsula, oasis agriculture and pastoral nomadism, but the Peninsula is surrounded on three sides by the sea. Arabs of the Peninsula not only developed means of survival in this hostile desert climate but also developed effective means of utilizing the sea, the third major economic activity. Oman, for example, has a long history of seafaring and was able to establish a large empire in East Africa and along the Gulf coast of what is today Pakistan. Omanis defeated the Portuguese and forced them out of the Indian Ocean in the 17th century. It is held that the inspiration for the story character of Sinbad the Sailor was derived from Omani sea captains from Salalah, who dominated much of the sea trade to the Spice Islands and China in the classical Islamic period. Omani and Gulf merchant families competed with those from Iraq, Iran, and India in the long-distance sea trade connecting the East Indies with East Africa and the Middle East. In the 19th and early 20th centuries pearling became an important part of the Gulf economy, bringing families from India and Iran to the Gulf emirates. Kuwait, Bahrain, and Oman still have active shipbuilding yards, although demand for the various types of dhows has decreased.

The combination of sea navigation and traveling through the desert helped establish the fourth major part of the Peninsula's pre-oil economy: trade. Arabs of the Peninsula conveyed expensive commodities from the east to the Mediterranean along with two items grown in Yemen and Oman: coffee and frankincense. Long-distance trade gave rise to several important pre-Islamic kingdoms in Syria-Jordan such as the Nabateans of Petra and more importantly for the modern world, the Quraysh of Makkah. The Prophet Muhammad was a member of the Quraysh tribe and worked in the long-distance trade taking merchandise to Syria. It was during these trips to Syria that, according to Muslim sources, two Christian monks recognized him as the last of God's prophets long before God called him to his service. Islam has a favorable attitude toward commerce, and Islamic law has developed several rules and regulations about ethical business practices.

ISLAM

The seventh-century Prophet Muhammad is one of the most influential men who has ever lived. Islam is the religion of more than one-quarter of all mankind. For Muslims, Muhammad's actions and sayings still hold weight in the everyday actions and sayings of believers. The humility, generosity, and love of man as demonstrated by the Prophet are the model for all Muslims today. Divisions in the Islamic community after the death of the Prophet into what have emerged as Sunni, Shi'i, and Kharaji forms are found among Muslims living on the Peninsula. Much of the difference has to do with disagreements over legitimacy of succession to the Prophet as head of the Muslim community, which have further divided over issues of law and legal procedures. Nonetheless, basic practices such as prayer, fasting during the month of *Ramadan*, and pilgrimage to Makkah are all held in common.

Western perceptions of Islam and popular stereotyping of the religion are perhaps the most important sources of continued misunderstanding. This is best illustrated when in 2008 the Archbishop of Canterbury suggested that the British parliament legalize aspects of personal law found in the *Shari'ah* or Islamic law for the country's growing Muslim community. What he was referring to are issues of marriage, divorce, inheritance, and the like that had already been legalized for Britain's Jews and are de facto practiced by many of the country's Muslims. The immediate outcry from the press was that Britain would be sanctioning stonings, whippings, and beheadings—not at all what the Archbishop had proposed. Such a response shows how little the general public knows about Islam and Islamic law—and the fear generated by the headlines of sensationalist press coverage of application of certain laws in Saudi Arabia, Taliban Afghanistan, or conservative areas of Pakistan or Nigeria. Such ultraconservative practices are not part of most Muslim countries today and are not that common even in Saudi Arabia.

Islam, like the other great world religions, teaches a universalism. In many ways Islam is closer to Judaism because legal codes based on religion regulate the way people are to live. Islam is tolerant of non-Muslims and legalized the interactions between non-Muslim communities with the Islamic state. The expansion of Islam into first the Middle Eastern provinces of the Byzantines and then Sasanid Iran brought large numbers of non-Muslim subjects to the new empire. The seat of government moved from Madinah to Damascus and then to Baghdad, and the Arabs of the Peninsula faded into the background as new Syrian, Egyptian, Berber, Persian, and Turkish dynasties emerged to rule parts of the empire.

The Arabs of the Peninsula who had spread Islam from the borders of China in the east and to the Atlantic Ocean in the west lost their importance in the large multi-ethnic empire they had created. Occasionally they would burst forth again, supporting egalitarian reform movements such as the Shi'ite Qaramitah in the ninth century or the Sunni Wahhabis that emerged in the 18th century and form the legal base for Saudi Arabia, Qatar, and the United Arab Emirates today.

Among the main stereotypes of Arabs and Muslims is the seclusion of women, and no one thing seems to annoy Westerners more than the veil. Veiling is an urban phenomenon and as a concept was borrowed from the urban elite of the Byzantine and Sasanid Empires where it had been a means to distinguish women of the higher classes from the poor. It is known that the Prophet's wives were veiled, but it can be debated what this meant. The Prophet's wife 'A'ishah led an army of rebellion against 'Ali ibn Abi Talib and from atop her camel gave inspiration to her army during battle. Various traditions mention her showing her face to let her men know that she was still commanding. Veiling can mean the complete cover or *munaqabah*—head to toe—or to wear a scarf or *hijab* to cover the hair. As such, the Muslim world has a wide variety of traditional garments that have developed to cover women in a "decency" or "modesty" garb. Such garments vary in not only the need to deal with climate but also class—women of the upper classes being able to afford massive amounts of fine-quality cloth with no need to have their hands and faces free for work.

For Westerners the veil is the sign of women's submission and oppression by patriarchal society, and it is believed that women will not be freed until they are unveiled. For many Muslim women the veil is a sign of coming of age—becoming an adult woman and therefore marking a woman's status in society. The veil expresses the need for respect for women as members of the Muslim community—and certainly is not a sign of their oppression. Studies of veiling among women working in public service offices in Egypt, for example, note that wearing the veil brings respect from men—and gives women a social space. It serves as a means to protect women from both verbal and physical harassment. Other anthropologists have noted that veiled women like the anonymity the veil can give them, and perhaps surprising to many in the West, the freedom of movement. A veiled woman is able to move about unrecognized (by men) and interact with strangers without compromising important personal and family honor.

Muslim women are often annoyed by the fact that Westerners focus on the garment and what it means in a Western context and do not look at the legal rights women have in Islam. Women have rights to personal property and income husbands cannot touch without a woman's permission. Women have always been involved in business—Khadijah, the first wife of the Prophet, was herself a wealthy merchant. Women had rights to inheritance when in the West women could only inherit if they had male guarantors (thus the basis for many Jane Austen novels). Muslim women have always had rights to initiate divorce, although is not easy to do. In Saudi Arabia a woman can write the right to divorce her husband (called *'ismah*) into the wedding contract before marriage.

Women in Saudi Arabia are not allowed to drive cars but do have the right to buy and own them. Since the 1990s Saudi women—and there are Saudi feminists—have protested this law by occasionally organizing to publicly break it. They can point to the women in all of the rest of the Arab and Islamic world who have been driving since the first importations of cars. They have even been successful in getting a ruling from the *'ulama'* stating that there is no Islamic reason for women to not be allowed to drive. The law is now more and more described as "cultural" and will be changed once Saudi society is "better able" to deal with women as drivers. The law is not part of the personal status codes, which are based on Islamic law, but is part of tradition. Initially the law was seen by Saudi men as a means of protecting the honor of the woman and her family, but today it is seen more and more as a hindrance to women's employment.

Another issue based in tradition and not supported by Islamic law is honor crime, in which a woman is killed for damaging the honor of the family. Honor crime is not unique to the Arabian Peninsula but is widespread in the Mediterranean region often called the "Patriarchal Belt." Honor crime is part of tradition, and Islamic law condemns such crimes as murder. However, for many in the region, the act of harming family honor is greater than the rights of any one person, and honor can only be restored by the death of the one who caused the family shame. Jordan is the only country in the Arab world dealing openly with the issue, and recently the Jordanian Parliament passed harsher laws to punish the men who are convicted of an honor crime. Jordan remains unique; no other country in the region is willing to openly talk about honor crimes.

Restrictions on women's rights to hold passports or to travel without the written permission of male relatives are widespread beyond only Saudi Arabia and the Gulf States. Many Muslim countries have the same laws but exercise a degree of tolerance depending on a particular woman's economic and social status. Such laws are based on Islamic principles whereby men are held responsible for the women of their family. They are part of the personal status codes that in all Muslim countries are based primarily on *Shar'iah*. Differences in how *Shar'iah* is applied has to do with the different legal schools or *madhahib* among Sunnis, Shi'ites, and Kharajis. According to Westerners, some of these legal schools are more "liberal" than others, meaning women may have more defined freedoms in one than in another.

Women's rights to child custody are also part of the personal status codes and are rooted in *Shar'iah*. For many Westerners the woman's limited rights seem unfair, but in the Arab and Islamic world children carry the name and even nationality of their father (not their mother), and thus it is seen as right and proper that the father take care of them. Fathers can give up their right to custody before a judge or a judge may deem him unfit in the role of father and grant custody to the mother. In most cases women's rights to custody are set by the age and gender of the child—boys needing to be with their fathers earlier than girls who need to learn skills from their mothers.

Muslim feminists point to these kinds of issues that touch on women's legal rights in Islam as being far more important than the issue of veiling or driving a car. The *Shar'iah* is not stagnant and unchanging but can be modified given new social, economic, and political conditions. Women have obtained the right to vote in Bahrain and have won similar rights in Kuwait. Women's political participation can be framed within Islam and does not have to be seen as a challenge to Islamic principles. For many Muslim feminists the issue is not that women do not have rights, but that women do not exercise their rights mainly because they are unaware of them. Women will become more active members of their own society once they are educated and understand what their rights are.

SOCIAL ORGANIZATION

Social equality as taught by Islam did not alter the social organization of most Arabs in the Peninsula. With few urban centers rarely touched by strong central governments, tribe remained an important means of organization for practical economic as well as political concerns for the Bedouin. A tribe is usually defined as a kin-based sociopolitical organization with weak leadership. Leaders lead by example and persuasion but are not able to force compliance because all members of the same tribe are equal (outsiders, especially non-tribal people, are not seen to be equals). "Nobility" is based on knowledge of descent from an ancestor who lived before the time of the Prophet. For Arab tribes this ancestor either traces to Qahtan, the Biblical Yoktan or Joktan (southern), or to Isma'il, the Biblical Ishmael (northern). Studies of tribes in much of the Arab world have greatly dispelled the long-held theory referred to as Segmentary Lineage Organization. Tribes are often unpredictable in their actions, which are often exceptions to the rule. Segmentary Lineage Organization does provide a useful tool for researchers in establishing connection between lineages and what should be the obligations or responsibilities of the individual to the group, but it can be argued whether it has further use. In some instances tribal political elite, especially once settled, have frequently tried to maintain political control, adding to their personal wealth by acquiring land or interests in trade. Today, many of the modern Gulf States were established by tribal political elite who maintain themselves by alliances with other tribal political and non-tribal economic elite. Tribal connections can be helpful even today in accessing jobs, especially in government service.

Although the rhetoric of many in the Arabian Peninsula may make use of cultural ideals of tribe, actual practice is often far from the way tribe is supposed to work; the problems between verbalized "ideal" and practiced "real" cause confusion for many Westerners.

Many people in the Arabian Peninsula are not organized into tribes, but the extended family is the most important form of social organization. As noted before, the Arabian Peninsula is part of a region referred to in many anthropological texts as the "Patriarchal Belt." This region includes the entire Mediterranean and the Middle East. The modern Arab family is quickly changing, but the ideal is still centered on the head of household who controls the lives of all others living with him, perhaps best typified in the character of *Ahmad 'Abd al-Gawad*, who is called *Si Sayyid* (meaning more or less Lord and Master) in the Najib Mahfuz novel *Bayn al-Qasrayn*, or *Palace Walk* (1946). The character *Si Sayyid* was played so skillfully by the Egyptian actor Yahya Shahin in the 1964 film based on the novel that for most Arabs the film's character *is Si Sayyid*. The head of the household dictates to the others and most interactions are in the form of orders from him to the others to obey. He is concerned with the honor of the family as a whole and it is his ability to "control" the others that notes whether the family will be judged as "good" or "bad." Behavior that could damage the good name of the family must be punished quickly, and rules are much harsher for girls than for boys. The inability to control his family is seen as a mark of general poor manners, and even bad morals.

Women hold the weakest position in a patriarchal society. Women gain power within the structure by producing sons. Mothers gain greater say and status in a family with the number of sons they have—sons they can count on to even challenge their father if need be. Bonds between mothers and sons are strong, stronger than between fathers and sons where the need to demonstrate manliness may put sons into conflict with fathers. Bonds between brothers and sisters are often the strongest of all. Sisters count on the support of their brothers even after marriage; brothers protect their sisters from abusive husbands, and no husband can prevent his wife from visiting her brothers.

The patriarch gives commands, but women can soften or even change them. Women do not generally challenge orders openly but use a time when they can privately appeal to reason. The strongest patriarch is still responsible to his mother, and should she not agree with one of his decisions, he is most likely to change it. Wives, especially mothers of adult sons, are also powerful behind the scenes and are able to effect changes in his decisions. If need be, a woman can involve her sons and brothers in action against her husband, forcing him to change his mind, but rarely does she do this in such a way as to openly challenge his position as head of household. The traditional family structure is feeling the pressure as more and more men and women are university-educated and seeking their own careers away from the family.

CONCLUDING THOUGHTS

As noted, education in the West in general has not included much information on the Arabs or Islam. It would be hard to find a social science, history, or world literature textbook with more than a chapter on the region. However, one can say much the same for the lack of much information about the West in the textbooks used by many of the public schools in the Arabian Peninsula. The exception would be the numerous private schools in Kuwait, Bahrain, and the United Arab Emirates. Many Arabs hold stereotypes of the West formed from watching American and European television series, Hollywood films, or music videos. Unless they have been able to travel or study in the West, these are the lasting images of Western society. The problem of poor textbooks is being addressed in countries such as Saudi Arabia, whose government was shocked in 2001 by the lack of knowledge demonstrated by their graduates and the fact that many of their teachers were choosing to not cover materials in the texts they had.

The Internet has made access to information much easier, but it has not made it easy to find quality information. The aim here is to provide quality information as well as references for further reading where topics can be explored in greater detail. The contributors to this encyclopedia hope that the information they have provided will help serve to give a better understanding to the peoples, cultures, traditions, and religions of the Arabian Peninsula.

Note on Transliteration
John A. Shoup

Transliteration of Arabic into Latin script is difficult, and several different methods have been developed over the years for German, French, English, and other European languages. This volume generally uses the system devised by the U.S. Library of Congress, which is the most accepted method of Arabic transliteration in North America.

The Arabic alphabet is composed of twenty-eight consonants and semi-consonants. The Arabic letter 'ayn is noted as ', and the hamzah (or glottal stop) is noted as '. The letter ghayn is written as *gh*; kha as *kh*. Arabic has several "double letters," a normal letter and an emphatic form. Thus, there is *d* and emphatic *d*; *dh* and emphatic *dh*, which is frequently written as *z*; *h* and emphatic *h*; *s* and emphatic *s*; and *t* and emphatic *t*. In the Library of Congress system the emphatic forms have a . underneath them, but this takes a special keyboard and typesetting; therefore, in this volume the distinctions have not been made. In addition, Arabic letters are divided into "sun" or *shamsi* and "moon" or *qamari* according to how they are pronounced when the definite article *al* is placed in front. When the *lam* or *l* of the definite article is elided into the first letter of the main word such as *ash-shams*, the letter is a *shamsi* letter, and when it is not as in *al-qamar*, it is a *qamari* letter. The Library of Congress system does not note pronunciation, and all words and names with the definite article are written *al-* as in *al-shams*.

Arabic has only three vowels: *a*, *i*, and *u*; the vowels *e* and *o* do not exist. Short vowels are marked by *harakat* or diacritical marks called *fathah* for *a*, *dammah* for *u*, and *kasrah* for *i*. Short vowels are rarely shown in most Arabic texts because the language works on a root system with ten regular means to expand the root into numerous nuances of meaning. In addition, there are three semi-consonants: *alif*, *waw*, and *yah*. These correspond to long *a*, *u*, and *i* when they are used as vowels. When they are consonants, *waw* corresponds to *w* and *yah* to *y*. An *alif* can take a *hamzah* riding above making the sound *u*; for example, in the name *Usamah*. It can also take one underneath, changing the sound to *i* such as in the word *Inglizi*, meaning English. There are two other diacritical markers: the *sukun*, where no vowel is pronounced, and *shaddah*, which notes the letter is to be doubled.

There are two diphthongs in Arabic: *ay* and *aw*. The *ay* is often popularly transliterated as *ai*, and although this is acceptable, the Library of Congress system uses *ay* because it is closer to the letters in Arabic.

In most cases, people are listed by first names—not by family names—because, in the Middle East, most people refer to others by first names, and family names can be that of a large tribal group and therefore are rather meaningless. Most people, if they need to be more specific, include the father's names, e.g., Muhammad *ibn* 'Abd al-Wahhab (Muhammad, *son* of 'Abd al-Wahhab). Thus, Muhammad ibn 'Abd al-Wahhab is found under M and 'Abd al-'Aziz ibn Al Sa'ud under A.

Titles such as *Sultan*, *Khalifah*, *Amir*, and *Shaykh* are italicized in the text. *Sultan* means the person who holds real political power, or *sultah*, and emerged as a political title when the *Khalifah* began to lose control over the political affairs of state. *Khalifah* means successor and as a political title emerged following the death of the Prophet Muhammad. The word has come into English as Caliph. The *Khalifah* held the *Khilafah* or successor ship to the Prophet. *Khilafah* refers to the Caliphate. *Shaykh* has a number of uses. It can be used as a term of respect for an older man, as a title for the leader of a tribe, a proper title for members of ruling families in the Gulf, and a title for a learned man of religion. *Amir* also has a number of uses meaning a military commander (someone who gives orders or *amr*) and more frequently today a prince. However, Sultan, Amir, and Khalifah are proper men's names, and when they are names rather than titles in this encyclopedia (as they are in this sentence), they are not italicized. In some countries, such as Oman, where the head of state has usually been called a *Sultan*, Sultan is also a common name; thus, it is possible to have *Sultan* Sultan. *Khalifah* is not only a man's first name, but the ruling family of Bahrain is the Al Khalifah. For these reasons it is necessary to distinguish when the word is a proper title and when it is a proper name.

Chronology

ANTIQUITY

5000–3500 BC (Neolithic)	Beginnings of agriculture and settled life
3200–330 BC	Dilmun civilization in Bahrain
3000 BC	Magan civilization in Oman supplies Mesopotamia with copper ore
750–115 BC	Sabaean Kingdom in Yemen
600–500 BC	Persia establishes authority over much of Oman
400–300 BC	Nabatean Arabs are established in southern Jordan and northwest Saudi Arabia
400–200 BC	Conquest of parts of Ethiopia by Yemenis and rise of Ethiopian Kingdom of Aksum
330 BC–622 AD	Tylos Hellenistic civilization on Bahrain
321 BC	Nabateans defeat Antigonus I Monophtlamus' attempt to include them in Hellenistic Syria
300 BC–200 AD	Hellenistic civilization on Faylakah Island off Kuwait (Faylakah is called Ikaros in Greek)
115 BC–40 AD	Height of the Nabatean kingdom in Jordan—Petra its capital city
115 BC–300 AD	Himyarite kingdom in Yemen
106	Nabatean Kingdom annexed by the Roman Emperor, Trajan
226–640	The Arab Bani Azd tribe gains control over most of Oman, slowly pushing Persians toward the coast

200–300	Bahrain accepts Christianity and eventually there are five Nestorian bishoprics on the island and the nearby Gulf coast
300	Rise of the second Himyarite kingdom; both Christianity and Judaism spread in the kingdom
330	King Ezana of Aksum converts to Christianity
400–500	Rise of Ghassanid Kingdom in Syria, allies of Byzantium; the Lakhamid Kingdom in Iraq, allies of the Persians; Kingdom of Kindah in Central Arabia dominates much of the Peninsula, allies with Byzantium against Persia in 530, but collapses in the second half of the sixth century
522	Ethiopia conquers Yemen
529	Lakhamid King Mundhir III kills King Hujr of Kindah and most of the Royal House, ending the Kingdom of Kindah; Prince Imru' al-Qays begins attempt to avenge his family and take back Kindah
531–578	Sasanian King Khosrow Anushirvan withdraws from most of Oman, keeping the important port city of Suhar (Sohar)
538	Massacre of the Christians of Najran by Jewish king of Yemen, Dhu Nuwas
535	Ethiopia begins to expand from Yemen into Central Arabia
540	Death of the last Prince of Kindah, the poet Imru' al-Qays

EARLY ISLAMIC PERIOD

570	Approximate date for the birth of the Prophet Muhammad; Ethiopia attempts to conquer the Hijaz
572	The Persian Sasanids expel the Ethiopians from Yemen and briefly rule both Oman and Yemen
610	First revelation to the Prophet Muhammad
615	The Prophet Muhammad sends a number of Muslims to the safety of the Christian king of Ethiopia
622	*Hijrah*, or migration from Makkah to Madinah
629	Bahrain's Christian ruler al-Mundhir ibn Sawa al-Tamimi accepts Islam
630	Makkah taken without a fight by Muslim forces; 'Amr ibn al-'As brings Islam to Oman
632	Death of the Prophet Muhammad
632–661	Rightly Guided *Khalifah*s; 632–633 wars of *Riddah* and final establishment of Islam throughout the Arabian Peninsula
661–750	Umayyad Dynasty rules from Damascus; expansion of the Islamic empire in North Africa and Spain in the west and into Pakistan, Afghanistan, and Central Asia in the east

684	Foundation of *Ibadi Kharajism* in Basrah, Iraq
750	Founding of the 'Abbasid dynasty replacing the Umayyads. Capital is moved from Syria to Iraq; election of al-Julandi ibn Mas'ud as first Ibadi *Imam* in Oman; establishes first independent dynasty of Oman, the Julandah, which lasts until 1435
793	Nizwa's main mosque first used for the election of the Ibadi *Imam*; used ever since
874	(?) Rise of the Isma'ili (Shi'ite) Qaramitah movement
886	Qaramitah established in Bahrain and Gulf coast
930	Qaramitah attack and take Makkah, carrying away the Black Stone[1] from the Ka'abah
951	Qaramitah return the Black Stone
973	Fatamids (Isma'ili) found Cairo as the capital of their rival Caliphate
988	Most of the Qaramitah communities are absorbed into the Fatamid state
1037–1138	Sulayhids rule Yemen
1154–1406	Nabahani dynasty rules much of Oman
1077	Sunni Saljuq Turkish forces bring a final end to the Qaramitah state in Bahrain

AYYUBID AND MAMLUK PERIODS

1174–1249	Ayyubids of Egypt rule the Hijaz
1181–1229	Ayyubids rule Yemen
1182	Crusader leader Renaud de Chatillon organizes a fleet to raid down the Red Sea coast, intent on attacking Makkah
1183	Fleet is caught and destroyed by Muslim fleet, and the survivors are sold into slavery in Egypt
1229–1451	Rasulid dynasty rules Yemen
1248–1517	Mamluks of Egypt rule the Hijaz
1258	Fall of 'Abbasid capital in Baghdad to the Mongols under Hülegü Khan
1260	Mamluks defeat Mongols at 'Ayn Jalut in Palestine
1435–1624	Oman ruled by a series of elected *Imams* who do not establish rule by one family

---

[1]The Black Stone was presented to Ibrahim (Abraham) by the archangel Jabra'il (Gabriel) when the Ka'abah was first built and is placed as a corner stone. It has subsequently been replaced each time the Ka'abah has been rebuilt. It is considered a special sign between man and God.

OTTOMANS AND PORTUGUESE

1507	Portuguese occupy Hormuz on the Iranian side of the Straights of Hormuz; Portuguese build forts at Masqat
1515	Portuguese occupy Julfar (near present day Ra's al-Khaymah)
1516	Ottomans defeat Mamluks near Aleppo and annex Syria (including today's Lebanon, Palestine, and Jordan)
1517	Ottomans defeat Mamluks near Cairo and annex Egypt and the Hijaz
1521	Portuguese occupy Bahrain
1530	First Ottoman occupation of al-Hasa
1550	Turkish fleet briefly takes the Portuguese forts in Oman
1581	Turkish fleet again takes the Portuguese forts, but again do not stay
1591	Bahrain joined to the Ottoman province based in al-Hasa
1592–1962	Zayidi *Imam*s rule North Yemen
1602	Bahrain comes under the Shah of Iran
1622	Portuguese lose Hormuz
1624–1741	Ya'rubah dynasty established in Oman
1633	Local rebellion forces the Portuguese to leave Julfar
1650	*Sultan* bin Sayf al-Ya'rubi takes Masqat forts from the Portuguese
1654	Oman oust the Portuguese from the Indian Ocean

RISE OF LOCAL RULERS, OTTOMANS, AND THE BRITISH

1700–1800	Arrival of the Qawasim in Ra's al-Khaymah and Sharjah and Bani Yas in Abu Dhabi; the Qawasim begin attacking British shipping and as a result the coast is labeled "The Pirate Coast"
1701	First brief occupation of Bahrain by the Al Khalifah
1720	Al Sabah establish themselves in Kuwait
1744	Muhammad ibn 'Abd al-Wahhab in Dir'iyah and allies himself with the Al Sa'ud
1749	Al Bu Sa'idi dynasty established in Oman and rule to the present day
1752	Al Sabah elect their first *amir*, who is the founder of Kuwait
1780	Saudi-Wahhabi expansion begins
1783	Al Khalifah firmly established in Bahrain
1797	Qatar and Bahrain accept Saudi authority
1801	Saudi-Wahhabi forces attack Karbala' in southern Iraq

1802	Saudi-Wahhabi expansion into the Hijaz
1806–1856	Rule of *Sultan* Sa'id bin Sultan bin Ahmad, who extends Oman's overseas empire to its greatest limits
1811	Beginning of Egyptian-Turkish campaign against the Saudis
1818	Egyptian troops occupy the Saudi capital Dir'iyah and end first Saudi state
1820	Britain attacks several of the *shaykh*doms of the Pirate Coast and forces the *shaykhs* to sign treaties; these treaties recognize the Gulf *shaykhs* as separate political entities
1824	Turki ibn 'Abdallah re-establishes the Saudi state with Riyadh as the capital
1831	Ottomans reassert control over Baghdad and Iraq
1835	Britain forces Gulf *shaykhs* to sign treaties of peace between each other; region renamed the Trucial Coast
1836	Al Rashid of the Shammar tribe establish their rule in central Arabia with Ha'il as the capital
1839	Britain occupies Aden
1840	*Sultan* Sa'id of Oman sends *al-Shaykh* Ahmad bin Nu'man al-Ka'abi to the United States, first Arab ambassador to Washington, D.C.
1849	Ottomans occupy the Red Sea coast of Yemen
1856	On the death of *Sultan* Sa'id, Oman's empire is divided between his heirs, one based in Oman and the other in Zanzibar
1867	*Shaykh* Muhammad bin Thani signs a treaty with the British, the first international recognition of Qatar's independence from Bahrain
1869	Suez Canal opens—vital link for the British to India
1871	Ottomans reassert authority in al-Hasa and 'Asir
1872	Ottomans occupy Sana'a in Yemen; *Shaykh* Jasim bin Muhammad Al Thani of Qatar signs treaty with the Turks; *Shaykh* Jasim begins policy of playing the British and Ottomans against each other
1890	Britain forces the *Sultan* of Zanzibar to agree to a British protectorate
1892	Britain signs exclusive agreements with most of the Gulf *shaykhs* that accepted British protection
1893	Al Sa'uds take refuge in Kuwait from the Al Rashid
1896	Mubarak Al Sabah assassinates his kinsman Muhammad and takes control of Kuwait

1899	Mubarak enters into a treaty with Britain that will establish Kuwait's independence from the Ottoman Empire when World War I begins
1902	'Abd al-'Aziz ibn Sa'ud retakes Riyadh from the Al Rashid
1903	'Abd al-'Aziz ibn Sa'ud takes the title of *Sultan* of the Najd
1904	Saudi conquest of Abha
1908	Young Turk Revolution ends effective political control by the Ottoman *Sultan*; *Sharif* Hussein ibn 'Ali declared *Sharif* of Makkah by the Young Turks
1909	Ottoman *Sultan* 'Abd al-Hamid II tries to regain control and is defeated and deposed; a kinsman placed on the throne as *Sultan* Muhammad V al-Rashad
1911	Treaty between the Turks and *Imam* Yahya in Yemen
1912	Start of the *Ikhwan* movement by 'Abd al-'Aziz ibn Sa'ud
1913	Saudi conquest of al-Hasa; Kuwait separated from the Iraqi province of Basrah; most of the tribes of Oman's interior refuse to recognize the succession of Taymur bin Faysal as both *Sultan* and *Imam* and elect Salim bin Rashid al-Kharusi as *Imam*, splitting Oman into the *Sultanate* of Oman and the *Imamate* of Nizwa

WORLD WAR I

1914–1918	World War I; Turkey sides with Germany
1914	Britain establishes a protectorate over Bahrain
1915	*Shaykh* 'Abdallah bin Jasim Al Thani oversees the withdrawal of Turkish troops from Qatar
1916–1918	Arab Revolt against the Turks
1918	*Sultan* Muhammad V al-Rashad dies and is replaced by a cousin, Muhammad VI Wahid al-Din, who is eventually deposed by Kamal Ataturk in 1922, ending the Ottoman dynasty and the position of *Khalifah*, or successor to the Prophet.

BETWEEN THE WORLD WARS

1918–1919	Turkish withdrawal from Yemen
1918–1920	*Imam* Yahya expands area under his control in Yemen
1921	Faysal ibn Hussein made King of Iraq
1924	Ta'if falls to the Saudis
1925	Jiddah falls to the Saudis
1927	*Ikhwan* Rebellion in Saudi Arabia
1930	Final defeat of the *Ikhwan* in Saudi Arabia

1931	Oil discovered in Bahrain
1932	'Abd al-'Aziz declares the country to be named the Kingdom of Saudi Arabia
1933	First oil concessions in Saudi Arabia
1934	*Imam* Yahya agrees with British on the border between North and South Yemen; *Imam* Yahya agrees with Saudis on the border between Yemen and Saudi Arabia
1938	*Sultan* Taymur dies and is succeeded by his son Sa'id as *Sultan* of Oman
1939	First oil discovery in Qatar, but not exploited until 1949; first oil concessions in Abu Dhabi, but area is disputed with Saudi Arabia
1945	Meeting of King 'Abd al-'Aziz of Saudi Arabia and American President Franklin D. Roosevelt

MODERN OIL STATES

1952	Buraymi Crisis, Saudi Arabia forced to give up its claims to Buraymi Oasis to the *Sultan* of Oman
1953	King 'Abd al-'Aziz dies and his son Sa'ud is declared King; Abu Dhabi signs oil concessions offshore and begins exports in 1962
1956	Suez Crisis; Yemen joins Saudi Arabia and Egypt in an anti-British pact
1956–1959	Jabal al-Akhdar War in Oman, eventually the *Imam* of Nizwa is defeated; Oman unified under the *Sultan*
1961	Kuwait's independence challenged by Iraq
1962	Free Officer's Movement in North Yemen deposes *Imam* al-Badr and starts civil war
1962–1975	Dhufar rebellion in Oman
1963	Zanzibar becomes independent, but one year later a bloody revolution brings the country into union with Tanganyika as Tanzania; many of Zanzibar's Omani families are either killed or leave for Oman
1964	Sa'ud forced to abdicate in favor of his brother, Faysal, who becomes the next King of Saudi Arabia
1966	Britain announces departure from South Yemen and Aden by 1968
1967	Britain forced to leave South Yemen because of popular Yemeni revolution
1968	Britain announces it will be leaving the Arab Gulf States in 1971

Chronology

1970	Yemeni civil war in the north ends; *Sultan* Qabus of Oman stages a palace coup and deposes his father, Sa'id
1971	Independence of Bahrain, Qatar, and United Arab Emirates
1972	War between North and South Yemen
1973	October War between Egypt, Syria, and Israel; King Faysal used the "oil weapon" by embargoing oil sales to countries assisting Israel
1975	A nephew assassinates Faysal; Khalid is made King of Saudi Arabia
1979	Saddam Hussein becomes President of Iraq; Mosque in Makkah attacked and briefly held by extremist group calling themselves *Ikhwan*; second war between North and South Yemen
1980	Expulsion of 40,000 Shi'ites of Iranian descent from Iraq; start of the Iran-Iraq War
1981	Gulf Cooperation Council established
1982	Khalid dies and another brother, Fahd, is named the next King of Saudi Arabia; stock market crash (*suq al-Manakh*) crisis in Kuwait
1986	King Fahd takes the title "Custodian of the Two Holy Mosques"
1988	End of Iran-Iraq War
1990	Iraq invades Kuwait; North and South Yemen unite to form Republic of Yemen, which sides with Iraq; Saudi Arabia and other Gulf States expel large numbers of Yemenis
1991	Gulf War I. United States and allies expel Iraq from Kuwait
1992	Usamah bin Ladin expelled from Saudi Arabia by Saudi authorities
1994	Saudi authorities revoke Usamah bin Ladin's citizenship
1996	Series of explosions set by terrorists hit the Kingdom of Saudi Arabia, eventually linked to *al Qa'idah*, Usamah bin Ladin's group
1998	U.S. Embassy bombings in Kenya and Tanzania linked to *al Qa'idah*.
1999	Saudi Arabia's yearlong centennial celebrations; *Shayhk* 'Isa, ruler of Bahrain, dies, and his son, Hamad, becomes the next ruler
2000	Attack on U.S.S. *Cole* in the Aden harbor linked to *al Qa'idah*
2001	September 11 attacks by *al Qa'idah* provoke U.S. invasion of Taliban-controlled Afghanistan; Usamah bin Ladin seeks refuge with tribal people in the Afghanistan-Pakistan border region; Bahrain becomes a kingdom and *Shaykh* Hamad becomes King Hamad

2002	Elections in Bahrain—women allowed to vote
2003	Gulf War
2004	Death of *Shaykh* Zayid of Abu Dhabi and President of the United Arab Emirates; succeeded in both positions by his son, Khalifah
2005	Kuwait's National Assembly expands voting to include women
2006	Elections in Bahrain and Shi'ites win forty percent of the seats in parliament; *Shaykh* Jabir Al Ahmad *Amir* of Kuwait dies and is succeeded first by *Shaykh* Sa'ad Al 'Abdallah, who resigns because of poor health, then by *Shaykh* Sabah Al Ahmad, who becomes the *Amir* of Kuwait
2008	UAE forgives Iraq's debt of $7 billion and appoints an ambassador to Baghdad; Bahrain appoints its first woman ambassador, Huda Nonoo—a member of Bahrain's very small but ancient Jewish community—as its representative to the United States; oil prices rise to record highs of $147 to $150 before stabilizing around $100 a barrel in July over fears of Iran's nuclear program and continued political unrest in the Middle East; UAE appoints its first female judge, Khalud Ahmad Jawan; during *Ramadan* Saudi Arabia's King 'Abdallah hosts an unofficial meeting between representatives of the Taliban and the Afghan government; Saudi, Kuwaiti, Bahraini, Qatari, and Emirati stock markets are all affected by the global credit crisis, and oil prices fall to below $50 a barrel in November; some countries are forces to institute similar bank bailouts as in the West; Oman is the only country in the region to not be greatly affected by credit crisis, stating its $3 billion infrastructure is not at risk

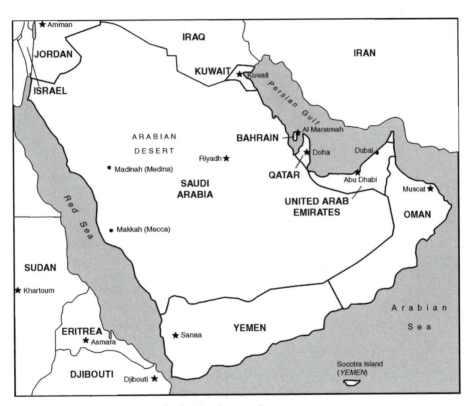

The Gulf region. Cartography by Bookcomp, Inc.

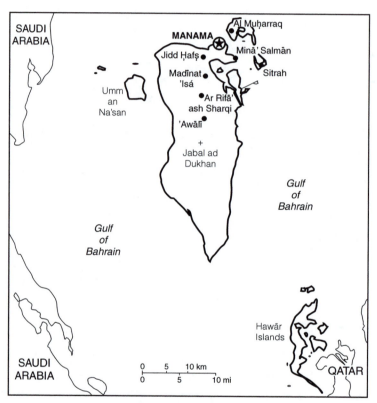

Bahrain. Cartography by Bookcomp, Inc.

Kuwait. Cartography by Bookcomp, Inc.

Oman. Cartography by Bookcomp, Inc.

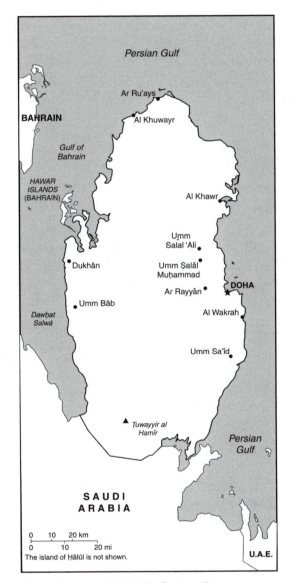

Qatar. Cartography by Bookcomp, Inc.

Saudi Arabia. Cartography by Bookcomp, Inc.

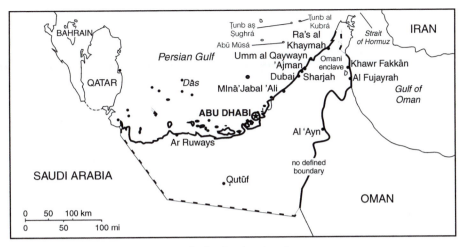

United Arab Emirates. Cartography by Bookcomp, Inc.

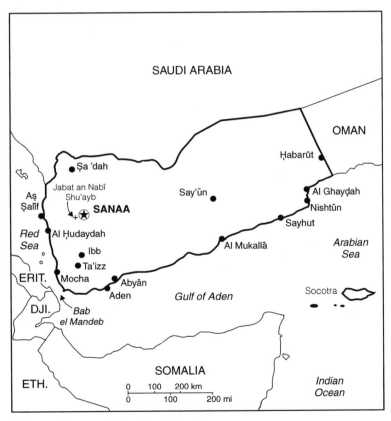

Yemen. Cartography by Bookcomp, Inc.

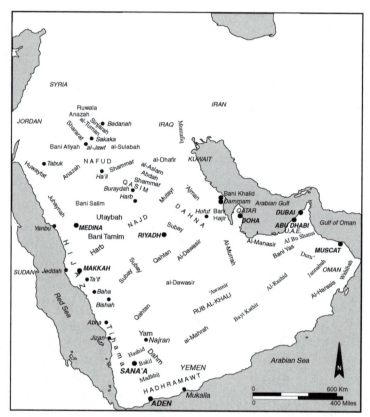

Approximate traditional locations of the main tribes of Saudi Arabia. Cartography by Bookcomp, Inc.

Saudi Arabia and the Gulf
Arab States Today

A

'Abd al-'Aziz b. Muhammad b. Sa'ud (1721–1803)

Sebastian Maisel

'Abd al-'Aziz b. Muhammad b. Sa'ud (1721–1803) was the son of the founder of the first Saudi state, Muhammad b. Sa'ud, and *amir* of an Islamic revival movement since 1766. He was also the son-in-law of the religious leader and initiator of the same movement, Shaykh **Muhammad b. 'Abd al-Wahhab**. His father and father-in-law signed the historic alliance with a **marriage** between their children, making him the first political leader of the **Al Sa'ud** and the religious reformers of the Al al-Shaykh. This pact is still regarded as the legitimization for the current rule of the Al Sa'ud in **Saudi Arabia**. With the occupation of large areas in central Arabia, he is considered as the founder of the first state of the Al Sa'ud dynasty and their historical rule in the **Najd**. After the death of Muhammad b. 'Abd al-Wahhab, he united the political and religious leadership of the movement under his control and took the new title of an *imam*, a religious leader of the Muslim community. His successful **military** campaigns added the areas of **al-Hasa** and **Hijaz** to the Saudi realm. The rulers of **Ta'if** and **Asir** joined them, and with the occupation of Karbala and **Makkah** (Mecca) in 1803 the area under Saudi control included almost the entire Peninsula. Everywhere he brought with him a new message of a purified Islam, cleansing the area from innovations such as worshipping saints, trees or tombs. As long as he operated only in Najd, the expansion went largely unnoticed. But after the destruction of **Shi'a** shrines in southern Iraq and the Prophet **Muhammad's** tomb in **Madinah** (Medina), the Ottoman Empire forced 'Abd al-'Aziz's troops out of the Hijaz and subsequently destroyed the first Saudi state. His legacy is also characterized by his unsuccessful attempts to unify the tribal society of Arabia, thus failing to create a centralized authority to rule the different nomadic and settled tribes in his region; however, he is known for his ability to deal with tribal leaders in the *majlis*, open meetings where all citizens had open access to the ruler. 'Abd al-'Aziz was killed and subsequently succeeded by his son Sa'ud, who continued the policy of religious purity.

FURTHER READING

Delong-Bas, Natana J. *Wahhabi Islam: From Revival and Reform to Global Jihad*. New York: Oxford University Press, 2004.

al-Rasheed, Madawi. *A History of Saudi Arabia*. New York: Cambridge University Press, 2002.

Vassiliev, Alexei. *The History of Saudi Arabia*. London: Saqi Books, 1998.

'Abd al-'Aziz bin 'Abd al-Rahman Al Sa'ud (1876–1953)

Sebastian Maisel

'Abd al-'Aziz was born in 1876 in **Riyadh** to 'Abd al-Rahman Al Sa'ud, then head of the **Al Sa'ud** family and ruler over parts of **Saudi Arabia**, who in the previous century consolidated its hegemony of large parts of central Arabia. However, in 1891 he and his family were forced by their biggest political rivals, the **Al Rashid** from **Ha'il**, to leave Riyadh and go into exile in **Kuwait**, where 'Abd al-'Aziz grew up to become a successful politician, warrior, and religious leader. He started his mission to reinstall the power and legacy of the Al Sa'ud with a bold and surprise attack on Riyadh in 1902, which he took from the Al Rashid, and a tactical maneuver that allowed him to snap **al-Hasa** from the Turkish control in 1913. As *imam* (or religious leader) of the **Wahhabi** reform movement, he became the religious and political leader of **Najd**. His natural political and **military** talent helped him to succeed with his mission of conquest in 1932 when he proclaimed the foundation of the Kingdom of Saudi Arabia. Several unique political strategies applied by 'Abd al-'Aziz ibn Sa'ud were extremely helpful in this quest. On one hand he was able to gain support from Britain without becoming completely dependent upon them. He used the rivalry among other Arab leaders to secure British funding and recognition, while on the other hand he utilized the military force of recently settled **Bedouins (Ikhwan)** to conquer al-Hasa (1913), Ha'il (1921), the **Hijaz** (1925), and **Yemen** (1934), that is, the main and central parts in Arabia. The Ikhwan became a powerful tool in his hand that he used to pacify Arabia and consolidate the control of the Al Sa'ud.

Through the friendship and personal relations with influential foreign politicians, intellectuals, and decision-makers such as Gertrude Bell, Ameen Rihani, Charles R. Crane, and **Harry St. John Philby**, 'Abd al-'Aziz b. 'Abd al-Rahman was able to gain political recognition and independence in a time period when the rest of the Middle East was split among the mandate powers and turned into semi-colonies.

Oil was discovered in Saudi Arabia in 1938, and through his British advisor, Philby, concessions were granted to U.S. **companies**. This brought the first revenues to the poor and undeveloped country, which 'Abd al-'Aziz decided to invest in the development of infrastructure. It also brought rapid social change to Saudi Arabia, particularly to the Eastern Province where most of the oil reserves are located. Although 'Abd al-'Aziz used the oil money to enhance his kingdom, for himself he chose a rather simple lifestyle. It became one of his major domestic policies to make Islam and its teaching and requirements compatible with the technological advances by preserving the special character of Saudi Arabia. 'Abd al-'Aziz died on November 9, 1953 in **Ta'if** and was succeeded by his oldest son Sa'ud.

FURTHER READING

McLoughlin, Leslie J. *Ibn Saud: Founder of a Kingdom*. London: St. Martin's Press, 1993.
al-Rasheed, Madawi. *A History of Saudi Arabia*. New York: Cambridge University Press, 2002.
Rihani, Ameen. *Ibn Sa'oud of Arabia*. Boston: Houghton-Mifflin Co., 1928.
Vassiliev, Alexie. *The History of Saudi Arabia*. London: Saqi Books, 1998.

Abha

Sebastian Maisel

Abha is a medium-size city with roughly 200,000 inhabitants located in the strategically important **Asir** Mountains in southwestern **Saudi Arabia**. The population belongs to several, mostly South Arabian, tribes, such as the Ghamid, Zahran, Asir, or **Qahtan**. The tribal groups in the Abha area originate from the central highlands and are called *sarat*. Generally, the people belong or are strongly connected to a larger **Yemen**-oriented culture.

Because of its elevation of approximately 7,200 feet (2,194.5 meters), abundant rainfall, and mild climate, it is a center for agriculture and **tourism**. Abha is also the political and administrative center of the Asir province and the seat of its governor, Prince Khalid Al Faysal. Several academic institutions are located in Abha, such as King Khalid University and Prince Sultan College for Hotel Management. One of the most liberal **newspapers** in Saudi Arabia, *al-Watan*, is edited and published in Abha.

Agriculture and irrigation played an important part in the city's development, where farming terraces and irrigation canals dominate the landscape. The traditional buildings in Abha, painted with bright colors, are made of several layers of stone and mud with a slight graduation from one layer to the next preventing the rainwater from saturating the walls.

Since the 1990s tourism has become a focal point in domestic diversification strategies with Abha being the capital of the primary tourist area in the kingdom. It offers hotels, amusement parks, cable cars, modern and traditional shopping centers, and other tourist infrastructure to explore the city and its surrounding areas. In 1981, the Asir National Park was established, which served as a catalyst to the booming tourist industry. During the summer, when temperatures are pleasant in comparison to most other areas, the annual Abha Festival with its exhibitions and concerts attracts many Saudi and foreign tourists, mostly from the Gulf State. Famous artists from all over the Arab world perform in Abha, and it was here where the "Sound of the Earth," all time-favorite 'ud-player Talal Maddah, died on stage in 2000.

In history, the medieval Muslim historian al-Hamdani mentioned the name of the city as home to the Asir tribe and a weekly marketplace, and it continues to be a political and economic center for the centuries to come. During the expansion of the first **Wahhabi** state around 1800, the area subsequently came under the control of the Ottomans and their **military** leadership from Egypt. The Al Aid, chief clan among the tribes in the area, ruled from Abha until another Turkish attack in 1887. After the end of World War I and the demise of the Ottoman Empire, **Yemeni tribes** under the Idrisis of Sabya tried to include Abha in their realm. The ruling clan of the Al Aid was finally defeated during several campaigns by the emerging power of King **'Abd al-'Aziz ibn Sa'ud**, who successfully managed to make Abha a bridgehead for further acquisitions of Idrisi territory and merged Abha and Asir into his newly established Kingdom of Saudi Arabia.

FURTHER READING

Abdulfattah, Kamal. *Mountain Farmer and Fellah in Asir, Southwest Saudi Arabia*. Erlangen: Fränkische Geographische Gesellschaft, 1981.

Philby, Harry St. John. *Arabian Highlands*. Ithaca, NY: Cornell University Press, 1952.

Reissner, Johannes. "Die Idrisiden in Asir: Ein historischer Überblick," *Die Welt des Islams* 21, no. 1–4 (1981): 164–192.

Saud, Noura bint Muhammad, Al-Jawharah Muhammad 'Anqari, and Madeha Muhammad Ajroush. *Abha, Bilad Asir: South-Western Region of the Kingdom of Saudi Arabia*. Riyadh: Antiquariaat Klondyke, 1989.

Abu Dhabi (City)
Carla Higgins

Abu Dhabi, which means "father of the gazelle" in Arabic, is the capital city of the **United Arab Emirates**. Abu Dhabi is on a **desert** island and connected to the mainland via two bridges. In 1761 water was discovered and settlement followed. By 1793 the shaykhs of the **Bani Yas** tribal confederation had arrived and made it their capital, led by the Al Bu Falah ruling family. Abu Dhabi grew because of **pearl** fishing and trade made possible by pearl wealth—almost daily caravans arrived from either the Liwa or Buraymi **oases**. As the pearl industry grew, a stratified society developed that required labor, and slaves were imported to work as domestic servants, to tend date gardens, and to pearl dive. **Bedouin** tribesmen began to stay in Abu Dhabi rather than migrate to their **camel** herds or **date** gardens. Migrants from other **Gulf** areas as well as Persia arrived to practice trades and crafts (see **handicrafts**) as the cash economy grew. Persians fared especially well and grew to control most shops in the market, as well as many trades and crafts. The British administration in Bombay took an interest in the security of maritime trade, hindered by piracy and regional rivalries, both also the concern of the tribal shayhks. The General Treaty of Peace was signed in January 1820 between the British and each ruler on the Arab coast—*Shaykh* Shakhbut bin Diyab signed for Abu Dhabi. British involvement in the area was thus codified, setting up Abu Dhabi as a minor ally and dependent of British India, and setting the stage for the British role as chief mediator in regional conflict and development.

The **pearling** industry severely declined by the 1930s, and economic stagnation set in. Within a few decades the newly established **oil industry** became the source of wealth and employment, far exceeding any single source of revenue. The London-based oil company, Iraq Petroleum Company, signed agreements with Abu Dhabi's ruler, *Shaykh* Shakhbut, in 1939 to gain rights to explore the emirate's onshore and offshore territories, but oil in commercially viable quantities was not discovered until the late 1950s. By 1966 tribal unrest caused by Shakhbut's reluctance to spend oil revenues led to his deposition by his brother, *Shaykh* **Zayid bin Sultan al Nahyan**. *Shaykh* Zayid soon demonstrated his commitment toward improving the lives of Abu Dhabi residents by investing in social infrastructure such as mosques, health services, **education**, markets, and housing.

In 1971, the birth year of the United Arab Emirates, Abu Dhabi became the capital of the federation. It is now a highly developed cosmopolitan city with

Mosque in downtown Abu Dhabi. The growth of high-rise buildings around the mosque attests to the rapid growth since 1970, when Abu Dhabi was mainly composed of barasti or palm frond huts. Courtesy of John A. Shoup.

spacious streets, gleaming glass buildings, and a stunning skyline. Because of *Shaykh* Zayid's efforts to green the emirates, Abu Dhabi hosts family parks and recreation areas. There is a building boom, and emphasis is upon developing **tourism**. New hotels, such as the Emirates' Palace, host film festivals, art exhibits, and international pop stars. Plans to develop the city focus on bringing cultural and arts institutions renowned in the west, such as the Gugenheim Museum and the Louvre.

Abu Dhabi (Emirate)
Carla Higgins

Abu Dhabi occupies eighty-seven percent of the **United Arab Emirates'** territory and is the largest emirate by far. Its area corresponds to the territory of the **Bani Yas**, a large tribal confederation that inhabited the area for centuries.

Dozens of islands exist off Abu Dhabi's north coast and were historically significant for the **pearling** trade, guano gathering, and **camel** fodder and today for hydrocarbons. Abu Dhabi's mainland is largely characterized as desert punctuated by gravel plains. In the north, salty mud flats known as *sabkah* stretch along the coast. Historically this area could not support vegetation, travel, communications, or settlement. Desert sands begin three to six miles (five to ten kilometers) from shore, extending south and westward into the vast Rub'al-Khali Desert of **Saudi Arabia**. There are three population centers: the Liwa **Oases**, al 'Ayn town, and Abu Dhabi city. The Liwa Oases are in the west and historically were critical to the economy because of their **date** gardens. Peoples of the Liwa survived on wells created from dew and occasional rains. The Liwa is the ancestral home of the Bani Yas and thus Abu Dhabi's ruling clan, the Al Bu Falah. To the east, the Hajar Mountains rise on the Abu Dhabi/**Oman** border, and provided water via an ancient system of irrigation called *aflaj* to a cluster of villages, amongst them today's village of al 'Ayn. Al 'Ayn is the second largest population center in the emirate, hosts a huge date palm grove, and became a power base for the ruling family during the nineteenth and twentieth centuries. Abu Dhabi city is the northernmost settlement, the capital of the emirate, flourishing on wealth from the pearling industry and recently from **oil** and investments made possible by oil wealth.

Abu Dhabi's economy was based on seasonal activities and migration—the economy was diversified into camel herding, trading, date cultivation, fishing, and pearling. Subsistence and survival were the goals, and all family members cooperated to exploit available resources at different times of the year, and in different areas of Abu Dhabi. Some manufacturing occurred, but all products were consumed locally. The ownership of date groves brought additional security and status, although dates were consumed locally and provided subsistence, not export. Only pearl diving brought revenue, grew the coastal settlement of Abu Dhabi city, created wealth and subsequent stratification, brought foreign traders and laborers to Abu Dhabi, and garnered the interest of foreign businessmen and governments interested in regional trade. The British administration in Bombay was interested in regional maritime trade, hindered by piracy and regional rivalries. Abu Dhabi signed British-sponsored treaties to protect and control trade, such as the General Treaty of Peace (1820), the Maritime Truce (1835), and the Perpetual Maritime Truce (1853). By 1892, British involvement in the area was established, eventually setting up Abu Dhabi as a minor ally of British India and setting the stage for British role as a chief mediator in regional conflict and development.

In the 1930s, the pearling industry failed, but Abu Dhabi's islands also lie over giant oil fields. Exploration by foreign oil **companies** began in the 1930s, and commercial quantities of oil were discovered in the late 1950s, offshore and onshore. In 1954 Abu Dhabi granted a concession to Abu Dhabi Marine Areas Ltd, who discovered oil on the island of Umm Shaif in 1958, and again on Zakum Island in 1963. Onshore, Abu Dhabi Petroleum Company discovered oil at al Bab in 1958. By the mid-1960s, five super giant fields had been discovered and now, because of hydrocarbon export, Abu Dhabi residents are some of the wealthiest citizens in the world. Today, there are approximately 1,000 producing wells in Abu Dhabi, providing almost unlimited funds for development.

In 1968, the British announced their impending withdrawal from the Gulf. In 1971, the federation of the United Arab Emirates (UAE) was created from seven independent emirates. Abu Dhabi played a key role in creating the federation, and Abu Dhabi city was made the provisional capital of the UAE, and the permanent capital in 1996. *Shaykh* **Zayid**, the **Emir** of Abu Dhabi, became president of the UAE and was not only the ruler of Abu Dhabi and architect of the UAE, but also directed oil wealth to improve the welfare of the emirates and the Arab world. From the mid-1960s Abu Dhabi has been building infrastructure in the smaller emirates and supporting other Arab and Muslim countries through the Abu Dhabi Fund for Development.

Today Abu Dhabi boasts modern roads and housing, a system of schools, modern **health** care, civil institutions, and a vibrant private sector. The emirate boasts clean, well-maintained, garden-filled, well-lit cities with a growing number of recreational, entertainment, and cultural opportunities for its citizens and the large multinational expatriate population that lives within it. Free **education**, from the primary levels up through higher education, as well as education abroad, is offered to Emirati nationals. Free housing is supplied to Emiratis. Major highways provide connectivity. Electricity and water are subsidized. Abu Dhabi citizens are primarily employed in government and own buildings and other real estate, cars, and taxis to garner income. The Abu Dhabi National Oil Company (ADNOC) plays a huge role in the economy and is a major employer of Emirati nationals. The Abu Dhabi Investment Authority (ADIA) is tasked with providing for a future without oil—ADIA invests oil revenue overseas and is believed to have built a diverse and substantial portfolio since initiated in 1976.

The obvious characteristic that now affects Abu Dhabi's future is its role as a major oil producer. This tiny emirate is now a world player by virtue of its extreme wealth, and its development now holds world attention. Abu Dhabi is challenged by issues common to other Gulf emirates and countries, such as labor and **human rights** for its population of relatively poor foreign workers, providing an education for its citizens, creating appropriate health care, building transparent and accountable institutions that provide services, and deciding how and when to adopt models of governance from other communities.

Agriculture: Traditional and Commercial

John A. Shoup

Agriculture in the **Arabian Peninsula** began in the Neolithic period (6000–8000 BC) with the domestication of both plants and animals. Archeological excavations in the **United Arab Emirates**, **Bahrain**, **Kuwait**, and **Saudi Arabia** indicate early trade connections in the **Persian Gulf**, with both Mesopotamia and the Indus civilizations that introduced other domesticated plant and animal species to the region, such as wheat from the north and zebu cattle from India. As the Arabian Peninsula

Openings along the line of *aflaj* or underground water canals are used to maintain the system. This *falaj* (singular of *aflaj*) helps irrigate the dense stand of date palms and other crops for the oasis of Adam in Oman. Courtesy of John A. Shoup.

began to dry up in the late Neolithic, the serious lack of permanent water sources concentrated agriculture in **oases** and encouraged pastoral nomadism.

OASIS AGRICULTURE

Most of the traditional agricultural production in the Arabian Peninsula came from the important oases that dot the landscape. The notable exceptions are the better-watered **mountains** in the **Asir** of Saudi Arabia, **Yemen**, and **Oman**, where other technologies such as terracing methods were introduced at an early period. Oases function with a highly developed system of irrigation tapping underground water supplies through two major methods: wells and a system of underground canals usually called *aflaj* in Oman or *qanat* in Bahrain, which may have been an early borrowing from Iran or Iraq. Wells used several methods to bring up large buckets of water: either with the bucket rope attached to a long pole with a heavy weight on the end to make it easier for a person to handle; or with the bucket rope harnessed to an animal such as a donkey, **camel**, or bullock and brought to the surface with a system of wooden pulleys. The water can be poured into a delivery ditch or directly onto the plants.

The *aflaj* (singular *falaj*) or *qanat* are underground canals that tap either surface water, such as a stream, or groundwater. A series of shafts are dug at intervals and the canals are dug connecting them. The shafts are used to help maintain the canals because they need periodic cleaning. The canals need to be at a constant slope that is not too steep, which would cause quick erosion, or too shallow, which would cause the canals to back up and stop the flow of the water. *Aflaj* can run for several miles before they open up into the oasis and the water distributed to individual fields by a strict accounting of time. Each field has a designated turn usually marked in number of hours and the whole system is controlled by a person (usually called an *'Arif*—plural *'Urafa'*—in most of the Gulf) who is knowledgeable about every person's inherited or purchased water rights.

The basic plant in the oases is the **date** palm tree. The date palm is heat- and salt-resistant, being able to thrive where daytime temperatures soar to over 120°F (50°C) and where the water quality is too salty for other plants to survive. The canopy provided by the date palms helps allow other more sensitive plants to grow and produce. Under the shade of the palm canopy the temperatures can be some ten to fifteen degrees cooler than outside of the oasis. A healthy oasis usually has a second layer of trees and shrubs such as olive, citrus, fig, pomegranate, henna, or mango that help keep the ground temperature cool and allow more sensitive vegetables to grow. The date palm is naturally a shrub rather than a tree and takes on the tall, treelike shape only with the interference of man. Trimming off the lower fronds causes the plant to continue to grow upward and careful yearly pruning is needed to produce the shade canopy. In addition, date palms produce more fruit when man helps with the pollination process by collecting the long pollen pods from the male trees and physically pollinating the female trees.

Livestock play an important role in traditional oasis production both as a major source of power/energy and of fertilizer. Livestock were kept in pens or stables near their owner's houses and rarely allowed to graze freely inside the oasis. Livestock were instead fed fodder raised by their owners or purchased from others in the markets. In some instances, oasis farmers contracted their livestock to pastoral nomads especially if they were from the same tribe. A particular tribe may have settled sections producing important products such as dates while other sections were pastoralists producing wool, hair, and milk. Such arrangements helped diversify the economy and minimize risk.

Oasis agriculture is by its very nature work-intensive and without the constant care of the farmers the system collapses and the land reverts to **desert**. Small plots of land are not only highly valuable but also highly productive, making oasis agriculture hectare-by-hectare some of the most productive agricultural land in the world. Nearly all land within an oasis is under cultivation and traditionally land has been privately owned. In addition, water rights are also privately owned and can be separate from land rights through complicated systems of inheritance based on Islamic principals. Land and water rights were strong factors encouraging families to prefer cousin **marriages** in order to not lose control over these valuable assets. Women were the most vulnerable to family pressures to give up their rights to inheritance in order to keep land and water from going to another family or lineage. Conflict over rights, especially to water, were settled by councils of lineage elders, although armed conflict was all too frequent even in the recent past.

PASTORAL NOMADISM

Pastoral nomadism is well adapted for the harsh dry conditions of the Arabian Peninsula. Sheep, goats, cattle, donkeys, **horses**, and camels are the main types of livestock raised yet today. Sheep, goats, cattle, donkeys, and horses need to drink at least once a day, which in the past limited the area where they could be raised. The need for water meant that they could not utilize the deeper desert areas except in the winter when rainwater forms pools and small lakes. Camels formed the economic and cultural basis for the great **Bedouin** tribes, whereas horses were important symbols of status and prestige because they were not only expensive to buy but also expensive to maintain. Horses were important in warfare and raiding because they are very fast and the Arabian horse is known for its speed and endurance qualities. Horses were also important to the Bedouin economy and Kuwait and Aleppo served as major markets for horses sold as cavalry mounts until after World War I mechanized army units were introduced.

Archeological records indicate that camels were first domesticated in southern Arabia between 3000 and 2500 BC and reached northern Arabia some time after 1100 BC. Camels gave pastoralists a greater range for migration and freed them from dependency on fixed water sources. Camel milk could be substituted for water for both people and horses whereas dates served as basic foodstuff for both. Although the camel gave the Arab Bedouin greater freedom of movement, the harsh desert conditions did not favor large populations; thus, they never formed the majority of people living in the Peninsula. Some Bedouin tribes tried to include areas with better-watered grazing lands in the north in Syria and Iraq and historically there has been a constant pressure by Bedouin from the south to move north.

The twentieth century brought rapid changes to many Bedouin, including a shift to more market-oriented production. Camels, although highly valued in Bedouin culture, were less demanded in the markets and many Bedouin began the shift to raising sheep and goats, but mainly sheep. Sheep have a quicker return on investment because they gain full adulthood in a year whereas a camel takes five to six years to mature. Excess male sheep are sold in local markets for meat and hides whereas females produce both milk and wool. Traditional migration patterns were disrupted with the introduction of motorized transportation in the 1950s, which sped up the amount of time needed to move between pastures. Large trucks not only replaced camels in moving people (and livestock), but also opened up the desert to sheep pastoralism. Water can be easily hauled from distant springs and wells in large containers or in specially built tanker trucks, making it possible to water large numbers of livestock on a daily basis. Camel herds are still kept by many Bedouin, even those who have settled, for their hair and milk or are raised as racers.

Those Bedouin who lived in the more rugged mountainous regions of the Peninsula or in the northern areas close to Syria and Iraq traditionally raised sheep, goats, and cattle. The goat breed developed over time is usually black in color with long hair. The hair was clipped in the late spring or early summer and was either sold in local markets or kept and spun into yarn used to make tent panels or as the warp for rugs and winter clothing. The sheep breed developed in the region is a fat-tailed variety with long, straight carpet wool. The wool is shorn in late spring or early summer and, like the goat hair, was sold in local markets or spun into yarn to make numerous household items such as bags, rugs, or clothes. Both sheep and goats are milked and a variety of yogurts and cheeses were, and still are, an important part of the Bedouin diet. Cattle were less commonly raised by pastoralists, although they were, and still remain, part of the agro-pastoral production system in parts of Oman and the Asir region of Saudi

Arabia. In the Jabal Akhdar of Oman, a dwarf breed of zebu was developed to deal with the environmental conditions and scarcity of fodder.

People in the Peninsula developed several land management systems in order to not abuse the limited natural resources. Much of the land outside of the oases was considered to be common or tribal lands open to all to use. Common lands were managed by a system called *hima* or *mahmiyah*, meaning protected or re-served under the control of the tribal or lineage elders. Lands were set aside for specific use such as for cattle or horses only or for a specific season of the year. Some lands were not to be grazed except during periods of drought or for the production of honey, which was used in traditional medicine. Both settled com-munities, and Bedouin improved natural pastures by building dams on seasonal streams that were used to water livestock, and when the water dried up, livestock were allowed to graze the meadow that was left behind.

COMMERCIAL AGRICULTURE

Following the discovery of **oil**, several Gulf countries and Saudi Arabia embarked on new agricultural policies in attempts to lessen dependency on imported foodstuffs. Deep wells were drilled to tap fossil water for large irriga-tion schemes and even desalinated water is used to irrigate new agricultural schemes; for example, in Saudi Arabia desalinated water makes up seventy per-cent of the total amount of the available potable water.

Saudi Arabia established the Directorate of Agriculture in 1948, which began by providing water pumps, building dams and irrigation canals, and providing loans to farmers to improve existing agricultural infrastructure. In 1953 the Directorate was made into a full ministry, the Ministry of Agriculture and Water. In 1964 the Saudi Arabian Agricultural Bank was established to assist farmers in financing new agri-cultural equipment and machinery. The Ministry instituted programs to provide technical advice as well as veterinary services and pest control through local centers.

In 1972 Saudi Arabia embarked on an ambitious scheme to produce large amounts of wheat and barley irrigated by large sprinkler networks that make some parts of the kingdom look like the Great Plains states such as Kansas. Almost 3 million hectares of land have been put under grain production and by 1985 the kingdom became self-sufficient, although the actual cost of production makes it among the most expensive grain in the world. During the 1980s and into the 1990s, Saudi Arabia became the sixth largest exporter of wheat. However, by 1996 the government began discouraging large-scale wheat production because it was quickly using up the supply of ground-water. Some sixty percent of the water used to irrigate the fields was lost to evapora-tion and the water table sank to depths of over 492 feet (150 meters). Saudi Arabian wheat farmers also began to have trouble finding skilled agricultural labor, adding to the production price of Saudi wheat. Saudi Arabia still produces around 2 million tons of wheat per year but production will be phased out by 2015 and the country will once again be dependent upon imported supplies of wheat.

Saudi Arabia and most of the Gulf States have embarked upon greenhouse production of fruits, vegetables, and even berries and fresh-cut flowers. Many of these are private investments by locals and are among the most sophisticated greenhouses, using the most up-to-date technologies. Produce is sold fresh in the

11

local markets or is processed in local factories. Cut flowers are shipped by air to markets in Europe on a daily basis and processed fruit juices are sold in markets throughout much of Africa.

Commercial livestock production has concentrated on cattle, sheep, and poultry (mainly chickens). Cattle are raised for their meat and hides, although since the 1960s dairy breeds have been introduced from Denmark and the Netherlands to supply fresh and processed milk and milk products. Dairy farms require expensive infrastructure, not only to guarantee quality and cleanliness, but also to maintain high levels of production during the hot months. European breeds of dairy cattle suffer from the heat and milk production is adversely affected by it; therefore, dairy barns need to be air conditioned or cooled with misters or sprinklers. Many of the counties in the region are now able to provide most of their needs for eggs and chicken, but still need to import red meat. Sheep, cattle, and camels are imported from nearby states such as Syria and Sudan or from Australia and the United States.

In addition to the newer sectors, commercial practices have also been applied to date production. Date groves have been improved with drip irrigation, which loses little water to evaporation. Tree management has also been improved to increase the level of production, making the Gulf and Saudi Arabia among the highest-producing regions of the world. Saudi Arabia alone has over 13 million date trees in production, producing over 600,000 tons of dates a year. Dates are processed and packaged locally and exported to other countries. There is a high demand for dates throughout the Muslim world, especially during the month of *Ramadan* when Muslims break their daily fast with dates.

FURTHER READING

Hansen, Eric. "Looking for the Khalasah" and "Carrying Dates to Hajar," *Saudi Aramco World* 55, no. 4 (2004): 3–8, 9–15.

Shoup, John. "Middle Eastern Sheep Pastoralism and the Hima System," in *The World of Pastoralism*, edited by John Galaty and Douglas Johnson. New York: Guilford Publications, 1990.

'Ajman

Sebastian Maisel

The 'Ajman is considered one of the most powerful tribes in the Eastern Province of **Saudi Arabia** and **Kuwait**. Currently, they are mostly living in Saudi Arabia (80,000), but large sections are found in Kuwait (30,000) as well as in **Qatar**. During the early eighteenth century, the 'Ajman moved from their original homeland in **Najran** through the Jabal Tuwayq into **al-Hasa**, where under the leadership of the *shaykhly* family, Bin Hithlayn, they replaced the ruling **Bani Khalid** as the strongest **military** force in the eastern **Arabian Peninsula**.

Enemies of the 'Ajman often describe them as Isma'ilis (i.e., **Shi'ites**) and they might have been originally, because Najran, where they originated, is home to the Bani Yam tribe of which the majority are Isma'ilis although some sections are

Sunnis. However, there is no evidence that the 'Ajman have any Isma'ili connection. Like their closest relatives, the **Al Murrah**, the 'Ajman claim descent from **Qahtan** and share the common descent from Hamdan of the southern Arabs through Yam.

The tribal area, or *dirah*, of the 'Ajman borders the tribal areas of the **Mutayr** in the north; the **'Utaybah**, Subay, Bani Hajir, and Bani Khalid in the west; and the Murrah in the south. It includes the famous Samman uplands, which after winter rains becomes excellent grazing land attracting Bedouins of the Mutayr, Bani Khalid, and Subay tribes.

The main divisions of the 'Ajman are the Marzuq and the Wubayr. Among the historical tribal leaders is Rakan bin Falah bin Hithlayn, a well-known poet and leader who inherited the position of *shaykh* from his uncle and ruled the tribe successfully for 35 years (1859–1892).

During the formation state of Saudi Arabia, the 'Ajman often sided with 'Abd al-'Aziz ibn Sa'ud but never fully joined his side. In the battle of Kinzan in June 1915, ibn Sa'ud's brother Sa'ad was killed by the 'Ajman. Their shifting loyalty made them a notorious distrusted enemy to the **Al Sa'ud**; however, that did not prevent them from joining the **Ikhwan** movement from an early time period and from settling in fourteen *hijra*s. During this era, their clients, the 'Awazim tribe, officially broke away and sided with ibn Sa'ud. Joining forces with sections from the Mutayr and 'Utaybah, the 'Ajman were a leading force in the rebellion of the Ikhwan against ibn Sa'ud between 1927 and 1929 under Didan bin Fahad bin Hithlayn. In May 1929, Didan was killed, and his cousin Nayif took his place as tribal leader.

The 'Ajman are famous for their **camel** and **horse** breeding, but because of the developing **oil industry** and **oil** production in their *dirah*, most of them gave up nomadism and took jobs with **Aramco**. However, they maintained their superior social position by keeping close marital relations with the royal families in Saudi Arabia and Kuwait. There appears to be no connection between the tribe of the 'Ajman and the emirate of 'Ajman.

FURTHER READING

al-Haddad, Mohammad S. "The Effect of Detribalization and Sedentarization on the Socio-Economic Structure of the Tribes of the Arabian Peninsula: The Ajman Tribe as a Case Study." PhD dissertation, University of Kansas, 1981.

Kostiner, Joseph. "Sa'udi Arabia's Territorial Expansion: The Case of Kuwayt, 1916–1921," *Die Welt des Islams* 33, no. 2 (1993): 219–234.

Raswan, Carl R. "Tribal Areas and Migration Lines among North Arabian Bedouins," *Geographical Review* 20, no. 3 (1930): 494–502.

'Ajman and Umm al-Quwayn

John A. Shoup

'Ajman and Umm al-Quwayn are two of the seven emirates that make up the **United Arab Emirates**. 'Ajman is the smallest of the seven emirates with a total area of only 100 square miles (260 square kilometers), most of which is immediately located around the capital, 'Ajman City. It also controls two small but important agricultural inland enclaves of Masfut and **al-Manamah**. 'Ajman is ruled by the Al Nu'aymi lineage of the Nu'aym tribe, which has been important in the history of the region. The Nu'aym (Na'im) tribe dominated much of the oasis of al-'Ayn/al-Buraymi in the past and were involved in the disputes over the **oasis** of al-Hatta in the nineteenth century. Part of the Nu'aym moved to **Bahrain**, where they were important allies (both **Bedouin** and **Sunni**) of the ruling **Al Khalifah** family. The Nu'aym were able to establish control over 'Ajman in the mid-eighteenth century, although the exact date is not known. There are no known dates for the first *shaykh*, Rashid ibn Hamid, and only the date of the death in 1816 of the second *shaykh*, Humayd bin Rashid, is known.

'Ajman was able to maintain its independence during the nineteenth century and was recognized by the British by a treaty with *Shaykh* Rashid ibn Humayd al-Nu'aymi signed in 1820. During the nineteenth and first part of the twentieth centuries, 'Ajman's economy was based on **pearling**, fishing, and oasis agriculture, much like the other emirates. 'Ajman's small territory has no **oil**, and in 1971 the ruling *shaykh*, Rashid bin Humayd, opted to join the United Arab Emirates, and Abu Dhabi's massive oil wealth was shared out by its ruling *shaykh*, **Zayid bin Sultan al-Nahyan**.

'Ajman's population also remained small, with only 36,000 in 1980. Building booms in **Dubai**, **Sharjah**, and to a degree **Ra's al-Khaymah** have recently affected the emirate. With the rising cost of living in the other nearby emirates combined with 'Ajman's close proximity and easy connection to the others, 'Ajman has become an important "sleeper community." In 2008 the population is estimated to have grown to over 361,000 people, of whom 347,733 live in 'Ajman City. 'Ajman's ruler *Shaykh* Humayd bin Rashid has taken Dubai's recent growth as a model and has opened 'Ajman to the same type of freehold property development in an attempt to draw investors. There are several developments scheduled, including one that is supposed to help protect the stand of mangrove trees in the shallows just off 'Ajman City's coast.

Umm al-Quwayn was established in 1775 by the first ruler of the Al Mu'alla lineage of the Al 'Ali. Like the other emirates, Umm al-Quwayn was recognized as an independent emirate by treaty with the British in 1820. The emirate is small, but nearly twice the size of 'Ajman with a total area of 289 square miles (750 square kilometers). Its population is the smallest of the seven emirates making up the United Arab Emirates with a total of only 62,000 people (2003 estimate), most of who live in the main city of Umm al-Quwayn.

'Ali bin Hussein bin 'Ali (1879–1935)

Sebastian Maisel

'Ali bin Hussein was the son of **Hussein bin 'Ali**, Grand *Sharif* of **Makkah** and King of the **Hijaz**. 'Ali succeeded his father and ruled the Hijaz for a short period of time. He was born in Makkah in 1879 and was the eldest son. Most of his childhood he spent with his family in exile in Istanbul, but after his father was appointed ruler of Makkah, he returned with his family to the Hijaz. Under his father he served as an army leader in the **Arab Revolt**. His brothers Faysal and 'Abdallah were rewarded for their participation in the anti-Turkish campaign with the thrones in Iraq and Transjordan. 'Ali inherited his father's throne as King of the Hijaz. In the years following World War I he unsuccessfully tried to stem the advances of **'Abd al-'Aziz ibn Sa'ud's** army on Makkah and **Jiddah**. After his father's forced abdication, 'Ali was proclaimed King of Hijaz on October 6, 1924. The Hijaz under his rule became a constitutional monarchy with a national representative council that included the nobility of the Hijaz, such as the *Sharifs*, religious scholars, and merchants. The area experienced a short renaissance in culture and **education** with the foundation of schools and **newspapers**. However, the rule of 'Ali was contested by ibn Sa'ud, who tried to expel the **Hashemites** (see **Al Hashim**) entirely and incorporate the Hijaz into his realm. After a long siege and realizing that the British were no longer willing to support him, 'Ali surrendered his last stronghold, the city of Jiddah, and left for Iraq, where his younger brother Faysal was king. 'Ali was married to *Sharifah* Nafisah bint 'Abd al-Ilah and they had five children: four daughters and one son, 'Abd al-Ilah, who became the regent of Iraq during the minority of King Faysal II. 'Ali died in Baghdad in 1935.

FURTHER READING

De Gaury, Gerald. *Rulers of Mecca*. London: Harrap, 1951.
Vassiliev, Alexei. *The History of Saudi Arabia*. London: Saqi Books, 1998.

'Anazah

Sebastian Maisel

One of the largest tribal confederations in Arabia is the 'Anazah, who live and migrate over several Middle Eastern countries, including **Saudi Arabia**, Jordan, Syria, and Iraq. It is estimated that the confederation numbers around 1 million. Their tribal territory spreads roughly within the area of Aleppo to the north, Damascus to the west, Baghdad to the east, and Taymah in the south, thus covering most of the Syrian Desert, but overlapping with other tribal areas, such as those of the **Shammar**. The boundaries of tribal areas in Arabia have been loosely fixed since the beginning of the eighteenth century.

The 'Anazah tribe has a long history going back to the pre-Islamic *jahiliyah* period and the time of the Prophet **Muhammad**. Originally located in al-Yamamah in southern **Najd**, their ancestors belonged the Rabi'a tribe, who was in opposition to the early Muslim community and had their area destroyed by the first Caliph, Abu Bakr. After the Qaramitah war in 1165, they started to move northward to the Harah of Khaybar from where they continued to the north and east in the fifteenth and sixteenth centuries. From the end of the seventeenth century they pushed to the north into their current territory leaving the sections of the Wuld Sulayman, Fuqarah and Wuld 'Ali behind in what later became Saudi Arabia. As the most powerful tribe of the region, next to the Shammar, they played an important role in the politics of the nineteenth century, but since the 1870s they fell under Ottoman influence through the system of allocating land and titles to the tribal leadership. In 1917–1918 they joined the British in World War I and submitted to the Mandate powers, and in 1925 to the *Sultan* of Najd, **'Abd al-'Aziz**. In the past they have been **camel** nomads, but since the beginning of the twentieth century they have mostly engaged in sheep farming. During the height of the **Ikhwan** movement, they founded several colonies in the **oasis** of Khaybar, where the tribe owned land and plantations. They did not participate in the Ikhwan rebellion, but remained loyal to ibn Sa'ud. After World War II they quickly abandoned nomadism and settled in rural areas.

The ruling family of Saudi Arabia, the **Al Sa'ud**, and the ruling family in **Kuwait**, the **Al Sabah**, both descend from the 'Anazah tribes; the Al Sa'ud family descends from the Wuld 'Ali branch. In 1710, formerly nomadic 'Anazah groups from central Arabia founded **Kuwait City**, and 'Abd al-Rahim of the Sabah lineage became *shaykh* in 1756, the first of the family that continues to rule Kuwait. The ruling family of **Bahrain**, the **Al Khalifah**, also claims descent from the 'Anazah through the 'Utub branch.

The name 'Anazah derives from the Arabic word *'anz* (goat), which leads to the assumption that the 'Anazah in addition to their camel herds also bred goats. In genealogical terms, the 'Anazah are of 'Adnan (northern) descent; however, there seems to be confusion regarding their subdivisions and branches about a regional division into a northern and southern branch. One approach defines the northern section, which denotes the groups of northern Syria and Iraq, including the Fid'an, Saba'ah, 'Amarat, and Khursah, and the southern section, which includes the Banu Wahab with the Hasanah and Wuld 'Ali and the Al Galas with the Ruwalah and Mihlif. A smaller section of the 'Anazah that remained in al-Yamamah and settled much earlier is also considered part of the southern branch. They include the Bani Hizzan (al-Hazazinah) and the Jumaylah in Aflaj. However, the latter mainly moved to the east under pressure from the Dawasir. The Ruwalah essentially became an independent unit within the confederation and often fought other clans over the supreme leadership, which was held for many years in the hands of the Al Sha'lan. Each group is headed by a tribal leader called *shaykh*, a position that can be inherited within an important family or lineage. The leading *shaykhly* families in the 'Anazah tribe are the ibn Hadhal of the 'Amarat, and the Ibn Sha'lan from the Ruwalah section, the latter being the fourth most powerful family in Arabia prior to World War II after the Al Sa'ud, the Hashimites (see **Al Hashim**), and the **Al Rashid**. The Ruwalah under Nuri Sha'lan participated in the **Arab Revolt**. Through intermarriage with the Saudi royal family, they are considered part of the social and partly the political elite of the kingdom. A member of the Sha'lan family made headlines in 2007 when he was accused of drug trafficking in France.

In general, like many other nomadic groups in the area, the traditional way of life has been severely affected by rapid modernization, **urbanization**, and industrialization. Although the prospects for the survival of their lifestyle are slim, their cultural and social impact on the society because of their sheer number and being the most numerous tribe in Saudi Arabia is still strong.

FURTHER READING

Ashkenazi, Touvia. "The 'Anazah Tribes," *Southwestern Journal of Anthropology* 4, no. 2 (1948): 222–239.

Ashkenazi, Touvia. "Social and Historical Problems of the 'Anazah Tribes," *Journal of the Economic and Social History of the Orient* 8, no. 1 (1965): 93–100.

Lancaster, William. *The Rwala Bedouin Today.* Prospect Heights, IL: Waveland, 1997.

Lewis, Norman. *Nomads and Settlers in Syria and Jordan, 1800–1980.* London: Cambridge University Press, 1987.

Musil, Alios. *The Manners and Customs of the Rwala Bedouins.* New York: American Geographical Society, 1928.

Shanklin, William M., "The Anthropology of the Rwala Bedouins," *Journal of the Royal Anthropological Institute of Great Britain and Ireland* 65 (1935): 375–390.

Arabian Gulf

John A. Shoup

The name of this major body of water differs from one shore to the other; it is called the Arabian Gulf or *Khalij al-'Arabi* by the Arabs and *Khalij al-Farisi* or Persian Gulf by the Iranians and most of the rest of the world. The classical Arab geographers called it *Bahr Faris*, or the Persian Sea, from which its modern name, the Persian Gulf, derives. To avoid any problem over the name, it is frequently called simply "the Gulf." The Persian Gulf lies between Iran on the north and the **Arabian Peninsula** on the south and is fed by the Tigris and Euphrates Rivers, which flow into its western end through the Shatt al-'Arab waterway. The Shatt al-'Arab is shared between Iran and Iraq and is separated from **Kuwait** by Bubiyan Island. The Gulf stretches about 600 miles (970 kilometers) from the Strait of Hormuz in the east to the Shatt al-'Arab on the west. The Strait of Hormuz is only thirty to fifty miles (forty-eight to eighty kilometers) wide and includes four islands: Qishm, which belongs to Iran; and Greater and Lesser Tunub and Abu Musa, seized from the **United Arab Emirates** by Iran in 1971. The dispute over these islands has been unresolved.

The Gulf has served as a major means of international transportation since the earliest periods, linking Mesopotamia with ancient **Oman** and the Indus civilizations. In more recent times it has been the main water route for **oil** shipments from Iran, Iraq, and all of the Arab Gulf countries. The Gulf coast is shallow and until the twentieth century most of the ports could only accommodate lighter vessels such as light, quick **dhow**s. This fact allowed several pirates to operate in what is today the United Arab Emirates. These pirates preyed on commercial shipping in the Arabian Sea and Indian Ocean from the sixteenth to nineteenth centuries. They were able to escape back into the shallow waters of the Gulf coast and avoid capture by the British Navy until 1820, when Britain imposed peace in the region by landing troops and burning several ships and forts.

The Gulf is home to some of the largest **pearl** banks in the world. The shallow nature of much of the Gulf, along with the relative warm temperature of the water, encourages several sea animals to flourish, including oysters and corals. Pearls were one of the major sectors in the local economy until the discovery of oil in the twentieth century. Coral was used as building material along much of the Gulf coast, where other building materials are scarce. Coral is light but strong, making it an ideal material for walls. The Gulf supports many fish and even today fishing is an important industry, although foreign workers, mainly from Pakistan and India, now do much of the hard labor.

The Gulf has several important oil fields, most of which are fully exploited by the countries who claim them. The importance of the region for the world economy is highlighted when there is a regional dispute or threat of war. World prices of oil are linked to events in the Gulf; a threat of war could close shipping through the Strait of Hormuz.

FURTHER READING

Beaumont, Peter, Gerald Blake, and Malcom Wagstaff. *The Middle East*. London: John Wiley & Sons, 1976.

Fisher, W.B. *The Middle East: A Physical, Social, and Regional Geography*. London: Methuen & Co. Ltd., 1971.

Arabian Horses

John A. Shoup

Faras or *khayl* in Arabic refers to a riding horse and one of *asil* or "noble" descent. The origin of the Arabian horse is lost in antiquity although among the cuneiform tablets discovered in ancient Mesopotamian sites are pedigrees of horses that note attempts to breed animals with the main characteristics of the Arabian. Popular Arab legend traces the purebred Arabian back to five mares that escaped the destruction of the Ma'rib Dam in **Yemen**, or from a horse presented to the Azd tribe by King Solomon. Other legends say that the Arabian horse was born from the wind and in popular terminology Arabian mares are still referred to as *Banat al-Rih*, or Daughters of the Wind. In the pre-Islamic period horses seem to have been rare in much of the Peninsula and held in high esteem for the purity of their bloodlines. Pureblood Arabian horses have very high social value among Arabs and their commercial value has also been very high. Veterinary medicine is among the Islamic sciences advanced in the classical period.

Horses were kept by the **Bedouin** and by the main ruling dynasties in the Peninsula and Gulf. The **Al Khalifah** of **Bahrain** remain avid breeders of race horses and developed their own substrain of the *Kuhaylan* unique to the island called the *Jallabi*. In the mid-nineteenth century the **Al Sa'ud** family owned over 600

18

purebred horses kept on their farm near **Riyadh**. Starting in the late eighteenth and during the nineteenth century, **Kuwait** was one of the major exporters of Arabian horses for the British **military** in India and horses from Syria and Iraq were brought there for sale. The **'Anazah** and **Shammar** Bedouin of the Syrian Desert and northern **Arabian Peninsula** were among the most important sources of purebred horses until the early twentieth century. European and American enthusiasts purchased horses for export back to their own countries, founding many of the main families of purebred Arabians in Europe and North America today. Alarmed by the large number of excellent horses being purchased by Europeans to improve their cavalry mounts, the Ottomans passed a law in the 1890s restricting the numbers of Arabian horses that could be exported and requiring personal written permission called a *firman* from the *Sultan* himself.

The Arabian horse is divided into five main strains, most of which descend from the *Kuhaylan*, considered the most noble of the strains, and frequently today the term *kuhaylan* is used to mean a purebred Arabian horse. The five strains are *Kuhaylan, Hadban, Hamdan, Saqlawi,* and *'Abayan*. In addition, each of these has several subfamilies and there are three other strains generally accepted as *asil* by most Bedouin, the *Umm al-'Arkub, Mu'aniqi,* and *Khlafah*. Each of the five main strains are known for a particular strength but all Arabian horses should have a small nozzle; wide forehead; dish face; thin throat; high head carriage; long, slim neck; short back; long, straight croup; high tail carriage; deep chest; thin but strong legs; and strong hooves. The horse is built to have stamina and run long distances and, although not as fast as its direct descendant the English Thoroughbred, is fast and agile. The qualities of the Arabian horse are such that they were eagerly sought after to improve larger, slower European breeds and the Arabian horse is the originator of all other hot-blood and warm-blood breeds. Arabians are excellent for endurance and dominate endurance racing everywhere in the world.

The ruling houses in Kuwait, Bahrain, and **Saudi Arabia** have long interests in breeding fine horses and in recent years the ruling families in the **United Arab Emirates** have also established horse farms. Unable to draw on local sources for horses, the Emiratis have imported purebred Arabians from Europe, the United States, and Australia. Horses are used in flat racing, where Bahrain dominated for nearly two centuries. The **Al-Maktum** family in the United Arab Emirates introduced endurance races in the 1990s. Since 1998, they have sponsored and competed in the 125 mile (200 kilometer) World's Most Preferred Endurance Ride held in **Dubai**. **Abu Dhabi** established an endurance racing center at al-Wathbah to promote the **sport** and the United Arab Emirates is also promoting endurance races in other Arab countries such as Bahrain, Syria, and Egypt. Bahrain and the United Arab Emirates have sponsored festivals centered on the Arabian horse, the first of these being held in Bahrain as one of the yearly cultural festivals sponsored by the National Museum. The festival in Bahrain focused on the importance of the Arabian horse in Arab history and culture. The United Arab Emirates now has a yearly horse festival that includes not only Arabian horse racing, but also the world's richest Thoroughbred race, the Dubai World Cup, worth $1 million.

FURTHER READING

Dickson, H.R.P. *The Arab of the Desert*. London: Allen & Unwin, 1949.

Jabbur, Jibra'il S. *Bedouins of the Desert: Aspects of Nomadic Life in the Arab East*. Translated by Lawrence Conrad. Albany: State University of New York Press, 1995.

Raswan. Carl. *Black Tents of Arabia: My Life among the Bedouin*. Boston: Little, Brown, and Co., 1935.

Arabian Peninsula

John A. Shoup

The Arabian Peninsula is shaped roughly like a quadrilateral, some 1,367 miles (2,200 kilometers) in length and some 746 miles (1,200 kilometers) in width. Its shape is frequently compared to that of the profile of a rhinoceros' head with the **Musandam** bulge as the horn and the **Qatar** Peninsula as the ear. It includes all of **Saudi Arabia**, **Yemen**, **Oman**, the **United Arab Emirates**, Qatar, and **Kuwait**; the island state of **Bahrain** is the only Arab Gulf country not physically part of the mainland. The Arabian Peninsula is bound on the north by the Nafud Desert and by the riftlike Wadi Sirhan, which is 186 miles (300 kilometers) long and 31 to 43 miles (50 to 70 kilometers) wide, separating it from historic Syria or *Bilad al-Sham* and from Sinai by the Gulf of 'Aqabah; bounded on the southeast by the Red Sea; on the east by the Arabian Sea and the Gulf of Oman; and on the northeast by the **Arabian Gulf** (Persian Gulf). In Arabic it is called *Jazirat al-'Arab*, or Island of the Arabs, and it in many ways is like an island, being separated from Syria by a definite physical division of the Nafud and Wadi Sirhan and making it an "island."

The main physical features include several **mountain** ranges along the Red Sea coast, Yemen, Oman, and the eastern part of the United Arab Emirates; a narrow subtropical coastal plain along the Red Sea coast; a vast inland plain that slowly descends to the Persian Gulf coast; the Persian Gulf coast, which includes large areas of salt flats and bogs in the south; and several sand **deserts**, of which the largest are the Great Nafud in the north and the Rub' al-Khali in the south. Although there are several valleys cut by water erosion, there are no permanent streams or lakes in the Peninsula. The climate is arid, with an average of only five inches (150 millimeters) of rainfall a year and some areas of the Rub' al-Khali not receiving rain for more than ten years at a time. Rain falls during the winter months in the northern and central parts of the Peninsula, but Yemen and parts of Oman receive summer monsoons. When rain does fall it can be torrential, causing flash floods. Summer temperatures frequently are above 100° F (37°C) and temperatures of 120°F (48°C) are not uncommon. The Red Sea coastal plain called the **Tihamah** is semitropical and the humidity during the summer is very high, making life difficult. Winter months can be cold and in the far north near the borders with Jordan and Syria it is possible to have snow on the higher peaks.

The main bodies of water that surround the Peninsula on three sides influence the winds. Although winds tend to be fairly constant from one direction, it is

**Jabal Kawar in the background is a prominent feature of the Jabal al-Akhdar moun-
tain range in Oman. The large tree is a ghaf tree that is used as fodder for camels,
sheep, and goats. The ghaf tree has a wide and deep root system, allowing it to live
and flourish where other trees cannot live.** Courtesy of John A. Shoup.

possible to have violent shifts in direction that can bring sandstorms. Sandstorms
can last from a few hours to several days and can be of such intensity that they
can disrupt air traffic. In Yemen and Oman the monsoon winds bring needed rain
rather than dust and sand. Winds cause sand dunes to shift and simple but effective technologies have been developed to help prevent dunes from burying **oases**,
or at least to slow the process. Interlocking fences of woven palm fronds trap the
sand and fix the dunes in place. Natural vegetation such as the *ghaf* tree grows
on the dunes and may also fix them in place.

There are several islands associated with the Arabian Peninsula in the Red Sea,
with the Persian Gulf, and off the coasts of Oman and Yemen. Many of these are
small and uninhabited coral reefs whereas others have been occupied for millennia. The Persian Gulf country of Bahrain is made up of over thirty islands but
only the main islands of Bahrain, Sitra, and **Muharraq** are inhabited year round.
The island of Socotra, located between Yemen and the Horn of Africa, has historically played an important role as a link between Arab culture of the Peninsula
and African cultures of the Horn and East Africa and may have played a major
role in the introduction of both the **camel** and zebu cattle to the Horn region
some 4,000 years ago. The small islands of Kuria and Muria only a few miles
from the Oman coast are important breeding grounds for sea turtles.

The Peninsula is separated from Africa by the narrow Bab al-Mandab Straits
and from Asia by the equally narrow Strait of Hormuz. Both straits are vital for
international shipping and Hormuz controls access to **oil** terminals for Saudi

Arabia, Kuwait, Iraq, Iran, Bahrain, and the United Arab Emirates, making it one of the most strategic narrows in the world. The straits are controlled by Oman and Iran although a very narrow international zone lies between them. Bab al-Mandab is shared by Yemen, Djibouti, and Eritrea, and in recent years Eritrea and Yemen have been in open conflict over several small islands in the Red Sea.

Arabic Language
Sebastian Maisel

Arabic is an ancient Semitic language, as are Hebrew and Aramaic. It is often referred to as Northern Arabic in contrast to Southern Arabic, which nowadays is only spoken among the Mahra tribe in northern Hadramawt as well as on the island of Socotra. Arabic is situated between the southern and northwestern Semitic languages, overlapping both in certain areas. Arabic is the most widespread Semitic language, with over 200 million native speakers and nearly 50 million second-language speakers, which makes Arabic one of the official languages at the United Nations. Arabic is the language of the Qur'an, believed to be God's divine revelation by almost 1 billion Muslims worldwide, and Muslims all know basic structures, passages, and prayers in this language.

The Standard Arabic of today is called Modern Standard Arabic, or *fusha*, and derives from Classical Arabic, the Arabic of the Qu'ran and literature of the early Islamic empires. Arabs speak a variety of local dialects that differ not only from Modern Standard but also from each other. Even in the pre-Islamic period Arabs spoke a number of dialects, but the language used by poets was considered to be the best. Poets were honored for their abilities in the language. During the pre-Islamic period all of the arts associated with language, recitation, and calligraphy were highly honored.

Starting in 610, the Qur'an was revealed in the same poetic language, but in the dialect of **Makkah** (Mecca), **Muhammad**'s birthplace. Later this version came to be known as Classical Arabic. There are few changes in syntax and morphology, but there are more in vocabulary even though Arabic has not borrowed heavily from other languages. *Fusha* tried to preserve the classical language of the Quran when Muslim linguists established a grammatical system that is still used with certain adaptations and transformations.

HISTORY

The history of Arabic is classified in four segments: old (proto) Arabic, early Arabic, middle or Classical Arabic, and Modern Standard Arabic. The oldest mention of Arabic and the Arabs are proper names found in Assyrian inscriptions from the ninth century BC. Aramaic and Assyrian influenced old Arabic. The following period from the third to the sixth century is called early Arabic. From this time the first self-contained scripts stem back from rock graffiti from 400 BC.

The phenomenon of diglots, in which two forms of the same language exist parallel to each other as colloquial and high language, goes back to that time period when colloquial dialects were competing with the language of the poetry. Classical Arabic evolved at the same time. Hundreds of Aramaic, South Arabian, and Persian loanwords entered the language through contacts between the Arab tribes and Christian and Jewish groups. Most early Arabic inscriptions trace back to Christian missionaries. Christian Arabic continued to develop, slightly deviating from classical Arabic. Jews in the Arabian Peninsula helped develop Classical Arabic as well, and it is said that Jews in Yathrib (**Madinah**) instructed Muslims to write Arabic. At the court of Hira, written Arabic was further standardized. In the sixth century, Arabic fully developed as the lingua franca in tribal Arabia on the basis of script that dates back to Aramaic and later Nabataean structures. Different writing styles developed, and a cursive style using diacritical markers prevailed.

The Arabic of poets originated among various tribes in central Arabia and prevailed as a purely literary dialect despite its rather archaic character in phonetics and syntax. Pre-Islamic poetry and the Qur'an are two examples of early Arabic merging with classical trends in its most extended form. Syntax, grammar, vocabulary, and pronunciation were clearly defined and a standard literary language, classical Arabic, was formed. Although Arabs continued speaking in their local dialects, all accepted classical Arabic for purposes of writing. On the basis of the "clear and eloquent Arabic" of the Qur'an, sayings of the Prophet **Muhammad**, speeches of the caliphs, and poetry samples, linguists and grammarians put together a list of authentic references and collected, studied, and commented on them. Arabic was heavily influenced by Islam, particularly the literary language. Having the holy book of the Qur'an revealed in God's own language, Arabic, was evidence and justification to give the language a superior role over others. Muslims strived to memorize, record, and preserve this sacred language as much as possible. Worries over variations in the reading and reciting of the text led to efforts to create a standard copy and final edition of the Qur'an.

During the Arabic-Islamic expansion from the seventh until the eleventh century, Arabic came in contact with other languages, cultures, and religions. The local non-Arab and even non-Muslim population adapted Arabic quickly and simplified syntax, word order, and vocabulary, creating a hybrid version that coexisted with the classical Arabic of the Qur'an and the **Sunna**. Arabic became the lingua franca for the Empire, especially in the field of scholarship, and it superseded Southern Arabic in **Yemen**. In Syria Arabic replaced Greek and Aramaic, in Egypt Coptic, and in Northern Africa the indigenous Berber languages. The Umayyad Caliph 'Abd al-Malik, who ruled from 645 to 705, made Arabic the official language for the administration of the Islamic Empire. The everyday language and local dialects as spoken by the different social elements within the Islamic Empire needed some sort of direction before going astray in the large and diverse area. During the eighth and ninth centuries, Arab grammarians laid out the basic grammatical guidelines and rules of classical Arabic, which are still applied today for modern standard Arabic. During the Golden Age of Islam, sciences and arts flourished, as did the use of Arabic among scholars, translators, intellectuals, scientists, and poets. Many of them were non-Arabs; however, it was during this time that the diglossia became apparent. On one hand the spoken language was corrupted by vulgarism and foreign infiltration, whereas the literary language became a privilege of the elite and required extensive training. Soon it was superseded by New Persian as the dominant language in the Muslim east. Concurrently, the Islamic Empire began to disintegrate and local, independent dynasties emerged. With the fall of the 'Abbasid Empire, the focus of classical Arabic shifted to Cairo, where the Mamluks established a new center of culture and literature; however, after the conquest of most of the Middle East by the Turkish-speaking Ottomans, the cultivation of Arabic reached a historic low point. A period of stagnation and decay for almost 300 years witnesses the fostering of the gap between the literary Arabic as the language of a very small elite and the emergence of the vernacular language in all other areas.

Napoleon's expedition to Egypt in 1798 began a long range of European involvement with the affairs of the Arab world. It sparked immediate attempts for political reform and led to an often deliberate adaptation of Western ideas and products. Arabs studied in Europe, and brought back home a sense of longing for identity, which was found in the Arabic language. Thus, schools were opened, an active **media** was founded, and intellectual ideas were exchanged on the basis of translations of European books into Arabic. In the second half of the nineteenth century, the idea of nationalism based on ethnic lines found its way to the Arab world and led to a revival in studies on the origins of Arabs and Arabic language and heritage. The movement started among Syrian/Lebanese writers like Ibrahim al-Yaziji or Butrus al-Bustani who relied on classical Arabic sources as well as modern European works. New words were created and adapted to the traditional root system, a modern press promoted and spread the new ideas and terms, and dictionaries and encyclopedias were put together. On the advent of a growing educational system and higher literacy rates, the interest of the general public in this movement and the language grew rapidly; particularly the issue of coining new terms was widely discussed and written about. In 1919, it led to the founding of the first scientific academy for Arabic in Damascus devoted to reform and modernizing the Arabic language. Followed by the Egyptian language academy in 1932, various publications wrote about new regulations and expansions. *Lughat al-'Arab*, the review of the language academy in Baghdad, became another influential voice for the efforts in developing terminology. However, it remained a major concern of how these new words and rules were accepted by the public. It turned out that some words quickly made it into the daily languages, whereas other creations were completely ignored.

During the *Nahdah* period, Classical Arabic was revived and a new hybrid, Modern Standard Arabic, was developed to address the challenges of modernity. Both continued to be applied among the general educated public, whereas dialects were used alongside for day-to-day communications; however, **education** became available for the masses, and thus with the opening of schools and implementation of curricula in Arabic countries, both literary forms, the old classical and the newer modern standard form, widely spread in the society. Now a uniform language is taught all over the Arab world, from Morocco to Iraq, and it is regarded by Arab people as a symbol of unity and identity. The vernacular coexists with Modern Standard Arabic, but neither will replace the other.

DIALECTS

Although Classical and Modern Standard Arabic are mainly used in literature and other forms of writing, everyday conversation is held in a vernacular or dialect. Sometimes referred to as colloquial Arabic, it differs from literary Arabic in syntax, morphology, vocabulary, and phonetic structures. A vernacular form of Arabic is spoken in a large, extended region ranging from the Atlantic Ocean and northern Africa to the Fertile Crescent and the **Arabian Peninsula**. In addition, isolated regions exist, such as Djibouti, Zanzibar, Cyprus, and Malta. Finally, there is a large Arabic Diaspora in North and South America as well as in West Africa.

Spoken Arabic emerged from old dialects in central and western Arabia, **Najd**, and **Hijaz**. The dialect of the **Quraysh**, the leading tribe in Makkah, contributed to the evolution of Classical Arabic, but continued to be applied among nomadic groups. Among the most noticeable differences between spoken and Classical Arabic is the absence of case endings; verbal inflexions; and the use of passive, dual, and feminine plurals. Phonetically, dialects offer a greater variety and flexibility in terms of vowel range. Dialects are predominantly oral, and with a few exceptions of proverbs and poetry, are not recorded but rather recited or narrated.

Arabic dialects are normally classified by geographical rather than linguistic terms. Other forms of classification look at lifestyle, religion, or education level. Five main dialect groups follow geographical boundaries from the Maghrib, Egypt and Sudan, the Mashriq, the Arabian Peninsula, and Iraq. Because of the well-known and popular Egyptian movie industry, Egyptian Arabic is the most prevailing Arabic dialect and is understood all over the Arab world. The dialect of the Maghrib, which includes Morocco, Algeria, Tunisia, and parts of Libya, is probably the most difficult to comprehend because it includes significant borrowings from French and Berber, Berber being the indigenous language of the area before the arrival of the Arabs in the seventh century. The Mashriq comprises all of Syria, Lebanon, **Palestine**, and Jordan, and the former region of Greater Syria, or *Bilad al-Sham* in Arabic. On the other side of the Syrian Desert, between the Tigris and Euphrates, is the dialect of Iraq, which forms the border to the area of Kurdish and Persian language. On the Arabian Peninsula, one widely understood dialect exists; however, regional versions are recognizable and mutually intelligible. Clear distinctions prevail indicating the origin of the speaker. Therefore, it is possible that a **Bedouin** from the remote Empty Quarter will have difficulties understanding the urban Arabic of **Jiddah**, which in addition is influenced by other languages and dialects. Yemeni Arabic is widely used in Somalia, and the Arabic of **Oman** made it to Zanzibar through extensive trade and religious relations between the two areas.

In Arabic-speaking countries, the difficult situation of diglossia prevails. People use Modern Standard Arabic for writing, literature, the news, formal settings, and scholarship, but speak their local dialect. The usage of either language often overlaps; for example, on formal occasions *fusha* speakers fall back into their home dialect after time and classical or modern standard lexical expressions and phrases are used in daily communication to express more complicated scenarios.

Native speakers learn the dialect first at home to study *fusha* at school. When communicating with speakers of other dialects they have difficulties understanding each other because Arabic dialects are not easily mutually intelligible with the exception of the Arabic of Cairo. In those cases, people will revert to *fusha* as much as they are able to.

SPREAD TO OTHER CULTURES AND RELIGIONS

Other languages use the Arabic alphabet with some graphical modifications, such as Persian, Kurdish (Sorani), Pashto, and Urdu, but mostly they rely on Arabic for Islamic worship and education. Other languages of predominantly Muslim people were strongly influenced by Arabia, such as Turkish, Swahili, or Hausa. Many words, especially scientific terms, found their way into European languages. Contact was established during the Arab period in Spain and Sicily long before the First Crusade in 1096, and words such as *alcohol*, *cotton*, *magazine*, and *genie* were directly borrowed from Arabic.

Within the geographical Arabic area, there are non-Arabic languages that have developed mutual and symbiotic relations. In Syria, Aramaic is still spoken (and lately written as well) in three remote villages. Circassians, Sunni Muslims originating from the Caucasus, live in Jordan and Syria. Armenians are found in Lebanon, Syria, and Palestine/Israel. One of the largest linguistic minorities in the Middle East is the Kurds, who speak an Indo-European language close to Persian. In Oman, a small community speaks the Persian dialect of Kumzari, and in the border area between Oman and Yemen modern south Arabian languages survived. Modern Hebrew is spoken in Israel and Palestine.

Although Arabic is the official and sacred language of Islam, other faiths use it for their liturgy and prayers. Fifteen million Christians from different denominations, especially Maronites in Lebanon and Cyprus, speak Arabic, whereas the Syrian Orthodox Church uses Karshuni (Arabic with Syriac letters). Some 2 million Jews from Morocco to Turkey speak Yahudi, a distinct form of Arabic. The Yazidi communities of Bashiqa and Bahzani in Iraq, although ethnically Kurds, adopted Arabic as their spoken and religious language.

STRUCTURE

Arabic is written from right to the left. The Arabic alphabet contains twenty-eight letters consisting of consonants and long vowels, and several diacritical symbols representing short vowels and other pronunciation and grammatical markers. Arabic script evolved from earlier Semitic alphabets such as Aramaic and Phoenician. Fully vocalized texts are rarely found with the exemption of the Qur'an and some poetry. The art of writing, calligraphy, became one of the most venerated forms of artistic expression among Muslims because of the sacred status of Arabic as the language of God and the general discouragement of depicting the human figure.

The vowel sounds are a, u, and i, both in a short and long form, in addition to vowel combinations and diphthongs. Stress is bound to the syllabic structure of the word. As a rule of thumb, stress falls on the heavy syllable before the last syllable of the word. It never moves beyond the third syllable from the end. The general syntax requires the attribute to follow the noun and to agree with it in gender, number, case, and status. The common word order is verb-subject-object, but nominal sentences with or without copula exist.

The typical feature of all Semitic languages, including Arabic, is the use of a root-and-pattern system. On the basis of a tri-letter root structure, words are formed by using additional markers such as prefixes, suffixes, long and short vowels, and other grammatical or phonological symbols. For example, the Arabic root d-r-s connotes the meaning of study. Adding a specific vocalization, a prefix, or doubling the stress creates other word types such as conjugation pattern, active or passive participles, places, adjectives, and so forth. *Darasa* means studying, *yadrus* he studies, *dirasah* study of, *madrasah* school, *mudarris* teacher (masculine), etc.

Arabic also borrows foreign words and assimilates them into the language. However, the first option is still to look for a word that can be derived from the existing Arabic root system. Sometimes linguists at the main academies go back to the classical period in their search for new words and meanings; for example, the word *jaridah* in old Arabic is a stripped palm branch used for writing that is now used to mean **newspaper**. Other strategies include literal translations (*qatala al-waqt*—he killed time), using prefixes like in Latin-based languages (*la-silki*—wireless), or adopting Western translations (*miknasah kahraba'iyah*—electric broom/vacuum cleaner).

USE IN ARABIA

Arabic is the native language for **Saudi Arabia** and the Gulf States. The Arabian Peninsula, covering a vast area and several cultural zones, is the birthplace of Arabic. Its early forms emerged and developed between ancient south Arabian kingdoms and north Arabian empires. In between, poets and merchants of central Arabia contributed to the uniformity the language, witnessed especially with the divine revelations to Muhammad in the very same language. As noted before, the center of language maturity moved away from Arabia into the Fertile Crescent only to return at the beginning of the twentieth century to the Hijaz. Vernaculars, however, remained strongly attached to the early forms. Although one can analyze the dialectical map of Arabia along geographical features, the different lifestyles of its people should also be considered. Hijazi Arabic is a very distinct form, and two separate versions are dominant in the area: the one of the urban settlers in Jiddah, Makkah, and Madinah; and that of the nomadic Bedouins tribes such as the Harb, Billi, and **Huwaytat**. Other subregions on the Peninsula include *Khaliji*, *Bahraini*, *Najdi*, and *Yamani* (Yemeni) Arabic. They encounter the same linguistic separation between nomadic and urban groups. Generally, Bedouin varieties are more conservative, whereas urban dialects tend to adopt both classical and modern features. Bedouin dialects have a common origin and are mostly intelligible amongst all Bedouin. Most tribes originating in southern Arabia moved northward to the Hijaz and from there spread into Najd and the Gulf area. Thus, tribes in eastern Arabia usually have no problems conversing with tribes from the western part. The dominant dialect on the Gulf is *Khaliji*, or Gulf-Arabic, with two main influences coming from the Bedouin tribes who moved to the area some centuries ago, as well as Mesopotamia and Iraqi Arabic, which was connected by trade relations and the same authority. A subdialect is *Bahraini* Arabic, which is considered a more indigenous form although it borrowed many words from Persian and Hindi. The dialect of Oman stretched out into southern Arabia and the Hadramawt as well as to eastern Africa, where close trade and cultural relations between Zanzibar and Oman existed for centuries. In the southern parts of Saudi Arabia, in the **Najran** and **Asir** region, Yemeni Arabic influences are easily identifiable.

FURTHER READING

Ingham, Bruce. *Arabian Diversions: Studies in the Dialects of Arabia*. Reading, UK: Garnet Publishing, 1997.

Holes, Clive. *Modern Arabic: Structures, Functions and Varieties*. London: Longman, 1995.

Holes, Clive. *Dialect, Culture and Society in Eastern Arabia*. Leiden, The Netherlands: Brill, 2001.

Prochazka, Theodore. *Saudi Arabian Dialects*. New York: Kegan Paul International, 1988.

Al-Tajir, Mahdi Abdalla. *Language and Linguistic Origins in Bahrain: The Baharnah Dialects of Arabic*. London: Kegan Paul International, 1982.

Versteegh, Kees. *The Arabic Language*. New York: Columbia University Press, 1997.

Arab Revolt

Sebastian Maisel

The Arab Revolt began as a rebellion of **Bedouin** tribes from the **Hijaz** and neighboring areas in 1916 led by Faysal bin Hussein, the son of the *Sharif* of **Makkah**, and **Thomas E. Lawrence**, a British agent, against the Turkish troops of the Ottoman Empire and their German allies. As the Arab Revolt moved north into the rest of the Arab Middle East, others joined its ranks. The domestic policy of the Ottoman Empire prior to World War I, especially after the takeover of the Young Turks, was characterized by favoring Turks and discrimination against the non-Turkish peoples of the empire, most notably against the Arabs and their quest for political participation or autonomy. With the outbreak of World War I those alienated forces were drawn to the side of the Allies, who in turn were looking for powerful, reliable partners to defeat the Ottomans. In a correspondence between *Sharif* **Hussein**, who wanted to break away from the Sublime Porte and create an independent entity in the Hijaz, and the British High Commissioner in Egypt, Sir Henry McMahon, the British vaguely approved the formation of an independent Arab kingdom under Hussein's leadership after the defeat of the Ottomans. In return, the *Sharif* promised to lead the people of the Hijaz in an open rebellion against the Turkish forces in the area. However, both sides interpreted the long-term obligations differently and the British made additional arrangements with both their French allies (Sykes-Picot-Agreement) and the Zionist movement regarding the establishment of a Jewish homeland (Balfour Declaration). But the British needed to counter the rising German influence in the Red Sea area and to gain control of the steppes, which was ruled by the **Shammar** tribe, a close ally of the Ottomans. It should also be mentioned that Britain, at the outbreak of the revolt, suffered several **military** defeats against the Ottoman army, such as at Gallipoli and Kut al-'Amarah.

Not being aware of the dispositions, Sharif Hussein proclaimed the Arab Revolt and named himself King of Hijaz. Bedouin tribes from the area started the campaign on June 5, 1916 with attacks against Turkish positions along the **Hijaz Railway,** the main re-supply route for the Ottoman troops. Hussein's sons Faysal and 'Abdallah became the military leaders of the revolt, but the Arab Bureau, the British representative in Cairo, sent Lieutenant Lawrence as a liaison officer to Hussein's army in order to assist their campaign. Lawrence was able to bring financial, military, and intellectual support and quickly advanced to become a peer to Faysal and 'Abdallah; Faysal was the acknowledged leader of the revolt. Faysal was mostly occupied with internal disputes, but his family served as the undisputed symbol of early Arab nationalism. Lawrence soon became a master of irregular, guerrilla warfare, often identifying himself with his cause by wearing local clothes, speaking Arabic, and learning how to live like the Bedouin.

From a military viewpoint, the Arab Revolt was successful because it bound thousands of Turkish troops, who otherwise would be dispatched to fight the British and Russians. They also contributed significantly to the **Palestine** campaign led by General Allenby and had one of their most important victories at 'Aqabah in July 1917, which they took by a surprise attack. With large support from the local population in Jordan and Syria and the British army, the Arab army pushed forward to Damascus, which they captured on September 30, 1918 without British support. Shortly afterward, the revolt was disbanded and its leaders became involved in the post-war reshaping and re-mapping of the Middle East. *Sharif* Hussein maintained his throne in the Hijaz and proclaimed himself the new *Khalifah* or Caliph, which was challenged by the rising power of 'Abd al-'Aziz ibn Sa'ud. Faysal and the Arab Nationalists had planned that he would rule the Arab kingdom from Damascus; however, the city and Greater Syria were promised to France, who forced him out after the Battle of Maysalun. Britain made him king in the newly established Iraq. His brother 'Abdallah was made *amir* in Transjordan, where the Hashemite still govern. Lawrence published a seminal book of his experiences during the revolt called *Seven Pillars of Wisdom* based on a more direct account he published earlier called *Revolt in the Desert.* The Arab Revolt played an important and controversial role in post-war negotiations, and in the decisions taken by Great Britain and France about the territorial divisions of the former Arab provinces of the Ottoman Empire.

FURTHER READING

Fromkin, David. *A Peace to End All Peace*. New York: Avon Books, 1989.

Johnson, Maxwell. "The Arab Bureau and the Arab Revolt: Yanbu' to Aqaba," *Military Affairs* 46, no. 4 (1982): 194–201.

Lawrence, T.E. *Seven Pillars of Wisdom: A Triumph*. London: J. Cape, 1935.

Thomas, Lowell. *With Lawrence in Arabia*. London: Hutchinson, 1933.

Aramco

Sebastian Maisel

The Saudi Arabian Oil Company, Saudi Aramco, is the most important and largest **oil** company not only in the Middle East but also in the world. The Arabian American Oil Company, known as Aramco, was founded in 1933 as California Arabian Standard Oil Company (CASOC), when Standard Oil of California signed a concessionary agreement with King **'Abd al-'Aziz ibn Sa'ud** over an area of 932,000 square kilometer for a period of sixty-six years. The concession included much of eastern **Saudi Arabia** as well as other offshore and onshore areas. British advisor, Harry St. John **Philby**, was vital in helping ibn Sa'ud to make this decision despite strong British competition. In 1973 the area was reduced to 220,000 square kilometers, including 31,000 square kilometers offshore. Shortly after, the first oil prospectors started to drill for oil and in 1938 well number 7 started to produce approximately 1,500 barrels a day. In 1936, Texaco Inc. joined the company when it bought fifty percent of the shareholdings. The first tanker with Saudi oil exported to the United States left the Gulf port of Ras Tanura in 1939 from a newly constructed pier. By the following year, production rose to 700,000 tons per annum. The company was essential in supporting King 'Abd al-'Aziz ibn Sa'ud during the financial hardships of World War II, creating a tight bond between the company, the United States, and the country. The company's headquarters and main operation terminals are located in **Dhahran** and the Eastern Province of Saudi Arabia. The current name was chosen in 1944. After two other oil **companies**, Standard Oil of New Jersey (later Exxon) and Socony-Vaccum Oil Company (later Mobil) merged with the company; shareholdings of 1948 were distributed as follows: Exxon thirty percent, Standard Oil of California thirty percent, Texaco thirty percent, and Mobil ten percent.

Saudi Arabia began to pressure Aramco in 1950 for better terms and was subsequently awarded with fifty-fifty net-profit sharing. Among the most productive oil fields are Ghawar and Safaniyah (the world's largest onshore and offshore fields, respectively), Abqaiq, Khursaniyah, **Dammam**, Marjan, and Khurais. Saudi Arabia is considered the country with the largest oil reserves worldwide, and Saudi Aramco, as the company was renamed later, owns almost all of it, about 260 billion barrels. In addition, Aramco is leading in the production of natural gas liquids, which are partly being used for domestic industry as well as for export.

The company was partly nationalized in 1973 and went fully into Saudi custody in 1980. Although government owned, it still functions like a commercial oil company, developing and acquiring new technologies, refineries, and oil fields. It invested in human capital by training and educating thousands of Saudi workers, for example through the well-known King Fahd University of Petroleum and Minerals in Dhahran, and employs over 50,000 Saudi and international workers. In the early days, the **Shi'a** population of Saudi Arabia concentrated mostly in the Eastern Province formed the core of skilled workers for Aramco in addition to a strong presence of American oilmen and their families. The current president, director, and CEO is Abdullah Jumah, and chairman is 'Ali

Saudi Aramco exhibition, Dhahran, Saudi Arabia. Courtesy of Sebastian Maisel.

al-Nuʿaymi, concurrently Saudi Arabian Minister of Oil and Petroleum. The company is a leading global economic player focused on investing in different industrial sectors in order to diversify the dependency on oil.

FURTHER READING

Brown, Anthony C. *Oil, God, and Gold: The Story of Aramco and the Saudi Kings*. Boston: Houghton Mifflin, 1999.

Hanrahan, Gene Z. *Secret History of the Oil Companies in the Middle East*. Salisbury, NC: Documentary Publications, 1979.

Nawwab, Ismail, Peter C. Speers, and Paul F. Hoye. *Aramco and Its World: Arabia and the Middle East*. Dhahran, Saudi Arabia: Aramco, 1980.

Stegner, Wallace. *Discovery! The Search for Arabian Oil*. Portola, CA: Selwa Press, 2007.

Yergin, Daniel. *The Prize: The Epic Quest for Oil, Money and Power*. New York: Simon & Schuster, 1991.

Archaeological and Historical Sites and Museums

Sebastian Maisel

The **Arabian Peninsula** is replete with historical and archaeological sites bearing evidence of a long history dating back thousands of years and giving the area another important label of a crossroad of civilizations. The people of the Arabian

Neolithic rock graffiti from the Empty Quarter, Saudi Arabia. Courtesy of Sebastian Maisel.

Peninsula have been vital as middlemen in overland trade along the coasts of the Red Sea and the **Persian Gulf** and with the domestication of the dromedary (**camel**) encouraged the lucrative spice trade between Southern Arabia and Syria or Egypt. The people of Arabia from early on contributed significantly to the development of early civilizations in Mesopotamia and Egypt. Many rock carvings, statues, and clay tablets depict the lifestyles and economic and social sophistication of the area. Hellenistic influence is found in former commercial centers along the coast of **Kuwait** and **Bahrain**, as well as in the oasis town of Thaj in **Saudi Arabia**. With the rise of Islam, another aspect contributed to the importance of the region. Although being a religion of city people and merchants, Islam spread rapidly throughout the Middle East.

Archaeological exploration in Arabia started in the nineteenth century, when European travelers began to study the ruins and inscriptions of places like Mada'in Salih, Taymah, or Ma'rib. In 1914, Jaussen and Savignac conducted the first thorough study of the **architecture** and epigraphs of the **Hijaz**. Later in the 1930s, Harry St. John **Philby**, through his unique position as advisor of King **'Abd al-'Aziz ibn Sa'ud**, surveyed large areas throughout the entire peninsula and also carried out small excavations at promising sites. Concurrent with his travels was a revived interest among local scholars in ancient antiquities and tribal origins. Hamd al-Jasir and 'Abd al-Quddus al-Ansari were the leading figures in the documentation of the archaeological heritage of Arabia. Their historic consciousness about the Islamic and pre-Islamic eras was a result of the Ottoman and other foreign rule in the area and the subsequent development of an Arabian cultural identity. In the 1950s a new period of archeological research started and produced large results predominantly in the epigraphy and rock art of Arabia. Possible links to the prehistoric cultures of the north were detected in the Negev and Sinai.

At the same time an international extensive survey and excavation program began along the coast of the Gulf, including Kuwait, Bahrain, **Qatar, Abu Dhabi,** and **Oman**, which unearthed material from the fifth to the second millennia BC and reconstructed the historical links of the area to Mesopotamia and India. Although no massive monuments or large cities have been discovered, the study showed the major role of the area in the development of maritime commerce along the Gulf for over 7,500 years. Trade relations with Mesopotamia around 5500 BC and long-distance commercial links with India by 3000 BC indicate the high level of shipbuilding and navigation skills among the people of the **Arabian Gulf**. The **pearl** industry looks back at a similar long history. **Ra's al-Khaymah's** archaeological program was conducted mostly by German experts, who first found evidence of settlement in the area dating back to the 'Ubaid Period (5000–3800 BC). Like the other states, Ra's al-Khaymah sponsored intensive projects through the Department of Antiquities and Museums, which is also in charge of the country's National Museum.

After half a century of archaeological research many historical and archaeological sites were discovered, restored, and analyzed. A premier location is Qariyat al-Faw in southern **Najd**, the place of a successful trading post on the frankincense route from south Arabia. For almost 1,500 years, until maritime routes became more prominent, it was a major stop for the caravans from **Najran** to the northern city of Mada'in Salih. A team of local archaeologists from King Saud University in **Riyadh** excavated this important site, which provides the main artifacts for the Archaeological Museum in Riyadh. The site shows the continuity of historical and cultural identity of the area. Some decorative and ornamental artifacts from Qariyat al-Faw have been excavated and incorporated into modern design and architecture.

Another site in the Eastern Province was accidentally discovered by **oil** workers, the Jawan Chamber Tomb, which included a variety of objects made of gold, iron, and ivory dating back 2,000 years. In the northern part of the kingdom near the town of Sakakah is the site of fifty groups of standing stone pillars dating back from the Neolithic period. Up to ten feet high (three meters), some of them have Thamudic inscriptions and are aligned to sunrise and sunset. In the 1950s, a Danish archaeological expedition identified the ancient trading post of Dilmun as located in Bahrain, the main port between Mesopotamia and India. Undoubtedly, the most significant archaeological site in the Arabian Peninsula is Mada'in Salih, the Nabataean city near al-'Ula in Saudi Arabia. Beginning in the third century BC until the second century AD, the Nabataeans ruled over an area that included present-day Jordan and **Palestine**. Along with the sister city of Petra, Mada'in Salih was the trading and political capital, strategically located on a cross point of several caravan routes. Today almost 100 rock-cut tombs are preserved, depicting the sophisticated achievements of the people who made a fortune on taxing the caravans en route to Egypt, Persia, or the Roman Empire. In 1968 a British team began to uncover artifacts and examples of the **material culture** as well as rock graffiti, some of them now on display in the National Museum in Riyadh. Early Islamic sites were surveyed and studied too; for example, the institution of Darb Zubaidah, the pilgrim caravan route from Mesopotamia to **Makkah** from the ninth century with its many housing complexes, wells, and artificial pools. A modern historical site is the **Hijaz Railroad**, which was built by the Ottomans before World War I and successfully damaged during the **Arab Revolt** under **Lawrence of Arabia**. Some of the tracks, bridges, and smaller stations are still intact, whereas two main stations, those in al-Ula and **Madinah**, were partly reconstructed and turned into open-air museums with old engines and buildings on display.

The concept of displaying art or artifacts is not alien; however, in correlation with the religious and social traditions, it is rather strange. Islam as the Peninsula's dominant religion does not prohibit the exhibition of artistic expression or specifically encourage it. Islam in Saudi Arabia and Qatar is connected with the teachings of **Muhammad 'Abd al-Wahhab** and his adherence to the traditional teachings of ibn Hanbal, which refuse all innovations to the religion, including the worship of saints and tombs, as well as the prohibition of portraying human figures.

Despite these difficult conditions, the Saudi Arabian museum environment has developed dramatically over the years. In the early 1970s, it took the first protagonists' patience and efforts to convince the authorities about the necessity to adopt an archaeological and museum-oriented policy. Anything that was related to the *jahiliyah* period, the pre-Islamic era before the Prophet **Muhammad**, was suspicious, and the creation of a permanent site to display these artifacts seemed impossible. Thanks to the restless efforts of the Department of Antiquities and Museums and its first director Abdallah Masry, a comprehensive archaeological survey was initiated in 1976 and the results were reported in *Atlal*, the Journal of Saudi Arabian Archaeology. The survey resulted in the discovery and beginning restoration of many archaeological sites and inscriptions throughout the kingdom, such as the Darb Zubaidah, the **pilgrimage** road from Baghdad to Makkah with its inns and wells built in the eighth century, or the Dir'iyah project, being the first capital of the Saudi state.

In the mid-1970s, the Department of Antiquities and Museums inaugurated the Museum of Archaeology and Ethnography in Riyadh, where for the first time a coherent chronology for the heritage, history, and archaeology of Saudi Arabia was developed and displayed. Since then other sites of historic importance have been restored, such as the former capital of the first Saudi state, Dir'iyah, the Qasr al-Murabbah, the Masmak in Riyadh, the Bait Nassif in **Jiddah**, or the 'Umar bin al-Khattab Mosque in Dumat al-Jandal. The government funded these preservation projects as well as a network of local museums in each of the five major regions of the kingdom, i.e., Taymah, al-'Ula, **Dammam**, Najran, and **Buraydah**. Each museum reflects the traditional heritage of the area, including numerous objects of the material culture of the nomadic, rural, and urban population as well as invaluable archaeological findings, thus demonstrating the important part Saudi Arabia has played in the development of culture.

Currently, nineteen museums are licensed in Saudi Arabia, eleven of them officially approved and sponsored by the Higher Council of Antiquities, which highlights the desire of merging history with politics. It is also seen in the future collaboration between governmental agencies such as the Agency for Antiquities and Museums and the Supreme Council for Tourism that aims at promoting the rich archaeological heritage to an increasing number of domestic and international tourists. Each of the kingdom's thirteen provinces is scheduled to have its own historical/archaeological/anthropological museum. In addition, several important historical sites, such as fortresses, palaces, or complete villages, are renovated and converted into open-air museums.

In the late 1990s, the Supreme Commission for Tourism discovered the so-called under-used treasure houses, as they were called by *Arab News*, the leading English-language Saudi **newspaper**, in its approach to boost domestic and international **tourism**, increase academic research, and redefine the image of the kingdom. One strategy is focused on the preservation of the cultural and historical heritage of Saudi Arabia. The council is currently taking over the administrative responsibility of all major public museums in the kingdom, including the National Museum in Riyadh. At present, there are more than sixty public and private museums located throughout the kingdom containing priceless collections ranging from historical tools to artistic masterpieces that capture the history and heritage of the kingdom. The variety of different types of museums includes cultural and heritage museums, history museums, and science museums as well as private collections of various sizes.

Similar trends can be observed in the Gulf States. In Kuwait, the Kuwait National Museum and the Tareq Rajab Museum are among the leading institutions, both predominantly focusing on local historical and ethnological material. One of the leaders in the Gulf region is Bahrain, whose National Museum not only serves as a place to display artifacts but also is actively engaged in both archeological excavations and training museum staff in the latest techniques. The Bayt al-Qur'an Museum in **al-Manamah** displays not only copies of the Qur'an but also includes Arabic calligraphy. Bahrain's museums also sponsor lecture series, films, and special displays for the National Independence celebrations. In Qatar, in addition to the prominent National Museum, several forts bear evidence of the country's **military** history. New museums have been built in the **United Arab Emirates** from additional oil revenues, including several focusing on local culture and history such as in al-'Ayn, **Dubai**, and **Sharjah**. Striving to make **Abu Dhabi** a supreme destination for tourism, major Western museums such as the Guggenheim and the Louvre will soon be opening branch museums. However, it is agreed that nothing offensive to the culture and religion of the Emirates, such as nudity or religious artifacts, will be exhibited.

Today, thousands of expatriates and locals, particularly the younger generations, visit these museums daily to become better acquainted with their heritage. However, many local ethnographic museums in remote areas suffer from marginalization and stagnation despite their enormous efforts in collecting, preserving, and documenting. Private museums often know little about maintaining and displaying their holdings. Furthermore, no institutional body exists to create a network between the museums and its staff. In the absence of a map detailing the location and contents of these places, a comprehensive survey should be conducted to document, manage, and facilitate the museums.

Efforts were made by national agencies and museums to return some artifacts that have been stolen from formerly unprotected sites and to prevent the smuggling of valuable artifacts and antiquities in or out of the country. Saudi Arabia, Oman, Kuwait, and Qatar are signatories of the 1970 UNESCO Convention on the Means of Prohibiting and Preventing the Illicit Import, Export and Transfer of Ownership of Cultural Property.

FURTHER READING

Bibby, Geoffrey. *Looking for Dilmun*. New York: Penguin Books, 1970.

Bidwell, Robin. *Travelers in Arabia*. London: Hamlyn, 1976.

Healey, John, and Solaiman al-Theeb. *The Nabataean Tomb Inscriptions of Mada'in Salih*. London: Oxford University Press, 1994.

Hoyland, Robert. *Arabia and the Arabs: From the Bronze Age to the Coming of Islam*. London: Routledge, 2001.

Al Khalifa, Shaykah Haya 'Ali. *Bahrain through the Ages: The Archaeology*. London: Kegan Paul, 1986.

Masry, Abdallah. "Traditions of Archaeological Research in the Near East," *World Archaeology*, 13, no. 2 (1981): 222–239.

Whalen, Norman. "Early Mankind in Arabia," *Saudi Aramco World*, 43, no. 4 (1992): 16–23.

Whitcomb, Donald. "The Archaeology of al-Hasa' Oasis in the Islamic Period," *Atlal 2*, (1978): 95–113.

Architecture

Sebastian Maisel

The architecture of Arabia is unexpectedly contrasting the prevailing image of **Bedouin** tents in a **desert** environment. Traditional architecture is by far not as sophisticated as other forms of artistic expression such as calligraphy or poetry; however, throughout the Peninsula distinct styles and various aesthetic features are found and still enjoy popularity. Arabian architecture combines aspects of art with the requirements of everyday living and the constant battle of the people to adapt to a changing environment. Life in the past was much less secure, as the defensive nature of many structures attests. The various forms of housing structures have been limited by several factors: climate, the availability of building material, and cultural/religious requirements; however, this limitation does not prevent a wide array of decoration and artistic details. But, when comparing quantities and qualities of architectural decoration in Arabia with those in other Middle Eastern cities, it shows a remarkable difference that can be attributed to the impact of puritanical religious beliefs. Among the main and distinctive features of buildings in Arabia are different means to control the heat. They include high and thick walls, covered yards, a few small windows, and special devices to channel the wind and keep water cool. A unique feature of the local architectural style is presented in the different ways to control the flow of air; for example,

Wind tower houses in the Bastakiyah District in Dubai are named for the towers called *barajil* (*barjil* in singular) that work as air conditioners, funneling even the slightest breeze into the house. Burlap or cloth sheets were wet and hung in the recesses of the towers, cooling hot summer winds as they passed through them. From the 1960s through the 1980s, most of the houses were cleared away to make room for more "modern" buildings. Today the few houses that were left have been restored, and Bastakiyah hosts hotels, restaurants, galleries, and craft shops. Courtesy of John A. Shoup.

through ventilation towers that were incorporated into the roofs of many of these buildings, or roof vents that were operated and controlled from the ground level. Carefully aligned to face the prevailing winds that sweep through the region, these features directed air into the inner recesses of the buildings, creating an airy and comfortable living environment in the hot summer months. Climate control was a major factor in the architectural design of the entire region.

The old Arabian architecture flourished during the Sabaeans in the south of the Peninsula as well as among the Nabataeans in the north. Rectangle or oval-shaped cities with massive walls, irrigation systems, sacral buildings, and cemeteries were common, and built from smoothly trimmed limestone blocks with flat, ornamental reliefs for decoration. The Nabataeans were skilled builders and craftsmen and carved amphitheaters, irrigation canals, and large tombs out of mountainsides and large rock outcrops. In central Arabia, the only important architectural evidence was the pagan sanctuary in **Makkah**, the Ka'abah, a large cubic structure. The main form of accommodation was either the adobe brick house or the tent for nomadic groups. With the development of Islamic cities, a new era for Arabic architecture began. The oldest Islamic building, Prophet

Restored house in Dir'iyah, Saudi Arabia, demonstrates Najdi architectural style. The building has two stories around a large central courtyard. It is made of sun-dried mud brick, and the outer layer is also made of mud. The water spouts are made of date palm trunks that are split into two and hollowed out. They drain water off of the roof and stick out far enough from the walls to keep water from damaging the structure. Courtesy of John A. Shoup.

Muhammad's house and place of worship in **Madinah**, introduced a new style of building serving two purposes: the religious and the profane housing needs, a mosque in simple style and first without minarets surrounded by a spacious yard. With the shift of Islamic leadership under the Umayyads and 'Abbasids to urban centers in the north, the architecture of the area remained unchanged for many centuries. Only in the eighteenth century is Ottoman influence visible in the cities along the Red Sea, and to a lesser degree in the Gulf area.

Prior to the discovery of **oil** in the 1940s, the architectural style in **Saudi Arabia** and the neighboring countries changed little with simple styles and forms that reflected the harsh conditions and poverty of the area. In the 1950s about forty percent of the population were nomadic and another forty percent settled in rural villages and **oases**. The remaining twenty percent consisted of the urban population of the few cities, such as **Kuwait, al-Manamah, Jiddah, Riyadh,** Makkah, Madinah, and **Ta'if**. However, **urbanization** did become a more decisive factor in people's decision where to live. The social distinction between nomadic and settler people was shown in the different forms of housing: the Bedouins, moving in search for pasture and water, preferred black goat-hair tents, whereas the people in the oases built largely with unfired sun-dried brick or pounded earth. In the **mountains**, mud was used together with stone. Along the coasts of the Red Sea and the Gulf, houses in the towns and cities were usually built with coral blocks. Other natural building material included wood from tamarisk and palm trees; however, it was only used for structural additions, such as doors, windows, roof beams, or sunscreens. In the hot and humid coastal areas, reeds, palm fronds, and branches were also used to build huts and other temporary shacks in the fields or for the animals.

Traditional architecture in Saudi Arabia can be broadly grouped into styles developed in the central **Najd** plateau, the **Arabian Gulf** coastal region, the **Hijaz** region along the Red Sea coast, and the **Asir** region in the southwest. Although starkly different, these various styles are all functional and simple, and each evolved to take advantage of the available building materials to create a comfortable living environment for the inhabitants, whether they lived in the hot and dry deserts in the central parts of the kingdom or the cool and wet regions of the southwest. After the discovery of oil, the kingdom's infrastructure and architecture transformed into modern styles using new technologies and building materials; however, more and more people are recognizing the need to preserve the remaining pieces of the kingdom's traditional architectural heritage.

NOMADIC ARCHITECTURE: THE BEDOUIN TENT

The traditional tent of the nomads in Arabia consists of several panels of coarse cloth made from goat hair and sheep wool sewn together. Goat hair is water-resistant and durable, lasting for several years before needing to be replaced with a new panel. The panels are then sewn together and form the roof and sides of the tent, which are supported by at least two poles. Ropes adjust the outside walls, which can be raised to allow air circulation and to provide cover and shade from the heat and wind. Usually, a colorful curtain divides the tent into a larger family section and a smaller men's section where guests and other visitors are entertained. During migration the tent and all of its contents are loaded on **camels** although today pickups and larger trucks have replaced camels. When arriving at a new campground, the women erect the tent and set up the site. Even after settling in villages and towns, many Bedouin keep tents next to their permanent houses. During the hot season, it serves as the sleeping room for the entire family. Although it is black, the loosely woven cloth allows heat dispersal and thus lowers the temperature about ten to fifteen degrees. Tents vary in size depending on the status of the owner and size of the family. Important tribal leaders have larger tents with additional poles, and the wealthy *shaykh*s of the 'Anazah and **Shammar** tribes own tents so large that they cannot be transported anymore, but remain at a permanent location and serve representative functions. Currently the more expensive goat-hair tent is becoming rare and has been replaced by industrial cotton/canvas tents, which are less airy and therefore require additional air conditioning. However, because full-scale nomadism has almost completely vanished, tents fulfill more recreational needs with additional comfort.

THE WESTERN REGION: HIJAZ

The western region of the **Arabian Peninsula**, known as Hijaz, includes some of the most important urban centers such as Jiddah, Makkah, Madinah, and Ta'if.

It is known for its long history in human settlement and urban growth. The unique architectural style of this region stands in contrast to other areas because of the appearance of multi-storied houses, sometimes up to five floors, that are built from blocks of cut coral rock and limestone and often reinforced with several layers of timber. The coastal region sits on a vast layer of coral left over from the era when the entire region was below sea level. Coral is not known for its ability to insulate from the heat, but its abundance made it the first choice. Buildings made of coral have to be repaired often because the humid and hot coastal climate destroys the stone rather quickly. Therefore, houses do not have a long lifespan and houses over 200 years old are very rare. The people of this region have been in constant contact with pilgrims from Islamic lands and therefore developed an indigenous architectural style that blended local and foreign elements. These houses show a distinct Ottoman influence that dominated the Middle East and much of North Africa from the sixteenth century to the early twentieth century. Ottoman period homes, such as those in Jiddah and Makkah, were several-story structures and featured decorative elements in plaster both inside and out. Having access to wood imported from India and other sources, the buildings in the Hijaz featured elaborately decorated doors and windows. Screens of carved wood called *rushan* placed over balconies allowed cooler air to pass as ventilation while at the same time ensuring the privacy of their occupants. These wooden balconies are the distinct mark of coastal architecture. Often highly decorated and sometimes painted, they extended over several floors. The vernacular building style of the Hijaz reflects the areas rich traditional building solutions combined with the impact of foreign styles that are brought in through **pilgrimage**.

THE CENTRAL REGION: NAJD

The most striking feature of Najdi architecture is its simplicity, making the size of a home the only distinction between the rich and the poor. The general image was one of seclusion, defense, and simplicity. The architectural style that emerged was based on the unique demands of life in a hot and dry climate. The principal building material was sun-dried mud brick; mud being collected from usually dry streambeds after the short rainy season. Limestone was not available. The earth was mixed with water, straw, and other items and made into bricks left to dry in the sun and then laid along horizontal layers for walls. The walls were deliberately made thick for added structural integrity. Tree trunks, most often those of the date palm, and palm fronds covered with mud formed the roofs. Windows were small both for privacy and to keep out the elements. The mud plaster was used to cover the buildings with added decorative elements for aesthetic purposes. The result was a structure with excellent insulation characteristics, remaining cool in summer and warm in winter.

ASIR

The **Asir** region is home to two distinct building styles, that of the **Tihamah** coastal plain with cylindrical huts made from reed and palm fronds (*usha* in Arabic), and that of the mountainous areas around **Abha** and Baha, where multiple-story tower houses are the typical feature. The outside is layered with courses of flat schist stones protecting the mud brick wall from eroding in the rain. Outside walls, rooflines, and frames were often decorated with white gypsum stucco, and doors were painted with bright colors and floral designs. Women painted the interiors in colorful geometric patterns.

THE EASTERN PROVINCE AND THE GULF COAST

The traditional architecture of the Eastern Province is identical with the style of the larger Gulf area, which in turn has significant Ottoman and Persian influences. Building material included coral blocks, dry or rubble stone, lime, mud brick, and wood from mangroves and palm trees. Pointed keel arches are a common feature of that style (found throughout the Gulf), and the use of *mashrabiyah* screens is another. Courtyard houses with separated family and guest areas were surrounded by thick walls for protection from the heat and were made from coral on the coast or limestone in the oases. Wind towers called *barajil* (*barjil* in singular, from the Persian word *badghir*) with openings to catch the breeze were added to the flat roofs. The cool air was then channeled into the lower rooms and provided ventilation. Wood was a rare building material and thus had to be imported. The exterior and interior were covered in plaster to keep out the humidity. The ruling class and wealthy merchants were able to add lavish stucco decorations, the styles of which were similar along the northern shore of the Gulf. More common were highly decorated doors, which by now have all disappeared. Gone too are small palm frond huts called *barasti*, which were common in the oases along the Gulf. Many traditional houses are still found in the **Muharraq** district of al-Manamah, such as the palace of *Shaykh* 'Isa **Al Khalifah** built in 1830 as the most prominent. In **Oman**, the traditional architecture of the Gulf has been preserved the most because of the country's isolation and resistance to modernization and Westernization.

RELIGIOUS ARCHITECTURE

Relatively little is known about religious buildings from the Peninsula, with the exemption of the two Holy Mosques in Makkah and Madinah. Although the birth land of Islam, Peninsula religious architecture cannot compete with the splendor of that from Egypt, Persia, or Turkey. Of the few remaining structures some characteristics emerge; for example, the absence of elaborate decoration and inscriptions. With extra funds available it seems surprising how little was preserved and much was built without looking back. As stated before, the mosques of Makkah and Madinah are different in this regard. Much has been done to rebuild, extend, and sometimes preserve the size and style of the *Haramayn*, the two Holy Places. In the past, rulers from beyond the Peninsula invested large sums and material to leave a trace in these sacred mosques. However, it was only with the Saudi kings that local interest paid for the extension of the mosques, making them a unique example of Islamic architecture with a Saudi Arabian touch that otherwise is not available in the kingdom. A valuable exemption might be the Umm Farasan mosque, which was built in 1347/1927–1928 and included many regional styles and techniques. Another fine example of old Islamic architecture is the mosque of 'Umar bin al-Khattab in Dumat al-Jandal in the northern part of the Saudi Arabia, which is believed to be built by the second caliph and has a very unusual style in its freestanding minaret. This absence is often attributed to the vigorous religious zeal of **Wahhabi** and/or early Islamic thought, which does not tolerate worshipping anything or anyone but God and is shown in its dislike for ornamental and highly decorative sacral buildings, shrines, or cemeteries. However, things changed drastically with the introduction not of oil but of concrete, which allowed expression of modern features, styles, and decors through the use of better material in mosques all over the area.

Outside the Wahhabi-dominated areas more ornate places of worships are found; however, mosques built before the nineteenth century rarely had minarets and simple columns, sometimes cylindrical and sometimes octagonal, supported the roofs. Shrines or tombs of saints and other venerated religious men are found in **Yemen** and **Dhufar.**

MILITARY ARCHITECTURE

The main cities of Arabia are mostly located on the coast and have served as seaports and trading hubs for centuries, but some bigger settlements in the interior developed into large urban centers. In addition to the **economic structures** of the ports, stores, and warehouses as well as the administrative and religious buildings, they all had to have defensive structures to provide protection from outside attacks, both seafaring and nomadic. Usually, a thick wall with several gates and watchtowers encircled the traditional Arabian city. Jiddah, for example, was a walled city until 1947 when the wall was demolished to expand the city. By the middle of the twentieth century, cities no longer provided safety from **military** conflict. In an effort to preserve the architectural heritage, many cities began to rebuild former military constructions, such as Riyadh's Masmak Fort, the walls of many Omani cities, the many smaller fortresses (*husn*) of Sharjah, and the watchtowers in the Asir.

MODERN ARCHITECTURE

The constantly rising revenues from the **oil industry** initiated an enormous building boom in the area, when most of the old cities were overtaken by new developments and sometimes rebuilt as completely new cities. At one point the whole population of the region seemed to be urbanizing, most notably the Bedouins, who gave up nomadism to settle in towns and take wage labor. The growing demand for housing was matched by the governments who provided Western-style accommodation, such as villas and apartment blocks at low or no cost to citizens. Open spaces quickly vanished under highways, industrial and housing complexes, airports, or stadiums. Architects and city planners abandoned the traditional setup of Islamic/Arab cities with their walled residential areas, narrow paths, courtyards, and palm gardens. Religious, economical, and administrative buildings used to have a central location around the marketplace, but with Western-inspired planning these have been placed in different areas. However, gender segregation, a dominant feature of Islamic architecture, seems to have survived even in luxurious villas and apartment complexes, where two distinct areas—one for guests and one for family members—are still found. Whoever can afford it buys a single-family home with high walls and separate entrances. Only the poorer classes and foreign workers reside in government-built apartment blocks. In recent decades, private contracting **companies** such as the UAE-based al-Nakheel began building luxury apartment high rises, condominiums, and gated communities that only the wealthy can afford. One common feature that changed in the architecture of the entire region is the method of climate control and replacement of traditional ventilation methods with electric-powered air conditioning.

In the 1990s approximately seventy percent of the population of the region lived in the urban centers. In the twentieth century and particularly beginning with the 1970s, contemporary European and American architectural plans have become a dominant feature, often designed by Western architects or Western-educated local architects. Generously stretched city plans for the fast-growing urban centers rivaled the rapid extension of infrastructure and new housing complexes and industrial, administrative, and cultural buildings. Because of almost unlimited financial means and significant central authority, it was possible to combine modern structures with traditional elements and materials, some examples being the Central Market (also called the Blue Suq) in Sharjah or several governmental buildings in Riyadh. Kuwait's architectural landmarks include the water towers and the National Assembly building.

The pace of change in Arabia over the last half century has been tremendous and is most notable in the modern look of the cities and infrastructure. Extensive building programs and large-scale **urbanization** gave the area an almost completely new appearance. The introduction of new building material such as glass and cement as well as new techniques in climate control changed the living experience. Government and the private sector now protect the region's architectural heritage and its influence is readily visible in the contemporary architecture of Saudi Arabia. Thanks to the current extra revenues from high oil prices, some countries in the Gulf region, especially the **United Arab Emirates**, have experienced an unparalleled architectural boom. The most prominent architects from all over the world are building ultramodern and enormous towers, hotels, and other administrative and business structures, making the area one of the leading global architectural trendsetters.

The traditional architecture of the Arabian Peninsula began to disappear in the 1950s. The remaining structures serve only as museums or heritage projects and are no longer inhabited on a regular basis. The modern, international architecture that was brought with oil revenues has changed the appearance of the entire region, although lately a growing awareness of the past should be noted, which is reflected in individual examples of adopting traditional regional or Islamic styles or restoring the few structures that are left.

FURTHER READING

Coles, Anne, and Peter Jackson. *Windtower*. London: Stacey International, 2007.

Dostal, Walter. *The Traditional Architecture of Ras al-Khaimah (North)*. Wiesbaden, Germany: Reichert, 1983.

Hillenbrand, Robert. "Traditional Architecture in the Arabian Peninsula," *Bulletin British Society for Middle Eastern Studies* 16, no. 2 (1989): 186–192.

Jodidio, Philip. *Architecture in the Emirates*. New York: Taschen, 2007.

Johnson, Warren. "Keeping Cool," *Saudi Aramco World* 46, no. 3 (1995): 10–17.

Kay, Shirley, and Darius Zandi. *Architectural Heritage of the Gulf*. Dubai: Motivate Publications, 1991.

King, Geoffrey. *The Historical Mosques of Saudi Arabia*. New York: Longman, 1986.

King, Geoffrey. *The Traditional Architecture of Saudi Arabia*. London: I.B. Tauris, 1998.

Lewcock, Ronald, and Zahra Freeth. *Traditional Architecture in Kuwait and the Northern Gulf*. London: Art and Archaeology Research Papers, 1979.

Raswan, Carl. *Black Tents of Arabia: My Life among the Bedouin*. New York: Creative Age Press, 1947.

Talib, Kaizer. *Shelter in Saudi Arabia*. New York: St. Martin's Press, 1984.

Asir

Sebastian Maisel

Asir (meaning difficult or hard in **Arabic**) is a region in southwestern **Saudi Arabia** between the **Hijaz** Mountains in the north and **Yemen** to the south and is named after the mostly settled tribes of the area who belong to the Asir confederation. The Asir highland has the most habitable climate in Saudi Arabia; it is cooler and has more rainfall than any other Saudi area. The main mountain range rises to heights over 9,842 feet (3,000 meters) and reaches its highpoint of 10,278 feet. (3,133 meters) at Jabal Sawda' near the region's capital, **Abha**.

The rugged western face of the escarpment drops steeply to the coastal plain, the **Tihamah** lowlands, the width of which averages only forty miles (sixty-five kilometers). Along the seacoast is a salty tidal plain of limited agricultural value, backed by potentially rich alluvial plains. The eastern slope of the mountain range in Asir is gentle, melding into a plateau region that drops gradually into the **desert** of the Rub' al Khali or Empty Quarter. Although rainfall is infrequent in this area, several fertile **wadis**, of which the most important are the Wadi Bishah and the Wadi Tathlith, make **oasis** agriculture possible on a relatively large scale.

Because of the higher frequency of rain in this region of Arabia, the area at large is very fertile. The heavier and relatively dependable rainfall has allowed the people of this region, for the most part, to live a settled life as farmers and herdsmen and provides for the cultivation of grains and fruits, in some parts **coffee**, and *qat* (a mild narcotic). It is mainly an agrarian culture of terraced farms on mountainsides that allows maximum land use. Because of the high level of rainfall, complex irrigation is rarely necessary and rain-fed agriculture is possible. The government has constructed more than forty dams to control the flow of water to farms, and farmers dig wells or build diversion dams in areas where the rain is less dependable. A variety of farming methods is used to grow crops on the terraced plateaus. Short-range, small-scale sheep or goat nomadism is noticeable in the eastern parts of Asir toward the steppes of **Najd**.

The people of Asir have a different appearance, custom, and temperament, which is attributed to the different environment compared with the rest of Saudi

Arabia. They are distinctly Yemeni in appearance and **dress**. The different regions are identified according to the dominant tribal group, their colors, patterns, and animal brands. The indigenous inhabitants are from the Khatham tribe, who were pushed back north from the Azd Sarat confederation that includes the Ghamid and Zahran. The Khatham, and among them the Shahran, maintained their position in northern Asir around Bishah and Turabah. The Asir confederation is a conglomerate of sections from the 'Anz (Bani Malik, Rufaydah) and Azd (Rijal Alma). Sections from the **Qahtan** are located in the southeast.

These agricultural communities enjoy a high standard of living that so far has not drastically changed their way of life or their traditional homes. The area is noted for its tower houses made from stone and mud that could be use for storage and defense. Exterior and interior sections of the houses as well as local clothing remain very colorful. Silver-making is a major local **handicraft**, and women traditionally wear a good deal of **jewelry**, similar to traditions in Yemen. African influences are clearly seen in the western part of Asir in the traditional **architecture** and very brightly colored clothing, as well as in many different ceremonies inspired from a mixture of traditions from Arabia and the Horn of Africa. However, transformations have already begun because of the inevitable influx of visitors, both Saudis and foreigners, as well as improved means of communication and infrastructure.

For centuries the Asir highlands were disunited because of intertribal warfare that was first challenged by **Wahhabi** expansion under their local leadership of the al-Rufaydah. After their defeat and the Ottoman withdrawal, the Bani Mughayd became the dominant group in the Asir for the next several decades. During most of the nineteenth century, Asir became the subject of heavy fighting between the Ottomans, the Wahhabi rulers of Najd, and local dynasties such as the Idrisis and the Zaydis of Yemen. After 1920, **'Abd al-'Aziz ibn Sa'ud** started the unification of central Arabia with the occupation of **Abha** and Asir through negotiations, treaties, and several **military** campaigns. In the treaty of **Ta'if** on May 20, 1934, Saudi hegemony over Asir and **Najran** was finalized.

Today, Asir forms an administrative region in Saudi Arabia that is separated from the Tihamah and Najran. The governor is Faysal bin Khalid Al Faysal, who is instrumental in the region's sustained development, focusing on extending road building and **tourism**. Saudi Arabia's first national park, a 1,000 square mile (over 1,600 square kilometers) natural reserve, opened in 1981. The domestic tourism industry in Asir offers great opportunities by providing employment to locals and keeping Saudi tourist riyals in the country. Tourists from Saudi Arabia and other countries enjoy the natural beauty, climate, and traditional hospitality of Asir. Both government and private sector money is being rapidly invested in numerous projects. The population is growing fast; foreign and domestic workers assist in the agricultural expansion.

FURTHER READING

Abdulfattah, Kamal. *Mountain Farmer and Fellah in Asir, Southwest Saudi Arabia.* Erlangen, Germany: Fränkische Geographische Gesellschaft, 1981.
Cornwallis, Sir Kinahan. *Asir before World War One: A Handbook.* New York: Oleander Press, 1976.

Eigeland, Tor. "Back to the Highlands," *Saudi Aramco World*, 31, no. 5 (1980): 2–21.
Mauger, Thierry. *Impressions of Arabia: Architecture and Frescoes of the Asir Region*. New York: Flammarion, 1996.
Philby, Harry St. John. *Arabian Highlands*. Ithaca, NY: Cornell University Press, 1952.

'Awamir

John A. Shoup

The 'Awamir tribe is a large Hinawi (southern) **Bedouin** tribe inhabiting much of the southern part of **Saudi Arabia** with sections in **Qatar** and **Oman**, whereas other sections live in the **United Arab Emirates**. The tribe originated in the region north of the Hadramawt of **Yemen** and at an early period seems to have begun moving to the north and east into central Oman where some sections settled. They had a long-standing quarrel with the **Duru'** tribe, who inhabit the area north of **Nizwa**, which was settled only in the 1960s. Because of their feud with the Duru', many of the 'Awamir moved with their *shaykh* to **al-Hasa** in Saudi Arabia in the 1940s where they eventually stayed. However, the majority moved into territory controlled by **Abu Dhabi** where they already had good relations with the ruling Al Bu Falah. Today they are split between those who consider themselves to be Saudi citizens and those who consider themselves to be Emirati citizens. The majority of 'Awamir in the Untied Arab Emirates follow **Ibadi Kharaji** Islam, as do those still living in Oman, whereas those in Saudi Arabia adhere to the more orthodox **Hanbali** school of **Sunni** Islam. Some remain pastoral nomads that depend on **camels**, but the vast majority have settled in special Bedouin settlements in Saudi Arabia or moved to the major towns in Oman and the Gulf.

FURTHER READING

Carter, J.R.L. *Tribes in Oman*. London: Peninsular Publishing, 1982.
Heard-Bey, Frauke. *From Trucial States to United Arab Emirates*. Dubai: Motivate Publishing, 2004.
Miles, S.B. *The Countries and Tribes of the Persian Gulf*. London: Frank Cass, 1966.

B

Bahla

John A. Shoup

Bahla is an ancient city located in the Dakhilah region of **Oman**. The origin of the city dates back into early antiquity and it served as a major administrative center for the Persians when they conquered the region during the reign of Cyrus the Great (550–530 BC). Bahla's citadel may have first been built during the Persian period and several of the major *aflaj*, or underground irrigation canals, date from the same period. Locally, it is held that the Persians introduced *aflaj* to Oman. Bahla remained a major urban center following the arrival of several major Arab tribes in the region following the collapse of the Ma'rib Dam in **Yemen** in the third century BC. The Bani Azd tribe was among the more important of them and they eventually threw off Persian rule.

Bahla served as a capital city for several Omani dynasties following Oman's independence from 'Abbasids in 796 and the establishment of the ***Ibadi Kharaji*** Imamate in Oman. It remained important city during the al-Ya'arbah dynasty (1624–1775). The Dakhilah region was the heart of the state and in 1670 the *Imam* Bal'arab bin Sultan built his palace, Husn Jabrin, between Bahla and Nizwa.

Today Bahla is a small town of around 30,000 people. Most are engaged in agricultural production in the small **oasis** that surrounds the town or are skilled craftsmen working in silver, making pottery, or making confections/candies. Bahla is famous throughout Oman for its fine silver **jewelry** and pottery, and the city has several very active craftsmen still engaged full-time in making items. The town is also a trade center for villages in the **mountains** that rise up behind it, although with the availability of modern transportation Nizwa has come to dominate local trade. Traditional **folklore** and legends say that Bahla's people are well known for magic and sorcery, which perhaps is linked to their high skills in crafts such as in silver.

The fortress of Bahla was first built by the Sasanian Persians in the sixth century and was subsequently rebuilt and expanded. Today it is a United Nations Educational, Scientific and Cultural Organization (UNESCO) World Heritage site. Courtesy of John A. Shoup.

FURTHER READING

Richardson, Neil, and Marcia Dorr. *The Craft Heritage of Oman*. Dubai: Motivate Publishing, 2003.

Bahrain

John A. Shoup

Bahrain is called *al-Bahrayn*, or "the Two Seas" in Arabic. The Kingdom of Bahrain is an island country consisting of the two major islands: Bahrain and **Muharraq**, and some thirty small associated islands, many of which are not permanently inhabited. The country is the only island nation among the Gulf countries and as a result has had a somewhat different history and ethnic composition.

Bahrain was the Dilmun mentioned in ancient Mesopotamian texts, a place of eternal life and happiness. Dilmun civilization arose around 3200 BC and lasted throughout much of antiquity. The island came under Greek influence following Alexander the Great's conquest of the Persian Empire in 330 BC. Bahrain was called Tylos by the Greeks, which most likely was a corruption of *Thilwun* or Dilmun. The Hellenistic period ended with the arrival of Islam in 629, when the Prophet **Muhammad** sent a letter to the ruler of the island, al-Mundhir bin Sawa al-Tamimi, asking him to accept Islam. Al-Mundhir accepted Islam, as did many of the island's people, although some remained Zoroastrian, Christian, or Jewish.

Bahrain was part of the **Shi'ite** Qaramitah movement and the island was more or less marginalized during much of the classical Islamic period. In 1602 the Persian Safavid Shah 'Abbas I took the island and Iran ruled it for the next 150 years. Iran lost Bahrian to **Oman** and it was administered by the Governor of Bushir, a major port on the Persian side of the Gulf controlled by Oman. Bahrain's modern history begins in 1701 with the arrival of the **Al Khalifah** family at the head of the Bani 'Utbah or 'Utub tribe of the **'Anazah** confederation. The Al Khalifah did not gain full control over Bahrain until 1783, when *Shaykh* Ahmad bin Khalifah (1783–1794) finally drove out the Omani governor Nasr al-Madhkur.

The Bani 'Utbah originally came from the southern **Hijaz** and first migrated to near **Qatar** and then moved north to al-Basrah in Iraq in the seventeenth century. The **Al Sabah** and their related lineages settled in what is now **Kuwait**, whereas the Al Khalifah and **Al Thani** migrated back south, taking control of both Bahrain and Qatar in the eighteenth century. The Bani 'Utbah were Arabic-speaking, Maliki **Sunni** Muslims, whereas the majority of Bahrain's people were Persian-speaking 12er Shi'ites. The Bani 'Utbah were from pastoral **Bedouin** background and have maintained the Bedouin speech partially as a means of social distinction. They settled in the central part of the main island and built a fort on the only bit of raised ground called al-Rifa'a, or "the Heights." The Shi'ites were mainly settled villagers and were concentrated in the north of the main island and on Muharraq close to numerous freshwater sources.

Bahrain's rich **pearling** banks attracted several other mainly Sunni Arab families or *Hawali* from the Persian side of the Gulf during the rule of *Shaykh* Salman bin Ahmad (1794–1821). With the help of the *Hawali*, many of the Bani 'Utbah became involved with pearling and shipping, which, because of their success, caused the anger of the *Sultan* of Oman. The Omanis attacked Bahrain in 1801 and the Al Khalifahs were supported by the **Al Sa'ud**, then a rising ruling house that was distantly related to them. The Omanis were defeated but attacks between the two continued for several years. In 1820 Bahrain signed an agreement with the British that served as the basis for the Protectorate that was signed into effect in 1914.

Bahrain has been different from its Gulf neighbors, being the first in several different fields. It allowed an American Christian mission to be established in 1893, which opened the first Western medical hospital in 1902. Bahrain opened the first post office in 1884, and the first telegraph office in 1916. In 1919 the government established the first public (non-religious) schools for boys and in 1924 opened the first girls' school. Bahrain also has the first elected representative body. In 1920 the city of **Manamah** was allowed to have a municipal council and by 1926 half its members were elected whereas the other half were appointed by the *Shaykh*.

Bahrain's economy was based on pealing and as long as the international demand for pearls was high, the economy did well. Bahrain attracted merchants from India who settled there, making the island unique with the only Hindu minority who are citizens and not guestworkers. In the 1930s cultured pearls began to enter the market and demand for natural pearls declined. In 1931 **oil** was discovered and Bahrain's **oil industry**, Bapco—a subsidiary of Standard Oil—began operation in 1932. Oil was able to replace pearls as the major source of national income.

Charles Belgrave dominated British involvement in Bahraini affairs during the 1930s to 1950s. Belgrave became the focal point of growing Bahraini anti-British sentiment after World War II and the rise of Arab nationalism embodied in Egyptian President Jamal 'Abd al-Nasir. In 1952 the Higher Executive Committee (composed of both Sunnis and Shi'ites) pushed for several political reforms and for Belgrave to be fired. The 1956 Suez Crisis brought things to a head and Belgrave "retired" rather than face being forced out of his position.

Shaykh **'Isa bin Salman** became the ruler in 1961 and *Shaykh* 'Isa moved his country toward independence and a more diversified economy. Bahrain decided to not join the **United Arab Emirates** and became an independent **Emirate** called the State of Bahrain in 1971. A Constituent Assembly was elected in 1972 and a constitution was issued in 1973 that authorized the election of a National Assembly. However, the National Assembly was dissolved in 1975 and the **Emir** ruled by decree.

Contemporary Bahraini history has been dominated by three major themes: the demands by the Shi'ites for a popularly elected government, conflict with Qatar over the Hawali Islands, and relations with the United States. The Shi'ites, many of Iranian origin, comprise around seventy percent of the population but do not share much of the nation's wealth. They tend to work in lower-paying jobs and feel marginalized politically. They form a distinct part of the population and are referred to as *Baharnah* (*Bahrani* in singular) rather than Bahrainis, which is applied to the Sunni Arabs. Several organizations emerged in the 1970s and 1980s (e.g., the Islamic Front for the Liberation of Bahrain and Hizballah Bahrain) that were involved in violent actions against the state. Some of the Shi'ite clerics were arrested for their open anti-government activities, the most important being *Shaykh* 'Abd al-Amir al-Jamri, who was arrested several times. In 1999 al-Jamri was sentenced to ten years in prison but the new Emir, *Shaykh* Hamad bin 'Isa, pardoned him, which started the progression toward more political openness.

Shaykh Hamad bin 'Isa succeeded his father as Emir in 1999 and in 2000 he appointed women and non-Muslims to the Consultative Council. In 2001 he held a referendum on political reforms that were overwhelmingly approved by the people. Bahrain became a kingdom as a constitutional monarchy and extended political rights to women. In 2002 Bahrain held the first elections and for the first time women were allowed to vote. The same year parliamentary elections were held and despite calls by Islamists to boycott them, more than fifty percent of the people voted. In 2004 the King approved Nada Haffadh as Minister of Health, the first woman minister. In the 2006 elections the Shi'ites won forty percent of the vote and for the first time a Shi'ite, Jawad bin Salim al-Urayd, was named the Deputy Prime Minister.

Bahrain and Qatar have disputed ownership of the Hawali Islands that lie between them. The conflict began in 1939 when Britain decided the islands belong to Bahrain. When both countries did not join the United Arab Emirates in 1971, the dispute became more important. Qatari troops briefly occupied two of the islands in 1986, trying to force the issue, but within a few months evacuated back to Qatar. In 1991 Qatar took the dispute to the International Court of Justice in The Hague, but Bahrain rejected the move stating the islands are legally part of Bahrain. Little was done with the case and in 1995 Britain refused to mediate the dispute. In 1999 the Emir of Qatar, *Shaykh* Hamad bin Khalifah al-Thani, visited Bahrain and the monarchs agreed to set up a joint Bahraini/Qatari commission to settle the issue.

Bahrain is a strong pro-Western state and has increasing ties with the United States. Since 1971 Bahrain rented naval and **military bases** to the United States, some of which had originally been British. In 1991 Bahrain, as part of the **Gulf Cooperation Council** Peninsula Shield Force, was an active member of the coalition in Operation Desert Storm against Iraq's invasion and occupation of Kuwait. Bahrain has pursued its relationship with the United States and signed a defense cooperation agreement in 1991 that set up joint military exercises and increased U.S. access to Bahraini port facilities. In 2004 Bahrain and the United States signed a free trade pact that was formalized by the United States in 2006. The free trade pact was not well received by other Gulf States, especially **Saudi Arabia**, who sees it as a means to break regional economic cooperation.

Since the beginning of King Hamad's rule, Bahrain has opened up politically to a great extent, although **media** is still subject to censorship. Nonetheless, MBC chose Bahrain as the location for its satellite channel MBC-2. The press is private; all three major Arabic dailies and the two English dailies are private. The state controls the local **television** station and radio with the exception of radio station Voice FM, which is aimed at the Indian listener.

Bahrain has become a major financial center since the late 1970s, and is called the Singapore of the Gulf. Oil production in Bahrain was never as high as in the other Gulf States and from the beginning Bahrain has tried to not be dependent on oil. Today, the oil sector amounts to close to thirty percent of the national economy. Banking, investments, shipping, oil refining, aluminum, and other such activities have a greater share. Bahrain is the least dependent on foreign workers of any of the Gulf countries and policies of "Bahrainization" have been in effect for decades. Only eight percent of Bahrainis are rural, the majority of which are Shi'ites and involved in agriculture, fishing, and traditional crafts such as pottery and weaving cloth.

FURTHER READING

Cooper, Robert. *Bahrain*. New York: Marshall Cavendish, 2000.
Khouri, Fouad. *Tribe and State in Bahrain*. Chicago: University of Chicago Press, 1980.

Bani Khalid

Sebastian Maisel

The Bani Khalid is a large Arab tribe who used to rule the eastern part of the **Arabian Peninsula** in the seventeenth and eighteenth centuries. To a lesser degree their influence stretched into **Najd** in Central Arabia. Today, most of the tribal members live in Najd and the Eastern Province of **Saudi Arabia**. In addition, many of them are found in **Kuwait**, **Bahrain**, Iraq, and Syria, and one section is found in Jordan. Tribal members are called Khalidi in the singular, and the plural form is Khawalid.

They are considered to be 'Adnani (northern—descendants of Isma'il), with a long, eventful history. Some scholars and tribal members trace the tribe to the famous Muslim commander Khalid bin al-Walid (592–642). However, not much is recorded about this early time, and they first show up on the written map of history in the fifteenth century, occupying large parts of Eastern Arabia. In 1534 they fell under Ottoman control until a successful rebellion by Barak bin Gharir al-Humayd led to the Ottoman expulsion from **al-Hasa** and **Qatif**. By then they ruled over Qatif, al-Ahsa, and **Qatar**, but not Bahrain. The Al Gharir as the most influential lineage of the tribe divided the area among the various groups and clans of the Bani Khalid.

Some groups extended the realm northward to Basrah. They opened up the area that is presently known as Kuwait by building settlements, ports, and fortifications. In Qurayn, the *shaykh* of the Bani Khalid erected a small fort (*al-kut* in Arabic), which became the core for the future state and city of al-Kuwait. Under their hegemony, smaller tribes settled in the vicinity of the fortress. One of them, the al-'Utub, quickly emerged as the new rulers and eventually founded the ruling dynasty of the **Al Sabah**. After internal power struggles, the Bani Khalid lost their influence over the area to the Al Sabah in the middle of the eighteenth century.

The Bani Khalid also extended their sphere of influence into al-Yamamah, the area of eastern Najd, where they gained many allies and tributaries such as the Al Mu'ammar, the rulers of 'Uyaynah. Here they first came in touch with the teachings of **Muhammad 'Abd al-Wahhab** and his movement to purify Islam that was also directed against **Shi'ite** Islam. Because many members of the Bani Khalid were Shi'ites, the tribe and its leaders challenged his teaching and tried to persuade the ruler of 'Uyaynah to kill Muhammad 'Abd al-Wahhab; however, he only expelled him to Dir'iyah, the capital of the **Al Sa'ud** area, in order to avoid unrest among his population. Almost a decade later, the movement grew stronger after signing a pact with the Al Sa'ud of mutual support and legitimization. After another period of internal power struggle, the Bani Khalid fell under the control of the first Saudi state in 1793 and had to pay the *zakat*, the Islamic charity tax, to the Al Sa'ud.

With the fall of the Saudi state to the Egyptian troops and anti-Saudi tribes under Ibrahim Pasha, the Bani Khalid were reinstalled as the rulers of al-Hasa until the second Saudi state again conquered this important oasis in the 1830s. The new Saudi rulers encouraged other tribes from **Qasim** in central Arabia to move into the *dirah* of the Bani Khalid to create a buffer zone and concurrently to weaken their rule in eastern Arabia by bringing in subjects loyal to the Al Sa'ud.

By the middle of the nineteenth century, the Bani Khalid lost most of its former influence in eastern Arabia to the **'Ajman**, **Mutayr**, and other tribes associated with the rulers of Kuwait. However, they participate in the *Ikhwan* movement, but only with insignificant numbers. Only two or three *hijrah*s, settlements for the *Ikhwan*, are known between **Dammam** and **Riyadh**.

The only other time the Bani Khalid made headlines was when King **'Abd al-'Aziz** married a girl from the *shaykhly* family, Wadhba bint Muhammad Bin al-Uraymir, who gave birth to Sa'ud bin 'Abd al-'Aziz, the second king of Saudi Arabia. Wadhba outlived her son Sa'ud and throughout her life worked on reconciliation between the two groups.

Among the most prominent sections of the Bani Khalid are the Al Humayd, from which are the Al Gharir and the *shaykh*ly family; the Al Jubur; the al-Mahashir; the Al Janah (in Qasim); the ad-Du'um in al-Qasab; and the al-'Umur and al-Qarsha in al-Jawf. Most of the Bani Khalid in Najd have been settled for centuries, whereas those in the eastern provinces only recently gave up nomadism.

FURTHER READING

Mandaville, Jon E. "The Ottoman Province of al-Hasa in the Sixteenth and Seventeenth Centuries," *Journal of the American Oriental Society* 90, no. 3 (1970): 486–513.

Vassiliev, Alexei. *The History of Saudi Arabia*. London: Saqi Books, 1998.

Winder, Bailey. *Saudi Arabia in the Nineteenth Century*. New York: St. Martin's Press, 1965.

Bani Tamim

Sebastian Maisel

The Bani Tamim is a large tribal group with an undisputed ancient descent living in central Arabia. Their progenitor Tamim ibn Murr lived around the first century AD and through him they trace their family tree back to 'Adnan and Isma'il. The meaning of *tamim* in Arabic is strong or solid.

In the distant past of pre-Islamic Arabia, the Bani Tamim maintained a dominant position among the Arab tribes because of their number and large territory. However, they never reached any paramount position, which is attributed to the fragmentation of their settlement pattern. They often share their tribal territory with other groups, mainly from the larger **Shammar** tribe, but through language and manners are distinguished from them. In contrast to the predominantly nomadic Shammar, the Bani Tamim were sedentary farmers who owned the land they cultivated in the **oases**. Their main product was **dates**, of which they possessed large plantations. Another economic activity was their participation in the local and regional market system. As settled farmers, they were no longer considered independent and had to acknowledge the authority of the leading Shammar family, the **Al Rashid**, over their territory. They did not participate in the raids and **military** expeditions organized by the Shammar, which placed them outside the value system and **honor** code of the Shammar.

In the fifth and sixth centuries, they belonged to the realm of Kindah, making al-Hira their political center. But the Bani Tamim was also closely connected to **Makkah**, where they helped established the dominant position of this city in tribal Arabia of that time period. Soon they adopted Islam and played an important role in the early conquest of Basrah and eastern Iran. A general move from the southwest to the northeast is noticeable in their history, which also led to the gradual diminishing of the tribe's importance staring in the ninth century.

However, they did not vanish from the tribal map of Arabia because they remained attached to the land of their palm groves. The descendants of the Bani Tamim settled in large numbers in central Arabia, particularly in their old domain between Washm and Sudayr. In the southern part, large contingents are found in al-Kharj and Hawta, but as mentioned earlier, a core part of their population lives in **Qasim** and the Jabal Shammar area.

A small elite of educated families arose from the mainly agricultural masses of the tribe. Among them are the founder of the religious reform movement, **Muhammad bin 'Abd al-Wahhab**, and the ruling ibn Mu'ammar family of his birthplace, 'Uyanah. This family served and still serve the **Al Sa'ud** in various political, economic, and cultural positions; for example, as the governor of **Ta'if** or currently the director of the National Dialogue. Another famous family is al-Bassam, who collaborated through many decades with European travelers, diplomats, and other foreigners. Some sources claim the ruling family of **Qatar, Al Thani**, also belongs to the Bani Tamim. Other segments of the Bani Tamim include the Nuwasir, Anajir, and Murshid. Today they are mainly located in **Najd (Saudi Arabia)**, Basrah (Iraq), and Khuzistan (Iran).

FURTHER READING

Al-Juhany, Uwidah M. *Najd before the Salafi Reform Movement*. Reading, UK: Ithaca Press, 2002.

Al Rasheed, Madawi. *Politics in an Arabian Oasis*. London: I.B. Tauris, 1992.

Vassiliev, Alexei. *The History of Saudi Arabia*. London: Saqi Books, 1998.

Bani Yas

John A. Shoup

The Bani Yas is a large tribal confederation of Hinawi (southern) origin that moved into the Gulf region from the **Najd**. They have no one single common ancestor but are composed of several groups who merged together in the past. They are composed of lineages that used to be fully nomadic pastoralists living in the **desert** and others who lived along the coast from fishing. Although they cannot point to a single common origin, by the beginning of the twentieth century the British described them as one of the "most compact and powerful tribes" in the Gulf.

During the eighteenth century the Al Bu Falah gained more or less the dominant position among the tribes of the confederacy, and their *shaykh*ly family, the **Al Nahyan**, became the main politically powerful voice. In 1761 water was discovered on **Abu Dhabi** Island, where the Al Nahyan settled and quickly a village grew up around them. The Bani Yas also took control of Liwa Oasis inland, which was an important source of **dates**. Although the Bani Yas were able to exercise rights over much of the land that is now the Abu Dhabi emirate, they shared it with several other tribes, including the **'Awamir, al-Murrah**, Manahil, and Manasir. The political acumen of the Bani Yas leadership was such that they were able to establish good relations with many of the other tribes, form alliances, and come to dominate others. In the later part of the nineteenth century, the Bani Yas leadership (the Al Bu Falah) were able to gain control over much of al-'Ayn Oasis by defeating the Dhawahir tribe in a war while establishing a good relationship with the Na'im tribe that lived in the oasis' other villages that were under the *Sultan* of **Oman**.

The end of the nineteenth century and early part of the twentieth century brought the Bani Yas into more conflicts with nomadic tribes, but these conflicts only increased the power of the Bani Yas. The Bani Yas consolidated their position, built forts, and appointed local leaders. Al-'Ayn became a second administrative center and tribes came to the Bani Yas leadership to help settle disputes. *Shaykh* **Zayid bin Sultan**, the first president of the **United Arab Emirates**, served as the *wali* or local governor of al-'Ayn during the 1940s and 1950s before becoming leader of the emirate in 1966.

FURTHER READING

Heard-Bey, Frauke. *From Trucial States to United Arab Emirates*. Dubai: Motivate Publishing, 2004.

Banking and Finance
Sebastian Maisel

In the Middle East and Arabia, moneylenders and changers existed in medieval times and served as the original model for the banks that arose in northern Italy, which enjoyed close relations with Egypt and Syria. Individual merchants or merchant groups normally owned them. In the mid-nineteenth century, branches of European banks, predominantly British and French or special Orient Banks of those countries, dominated the Arab finance sector. Many of them were located in **Jiddah**, **al-Manamah**, and **Kuwait**, the economic centers of the Peninsula.

Currently, all Gulf States have a highly developed and sophisticated banking system with a central banking or other official monetary institutions. In connection with the general economic boom and increasing revenues from exporting **oil** in the 1970s, many banks were either nationalized or newly established. In the 1980s, the annual growth rate for approving new banks was over thirty percent. **Saudi Arabia** and Kuwait were among the most important banking centers in the **Gulf** as well as in the entire Middle East, and the National Commercial Bank of Saudi Arabia and the National Banks of **Dubai** and **Abu Dhabi** are counted among the largest Arab banks. More and more Western banks entered the financial market of the Gulf and formed joint ventures through minority stakes such as the Saudi American Bank or the British Bank of the Middle East.

In addition to the Western-oriented banks, many banks in the area follow the Quranic prohibition of usury and charging interest, *riba* in Arabic. They also follow the simple principle of sharing profit and loss and give mortgage or car loans that are similar to leasing contracts. Other rules that Islamic banks are trying to implement include the prohibition of gambling, bulling the market, and investments in the following sectors: pornography, prostitution, alcohol, and pork, because they are considered *haram* (i.e., unlawful and unethical in Islam). Several private Islamic banks have been entering the market successfully, such as Rajih Bank from Saudi Arabia, Dubai Islamic Bank, and Kuwait Finance House. The Islamic Development Bank is a multinational developing bank based on Islamic financial jurisprudence and is owned by the governments of several Arab Gulf and other Islamic states.

Generally, the finance system of the Gulf States has been highly centralized from early on. Money sources included different taxes, tributes, foreign subsidies, and revenues from exporting oil and gas. The administration of the finances was in the hands of the government, which in turn was controlled by the ruling family. Therefore, members of the ruling family mostly owned the large national banks. Private financial institutions depended on the official banks to maintain their liquidity. If the government ran into financial difficulties or deficits, it also borrowed from the central banks. Individuals continued relying on the traditional moneychangers, even after modern banks opened in the 1950s. With the growing oil revenues, larger state budgets, and closer affiliation with the Western market system, the introduction of matching standards was required. In Saudi Arabia this took additional time in comparison to other Gulf States because of the resistance of Islamic scholars.

The central financial authorities maintain their control over the market even after the founding of the **Gulf Cooperation Council** (GCC), hoping to regulate the banks and to limit the risk of financial crises and disasters. Therefore they closely supervise the system and work toward matching international standards. The long-lasting debate over the introduction of a common GCC currency has to be viewed in this regard. A common currency binds the member states and their economies closer together while boosting it at the same time. The introduction of a common currency is scheduled for 2010, and once in place, the new currency, which does not have an official name yet, will represent a very strong economic block in which private investments and ownership are encouraged. Private banks began to invest in all major economic sectors. Because of mergers, joint ventures, and other collaborative agreements between central, private, domestic, and international authorities in the financial sector, it is no longer easy to define the status of such institutions.

FURTHER READING

El-Gamal, Mahmoud. *Islamic Finance: Law, Economics, and Practice*. Cambridge, UK: Cambridge University Press, 2006.

Gause, F. Gregory. *Oil Monarchies: Domestic and Security Challenges in the Arab Gulf States*. New York: Council on Foreign Relations Press, 1994.

Hussain, Mostaque et al. "Banking Policies and Regulations: Comparative Study of Kuwait, UAW, and Qatar," *International Journal of Financial Services Management* 2, no. 3 (2007): 214–234.

Ramanathan, Ramakrishnan. "Performance of Banks in Countries of the Gulf Cooperation Council," *International Journal of Productivity and Performance Management* 56, no. 2 (2007): 137–154.

Banking, Islamic

Jack Kalpakian

Islamic banking is banking with interest rates explicitly absent but implicitly present. It is centered on the idea that interest inherently constitutes *riba* (usury) and that the Qu'ranic prohibitions against *riba* apply to interest rates charged by conventional banks today. There are some basic issues to consider: the nature of money today versus at the time of the appearance of Islam; the time value of money; and finally the use of devices that veil interest rates behind several terms that include fees, buyback agreements, and profit-sharing arrangements. Money at the time of Islam's appearance was based on specie—gold, silver, or copper. It could also be in the form of other commodities or resource-use rights. This continued to be the case for nearly all human civilizations until fairly recently. Even when countries and states issued paper notes, they were backed with specie. Paper Ottoman *lira* could be redeemed for gold or silver as were the monies issued by other Muslim and non-Muslim governments. The direct and indirect use of gold as the basis of money continued until the collapse of the Bretton-Woods system in 1971. Some forms of Islamic jurisprudence have not yet come to terms with the full implications of the delinking of commodities and money, but this is not the case universally. Today's money has value because of two factors: the government's compulsion of its use and the interest rate charged for borrowing it. Banking, writ large, is not possible without increasing the money supply by creating loans and charging a price for the money. Even if the money were ultimately backed by specie, banking activities tend to create more money, thereby resulting in slow inflation, which means that a *dirham*, dollar, or *dinar* borrowed today and paid back next year will always buy fewer goods than it originally did, and this has implications for investing and lending—the time value of money.

Ironically, one of the most traditional Islamic jurisprudential institutions realized this early on, and conventional banks had no opprobrium attached to them at the late nineteenth century when they began to appear in and work in Islamic countries. Indeed, al-Azhar, Egypt's premiere Islamic seminary and a leading authority on **Sunni** Islam, has consistently emphasized that interest rates do not equal *riba*. Azhar scholars have argued that because money today is based on state fiat and because interest is paid to depositors there is no harm and the charge of *riba* cannot be substantiated. Furthermore they have argued that state bonds and home loans, because they further the good of the community as a whole and because they further family housing, are not expressions of *riba*. The *Azhar* continues to argue this perspective today, and it has recently began re-emphasizing the issue given all of the controversy that has surrounded conventional and Islamic banking; under its definition, as long as the bank does not invest in alcohol-related activities, gambling, the pork industry, pornography, or prostitution, its activities are within the spirit and the letter of Islamic law.

Other Muslim scholars argue that whenever issues related to the time value of money are invoked, *riba* is present. This second perspective dominates in **Saudi**

Arabia and the other **Gulf Cooperation Council** (GCC) states with the notable exception of **Oman**; it is the activities of banks catering to the region, peoples, and countries influenced by its culture elsewhere, and to others who accept the idea that interest is usury that have come to dominate the meaning of the term "Islamic banking." This includes significant numbers of people. It is estimated that the industry is worth about $500 billion, and a closer look reveals a whole set of devices designed to extract profit for the bank; that is, interest with another name. Some of the common ways that this takes place include rent-to-own agreements, where the borrower "rents" the assets he or she borrowed the money to buy for a fixed period of time and then makes payments on the principal.

Other methods of collecting the equivalent of interest include repurchase agreements that set the price lower than the original cost and depreciation. Other devices include profit sharing, payment in kind, joint venture, insurance purchases, securitization, and forthright charging of processing fees. Also included are the payment of "gifts" to depositors and lenders. These approaches have led to two sorts of criticism. The first came from conventional bankers who first argued that Islamic banking is nothing but a label and an advertising gimmick designed to deprive them of market shares, but have now taken the initiative and are opening Islamic banking units. The second source of criticism came from those who classify its profit-making methods as *riba*. The first Islamic banks were established in Egypt but reached the apex of success in the GCC states where **oil**-based cash reserves and piety were in abundant supply. Some experts expect the market to grow by about twenty percent a year for many years to come, and it is indeed likely that Islamic banking and finance will become universal options for devout Muslims who do not wish to be guaranteed interest payments for their deposits. Islamic banking will also be one of the instruments used by governments and firms to tap into the savings of the Gulf region, thereby entangling it further into the global economy.

FURTHER READING

Chraibi, Khalid. "Mixed Message on 'Riba' Leaves Muslims Trapped between Usurers and Lenders," *ArabLife.org*, April 24, 2007. Available at http://www.arablife.org/index. php?option=com_content&task=view&id=727&Itemid=187 (last accessed October 8, 2008).

El Diwany, Tarik. *The Problem with Interest*, 2nd ed. London: Kreatoc Ltd., 2003.

Kuran, Timur. *Islam and Mammon: The Economic Predicaments of Islamism*. Trenton, NJ: Princeton University Press, 2005.

MacLean, Aaron. "Islamic Banking, Is It Really Kosher?" *The American*, April/March 2007. Available at http://www.american.com/archive/2007/march-april-magazine-contents/islamic-banking-is-it-really-kosher (last accessed October 8, 2008).

Wilson, Rodney. *The Politics of Islamic Finance*. Edinburgh: Edinburgh University Press, 2004.

Al-Batinah

John A. Shoup

The al-Batinah region of **Oman** extends along the coast of the Gulf of Oman between Khatmah Malahah in the north (near the border with the **United Arab Emirates**) to Ra's al-Hamra' in the south and bounded on the west by the Western Hajar **Mountains**. It is only six to forty-three miles (ten to seventy kilometers) wide. The region is arid, receiving around only four inches (100 millimeters) of rainfall a year along the coast and only one inch (thirty millimeters) in the highlands. The region gets progressively more arid as one proceeds south.

The region has eight governates today and three of them have major historic cities: **Suhar**, Sur, and al-Rustaq. Suhar was a major shipping center in the past, and the ancient city was some three times the size of the modern city. Al-Rustaq served as the capital of Oman in the medieval period and today is best known for its spectacular fort Qala'at al-Hazm.

The region produces agriculture despite the arid climate. Agriculture is fed by a few seasonal streams that flow from the Western Hajar Mountains and from tapping underground water sources using *aflaj*. The people are able to produce **dates**, grapes, citrus, and quince as well as raise livestock, including **camels**, cattle, sheep, and goats. Several of the towns are famous in Oman for their interest in learning, fine manners, and ability in composing poetry. Communities on the coast engage in fishing and shipbuilding.

Bayt Kathir

John A. Shoup

The Bayt Kathir is a large tribal confederation living mainly within the borders of the modern states of **Oman** and **Yemen**. The Bayt Kathir is composed of the Bayt Kathir proper, Al Kathir, the Kathir of **Dhufar**, Hadramawt, and related or dependent tribes, including the **'Awamir**, Rawashid or **al-Rashid**, Shanafirah, 'Afar, and **Harasis**. Together these tribes are called the Kathir al-Ghathamah. Most of the confederation is composed of Hinawi (southern) lineages, but the Kathir of the Hadramawt are considered Ghafiri (northern) in origin. Each of these major divisions of descent lines have subsections and even sub-subsections, yet there is a strong feeling of "connection" to all who are Kathiri.

The Kathir are composed of both settled (*Hadar*) peoples who farm **oases** in the Hadramawt and Dhufar and those who were, or still are, pastoral nomads. Both settled and nomads harvested frankincense from the wild *boswellia* tree that grows almost exclusively in Dhufar and Hadramawt. The Kathir ruled the small state (sultanate) that was based in the city of Say'un in the Hadramawt until its incorporation into South Yemen in the 1960s. Thus, it is possible to talk about a "Greater Kathiri" population and identity with wider applications than for many of the other tribal groups in the southern **Arabian Peninsula**.

The British travelers/explorers Bertram Thomas (1930–1931) and Wilfred Thesiger (1945–1946) were assisted by guides from the Bayt Kathir, but Thesiger found them too "tame" for his liking and in his subsequent trips across the Empty Quarter chose instead guides and companions from the Rashid whom he considered to be the true **Bedouin**, untouched by the softness of urban life.

Since the discovery of **oil** in the Dhufar region of Oman in the late 1940s and early 1950s, the tribes of the region have mainly settled around the pumping stations and new towns that have sprung up to support the oil fields. Many of the younger men work for the oil **companies** or the Omani government as drivers, as guides, or on the oilrigs. Pastoralism is still a major source of income for a good many of the Bedouin who sell their livestock or livestock products in **Salalah** or **Nizwa** in Oman or in the ancient towns of the Hadramawt in Yemen.

See also **Travelers and Explorers**.

FURTHER READING

Carter, J.R.L. *Tribes in Oman*. London: Peninsular Publishing, 1982.
Thesiger, Wilfred. *Arabian Sands*. London: Readers Union Longmans, Green & Co., 1960.

Bedouin Culture
Sebastian Maisel

Bedouins are Arab, tribally organized, nomadic groups that live in the **deserts** and steppes of the **Arabian Peninsula** and adjunct areas. The Arabic word *badu* describes pastoral nomads who share a common sense of tribal origin, values, and qualities. Among the most important Bedouin tribes in the Peninsula are the **Shammar**, 'Amarat, Ruwalah, **Huwaytat**, **Mutayr**, **'Ajman**, **al-Murrah**, **'Utaybah**, Dawasir, **Qahtan**, and Manahil. During the 1960s, when the area began to undergo significant social and economical changes, the nomadic population of **Saudi Arabia** was twenty percent, in **Kuwait** was thirteen percent, and was less in the other Arabian Gulf States. Since that time, a constant decrease in numbers is noted, partly initiated by government settlement programs and partly by the irreversible degrading of their living areas.

In addition to **camels**, Bedouins raised sheep and goats and lived off of their meat and milk products. During long periods of drought, they lost many animals, but usually managed to survive. Their annual migrations in search of optimal grazing grounds and water were done in seasonal moves. Ownership of wells and pasture was often contested and constant fighting led to the expulsions or invasions of entire tribes. However, since the late eighteenth century, most tribal territories (*dirah* in Arabic) were clearly established with recognized summer and winter grazing grounds. Water and pasture were in the collective property of the tribe, whereas the animals belonged to the individual families. The system of

Murrah Bedouins, Saudi Arabia. Courtesy of Sebastian Maisel.

tribal territories was abolished by **'Abd al-'Aziz ibn Sa'ud**, who turned them into state land without privileges for any tribe.

A distinct classification or hierarchy within the tribal group distinguished between the tribe (*qabilah*), tribal section (*'ashirah*), clan (*fakhd*), lineage (*hamulah*), and extended family (*bayt*). Every section claimed descent from a common ancestor and shared a defined territory with pasture, water, and other resources. Each group was headed by the most prominent and reputable member (*shaykh*), and very large tribal confederations were led by a supreme *shaykh* called the *shaykh al-shuyukh*. The title can be hereditary; however, in theory, the *shaykh* is selected for his ability as a first among equals with limited authority. Only certain Bedouin groups enjoyed status as *asil* or noble tribes. Others are considered inferior because they were unable to trace their origins back to the two main ancestors, 'Adnan and Qahtan, and they were engaged in less noble professions, such as sheep breeding or farming. The tribes of noble descent used to marry only among themselves. Among the noble tribes are the Shammar, **'Anazah**, **Dhafir**, and Harb. Less noble tribes had to pay tribute and were excluded from many acts and deeds. Among them are the Shararat, Hawazim, and Hutaym. Traditionally, the powerful camel herders imposed such payments on the weaker tribes, which in return guaranteed several rights such as grazing and camping privileges, water rights, and protection and defense. The tribute was paid in cash or kind. At the bottom end of the Bedouin society were the **Salubah**, hunters and artisans without a tribal origin. They were considered too inferior to mix with; therefore, no true Bedouin would marry with them. They did not participate in tribal warfare and raids and their possessions remained untouched.

Raiding other Bedouin and settled groups in order to steal their herds is often described as an important economic exchange among tribal groups. This method of weakening neighboring groups and enhancing personal wealth and reputation was an honorable, social institution in pre-Islamic Arabia. Every raid (*ghazu* in Arabic) was organized and headed by a special leader, *qa'id*, who received the biggest share after the successful campaign. **Customary law** prohibited raids from turning into massacres, and the adherence to those rules was strongly enforced by all tribes. Because every raid was cause for retaliation by the injured party, travelers noted a constant state of warfare in the Bedouin territories. After the introduction of firearms, raids often turned into violent tribal wars and were subsequently suppressed by the central governments when possible.

Other activities included hunting with falcons and special hunting dogs or collecting desert truffles in the spring. Women, on the other hand, were always busy with chores around the camp such as making food, making clothes, and weaving. Children were spared from work until they reached the age of five or six, when their male relatives began to teach young boys the important intellectual features and material aspects of Bedouin culture: proper behavior, respect, **honor**, tribal history, and poetry. Boys were allowed to sit with the elders in the *majlis* and listen to the stories and discussions of the news. Bedouin girls supported their mothers and female relatives with daily chores, but they also received lessons on honorable and proper behavior and respect of the elders.

The material possession of Bedouins was traditionally limited to a minimum of durable and easy-to-transport items. The ideal type of accommodation was a tent made from camel and goat hair. It was divided into two sections, one for the family and the other for guests. The family section was reserved for the women and children, whereas the men of the family spent most of their time in the guest section where they entertained guests or chatted with friends and relatives while drinking tea and **coffee**. The tent was a sleeping room, kitchen, and workshop in one; however, most of the time, the inhabitants were busy working away from it. The tent was always open for visitors and guests because hospitality was a major feature of Bedouin culture and an important survival tool in this harsh environment. Guests have almost unlimited rights and the Bedouin host did everything to provide a comfortable, safe stay. Even if the guest was an enemy or someone who committed a **crime** against the host, he still received the same splendid reception.

Their main form of artistic expression was poetry and tribal poets still enjoy a high reputation. Islam influenced moral values; however, many are of pre-Islamic origin, such as the concept of honor and shame, and became part of the current identity of the people of Arabia, Bedouin or not. Prior to their Islamization, they believed in demons and spirits as well as in tribal deities, which were worshipped through idols, sacred rocks, and trees. Some tribes converted to Christianity and Judaism. The legal system was transmitted orally and based on tribal norms of collective responsibility and reconciliation. Professional judges held courts and passed judgments according to the unwritten customary law or *'urf* of the tribes. Public opinion and pressure helped enforcing punishments. Among the most important aspects of customary law were regulations for hospitality, raids, mutual protection, collective punishment, and honor crimes. Although blood revenge and retaliation were common, they were not the main forms of conflict resolution. Mediation and reconciliation between the two parties was more important.

Pastoralism developed with the domestication of the camel around 1500 BC. With the introduction of the **horse**, the Bedouin gained **military** supremacy in the area. They usually lived in small camping units of closely related families called *khamsah*, but merged with other lineages for political, economical, and military purposes. Bedouins distinguished themselves from the sedentary population, stressing the different identities of *Badu* versus *Hadar*. This distinction was embedded in the notion of inequality with regard to status, origin, and power, maintaining that Bedouin were in a superior position to that of the *Hadar*.

Bedouin were always in close contact with the settled population of the **oases** and neighboring cultural areas. During raids, long migrations, or military campaigns they penetrated urban areas and sometimes settled. In the past, Bedouin from Arabia invaded the Fertile Crescent and **Yemen**, where they established local dynasties, for example, the Ghassanids and **Nabateans**. To be protected from Bedouin raids, villagers and those living in oases often paid tribute and taxes, similar to caravans traveling in tribal territory. During the Islamic conquest and expansion, Bedouin often formed the core of the Muslim armies, which brought them to Central Asia and North Africa. Until modern times, Bedouin took over large settled areas and subjected farming populations to their rule. In central Arabia, they formed the military forces of the **Wahhabi** movement and helped to expand the first and second Saudi states. At the beginning of the twentieth century, 'Abd al-'Aziz ibn Sa'ud used Bedouin to create a standing army of loyal subjects called the **Ikhwan** based on settlements called *hijrah*. The *Ikhwan* were required to give up their nomadic life and settled in small, agricultural hamlets where they were taught Wahhabi ideology and used as the main military in **'Abd al-'Aziz ibn Sa'ud's** cause of unifying the country. Bedouin contributed most of the fighters for the **Arab Revolt** from 1916 to 1918. Neither attempt was successful from the Bedouin point of view, which in the end had to submit to the superior force of central authority represented by King 'Abd al-'Aziz and other rulers from the Gulf. After a revolt the *Ikhwan* were disbanded, and the Arab Revolt was betrayed by European colonial ambitions.

Today, Bedouin culture faces enormous challenges to their lifestyle and values. The entire area has undergone substantial economic, political, and cultural change. For the Bedouin this meant the end of their age-old way of life of annual migrations and practicing their customs and traditions. The introduction of motor vehicles and the drawing of permanent political borders were arguably the two most influential aspects that irrevocably changed their world. All governments of the Gulf States undertook large measures to subdue and control their nomadic population. A nomadic way of life was incompatible with nation states, modern societies, and economies. Today Bedouin are incorporated into the modern global economy, but they often maintain aspects of their traditional way of life as insurance against an uncertain future. Bedouin are able to adapt to extreme conditions, but they willingly accepted the improvements in their life such as access to health care, **education**, and religion. The price they had to pay for this was the detribalization of their society. What remains untouched is the impact that Bedouin culture has on the formation of national identity. Moral values, traditions, and customs of the Bedouin are now increasingly promoted and largely accepted in the entire society of the Gulf and Saudi Arabia. Kin-affiliated networks still exist and provide an arena in which Bedouin culture with all of its linguistic and cultural markers, customs, traditions, and different concepts of central rule are continuously practiced. They no longer represent an economic lifestyle, but rather function as the social conscious of the greater Arabian society.

FURTHER READING

Chatty, Dawn (ed.). *Nomadic Societies in the Middle East and North Africa Entering the 21st Century.* Leiden, The Netherlands: Brill, 2006.
Ingham, Bruce. *Bedouin of Northern Arabia: Traditions of the Al-Dhafir.* London: KPI, 1986.
Kurpershoek, Marcel. *Arabia of the Bedouins.* London: Saqi Books, 2001.
Mauger, Thierry. *The Bedouins of Arabia.* Paris: Souffles, 1987.

Buraydah
Sebastian Maisel

Buraydah is a medium-size provincial city with approximately 500,000 inhabitants in the **Saudi Arabian** district of al-Qasim. Although physically separated throughout history, Buraydah is also known as the twin city of neighboring rival **'Unayzah**. They are both located in the Wadi Rimmah on the route from Basrah to **Madinah**, and therefore have always been major trading centers. The cities in **Najd** have often been described as autonomous from central state control, but as areas of settled farmers and merchants, they have also attracted outside powers to plunder or control. As such, Buraydah was attacked since the beginning of the formation of Saudi states, but soon the newly created religious movement of the **Wahhabis**, combined with the military might of the **Al Sa'ud**, included the city into their realm. The city and its rulers remained loyal to the Saudis even after their expulsion by Egyptian troops under Ibrahim Pasha and the following occupation. During the time of Saudi internal power struggle, they sided with Faysal against Mishari. With the **Al Rashid** of the **Shammar** tribe, they were engaged in a long-lasting battle over the caravan routes that crossed central Arabia and their protection. During that time period, the population of Buraydah, which numbered some 10,000, lived mainly by farming their **date** groves and from **camel** caravans. Until the mid-nineteenth century, the Al 'Ulayyan, one of the most potent families in the region, ruled the city. However, local feuds over power and resources prevailed for almost half a century. Most prominent was the rivalry between the Al 'Ulayyan and the Al Muhanna, which both were able to gain power for limited periods. Rebellions against the local and regional leadership were common, but they have to be evaluated in the shadow of a larger struggle over hegemony of central Arabia between the Al Rashid and the Al Sa'ud, who sought out allies from both ends and often change these alliances on the basis of tactical and political reasons. In June 1904, **'Abd al-'Aziz ibn Sa'ud** captured Buraydah with the help of local population from the Shammar. Again, the local **emir** from the Al Muhanna tried to eliminate all foreign influence and sided with the Turkish army. Subsequently, the area depended administratively on

Basrah, but ibn Sa'ud returned two years later and took control of the city. Over the next decade with the constant weakening of the Al Rashid, he was able to consolidate his power in **Qasim** and added it to its stronghold in Najd.

After the unification of Saudi Arabia, King 'Abd al-'Aziz invested largely in religious and formal **education**. In the 1930s, new schools were founded in all major towns of the kingdom, and so in Buraydah. First, only classes for boys were offered, but starting during the reign of King Faysal, female education gained support and influence. With the rise of pan-Arabism under Egyptian president Jamal 'Abd al-Nasir and radio propaganda from Cairo, people began to organize themselves in labor and student associations, such as the school student's organization of 'Unayzah, Buraydah, and Shaqra in 1956. One of their main demands was to decrease the influence of the League of Public Morality, a religious-motivated police force. In the following clashes between the two parties in Buraydah, dozens were arrested and whipped. But the government opened additional schools, university branches, and vocational schools. Students, who formerly had to move to **Riyadh** or **Jiddah** to complete their higher education, can attend local branches to continue with their education.

In the early 1960s, agricultural cooperatives were created in Buraydah and other cities, which led to a significant increase in the agricultural production; particularly, poultry farms and date plantations produced large quantities for the market, both local and regional. Until World War II, most of the local trade between Buraydah and the surrounding cities was carried out by camels. The people engaged in this kind of transportation and trade were called *jammamil*, and became famous all over the **Arabian Peninsula** and even in Syria and Egypt. Another large-scale operation, the buying and selling animals, mostly camels throughout Arabia, was performed by the *'Uqaylat* (people from the Qasim area and particularly from Buraydah). Today, agriculture is still one of the prominent areas of employment and provides enough food to export the surplus to other areas. Traditional crops such as dates and fruits are still grown, but after the introduction of irrigation systems using fossil water wheat became the cash crop of the region and helped to make the kingdom free from international food imports, although because of the depletion of the water sources this wheat production is scheduled to end by 2015. With the development of infrastructure, paved roads, airports, schools, hospitals, and mosques, life in Buraydah started to change in the 1960s. It also initiated bilateral labor migration (locals moving to other parts of the kingdom); for example, the Eastern Province to work in the oil sector, and foreign guestworkers coming to work in the service sector of Buraydah.

FURTHER READING

Altorki, Soraya and Donald P. Cole. *Arabian Oasis City: The Transformation of 'Unayzah*. Austin: University of Texas Press, 1989.

Al Rasheed, Madawi. *Politics in an Arabian Oasis*. London: I.B. Tauris, 1992.

Vassiliev, Alexei. *The History of Saudi Arabia*. London: Saqi Books, 1998.

Al Bu Sa'idi

John A. Shoup

The Al Bu Sa'idi family gained control of **Oman** in 1749 when Ahmad bin Sa'id was elected *Imam*. The Al Bu Sa'idi was a prominent family from the **oasis** of Adam located near **Nizwa**. The current ruler of Oman, *Sultan* **Qabus bin Sa'id**, is the twelfth of the dynasty to rule the country. Under the Al Bu Sa'idi dynasty Oman was able to expand into the Indian Ocean and the African mainland occupying the Island of Lamu and the city of Mombasa in the last decades of the eighteenth century. The Al Bu Sa'idi were challenged by the growing power of the **Wahhabi** movement in the **Najd**, and Wahhabi forces composed of mainly **Bedouin** tribesmen took the oasis of al-Buraymi from Oman in 1800. The Wahhabi presence and Saudi claims to the oasis lasted until 1952.

During the nineteenth century Oman's power in the region grew, and the *Sultan* Sa'id bin Sultan bin Ahmad, the fourth ruler of the dynasty (1806–1856), ruled over a vast empire that included much of the Gulf coast of southern Iran, Baluchistan (Pakistan), and much of the coast of East Africa. In 1840 *Sultan* Sa'id sent *al-Shaykh* Ahmad bin Nu'man al-Ka'abi to the United States, where he became the first Arab ambassador to Washington, D.C.

For administrative reasons, Zanzibar was made a second capital of the empire shortly before the death of *Sultan* Sa'id. The Omanis introduced clove production and expanded agricultural areas on Zanzibar, Lamu, and Pemba. Following the death of *Sultan* Sa'id in 1856 the Omani empire broke up into two parts: Zanzibar and the African coast under his son Majid, and the Omani mainland and the Gulf regions under his son Thuwayni. European colonial interests, mainly British and German, undermined Omani influence in the Indian Ocean, and the Al Bu Sa'idi lost control of most of its African mainland possessions. In 1890 the *Sultan* signed an agreement with the British that made the Zanzibar *Sultanate* a British Protectorate, mainly to thwart the Germans in Tanganyika. Zanzibar remained a British Protectorate until 1963, and in 1964, after a bloody revolution, the Al Bu Sa'idi ruler was overthrown and the islands joined the recently independent country of Tanganyika as the new state of Tanzania.

The Al Bu Sa'idi dynasty in Oman also lost most of their overseas possessions mainly to the British and during the second half of the nineteenth century lost much of their control over the inland parts of Oman as well. When *Sultan* Faysal bin Turki died in 1913, many of the tribes in the interior of the country refused to recognize his son and heir Taymur as the *Imam*. In 1920 Taymur signed an agreement with the *Imam* of Nizwa at Sib, which split the country effectively into two: the *Sultanate*, which ruled the coastal regions; and **Dhufar** and the *Imamate*, which controlled much of the interior around Nizwa. When Taymur died in 1938 the state income had dropped to £50,000 a year and the state was in deep debt. Taymur's successor, Sa'id, began a policy of isolation in order to reduce the state's debt and reduce the country's dependence on British advisors. Starting in the 1940s Sa'id began trying to extend his authority among the tribes in the interior, which eventually brought him into conflict with the *Imam*. The discovery of oil fields in areas under the *Imam* brought the conflict to a head and sparked the **Jabal al-Akhdar War** (1954–1959), which ended with Sa'id's defeat of the *Imam* Ghalib bin 'Ali al-Hina'i. He was also able to force the Saudis to withdraw from al-Buraymi Oasis in 1952. Following the conclusion of the Jabal al-Akhdar War, Sa'id became more and more withdrawn and cut Oman off from the outside world. Sa'd personally approved entry visas for the few foreigners that were allowed into Oman.

In 1970 his son, **Qabus**, led a palace coup to replace Sa'id. Qabus was faced by a number of major problems, including the festering war in Dhufar, where the **Dhufar Liberation Front** (DLF) was battling government control. Qabus brought in Iranian and British **military**, which defeated the DLF by 1976. He also opened the country up to economic and educational reforms which were paid for by the growing income from oil exports.

Qabus is a charismatic leader who has been successful in combining the qualities of a traditional ruler with those of an astute modern politician. He has brought his country through several international crises and has been able to remain on good terms with Iran, **Saudi Arabia**, Egypt, the United States, and the Europeans. His brief **marriage** ended with no children, and succession will fall to the children of his uncles (the children of his uncle, Tariq, being thought to be the most likely candidates) to be selected by the Ruling Family Council within three days of his death.

See also **Oases**.

FURTHER READING

Allen, Calvin, Jr., and W. Lynne Rigsbee II. *Oman under Qaboos: From Coup to Constitution, 1970–1996*. London: Frank Cass, 2000.

Carter, J.R.L. *Tribes in Oman*. London: Peninsular Publishing, 1982.

Al Bu Shams
John A. Shoup

The Al Bu Shams is an Arab, Sunni, Ghafari (northern) tribe inhabiting the region between the town of Dhank in **Oman** and the oasis (see **oases**) of al-'Ayn/al-Buraymi, which today is shared between the **United Arab Emirates** and Oman. Until the late nineteenth century the Al Bu Shams were considered to be the pastoral nomadic section of the Na'im tribe, which still today makes up the largest portion of the population inhabiting the separate villages that comprise the al-'Ayn/al-Buraymi and are found in the coastal towns such as **Dubai**. The Na'im, including the Al Bu Shams, adopted the **Wahhabi** doctrine in the early part of the nineteenth century but assisted the Al Bu Falah of **Abu Dhabi** in gaining firm control over al-Buraymi in the first part of the nineteenth century by pushing out Wahhabi forces loyal to the **Al Sa'ud** family.

Several of the Al Bu Shams tribe still remain pastoral nomads today, but many have settled in the villages of Hafit, Qabil, and Sanaynah, which are associated with al-Buraymi where they farm **dates**. The Al Bu Shams have been able to exercise greater independence from the Na'im leadership for the past fifty years, but still consider themselves ultimately to be responsible to the Na'im *shaykh*s. During the conflict between the United Arab Emirates (then the Trucial States), Oman, and **Saudi Arabia** over al-Buraymi in the 1950s (the dispute ended in 1955), several of the leading families from the Al Bu Shams sided with Saudi Arabia and subsequently have left for **Dammam**, but the majority of the tribe sided with the Trucial States and have maintained good relations with the ruling family of Abu Dhabi. The Al Bu Shams continue to move away from the Na'im leadership and are emerging as their own tribal entity. Both Oman and the United Arab Emirates treat them as a separate, independent tribal group.

FURTHER READING

Heard-Bey, Frauke. *From Trucial States to United Arab Emirates*. Dubai: Motivate Publishing, 2004.

C

Calendar, Islamic

Sebastian Maisel

The recorded history of the **Arabian Peninsula** is riddled with large gaps, but from an Islamic perspective it is clearly divided into two periods. With striking similarity to the way the Christian calendar divides history into the age before Christ and the age after Christ, the Islamic, or *hijrah*, calendar divides it into the period before the birth of Islam, called *Jahiliyah* (the age of ignorance), and the period after the birth of Islam. In 622 AD, **Muhammad** and his followers emigrated from **Makkah** to **Madinah** because of the ongoing persecution of the young Muslim community. The journey is called the *Hijrah* (the migration) and marks the beginning of the lunar *Hijrah* calendar. The Islamic calendar is a lunar calendar based on the cycles of the moon phase. The Islamic year has twelve months: *Muharram, Safar, Rabi' al-Awal, Rab'i al-Thani, Jumada al-Awal, Jumada al-Thani, Rajab, Sha'aban, Ramadan, Shawwal, Dhu al-Qa'idah,* and *Dhu al-Hijjah.* The months begin when the first crescent of a new moon is sighted. Each month consists of twenty-nine to thirty days, which makes the Islamic year eleven to twelve days shorter than the solar year. Islamic dates migrate through the year. Like solar calendars, it follows the seven-day week concept.

All Islamic celebrations, such as the *Hajj*, or Great Pilgrimage to Makkah, and the month of *Ramadan* are determined by the Islamic calendar. *Ramadan* is the ninth and *Dhu al-Hijja* the twelfth month of this calendar. On the tenth of *Dhu al-Hijja*, Muslims celebrate their most important holiday, the *'Id al-Adha*. The other major holiday is *'Id al-Fitr* at the end of *Ramadan*. The feast is actually celebrated on the first day of *Shawwal*. Most Islamic countries observe *Mawlid al-Nabi*, the birthday of the Prophet **Muhammad**, on the twelfth day of *Rabi' al-Awal* as a state holiday; however, conservative/puritanical interpretations, such as that of **Wahhabis** in **Saudi Arabia**, consider this idolatrous and heretical. **Shi'ite** Muslims consider the tenth of *Muharram* equally important, when they commemorate *'Ashurah*, the death of Hussein bin 'Ali in 680 at the Battle of Karbala, Iraq.

In pre-Islamic Arabia, an intercalary system based on seasons, particularly the rainy season, was in use that later was prohibited by Muhammad on the basis of a divine revelation. He introduced a new model that was very similar to the previous one; for example, it continued the rule of four "holy" months in which fighting was prohibited, but he discontinued the tradition of inserting an additional month when needed. According to historical Islamic sources, it was the second caliph 'Umar bin al-Khattab who introduced the new calendar in 638, the year 16 AH, anno Hegirae, or Year of the *Hijrah*. What continued in local tradition was naming a year after an important event that happened during this time, for example, the *Year of the Floods* or the *Year of the Locusts*. In addition, especially among the rural and nomadic population, the calendar did not prevail because of its impracticality for agriculture.

Saudi Arabia is currently the only country that uses the Islamic calendar as the official calendar for governmental and business affairs. The country is also unique for the creation of official institutions to sight the lunar crescent, *hilal*, which determine the beginning of the new month. In the past the individual observation of the *hilal* led to confusion over the dates to begin or end the **pilgrimage** or fasting. Other Muslim countries only observe the moon, and still others use different astronomical techniques to mark the dates of the calendar in advance.

Conversion tables between the *Hijri* and the Gregorian dates are available on the **Internet**, which replaced the former research tool of the Wüstenfeld'schen tables. To get a rough estimate, multiply the *Hijri* date by 0.97, then add 622 to get the Gregorian year.

FURTHER READING

Birashk, Ahmad. *A Comparative Calendar of the Iranian, Muslim Lunar, and Christian Eras for Three Thousand Years: 1260 B.H.-2000 A.H./639 B.C.-2621 A.D.* Costa Mesa, CA: Mazda Publishers, 1993.

Al-Gailani, Noorah, and Chris Smith. *The Islamic Year: Surahs, Stories and Celebrations.* Stroud, UK: Hawthorn Press, 2002.

Camels

Sebastian Maisel

The camel has a unique position and importance for the cultural, historical, and economical development of Arabia. The dromedary, *Camelus dromedarius*, is a one-humped and even-toed ungulate. Its hair color ranges from dark brown to almost white. It is adapted to life in a **desert** environment and manages to live without water for several days. Their body temperature can fluctuate six degrees Celsius. Special body functions help cool down the body temperature, such as enlarged mucous membranes, blood vessels, and a thick fur. They usually do not pant and perspire very little. During sand storms, they are able to cover their nostrils. Thick calluses on the soles and knees allow them to walk and lay on hot and stony grounds. Full-grown male camels weigh around 1,100 pounds (500 kilograms), females less. Depending on how much water they have digested (up to thirty percent of their body weight), they can drink a maximum of fifty gallons (190 liters), storing fat and other energy sources, but not water, in the hump.

As the most important livestock of the **Bedouins**, it gives milk (up to three gallons, or eleven liters, a day), hair, meat, skins, and dung for campfires. The

Camel in the old camel market in al-'Ayn (the market has been moved due to urban growth). This is a riding camel and is in full riding harness, showing the Fulani or Omani riding saddle behind the hump. Courtesy of John A. Shoup.

urine is occasionally used for medical and cosmetic purposes (e.g., against body lice). First and foremost, the camel is used for transport and fieldwork, distinguishing the smaller and faster riding camels and large and heavy working type. Riding camels can cover distances up to seventy-five miles (120 kilometers) per day; those carrying goods up to 440 pounds (200 kilograms) and go thirty-one miles (fifty kilometers) a day. The normal lifespan for camels is forty to fifty years. Reproduction age is three years for females and five for males. They are kept in gender-segregated herds, with the bulls often fighting over leadership.

The different breeds of camels are named after tribal groups famous for their camels or the area of origin; for example, the *Mahriyah*, *'Umaniyah*, and *Hutaymiyah* are known for their speed. In all Gulf States camel racing declined after the introduction of motor vehicles and planes in the beginning of the twentieth century, but they have become popular again. Breeding and trading camels continued to be a major occupation and large camel markets are frequented in all major cities of Arabia. Because of the popularity of the races and **Bedouin** lifestyle in general, enormous sums are paid for some racing camels. The races are seen as a form of re-distributing wealth to the Bedouin, a component in the formation of national identities, as well as an expression of preserving traditional heritage and cultural identity in the wake of globalization.

Camels are still used for farming, pulling ploughs, or turning water wheels to irrigate the fields, but mostly they are kept for racing, hair, meat, and milk as well as prestige. In pre-Islamic poetry, camels were described as the most valuable possession of the Bedouin. The image of camels was used for praise, love, and other metaphors. A rich vocabulary with several hundred words is associated with the camel to describe gender, color, age, and body shape. Two types of riding saddles are common in Arabia: the *shaddad* in northern Arabia and the *hawlani* in the south. The *hawdaj* is a special riding litter for women and children as well as ceremonial purposes. The ownership of a camel is marked with specific brands or *wasm*, of which each tribal group has a unique pattern. Camels were given away as a dowry or to solve conflicts, with exact amounts of camels to be paid for every **crime**.

The domestication of the camel was an important prerequisite for the inhabitation of Arabia and the emergence of the Bedouins. Archaeological evidence suggests that Arab nomadic groups first domesticated the camels around 1500 BC, and with the invention of the saddle camels were used for riding. They are mentioned in the Old Testament and later were used by Assyrian, Persian, and Roman troops during their campaigns on the Peninsula. Among the camel-herding Bedouins of Arabia, the animals were considered the most valuable asset. To own large camel herds meant having enough food as well as reputation and power. Bedouin raided each other to steal camels. For special occasions, weddings, births, or peace settlements, camels would be slaughtered and served to the guests. Camels are reared for their milk, which is very nutritious and normally drunk fresh. The hair was used to make tents, rugs, robes, and other garments; the dung was collected to light the campfire.

FURTHER READING

Agius, Dionisius A. *In the Wake of the Dhow: The Arabian Gulf and Oman*. Reading, UK: Ithaca Press, 2002.

Bulliet, Richard W. *The Camel and the Wheel*. New York: Columbia University Press, 1990.

Khalaf, Sulaiman, "Camel Racing in the Gulf: Notes on the Evolution of a Traditional Cultural Sport," *Anthropos* 94, no. 1–3 (1999): 85–106.

Saltin, Bengt. *The Racing Camel (Camelus Dromedarius): Physiology, Metabolic Functions, and Adaptations*. Oxford: Blackwell, 1994.

Charitable Organizations
Sebastian Maisel

To support those who are in need and less fortunate is one of the main doctrines of Islam. One of the five pillars of Islam, *zakaat*, requires Muslims to give alms to the poor. Thus, philanthropy has a high status and long tradition in Islam. For this reason, each Muslim is obliged to give a percentage of his possession to institutions that are specialized in this field. Usually *zakaat* is 2.5% for a **Sunni** Muslim and ten percent for a **Shi'a** and is donated to the local mosque or directly to charitable organizations.

However, larger nongovernmental institutions are set up to deal with issues of the global Muslim community and international Islamic relief. Those agencies distribute food, water, medical supplies, medicine, and other financial and infrastructural assets to communities in need. Charitable organizations in the Gulf States focus on social and economical issues and support all disadvantaged groups, such as children, orphans, women, the blind and disabled, and senior citizens. Even occupational support organizations exist, which are similar to unions and provide service and welfare to specific workers. In addition, they provide financial, legal, and other economic help in times of national or international disasters such as earthquakes, cyclones, tsunamis, or plane crashes. In times of war, some organizations provide food, water, and medical supplies to the people of Kosovo, Chechnya, **Palestine**, and several African countries. However, there are Islamic charitable organizations that favor helping Muslim communities. At home, help is provided with housing, **education**, **health care**, and administrative support. Special centers for orphans and the handicapped are built. In **Saudi Arabia**, one of the largest charitable foundations is the Prince Sultan ibn 'Abd al-'Aziz Charity Foundation. In addition to their domestic programs to construct housing units for the needy, they support humanitarian efforts worldwide, such as a school for orphans in Pakistan, Islamic centers in Japan and Germany, a hospital in India, and a disease center in Morocco. In **Qatar**, the *Khayriyah* Foundation is the oldest and largest voluntary organization and focuses on three main projects: education and culture; family, women, and children; and religious endowments (which are to be used to support the needy). The Muhammad Bin Rashid Al Maktum Foundation from **Dubai** specializes in education, entrepreneurship, and cultural exchange and grants billions of dollars every year to schools, universities, and other educational institutions as well as scholarships. They are affiliated with major international relief institutions such as UNICEF, WHO, and the U.N. High Committee for Refugees. As such they support displaced refugees in international conflict zones such as Palestine, Somalia, Lebanon, or Sudan.

However, raising money and investing it properly is something that Arab Gulf States look at differently from the West. In recent years after the attacks of 9/11, funds from some institutions have been transferred and used by radical Islamic organizations to finance activities that often include violent attacks against Western nations or administrations in Islamic countries that are considered illegitimate. Since 2004, the government of Saudi Arabia has stepped up to monitor the activities of almost 300 charitable organizations, setting up regulations of conduct and supervision. Some notoriously suspicious organizations, such as the *al-Haramayn* Foundation, were largely dismantled and a new official entity, the Saudi National Commission for Relief and Charity Work Abroad, was established. The strive for transparency and control goes as far as banning schools from collecting donations for aid projects because of fears that the money might support unlawful activities. Other Gulf States followed suit and through new legislations began to regulate the financial activities of selected organizations.

FURTHER READING

Alterman, Jon, and Karin Von Hippel. *Understanding Islamic Charities.* Washington, D.C.: Center for Strategic and International Studies, 2007.

Burr, J. Millard, and Robert Collins. *Alms for Jihad: Charity and Terrorism in the Islamic World*. London: Cambridge University Press, 2006.

McChesney, R.D. *Charity and Philanthropy in Islam: Institutionalizing the Call to Do Good*. Indianapolis: Indiana University Center on Philanthropy, 1995.

Citizenship in Kuwait

Adnan Al-Ghunaim

Kuwaiti citizenship stemmed from the 1959 Nationality Law, which differentiated between Kuwaitis by origin ("by origin" or *bil-asl*) and Kuwaitis by naturalization ("by naturalization" or *bil-tajanus)*. Among the former are the ruling **Al-Sabah** family and those whose ancestors lived in the country before 1920. The latter comprise mainly **Shi'a**, **Sunni**, and Christian Arabs from states surrounding Kuwait, and non-Arabs who came to the country before its independence in 1961.

Since the mid-1960s the government has used article 5 of the Nationality Law, which allows it to grant citizenship by decree to those who render particular services to the country. As a result, many **Bedouin** tribes from **Saudi Arabia** and other parts of the **Arabian Peninsula** who traditionally conveyed loyalty toward the ruling family have been granted Kuwaiti citizenship through mass naturalization. Also used as a political motive, the naturalization of pro-Al-Sabah tribal groups secured a higher turnout in favor of pro-Al-Sabah candidates in different parliamentary terms. Many Bedouin of Kuwaiti background serve as royal guards and form a large part of the Kuwaiti **military**.

Until 1996, the Kuwaiti citizenry was divided into two groups. The "by origin" or *bil-asl* Kuwaitis were an exclusive category whose members were given substantial economic and social rights, but political rights prior to 2005 were given to males only. However, "by naturalization" citizens who could not prove ancestry in Kuwait before 1920 as required by the Nationality Law enjoyed most of the rights as the "by origin" Kuwaiti group and its benefits, except that "by naturalization" males were not allowed to vote. Despite their division, which no longer exists, as will be discussed below, all Kuwaiti citizens enjoyed the privileges of a generous "cradle-to-grave" welfare system offered by the state.

Political change in regard to citizenship status in Kuwait has been slow. From the first elections in 1920 (involving a few dozen notables), suffrage was gradually extended, until by 1996, following internal demands for equal citizenship, most adult males were allowed to vote in the 1996 parliamentary elections, but women were still excluded from having political rights because of Kuwait's electoral law. On May 16, 2005, the parliament, after a long and complicated fight, voted to amend Kuwait's electoral law to give women suffrage and the right to run for Parliament for the first time in the 2006 elections. However, certain groups such as recently naturalized citizens and the stateless inhabitants of Kuwait known in Arabic as the *Bidun* ("without citizenship") are still excluded.

The case of the "stateless" *bidun* has historical foundations. Today they number approximately 125,000, approximately half the number of the period prior to the

1990/91 Gulf War. Prior to 1986, the *bidun* population had been included as part of the Kuwaiti citizenry population in the government's official statistical figures.

The origins of the *bidun* are disputed. Some observers claim that they remained itinerant for both traditional and tax reasons and, because they did not register in the 1957 census, they were rendered stateless. Others argue that their numbers included unofficial pre-war immigrants from neighboring countries (mainly Iraq) that wished to take advantage of the country's abundant welfare services. Today, despite their substantial contribution to Kuwait's military effort in 1990–1991, they are still regarded as illegal residents.

The status of the *bidun* in Kuwait was imprecise: they were separate, being recognized as Kuwaiti subjects but not as Kuwaiti citizens. Before 1986, they enjoyed similar citizenship rights to Kuwaitis except suffrage. The *bidun* problems increased during the **Iran-Iraq war**, when restrictions allowed their detention without charge for six months for "state security" reasons. In late 1985, following claims of an attempt by a small group of *bidun* to overthrow the government, it was decided that there would be no group called *bidun*; its members would be either Kuwaitis or non-Kuwaitis.

The claims and their consequences had a serious effect on the lives and affairs of the *bidun*. Subsequently, *bidun* rights further deteriorated. Educational and employment restrictions aimed at compelling them to reveal and prove their official identity were imposed. Travel restrictions were imposed in 1986, and in the same year the production of valid passports was made compulsory for both government and private sector employees. However, many insisted that their families, being nomads, had neither nationality nor documents. In the following two years, *bidun* were prevented from renewing their driving licenses and were prohibited from attending Kuwait University.

Only those *bidun* serving in the army and the police were issued with residency papers. Such employment proved particularly attractive because it offered one of the only means of political, social, and economic stability available to *bidun* in Kuwait. On the eve of the Iraqi invasion, *bidun* made up approximately three-fourths of Kuwait's total army force.

Despite their persecution, most *bidun* actively resisted the Iraqi occupation of Kuwait. In many cases they were subjected to pressure from both sides. Conscripted to the occupying army under the threat of death or imprisonment, they faced the possibility of being charged with collaboration after the war. Others were dismissed from government employment, deported, or not allowed to return. After the liberation of Kuwait in 1991, their number dropped to about 117,000 because many of them either left the country or declared another nationality.

The courage of those who opposed the occupation went unrecognized for a decade. Recently some of the restrictions on the *bidun*, such as those on **education** and movement, have been eased, and some of them have been granted citizenship. In May 2000, the parliament approved a law to grant citizenship to 2,000 adults and their families every year. According to the law, approximately 35,000 *bidun* have qualified for Kuwaiti citizenship, albeit granted only after exhaustive tests. There is also an increasing public awareness of their situation. However, many still do not have Kuwaiti citizenship. Unfair official practices and lack of influence and finances have ensured that even the children of the martyrs who fought for Kuwait in previous wars prior to and during the invasion are still deprived of this basic human right.

FURTHER READING

Bencomo, C. "Kuwait: Promises Betrayed: Denial of Rights of Bidun, Women, and Freedom of Expression." *Human Rights Watch Report* 12, no. 2E (2000). Available at http://www.hrw.org/reports/2000/kuwait/#P58_1426 (last accessed October 8, 2008).

Boghardt, L.P. *Kuwait amid War, Peace and Revolution: 1979–1991 and New Challenges.* (St. Anthony's). Basingstoke, UK: Palgrave Macmillan, 2006.

Crystal, J. "Public Order and Authority: Policing Kuwait," in *Monarchies and Nations: Globalization and Identity in the Arab States of the Gulf*, edited by P. Dresch and J. Piscatori. London: I.B. Tauris, 2005.

Longva, A. "Nationalism in Pre-Modern Guise: The Discourse on Hadhar and Badu in Kuwait," *International Journal of Middle Eastern Studies* 38 (2006): 171–187.

Maktabi, R. "The Politics of Citizenship in Kuwait—Membership and Participation in a Rentier State." Paper presented at the 13th Annual National Political Science Conference, Hurdalsjøen, Oslo, Norway, January 5–7, 2005. Available at http://www.statsvitenskap.uio.no/konferanser/nfkis/kp/Maktabi.pdf (last accessed October 8, 2008).

Al-Najjar, G. "Human Rights in a Crisis Situation: The Case of Kuwait after Occupation," *Human Rights Quarterly* 23 (2001): 188–209.

Salem, P. "Kuwait: Politics in a Participatory Emirate," Carnegie Papers, Carnegie Endowment for International Peace, Carnegie Middle East Center, no. 3 (2007). Available at http://www.carnegieendowment.org (last accessed October 8, 2008).

Tetreault, M., and H. al-Mughni. "Gender, Citizenship and Nationalism in Kuwait," *British Journal of Middle Eastern Studies* 22, no. 1–2 (1995): 64–80.

Climate

John A. Shoup

The climate of the **Arabian Peninsula** is arid, receiving on average around five inches (150 millimeters) of rainfall a year, and it has no permanent river systems or lakes. Most rain falls in the winter, which lasts from November to March. The Peninsula is affected by the same weather systems that emerge first in the Atlantic and move eastward across the Mediterranean. The northern part of the Peninsula receives more moisture than the central regions, where more than ten years can pass without more than a trace of rainfall. Winters are cold and higher elevations can have moisture fall as snow; in the central region nighttime temperatures can hover close to freezing. In the **Asir** region of **Saudi Arabia** it is not uncommon for the nights to be below freezing and morning fogs so thick that all traffic comes to a halt. Cold fronts originating in continental Europe can drop as far south as the Peninsula, either moving across the Black Sea and then into Anatolia or from Russia and moving across Iran or Afghanistan and Pakistan, affecting even the Gulf coastal cities such as **Dubai**, **al-Dawhah**, **al-Manamah**, and **Kuwait City**. The Hajar **Mountains** help shield **Musqat** and other **Omani** cities, which also receive the warmer sea breezes from the Indian Ocean and the

Arabian Sea. The winter rains cause the **desert** to turn green, and this is when pastoral nomads can disperse to their widest range of grazing areas for their livestock.

The southwestern corner of the Peninsula is affected by the summer monsoons, which begin in the Ethiopian Highlands and then pick up moisture as they head across the Indian Ocean to the Indian Subcontinent. The highlands of **Yemen** and the southwestern corner of Oman are able to get some of this moisture and the Qarah Mountains in Oman become lush gardens with rushing water in September, whereas the rest of Oman still suffers from summer heat. Some of the monsoon's moisture is able to move further north and can cause late summer thunderstorms with brief and localized heavy rainfall.

The summers last from April to October and most of the Peninsula is hot and dry with daytime temperatures well above 100°F (37°C). In many places daytime averages are over 104°F (40°C) for months on end. Hot winds blow off the deserts, creating sand storms that can last several days. These winds have several different names in the Peninsula, some denoting main direction where they come from and others about their stifling nature. The sand and dust can be so thick as to cause airports and sea harbors to close. Along the Gulf and Red Sea coasts summers are humid as well as hot, making it difficult to breathe for those not used to the conditions.

Spring and autumn are both short seasons, so short that they can pass by hardly noticed by the people; each can last for literally a few weeks at most. Traditional **architecture** in the Peninsula is built to deal with the extremes of summer heat and winter cold, although it is more important to deal with the heat. Because rainfall is rarely a serious concern, many of the regional architectural styles use thick mud walls as a means to create a cool, shady environment for the people. Light is diffused through small openings that also allow air to circulate. Other styles make uses of palm fronds as the main building material, which again allows people to create a cool living space. *Barajil* (*barjil* in singular) or wind towers, an invention on the Iranian side of the Gulf, were introduced to several Gulf cities and these provide a form of air conditioning that helps with the heat and humidity of the coastal summers.

FURTHER READING

Beaumont, Peter, Gerald Blake, and Malcom Wagstaff. *The Middle East*. London: John Wiley & Sons, 1976.

Coles, Anne, and Peter Jackson. *Windtower*. London: Stacey International, 2007.

Fisher, W.B. *The Middle East: A Physical, Social, and Regional Geography*. London: Methuen, 1971.

Coffee: Arabic and Turkish
John A. Shoup

Coffee (*Qahwah* in Arabic) is the bean of the madder tree that grows naturally in the Ethiopian Highlands. Its narcotic properties were discovered by chance according to popular legend when a goat herder noticed the energetic activities of his animals after they had eaten the beans. Coffee was first spread in the Arab world by members of the Shadhili Sufi order and was drunk to allow them to stay

Arabic coffee is the coffee of the Bedouin. Here coffee is being prepared over an open fire in expectation of the arrival of guests in Abu Dhabi. Courtesy of John A. Shoup.

up all night for their *dhikr*s (*dhikr* means literally "remembrance" and refers to the gatherings of religious mystical groups in Islam). Coffee was banned by some Muslim religious authorities and was not accepted as a legal drink until the late sixteenth century. **Yemen** became the main producer of coffee beans, and its port Mukha lent its name to the drink as mocha. By the nineteenth century coffee had been introduced as cash crops in the Dutch East Indies (Indonesia), Colombia, and Ecuador and in the early twentieth century to British East Africa (Kenya and Uganda). Coffee is still one of the major export crops from Yemen.

In the **Arabian Peninsula** two main types of coffee are prepared: Turkish and Arabic. Turkish coffee, or *qahwa Turkiyah*, is strong, thick, and bitter unless large amounts of sugar are added. Generally speaking Turkish coffee is the drink of the **coffeehouses** and urban people. Turkish coffee is prepared in a special brass pot called a *kanakah*. It is made by measuring one demitasse cup of water per cup of coffee plus one heaping teaspoon of finely ground coffee beans and one equally heaping teaspoon of sugar per cup. The coffee is allowed to come to a boil several times before it is poured into a demitasse cup and served.

Arabic coffee, or *qahwa 'Arabiyah*, is prepared differently and is lighter in color, although perhaps as strong as Turkish coffee. Proper preparation of Arabic coffee begins with roasting the coffee beans over an open flame. The beans are allowed to cool in a special wooden dish called a *mabrad* or *mubarrad* and then once cooled are poured into a large wooden mortar called a *mihbaj*, where they are ground into a fine powder with a long wooden pestle. The person grinding the beans uses the pestle to beat out known rhythms that tell neighbors coffee is being made. The ground beans are then put in a brass pot made specifically for making coffee called a *dallah* along with several cardamom pods for added flavor and aroma. The coffee is served in small handleless cups called *finjan*. According to custom, it is proper to take three cups of Arabic coffee and no more. A person signals to the host or the person serving that enough has been served by shaking the cup from side to side and saying *da'iman*, meaning to remain blessed.

Coffeehouses
John A. Shoup

Coffeehouses (*Maqha* in Arabic) in the **Arabian Peninsula** serve several important social functions, and many are seen as male clubs where the same customers come every day. Coffeehouses were first established in Cairo during the first part of the sixteenth century and spread to Syria by the middle of the century. The first coffeehouses were established in Istanbul by the end of the same century. Muslim religious authorities debated the legality of **coffee** because it has obvious narcotic properties, including addiction. In the end, most Islamic jurists ruled in favor of the drink and coffeehouses were established in much of the Islamic world.

Coffeehouses were built near places of business and even today real business may be conducted from a coffeehouse and not in an official office. Early in the history of the institution, coffeehouses offered entertainment such as recitations of epic tales by professional storytellers who accompanied themselves on a one- or two-string fiddle and a chorus playing percussion instruments. Coffeehouses also offered a place where one could smoke and many offered a variety of flavored tobaccos that were smoked in a water pipe called *narjilah* or *shishah*.

Coffeehouses are urban institutions but they are popular enough that even small villages may have one. They remain a male space and very few allow women to sit; however, this is changing in several of the Gulf States where "faux" coffeehouses have become part of *Ramadan* celebrations. These faux coffeehouses offer traditional coffees, teas, and water pipes, but also several special drinks such as *sahlab* (made with arrowroot, nuts, coconut, and hot milk) and *karkadah* (made from boiled hibiscus flowers) that have been introduced from Egypt and Syria. In these coffeehouses, women and even families come to relax after breaking the day's *Ramadan* fast and enjoy traditional entertainment such as classical Arabic **music** and poetry recitations, or watch game shows on large-screen **televisions**.

Committee for the Promotion of Virtue and Prevention of Vice
Sebastian Maisel

Some Islamic countries employ a special control force that deals with the implementation of the rules and rituals according to Islamic law. According to the Qur'an, their main, general objective is to promote the virtue among the faithful and prevent vice, in Arabic: *al-amr bi'l-ma'ruf wa' l-nahi 'an al-munkar*. Their local name is **mutawwa**, or volunteer, and they are considered a **Shari'ah** law enforcement institution to control the public and private sphere of residents in **Saudi Arabia**.

The "sixth" pillar of Islam, *jihad*, refers to this concept, in which the individual and the society are obliged to encourage virtues and resist evil, by force if necessary. The modern interpretation of *jihad* in Saudi Arabia is strongly connected to the idea of members of the committee enforcing their understanding of Islam on others, as their way of *jihad*. The nonmilitary manifestation of this force is a large group of volunteers, some of them being organized in the committee and often addressed as the religious or morality police of Saudi Arabia. Most volunteers have an educational background in some aspects of Islamic law and studied at one of the Islamic universities of the country. Similar to Islamic teachers, judges, and scholars, they are considered a fundamental part of maintaining the Islamic character of the whole society; therefore the government, who has the same goal, funds them. However, with the current population growth and rising **unemployment** it becomes more difficult for the government to provide jobs for university graduates in general. Those graduates from Islamic universities usually join the committees and help to force the population to conform to Islamic social norms.

Approximately 5,000 members are employed and the director, *Shaykh* Ibrahim al-Ghayth, reports directly to the Minister of Interior, Prince Nayef bin 'Abd al-'Aziz. They usually patrol the streets together with members of the regular police force in order to inspect public behavior and appearance. An internal department deals with cases related to alcohol and **drugs**. During Valentine's Day, members of the committee enforce the restraint order not to sell red roses, toys, or presents in order to prevent the population from performing pagan rituals. In addition, between 2006 and 2007, they arrested more than 100 "sorcerers and witches," people who provide love potions and fertility amulets. Other tasks include tracking and persecuting homosexuals, prostitutes, and violations of prayer times. They also crack down on non-Islamic worship and the display of non-Islamic religious signs.

The committee and its actions are viewed controversially in present-day Saudi society. They added to their often negative image in March 2002 when they prevented schoolgirls from escaping their burning school building because they were not properly covered, which led to the death of several girls in the building. Small-scale corrections were implemented, but the overall attitude and behavior have not changed, and it is often viewed as anti-modern, conservative, and zealous.

FURTHER READING

Cook, Michael. *Commanding Right and Forbidding Wrong in Islamic Thought*. Cambridge, UK: Cambridge University Press, 2000.

Vogel, Frank. "The Public and Private in Saudi Arabia: Restrictions on the Powers of Committees for Ordering the Good and Forbidding the Evil," *Social Research: An International Quarterly of Social Sciences* 70, no. 3 (2003): 749–768.

Companies

Sebastian Maisel

The economy of the countries in the area of the **Arabian Gulf** is mainly **oil**-based with the governments controlling most of the sector. The dominance of the state-owned oil sector has often led to the private sector being overlooked. But the area is home to many national and multinational companies in different industrial sectors. Most of them are related to the oil and petrochemical industry, but because of efforts to diversify the economical base of the countries, more and more non-oil-related companies emerge. However, as a major aspect of **globalization**, many of those companies are no longer recognized as individual entities specialized in a specific area, but they are part of larger international consortiums operating all over the Gulf or even on a global level. The trend goes to companies, which can offer a variety of services and products under one brand name. Joint ventures in the form of multinational companies are the most common form of business ownership. They are popular because the economic climate in the Gulf encourages their formation and operation. The private sector is rapidly growing, while at the same time the dependency on the oil-dominated public sector is lessened. Entrepreneurs no longer simply look for government contracts, but for investment opportunities for their own private capital. As such they enter the global economy with its pros and cons, but this new trend still is regarded as one of the most positive stimulants in the Gulf economy. All major companies are listed on the various stock exchange markets, with the Saudi *Tadawul* being the largest and most influential for the region.

SAUDI ARABIA

The government of Saudi Arabia owns Saudi **Aramco**, the largest company in the kingdom, which concurrently is the largest oil company in the world. The company is headquartered in **Dhahran**, Saudi Arabia, and produces large amounts of crude oil and natural gas as well as manages over 100 oil fields in Saudi Arabia. In addition, the company is involved in other activities around the oil production, such as exploration, drilling, refining, and distribution.

The other gigantic public company in Saudi Arabia is SABIC (Saudi Basic Industries Corporation) with its headquarters in **Riyadh**. Most of the operations are managed from Jubayl. SABIC is a diversified manufacturing company with additional holdings in hydrocarbon-based industries. They are a leading producer of chemicals, industrial polymers, fertilizers, and metals.

Saudi Oger is a construction company with knowledge and expertise in prestigious and complex building, operations and maintenance, real estate development, utilities, IT services, and power and telecommunication projects throughout the Middle East. The company's original paid-up capital of SR 1 million has now grown to almost SR 1 billion. Rafik Hariri's family owns the company. Hariri was the former Lebanese prime minister who lived in exile in Saudi Arabia during much of the Lebanese Civil War (1975–2000) and who was

81

assassinated in 2005. The company enjoys close relations with leading governmental and private institutions and individuals from the **Gulf Cooperation Council** (GCC), which in return provides them with lucrative contracts.

The founder of Olayan Group, Sulaiman Olaiyan from **'Unayzah**, is considered one of the most successful Saudi businessmen with private assets worth some $8 billion. He started his company in 1950 with early investments in and representations of foreign companies. He is a major stockholder at Chase, Occidental, Saudi British Bank, and Credit Suisse First Boston. He is also the most important Saudi partner for Coca-Cola. His four children, including his two daughters Hutham and Lubna, are all in leading managing positions. In addition, he maintains business relations with Khalid Bin 'Abdallah **Al Sa'ud**.

The Saudi Bin Ladin Group is an old, large construction and holding company based in **Jiddah**. Founded by Yemeni Muhammad **bin Ladin**, the company expanded through lucrative government contracts in infrastructure construction, including the expansion of the Holy Mosque in **Makkah** and in 2005 the building of King Abdallah Economic City.

Kingdom is a semi-public holding and investment company founded in 1980 and currently controlled by Prince Walid bin al-Talal, the chairman and CEO. The company's headquarters is the Kingdom Tower, a landmark in Riyadh. Among the diverse areas of investment are banking, computer technology, **tourism**, retailing, entertainment, telecommunication, and real estate. The company invested in international corporations such as eBay, Ford, Apple, and Pepsi.

Founded in 1948 by *Shaykh* Ahmad Juffali, the Juffali Company established itself as a leading business corporation in the region. They started in electric appliances, construction, telecommunications, and joint ventures with international partners such as Siemens, Daimler-Benz, and IBM. Juffali's sons and cousins currently run the private company.

Dallah al-Barakah is one of the largest private companies in the Middle East and is owned by *Shaykh* Salih 'Abdallah Kamil. It started as a maintenance and service company before becoming specialized in construction, especially airports. They won several major contracts with the Ministry of Defense. Lately, the company started to invest in different areas, such as **media**, real estate, and tourism.

Almarai is the largest dairy company in Saudi Arabia and the wider Middle East. The word *al-mara'i* in Arabic means green pasture and represents the policy of the company of turning the **desert** into pasture. It employs approximately 10,000 people and is headquartered near the city of al-Kharj. This is also the site of the main manufacturing and central processing plants. The company operates three farms producing feed crops and five high-tech dairy farms housing about 33,000 Saudi-bred American Holsteins. Among the main products that are freshly produced daily are milk, *laban* (yogurt), *labanah* (sour cream), cheese, fruit yogurts, juices, and other desserts. Almarai operates its own fleet of refrigerated trucks that deliver to all countries of the GCC. The company started its operations in 1976 under the leadership of HRH Prince Sultan bin Muhammad bin Sa'ud Al-Kabir.

Saudia Airlines is owned by the Saudi government and was founded in 1945. By 2007, the first steps were made to turn Saudia into a privatized corporation with plans that ground services, cargo, catering, and the Prince Sultan Aviation Academy become part of a holding company. The airline operates over seventy destinations worldwide with their peak season around the time of the Muslim **pilgrimage** to Makkah and **Madinah**.

KUWAIT

Kuwait's economy is dependent on the **oil industry**. The main public oil company is Kuwait Petroleum Company, founded in 1980 with several large subsidiaries. Since the Iraqi occupation, important steps have been taken to strengthen the private sector and diversify the industry. Especially in the telecommunications sector, competition between private and semi-private companies is noted. Zain Group, formerly known as MTC, is specialized in mobile telecommunications, broadband, and **Internet** services. Headquartered in Kuwait, it has branches in twenty-one countries in the Middle East and Africa. The Sultan Center was founded 1976 by Jamil Sultan and is a leading company in self-service retail, groceries, and catering. Al-Mulla Group is an old and prominent business group specializing in various sectors, such as manufacturing, trading, and financing services. It held several dealerships and was the main distributor for Chrysler. Today it is successful because of its diversified trading opportunities.

BAHRAIN

In contrast to other Gulf States, Bahrain has few revenues from oil and gas and therefore transformed its economy toward other sectors, such as banking, heavy industry, telecommunications, and retail. Among the largest industrial projects were Aluminum Bahrain, the Arab Shipbuilding and Repair Yard, and the Arab Iron and Steel Company. Bahrain Telecommunications Company (Batelco) is the leading provider for telecommunications and information services in Bahrain. The shareholding company was established in 1982. Investcorp is a globally renowned company that provides and manages investments for both private and institutional clients. They deal in private equity, hedge funds, real estate, and technology. Recently, they launched a regional business line for investments primarily in the GCC area. Yusuf bin Ahmad Kanoo is the oldest pan-Gulf transportation and shipping company, as well as the leading travel agent. The company's background and policies are viewed in contrast to the large state-owned corporations.

QATAR

The economy of Qatar is heavily based on oil and even more on natural gas. The country has the world's third largest reserves and the state-owned Qatar Petroleum exploits the resources and manages the facilities. Modest plans were made to diversify the economy, and joint ventures for foreign investment in heavy industry projects are being formed. The government built chemical plants for fertilizers, steel, and cement and recently expanded the fishing industry focusing on shrimp.

OMAN

Petroleum Development Oman represents another example of a company in the Gulf region with joint ownership between the Omani government (sixty percent) and foreign capital (Royal Dutch Shell, Total). It is the main exploration and production company of the country, which depends heavily on the oil industry for its gross domestic product. Oman Telecommunication Company (Omantel) is the country's largest Internet and mobile phone provider. The government owns seventy percent of Omantel.

UNITED ARAB EMIRATES

The United Arab Emirates have been working on diversifying their industry for the last two decades, especially in the field of light industry, food processing, and some heavy industry, with **Dubai** Aluminum Smelter being the largest single investment. DUBAL is a conglomerate that includes the smelter, power plants, and desalination plants. The government owns some of the largest companies that have been founded during an ambitious phase of economical development turning the Emirates into a banking, media, and tourism center for the region. Among these companies are giants like Arab Media Group, **Dubai Media City**, Dubai World, or the Jabal 'Ali Free Zone. One of the largest public corporations not only in the Emirates but also on the global level is Etisalat, the country's main telecommunication and Internet provider. Although the market is highly restricted, a major competitor, Du Telecommunication, entered the market in 2007, breaking the monopoly of Etisalat. The United Arab Emirates' government is a major shareholder in both companies.

FURTHER READING

Gause, Gregory F. *Oil Monarchies: Domestic and Security Challenges in the Arab Gulf States.* New York: CFRP, 1993.
Field, Michael. *The Merchants: The Big Business Families of Saudi Arabia and the Gulf States.* Woodstock, NY: Overlook Press, 1985.
Mababaya, Mamarinta. *The Role of Multinational Companies in the Middle East: The Case of Saudi Arabia.* Westminster, UK: University of Westminster, 2002.
Marcel, Valerie and John Mitchell. *Oil Titans: National Oil Companies in the Middle East.* London: Chatham House, 2006.

Crime
Sebastian Maisel

Saudi Arabia and the Gulf States have a very low crime level, considerably lower than in many Western countries. Street crimes are rare and used to be unknown. This was mainly attributed to two factors. First, the area is the birthplace of Islam and the aspect of pure faith is significant for the application of right or wrong. Saudi Arabia in particular has adopted many legal measurements from the Qur'an and the code of law strongly relies on Islamic Law as it is codified in the *Shari'ah*. It can be suggested that the prevalence of Islamic values among the people of Arabia contributes to the respect and adherence to law and order in these nations. With *Shari'ah* comes a straightforward code of penalties with clear regulations and little room to appeal. Penalties are rigidly enforced, often in public in order to make an example and deter other future criminals. The occasional enforcement of harsh penalties for a variety of crimes contributes much to what is referred to as a high standard of public safety.

Prior to the unification of Saudi Arabia, crimes such as robbery or raids were so common that people felt relieved after King **'Abd al-'Aziz ibn Sa'ud** began to enforce Islamic law in all newly incorporated territories. Crimes rates dropped dramatically because of a prompt and harsh enforcement of penalties, which then were regarded as offenses not only against human law but also against the divine will.

Another aspect was the homogeneity of the population, a tribally organized society with strict rules and penalties. This type of **social organization**, in which everyone knows everyone else and is somehow dependent on each other, encourages noninvolvement in criminal activities. This traditional system has been weakened with the opening of the countries to foreign **companies**, workers, and visitors. Therefore, in local statistics, the rise of petty crimes is often attributed to unemployed foreign guestworkers and residents who are excluded from social solidarity. On the other hand, public institutions such as schools, mosques, security forces, police, and *mutawwas* in Saudi Arabia are busy with teaching legal and behavioral aspects of Islam, allowing maximal and constant indoctrination with all necessary rules of living together in a Muslim society. They combine informal (family), semi-formal (religion), and formal (school) social control over the population.

The most common crimes in Saudi Arabia are theft, offenses related to alcohol (production, sale, and consumption), altercations, and moral/honor crimes. Penalties are classified into *tazir* (prevention or correction)–penalties that are up to the discretion of the judge; *hadd*–penalties that are regulated by *Shari'ah*; and *qisas* (retribution), or fixed compensations for murder and battery. Most serious are the *hadd* (limit)-penalties for Islamic capital crimes such as adultery, false accusation of adultery, theft, highway robbery, and alcohol-related cases. Some legal/religious scholars add apostasy to the list. Penalties include flogging, amputations, and executions. In same case, capital punishment is applied for rape and armed robbery. The four main schools of Islamic law differ on the number of crimes and the execution of penalties. Saudi Arabia, **Qatar**, and the **United Arab Emirates** follow the Hanbali School, whereas in **Kuwait** the dominant school is Maliki; **Bahrain** is Maliki for the Sunnis and Ja'afari for its **Shi'ite** population, and **Oman** is mainly **Ibadi Kharaji**.

Newer charges include corruption and drug-related cases, in which the latter are punished severely in all Gulf States, some of them applying capital punishment for drug trafficking. These harsh laws help keep the number of drug addicts and drug-related crimes very low. Combating cyber crimes and software piracy is an issue that is discussed on the regional level of the **Gulf Cooperation Council**, where a common law is drafted based on experiences from the United Arab Emirates.

However, the picture of a peaceful, harmonic country is changing. Official reports stated that between 1990 and 1996 the crime rate among young unemployed Saudi rose some 320% and forecasted an additional 136% by 2005. The link between economic and social problems with an increase in crimes is possible and if correctly applied raises concerns about the safety of the country in the near future. Saudi Arabia has the highest car theft rate in the Middle East. To work with crime statistics in Saudi Arabia and the Gulf States is difficult because many cases are not brought to court but are instead dealt with internally on the family/tribal level.

See also **Madhhab**.

FURTHER READING

Crystal, Jill. "Criminal Justice in the Middle East," *Journal of Criminal Justice* 29, no. 6 (2001): 469–482.

Hamzeh, Nizar. "Qatar: The Duality of the Legal System," *Middle Eastern Studies* 30, no. 1 (1994): 79–90.

Helal, A., and C. Coston. "Low Crime Rates in Bahrain: Islamic Social Control," *International Journal of Comparative and Applied Criminal Justice* 5, nos. 1 and 2 (1991): 125–144.

Souryal, Sam. "The Role of Shariah Law in Deterring Criminality in Saudi Arabia," *International Journal of Comparative and Applied Criminal Justice* 12, no. 1 (1988): 1–25.

Vogel, Frank E. *Islamic Law and Legal System: Studies of Saudi Arabia.* Leiden, The Netherlands: Brill, 2000.

Wardak, Ali. "Crime and Social Control in Saudi Arabia," in *Transnational and Comparative Criminology*, edited by James Sheptycki and Ali Wardak. London: Glasshouse, 2005.

Cuisine

Sebastian Maisel

Arabs in pre-Islamic times were either nomads, who lived off the products of their **camels**, particularly the milk and its byproducts; or farmers in the **oases**, who harvested **dates**, which could be preserved for a long time and therefore were also popular among the **Bedouin**. Coastal people lived mainly off fish and seafood, whereas bread and other dishes made from grain were hardly found. With the rise of Islam, several dietary taboos were introduced, such as pork and alcohol. Islam classifies all food into *halal* (permitted) and *haram* (prohibited). Other requirements were made with regard to butchering animals. However, with the integration of different **ethnic groups** into the Muslim community, new eating and dietary habits were adopted. This became primarily visible during the *Hajj* (**pilgrimage**), when different people came together for an entire month and shared their traditions and customs with each other and the local population of the **Hijaz**.

It is remarkable that despite the homogeneity of Arabian culture, specific local and regional tastes and cuisines exist. In **Saudi Arabia**, dishes that shape the

Kabsah, a popular dish of meat (lamb or chicken) and rice in central Arabia, is served. Courtesy of Sebastian Maisel.

national cuisine most were those from the Hijaz. The sophisticated merchant families adapted many foreign dishes that came to the area with the pilgrimage and assimilated them so completely that it is hard to imagine these dishes are actually foreign.

Except for a few areas in southwest Arabia in the **mountains** of **Asir** and in the oases along the **Gulf**, water is scarce and the annual precipitation did not allow rain-based farming. It was therefore necessary to irrigate the fields with ancient techniques. Despite irrigation, the quantity and variety of produce were limited. Traditional produce included grain (wheat and barley), vegetables (tomatoes, cucumbers, onions), and of course dates, which is the fruit that is most suitable to this climate. The Bedouins and sedentary animal breeders provided meat. In the coastal region fish and other seafood were an important part of the daily diet. Since ancient times, the people of Arabia traded with India, East Africa, Europe, and East Asia and imported spices and tea from those areas. During the last two centuries, **coffee** and rice were added to the list of purchased items. Local beekeepers produced honey, the natural sweetener, but sugar was frequently used and therefore was bought from the market.

Almost everywhere on the **Arabian Peninsula** grain products were the main staple. Unleavened bread, pies, and sweets were made from wheat, whereas barley was used to make *burghul* and *jarish*. Milk continued to be another important staple. Butter, yogurts, laban, and a variety of cheeses were made from goat, sheep, or camel milk. Vegetables were always more important than meat. People ate them raw, steamed, fried, and pickled or as salads. Common vegetables and legumes were onions, garlic, carrots, cucumber, tomato, pepper, lettuce, parsley, lentils, chickpeas, eggplants, zucchini, and okra. Meat, especially mutton, goat, chicken, and camel, was eaten less frequently. The meat was either ground up or cut into small pieces, but usually not served as steak, and then grilled over charcoal. It was common to spice the meat with salt, pepper, garlic, thyme, and coriander or to marinate it in vinegar, oil, or rose water. Popular fish dishes included tuna, shark, mackerel, bass, and mahi mahi. They were often fried, baked, or grilled. In addition, shrimp, crabs, lobster, turtles, and dolphins were eaten.

Very important for the preparation as well as the preservation of food were oils, spices, and fat. Olive oil was the most common, followed by sesame oil and coconut oil. Spices and seasonings were used in abundance. Standard choices included salt, pepper, onion, paprika, and garlic. Garlic was considered helpful for general health and virility. In addition, thyme, coriander, cumin, sumaq, anise, fennel, cardamom, cinnamon, cloves, and peppermint were used frequently. Saffron was popular more for its coloring effect than its taste.

Fruit was served at almost every meal. Local fruits included dates, oranges, melons, figs, grapes, lemons, pomegranates, peaches, apricots, and apples, whereas in some areas with a more tropical climate bananas, mangos, and papayas were grown. Most fruits were eaten fresh, except for dates and figs, which were usually dried. Some fruits such as dates, figs, apricots, and grapes were used for pie filling and jams. The date was probably the most versatile staple with large varieties in size, taste, and preservability. The Arabic preference for sweets was shown in the substantial use of sugar in hot beverages and for baking. In addition to small cookies and other pastries, the people of Arabia loved to chew on nuts and other seeds such as almonds, hazelnuts, pistachios and melon, sunflower, and pumpkin seeds.

Milk and water were traditionally the most common beverages. During the Ottoman rule, coffee and tea were introduced and quickly became popular. Wine and Arak, although prohibited by Islam, have a limited importance.

People used to eat three times a day and continue to do that today. Mealtimes are coordinated around prayer times. The traditional social stratification of the society in urban, rural, and nomadic groups was also recognizable at the dinner table. People from the countryside ate different things than those in the city and those on the move. For breakfast in the city, the obligatory bread was accompanied by yogurt, *laban*, olives, eggs, and sometimes jams, whereas in the countryside people ate clarified butter, dates, and goat cheese with their bread. Bedouins had only dates and camel milk. In the settlement, tea was very common for breakfast. For lunch, on ordinary days main courses with variations of rice dishes with some kind of meat were common, whereas in the cities rice was replaced with cracked wheat in addition to fresh salads of tomatoes, cucumber, and parsley. In the evening, the entire family gathered for a light snack, often the leftovers from lunch. Usually, people in Arabia did not eat from a table but preferred to sit on the floor and share the food. They ate from the same bowl and instead of silverware used flat bread or the fingers of the right hand. Traditionally, men ate first, separate from the women and children of the family.

On special occasions, such as birth, circumcision, or a wedding, a sheep or young camel was slaughtered and served on large trays with rice and different spices such as saffron, coriander, and pinenuts. After dinner, tea and coffee were served in an exactly prescribed ceremony. Visitors were first served tea and coffee upon leaving; however, the coffee was not the Turkish kind (i.e., strong and sweet), but the Arabian brew (i.e., bitter, brown, and spiced with cardamom and cloves). Because of the commonness and frequency of the ceremony, every family had several sets of coffee and teapots and cups available.

It was difficult to label a recipe a traditional recipe from Arabia because of the constant influx of new trends and tastes and the mixture of lifestyles. Arguably the dish that was considered the national dish of Saudi Arabia and its neighbors was *kabsah*, a rice casserole with roasted lamb or chicken. Often associated with the central region, today it is found all over the Peninsula. Basic ingredients included rice with saffron, tomatoes, onions, spices, and the meat. In some northern areas, the dish was known as *mansaf*. For a long time, chicken was considered a delicacy until modern technologies enabled the establishment of large poultry farms throughout the area. *Mataziz* is another popular dish from **Najd** and is made from lamb and vegetable dumplings and served with white rice. In the Eastern Province and along the Gulf shore, *muhashshah*, a traditional rice dish, was served with fried fish. Fried mackerel with rice and salad was called *hubul*. Popular dishes that were of non-Arabian origin, but nevertheless Arabic, included *falafal* (deep-fried chickpea balls) and *shawarmah* (sliced lamb or chicken sandwiches). Saudis in the Eastern Province called rice *caysh* (life in Arabic), indicating the importance of this staple for the region; usually '*aysh* is used to refer to bread.

Some dishes were only made for certain occasions such as religious holidays; for example, the holy month of *Ramadan*, during which Muslims were not permitted to eat, drink, and smoke during the daytime. Nighttime, however, was a time to celebrate the accomplishment and this was done with special food such as *ful madammas*, fava beans in a sauce of clarified butter, cumin, and lemon juice; *minazzalah*, pieces of lamb, chopped tomatoes, and *tahinah*; and *qatayif*, small turnovers fried on one side and stuffed with nuts, fruits, and sweet spices and dipped in sugar syrup. People ate only twice a day during *Ramadan*: the *iftar*-meal after sunset and the *suhur*-meal before sunrise when fasting begins. For the 'Id al-Adha feast, immediately following the conclusion of the pilgrimage another special dish was prepared in **Najd** called *baydiyah*, a dish of wheat cooked in lamb broth and topped with onions. The whole dish was wrapped in dough that was topped with saffron, rose water, and lamb and garnished with eggs and additional vegetables. For the preparation of this dish, neighbors and relatives got together to help each other.

Changes in the eating habits did not start with the **oil** boom, but were noticeable before, particularly in the Hijaz during the pilgrimage. Because most of the **oil industry** with its many foreign workers and customs was located in the Eastern Province along the Gulf coast, stronger influences by other mostly Western cultures were observed. Only in the interior of the Peninsula, in Najd, **Najran**, or the mountains did the old dietary customs prevail due to the isolation of the area. Thanks to modern technology different methods to preserve, store, transport, and freeze food were available and led to an increasing consumption of meat and fish. Traditional food preservatives such as vinegar were now only used for the taste.

Arabic and other international cuisines (e.g., Lebanese, Egyptian, Indian, or Thai) entered the food market of the Gulf countries through migration and guestworkers. Particularly, influences by Indo-Malayan cuisine and their frequent use of soy and curry were seen along the Gulf. However, the biggest change came with the acceptance of Western eating habits. Today, large supermarkets and fast-food restaurants shape the picture of virtually every large city. Jiddah, **Dubai, Kuwait, Masqat,** and cities in the Peninsula are now Westernized, and international restaurants are found in each of them. They opened in the 1970s when oil revenues increased and were invested in the local infrastructure. **Urbanization,** the trend to move to the cities in search of better living conditions, increased rapidly during this time period and the old ways of providing for the local population were no longer sufficient. Traditional markets for vegetables or meat were pushed aside or began to offer imported processed goods. Those new products were in high demand, especially in the urban setting. The younger generation, comprising more than half of the entire population, was attracted to Western eating habits and products, and they adopted hamburgers, sodas, and french fries as the main staple. Coffee shops, offering Western coffee and pastries, became even more popular, because drinking coffee together while communicating had always been an important aspect of the daily lifestyle. Another way of adjusting traditions to the new way of life was to provide segregated eating areas for families and women in restaurants. Although ingredients and dishes have changed, other traditions remained intact. Where, when, and how one eats were still the same—only what one ate was different. Because foreign food items were usually not separated from local products, they were quickly accepted by the consumers.

Although it was fair to speak of an Arabic cuisine of the Gulf area, each country had its unique and traditional recipes and dishes. The small island of **Bahrain** lived off wheat, dates, and seafood that were seasoned with spices from India and Iran. The national dish of Kuwait was *kuzi* (roasted lamb stuffed with rice, eggs, and chicken). The cuisine of Kuwait combined traditional aspects of Bedouin lifestyle with that of a settled population and international guestworkers. Most people in **Qatar** lived off seafood, fish, as well as rice, dates, and sheep. However, in Oman, fish and rice were the most important staples. The country enjoyed close relations with eastern Africa, particularly Zanzibar, a center for the spice trade. Many spices were brought from there to Oman and then made into a special blend of cloves, coriander, nutmeg, pepper, cardamom, and cinnamon called *baharat.*

FURTHER READING

Long, David, *Cultures and Customs of Saudi Arabia.* Westport, CT: Greenwood Press, 2005.

Nawwab, Nimah Ismail. "The Culinary Kingdom," *Saudi Aramco World* 50, no. 1 (1999): 88–97.

Riolo, Amy. *Arabian Delights: Recipes and Princely Entertaining Ideas from the Arabian Peninsula.* Herndon, VA: Capital Books, 2008.

Al-Zayani, A.R. *A Taste of the Arabian Gulf.* Bahrain: Ministry of Culture, 1988.

Zubaida, Sami, and Richard Tapper (eds.). *Taste of Thyme: Culinary Cultures of the Middle East.* New York: I.B. Tauris, 2000.

Cultural Heritage

Sebastian Maisel

The culture of the **Arabian Peninsula** is homogenous and multifaceted at the same time. It emerged over a period of several thousand years. For a long time, nomadism, **oases** farming, long-distance trade, and different forms of worship characterized life in Arabia. With the revelation of Islam a new layer was added that significantly influenced all aspects of daily life. Islam in Arabia both expanded into other cultural areas, often assimilating with local cultures, and received foreign influences from Muslim pilgrims coming to perform the **pilgrimage** to **Makkah** and **Madinah**. The interaction with different ethnicities and cultures certainly enriched the culture of the Arabs and remains a source of inspiration and identity in modern times. Focusing on specific aspects of this heritage such as clothing, language, and core values added a sense of stability to the historically young states along the Gulf coast. Globalization has had a strong impact on the societies of those states since the middle of the twentieth century. Since that time the area underwent rapid modernization and development that almost led to the extinction of traditional customs, crafts, and objects. Recognizing this threat and starting to preserve and protect what was left comprise a process that evolved slowly, and only in recent years, **Saudi Arabia** and the Arab States of the Gulf began to recognize the importance of their rich cultural heritage as part of their manifestation of national and regional identities. Cultural heritage is also needed as a form of legitimization for the ruling families as well as a source to promote **tourism**. The attention given to cultural heritage is not limited to tangible items such as **material culture** or **historical sites**; it included intangible assets like language (see **Arabic Language**), poetry, and traditional customs. Other sectors include antiquities, archaeological sites, museums, **architecture**, and **handicrafts**. The preservation and promotion of cultural heritage is a major objective of the countries' domestic and regional policies. Several governmental organizations and institutions are working in the sector; for example, in Saudi Arabia they are as diverse as the Supreme Council for Tourism, the Deputy Ministry of Antiquities and Museums, or the National Guard. These stakeholders do not often cooperate in a successful manner. However, they are all sponsors of major heritage institutions and events. In addition, the **media**, both print and broadcast, discovered the topic of discussing the situation of cultural heritage as a favorite theme to report critically on local affairs. The mass media is actually the leading agent in promoting the recent heritage revival in the societies along the Gulf.

The public cultural reawakening is manifested in art galleries, **dance** and **music** groups, large-scale festivals, open-air museums, and other state-sponsored activities; poetry as the main form of literary expression is outselling prose on the book market; heritage is celebrated for and by the local population. In Saudi Arabia the main event is the two-week long **Janadiriyah Heritage Festival**, in which artists and artisans from all regions of the kingdom exhibit and perform their arts and crafts. Traditional folk music, **camel** races, and Qur'an and poetry

Emirati women prepare traditional wafer-thin bread at the Heritage Village in Dubai. Older women have been left out of much of the rapid development since 1970 in the United Arab Emirates, and their knowledge and skills have been devalued. The Heritage Village is an attempt to reconnect the younger generation with life before oil. Courtesy of John A. Shoup.

recitals attract hundreds of thousands of visitors every year. On certain days only women and families are permitted entrance and various events focus on women's culture. This is also the place where national cultural heritage is shaped into a homogenous form that sometimes omits or excludes regional varieties. In **Dubai**, a special heritage center was built to depict the story of **pearling**, which was once the main source of income in the area. In **Kuwait**, the National Council for Culture, Arts, and Letters is a good example of governmental interest in the encouragement of cultural heritage. The council sponsors literary and historical publications; hosts art exhibitions; restores old architectural structures; and organizes an annual cultural festival, al-Qurayn. In **Abu Dhabi**, a special authority for culture and heritage was established that sponsors cultural and intellectual activities. On an international level, Saudi Arabia is applying for its major archaeological site of Mada'in Salih to be added to the World Heritage List.

Most Gulf States are member states in UNESCO's program to protect intangible cultural heritage. However, in general there is little legal protection for those assets. Some regulations have been passed for antiquities, but few have been passed to protect historical buildings, traditional crafts, and customs. All of these areas are under enormous pressure from the current trend of modernization. Although the countries began to realize the importance of ancient artifacts, the situation for traditional crafts and the practice of many customs is deteriorating.

Another threatening aspect for some areas of cultural heritage, particularly architecture, is the unfavorable view of it by some religious scholars in Saudi Arabia who are afraid that these sites could be used for idolatry or the veneration for other worldly things such as tombs, shrines, or locations related to famous Muslims of the past. The very puritanical **Wahhabi** ideology led the destruction of several historical religious sites in the **Hijaz**. As early as the beginning of the eighteenth century, Wahhabi conquerors demolished such sites as the grave of Eve, or the houses of **Muhammad**'s mother Aminah and wife Khadijah. Initially, conservative scholars had issues with displaying artifacts in museums, especially those objects that depict human figures or were related to pre-Islamic times. But today, public and private museums have emerged all over the area with large collections of material culture and other ethnographic and archaeological evidence. **Riyadh** has a state-of-the-art National Museum; similar places were built in **al-Manamah**, Kuwait, and **al-Dawhah**. An active schedule of finding, preserving, and analyzing historical sites provides additional evidence of the region's cultural heritage.

Regarding intangible items, oral history and *nabati* poetry are among the most popular areas of preserving the heritage for future generations. Narratives from the older generations are recorded, and poems are collected. The ongoing struggle of what is considered part of the official heritage prevents the massive collections from being researched thoroughly because they might contain material that indicates a different regional opinion. With all of the funds devoted to the heritage preservation industry, it is still their main objective to create a national identity conforming to the ruling elite's understanding of history and legitimacy. Societies in the Gulf counter modernization and Westernization not only by attending closely to religion, but also to their heritage that lies in the tribal **Bedouin** tradition as well in Islam. Processes of **globalization** and preserving heritage in the Gulf area are now inseparable. Although the economy is booming, the states put large funds aside to invest in heritage industry, large theme parks, festivals, or museums, which are frequented by locals and foreign residents alike. This all contributes to the building of an environment that is an image of what the ruling elites want it to be.

FURTHER READING

Cernea, Michael. *Cultural Heritage and Development: A Framework for Action in the Middle East and North Africa*. Washington, D.C.: The World Bank, 2001.

Gugolz, Alessandro. "The Protection of Cultural Heritage in the Sultanate of Oman," *International Journal of Cultural Property* 5, no. 2 (1996): 291–309.

Khalaf, Sulayman. "Poetics and Politics of Newly Invented Traditions in the Gulf: Camel Racing in the United Arab Emirates," *Ethnology* 39, no. 3 (2000): 243–261.

Customary Law
Sebastian Maisel

Customary law is considered an integral part of the social order of tribal groups. In the past, tribes formed an important part of the population in Arabia, and today they still enjoy a disproportionate reputation in the larger society. Blood and kinship ties create close relations among tribal members. They are furthered by ritual interaction, **marriage**, housing pattern, and a common legal system that is based on the concepts of solidarity and loyalty. Tribal groups survive and exist based on notions of togetherness that often overrule the rights of the individual. However, if an individual is treated badly, the entire group is affected by this and reacts. If an individual commits a **crime**, then the entire group is likewise responsible for the deeds of the single member. The interactions within the group as well as with members of other tribal units or non-tribal members are regulated by a codex of law, which in its entirety originated many hundreds if not thousands of years ago. However, because of constant interaction and coexistence with other lifestyles and legal systems, this codex has been adapted to new circumstances.

In Arabic, the law that was prescribed by local traditions and customs is called *curf*. It goes back to pre-Islamic times but today covers areas that are under the jurisdiction of other legal systems, most notably Islamic law. The main source of customary law is embodied in a set of "texts" or poems and narratives that were mostly transmitted orally and rarely written. This customary law was applied by tribal groups that followed a nomadic or semi-nomadic lifestyle, but it was also found among sedentarized groups. As such it was often in contrast to the prevailing religious or state law, because both legal systems (nomadic and sedentary) stood for different social and legal rubrics when evaluating right from wrong. The opposition to another legal system was therefore connected to conflicting ethical and moral perceptions. At large, those tribal moral values still enjoy a large popularity among the people on the **Arabian Peninsula**, although they are officially eradicated in states such as **Saudi Arabia** or at least seen as outdated and "ignorant." However, up to this day, many prefer to use customary law to the other legal system when regulating conflicts because of its simplicity, flexibility, and decency. Another often heard argument in favor of customary law is the fact that it intends to reconcile between parties rather than punish one party. Moral convictions and common actions by the whole unit thus form the basis for conflict regulation and not sheer force or violence. In theory, customary law is strictly directed to peaceful reconciliation and avoiding further bloodshed.

The enforcement of customary law requires the acceptance by the tribal group and not the power of a central tribal authority. Several driving forces within the group such as public opinion, reputation, rationality, solidarity, and mutual responsibility constitute the acceptance. The bottom line is the collective legal responsibility of the *khamsah*, the kin group over five (*khamsah* in Arabic) generations. Customary law is applied for the following crimes: murder, rape, battery, manslaughter, adultery, kidnapping, theft, trespassing, and cases on land, water, and pasture, as well as **honor** crimes. Cases follow a strict and detailed code of procedure that includes judges, witnesses, evidence, investigations, rulings, appeals, and enforcement of the ruling. Judges are normally well-respected and trained members of the tribal community who apply analogies and consensus to find their judgment. Tribal judges are classified according to their special area of expertise; some deal with capital crimes and others with property cases. Arguments, evidence, and witnesses are brought up in front of the panels of judges. Oath and confessions are important means of reasoning between the parties, but the judge has additional ways of fact-finding if there were no witnesses (e.g., the ordeal). The accused is asked to prove his innocence by licking a hot metal spoon or stick several times. Afterward he clears his mouth, which is then inspected by the *mubashi'*, the tribal official that performs and analyzes the ordeal. If the tongue was not scratched, he declares the accused innocent. The *bisha'* ceremony is illegal in religious and state law in Saudi Arabia; however, it is still practiced among tribal groups and considered an effective investigative tool in customary law and is legal in other Arab states such as Egypt.

Other regulations provide protection and safety for those involved in legal disputes. Immediate safety is granted to everyone, and it is demanded by touching the tent, cloths, or head cover of the protector. Guest and neighbors enjoy similar rights. Any offense against a protégée is punished twice, because it affects the protector as well, whose honor was blackened by attacking someone under his protection. Generally, the concept of honor and shame contributes much to the application of customary law. Every individual and group has honor; they can lose it or increase it. Crimes usually are considered shameful, not just because something was stolen or someone was hurt, but also because the victim's honor was discredited. In addition to the punishment for the crime, the guilty party must "clean" or "whiten" the face of the injured party from any shame by whatever additional measures are imposed by the judges.

Reconciliation is the mother of all judgments. This ancient proverb highlights the importance of tribal conflict resolution by applying customary law. Most legal cases end with the reconciliation of the parties involved. Arbitration is carried out by the notables of both parties, usually elder and well-respected tribal members, and sometimes by members of the ruling families who negotiate the final ruling and compensation. Afterward a hug banquet is given and white flags are raised indicating that the honor is restored and the case is closed.

In the present-day society of the Arab Gulf States, customary law is still applied in rural areas. Some aspects have been incorporated into religious law, and even political rulers occasionally refer to it when solving tribal conflicts in their areas. However, the trend goes toward a joint application and parallel existence of customary with other legal systems.

FURTHER READING

Meeker, M. *Literature and Violence in North Arabia*. Cambridge, UK: Cambridge University Press, 1979.

Serjeant, Robert. *Customary and Shari'ah Law in Arabian Society*. Brookfield, VT: Variorum, 1991.

Serjeant, Robert, and G. Rex Smith. *Farmers and Fishermen in Arabia: Studies in Customary Law and Practice*. Brookfield, VT: Variorum, 1995.

Sowayan, Saad. "Customary Law in Arabia: An Ethno-Historical Perspective." Paper presented to the Conference on Customary Law in the Middle East and North Africa, Princeton University, May 13–14, 2006.

Sowayan, Saad. *The Arabian Oral Historical Narrative*. Wiesbaden, Germany: Harrasowitz, 1992.

Stewart, Frank. "Tribal Law in the Arab World: A Review of the Literature," *International Journal of Middle East Studies* 19 (1987): 473–490.

Stewart, Frank. *Honor*. Chicago: University of Chicago Press, 1994.

Stewart, Frank. "Customary Law among the Bedouins of the Middle East and North Africa," in *Nomadic Societies in the Middle East and North Africa*, edited by Dawn Chatty. Leiden, The Netherlands: Brill, 2006.

D

Dammam

Sebastian Maisel

Al-Dammam is a large **Saudi Arabian** seaport city on the southern rim of the Tarut Bay on the Persian Gulf. Two separate meanings for the origin of the name are recorded. One is the onomatopoeic sound of an alarm drum that produces a melody called *damdamah*, whereas the other relates to the Arabic word *dawwama*, or whirlpool, indicating the nearby waterway that ships had to avoid.

Historically, the area belonged to the **oasis** of al-Qatif. In 1923, some **Bedouin** of the Dawasir tribe coming from **Bahrain** settled here and founded a small fishing and **pearling** village. With the discovery of **oil** in large quantities in 1938, the city developed and grew into an important regional industrial, educational, and administrative center. Today, the city limits cover some ten square miles (fifteen square kilometers) with overlapping borders to neighboring cities of **Dhahran** and Khobar. Approximately 1 million people live in Dammam, which also is the capital of the Eastern Province. However, since the mid-1980s the three cities were formally connected to form the tri-city area, but they have maintained their functional independence. As a comparatively young city, most of the population recently moved to the city, which indicates the absence of a traditional elite and a large amount of foreigners among the inhabitants. The new image of Dammam is also visible in the layout of the city with its rectangular setup that contradicts the traditional layout of a traditional Islamic city. Most of the city's inhabitants work for **Aramco** and the **oil industry** continues to be a major factor in the development of the master plan of the city.

The development of the city is closely related to the growth of the oil industry. When the first concessions for oil exploration in Saudi Arabia were granted, they started to drill in what is today the city of Dammam. In 1936, well Dammam number 7 was the first to produce oil in commercial quantities. For this reason, the area was selected as company headquarters for Aramco, the main oil company in Saudi Arabia. After a period of stagnation during World War II, the area began to grow quickly in the 1950s. Between 1946 and 1950 the ten-kilometer-long pier in Dammam was built in order to land supplies and equipment. In 1962, the facilities were enlarged with the construction of the King ʿAbd al-ʿAziz Port that consists of four additional piers. Around the port area, several industrial complexes (e.g., Saudi Arabian Fertilizer Company, the first petrochemical concern) and **military** installations were built.

The growing importance of Dammam was symbolized by transferring the province's capital from Hufuf to Dammam in 1963. King Faysal University has a large campus for medical studies and engineering in Dammam. Since 1952, Saudi Arabia's only railway links Dammam with the capital **Riyadh**.

FURTHER READING

al-Doussari, Mohammad Hasan. *Evolution of Urban System in the Eastern Province of Saudi Arabia, 1900 to 1970.* Al-Ahsa, Saudi Arabia: King Faisal University, 1999.

Facey, William. *The Story of the Eastern Province of Saudi Arabia.* London: Stacey International, 1994.

Moody, Burnett. "A Boys-Eye View of Dammam Port," *Saudi Aramco World* 14, no. 2 (1963): 3–7.

Dance, Traditional

Sebastian Maisel

The people of the **Arabian Peninsula**, both townspeople and nomadic, possess a rich history in performing arts. One of the most authentic and popular features of traditional musical artistic expression is traditional dance, which blends together unique movements with songs and poetry. The origin goes back to pre-Islamic times and derives from various ethnic traditions, mainly Arab and Persian. It existed and developed in the tribal setting of Arabia as a form of entertainment and to celebrate major events in the rites of passage. Dances are usually interactive, allowing the audiences to attend and participate. Generally, similar to the folk **music** of the area, dances are rather monotonous and include simple and repetitive movements; however, they do occur in a variety of settings, both formal and informal. Formal venues include those occasions that are connected to rites of passage (e.g., births, circumcisions, weddings, and religious holidays), whereas informal dances are performed at home, in the fields and campsites, or even at sea, as in the case of the **pearl** divers in the Gulf. Lately, dances are also performed at official gatherings such as national celebrations, state visits, or sporting events. On the other hand, a conservative attitude discouraging dancing is found among people with a traditional religious focus who are concerned about the possible immorality of the dances. However, dances are seen as communal performances associated with certain religious, social, or national occasions and utilize several **folklore** genres. Moreover, traditional dances are considered as modes of communication for both the conservative and the innovative parts of the Gulf's societies. Dance is also a process that includes producers, performers, and sometimes musicians and depends on acceptance or rejection from the audience. Some dances enjoy prominent status, whereas others are considered of lower status. Among the dances with a high reputation are those involving weapons, such as rifles, swords, and daggers that are spun and thrown above the heads of the dancers. The *'ardhah* sword dance is perhaps the

Among the traditional dances of the Gulf, the Liwa brings the audience to its feet to participate, as at this performance at a festival in Dubai. Courtesy of John A. Shoup.

singlemost important dance of the **Peninsula** and performed by men holding up their weapons and moving slowly to the beat of drums. Originally performed before going to war, it is now considered the national dance of most Gulf States and as such is performed by political leaders at all major public occasions.

The traditional society of the Gulf State requires gender segregation in public and private spheres. In some states, particularly **Saudi Arabia**, the separation of men and women is almost considered a national and religious obligation, at least in the way it is enforced by some authorities. Most other Gulf States follow a more liberal approach, yet within their clearly defined limits both genders can practice and perform music and dance. Probably the most common arena for dances is the traditional wedding party, which is also celebrated separately. Female musicians perform for a female-only audience, some of which actively participate in dance and song. During the wedding party hired musicians play popular songs and younger women usually perform the traditional dances of their area, oftentimes wearing traditional dresses called *thawb nashal*. Most of the movements are from the shoulders and the head. There is a little shimmying in the shoulders, small drops with the hips, and gliding of the feet. One distinct movement is called *na'ish*, or tossing the hair, in which women loosen their waist-long hair and swing it in circles, which is considered a higher and more en-thusiastic level of performance. *Na'ish* is said to have originated from the **Bed-ouin** tribes and is performed along the Gulf coast. Slowly other women join the dance; and it is expected that all guests at one point participate in the dances. Another occasion of extensive dancing is *laylat al-hanna*, the henna night prior to the wedding. Here, family members and friends dance to entertain the bride, who has to sit patiently in order for the henna dye to dry. At the groom party, young men and teenagers often get excited and start to dance on their own, imitating popular moves and steps, some of them clearly labeled as female movements. Unlike in other Middle Eastern cultures, men in the Gulf States in urban settings are much less attracted to communal dances during weddings. Nevertheless, dances have their proper place, for example, at tribal gatherings or weddings in the countryside.

The governments of Saudi Arabia and the Gulf States generously support traditional folk arts such as music and dances as long as they are performed in accordance with the requirements of public morality. Performances of music and dance draw large audiences at regional or national festivals for folklore and traditional culture. Women are encouraged to participate in these state-sponsored activities, but they have to present their shows at separate events. For example, at the National **Janadiriyah Heritage Festival**, selected occasions deal with music and dance from the women's point of view. Performances by female groups in front of female-only audiences are held to portray the regional dance tradition. Every region in the Arabian Peninsula has its unique dances with its own steps and movements. Some are more graceful, whereas others imitate male dances holding a dagger and stamping on the ground.

The most popular dance in the **United Arab Emirates** is 'ayalah, which derives from the Arabic word meaning "to attack." 'Ayalah migrated to the Emirates during the nineteenth century from central Arabia as a version of the 'ardhah. The entire atmosphere, its steps, and the name indicate that this used to be a war dance and as such it simulates battles scenes. Sometimes up to 200 male dancers form two rows that are accompanied by musicians with the drummers and sword dancers in their midst. The dancing movements go back and forth until the "invading" party admits defeat. Sometimes in the middle of the dance a group of young women called na'ashat perform a hair dance, exhibiting and swirling their hair around to motivate the men to protect them. Because it is clearly a male dance, it can be performed without the na'ashat segment. No private or public event is celebrated in the United Arab Emirates without the 'ayalah dance. Emirati soccer players sometimes perform it spontaneously as a victory dance. As a national dance it contains steps symbolizing social and tribal aspects of life in addition to lyrics and songs that glorify the nation's identity and values. A very reserved and dignified version of 'ayalah in **Ra's al-Khaymah** and **Fujayrah** is called wahhabiyah. Here too men dance in two lines holding weapons or sticks indicating their readiness to defend. No musical instruments are used; the dance lives by the lyrics of its songs. The name wahhabiyah suggests a link to the dominant religious belief in Wahhabi, which in fact might be true. Wahhabi Islam as a religious practice spread quickly in much of Arabia, and several other states in addition to Saudi Arabia have adopted **Wahhabism** as the official form of Islam. A different war dance is called harbiyah and it is performed without musical instruments but includes both singing and dancing. The lyrics of the song control the movement of the dancers. The theme of the dance also reflects notions of war, defense, and **military** parades. Often, na'ashat dancers perform in harbiyah dances to encourage and motivate the male dancers.

Another popular dance along the southern Gulf coast is called malid, a derivative from the Arabic word mawlid, which is a term used to refer to the observance of the birthday of the Prophet **Muhammad**. It consists of two parts, the first being a reciting of the *sirah* (story of life) of Muhammad, whereas in the second part (*sama'a*—hearing), the participants respond by forming two rows facing each other and exchange and repeating phrases to the beat of tambourines.

In **Bahrain** and all other Gulf States, the very popular *'ardhah* sword dance represents the folkloristic dance tradition. Accompanied by songs and drums, male Bahrainis often perform this dance during public events. Only members of the pearl diving community perform a special form of *'ardhah* that is called *fijiri*. Belly dancing, *raqs sharqi* in Arabic, although very popular is not considered a traditional dance of the region but was imported from Egypt for cabaret performances. Because of conservative and spatial constraints, this type of dance takes place only in separated and private settings. Talented dancers started to include traditional dance moves from the Gulf into their belly-dancing performance in order to please their predominantly Gulf audience.

A new type of female dance is called *ma'layah* or *daqni*. Arabs claim that it originated in Iran, and it is very similar to a folk dance from southern Iran called *Bandari*, meaning "port" or "harbor dance." The reason why they do not want to be associated with it is the obvious sensual character of the movements, including fast and vibrant shaking of the buttocks and backside. Along with a small band and a singer, two or more women entertain a mostly male crowd by swinging their backs up and down individually or as a group right in front of their faces. In the past, it was traditionally part of the wedding celebrations and customs but recently has turned into a popular trend among the younger generation.

In **Oman**, the heritage of dance is cultivated through many performances on the local and regional level with distinct themes and moves. Omani dances include sword dances; religious dances (resembling Sufi practices); specific dances on the coast and in the **desert**; and dances for social events and other occasions, such as the *dan*, the Omani dance of death. During this ritual lamentation, mostly women dancers move around slowly to a seven-unit rhythm to reach an ecstatic stage and symbolically throw off an article of clothing, expressing their grief and sadness. Dances follow the rhythm of the accompanying music. Whereas Arabian folk music is usually monorhythmic, local dances are sometimes performed on a polyrhythmic base. For example, the *rawah* dance from the **Musandam** Peninsula combines the two-unit rhythm for the body movement with the three-unit rhythm for the drums. The *sawt silam* dance from **Dhufar** requires skills and concentration to perform the polyrhythmic moves. In Dhufar in another unusual dance form, the *shubbaniyah*, male and female dancers perform together but along different cycles and rhythms.

Dancers can perform the dance and simultaneously produce sounds and music using bells, small drums, and other rhythmic instruments. A necklace or string of whistles and bells wrapped around the dancer's body produces idiophone sounds that do not accentuate the basic rhythm of the dance. The unity of dance and music is also shown in some musicians that dance while playing their instrument.

The area's rapid modernization is often seen as a threat to traditional arts, particularly to music and dance. However, because folk dances are deeply embedded into the **cultural heritage**, and the heritage is strongly supported by officials and the local population, the traditional dances of Saudi Arabia and the Gulf States will be continuously performed and preserved. Every country of the area sponsors national dance troops to represent the heritage of the country both locally and internationally. In addition to national support of the preservation of traditional dances, local dance groups also enjoy a great popularity as an essential means to express tribal and regional identity.

FURTHER READING

Campbell, Kay Hardy. "Folk Music and Dance in the Arabian Gulf and Saudi Arabia," in *Images of Enchantment: Visual and Performing Arts of the Middle East*, edited by Sherifa Zuhur. Cairo: American University of Cairo Press, 1998.

Campbell, Kay Hardy. "Saudi Arabian Folk Music Alive and Well," *Saudi Aramco World* 58, no. 2 (2007): 2–13.

Corona, Vicky. *Women's Dances of Kuwait: Beginner Steps, Thobe Actions, Choreography*. Video recording. North Hollywood, CA: Dance Fantasy Productions, 1989.

Hurreiz, Sayyid H. *Folklore and Folklife in the United Arab Emirates*. London: Routledge, 2002.

Kaisha, N.B., and K.M. Hakubutsukan. *The JVC Video Anthology of World Music and Dance. Book V, Middle East and Africa*. Video recording. Tokyo: JVC Victor Co. of Japan, 1988–1990.

Mahmood, Reem. "Folk Dances of the United Arab Emirates," *al-Shindagah Magazine* (1997). Available at http://www.alshindagah.com/may/dances.htm (last accessed 2008).

Dates

John A. Shoup

A date (*tamr* or *balah* in Arabic) is a small, dark, oval fruit with a pit, and is an important part of Arab social customs. Dates are served to guests as part of the required hospitality and display of generosity as well as part of the traditional practices to break the *Ramadan* fast. The Prophet **Muhammad** established the tradition of breaking the *Ramadan* fast with dates and milk. In Arabia and the Gulf region, dates and date products are not only an important part of the diet, but also until the discovery of **oil** one of the most important domestic products. Dates are sold as the whole fruit (*tamr* or *balah*), as a sweet, thick syrup or molasses (*dibs*), or as a paste (*'ajwah*). The palm tree (*nakhlah*) can be tapped for its sweet sap, which can be drunk as is or allowed to ferment into an alcohol (*labqi*).

Dates were domesticated during the Neolithic in Iraq and the **Arabian Peninsula,** and people began to understand that assisting with pollination between the male and female trees could enhance fruit production. An Akkadian cuneiform text dated 2500 BC is one of the oldest to specifically mention the cultivation of dates, and archeological evidence from **al-Hasa** indicates it has been an established **oasis** for the cultivation of dates for more than 4,000 years. Dates are drought resistant, actually liking the heat, and can grow where the water supply is brackish. Intensive date-farming methods improve productivity and include innovative systems of irrigation, pruning, and spacing of the trees, in addition to assisting fertilization of female trees.

Many varieties of dates are grown in the Middle East and North Africa and still form an important part of agricultural production. Date varieties are distinguished by the amount of sugar and the size, moistness, and color. There are 600 varieties grown in the Arab countries, and Arab countries account for 64 million of the 90 million trees in the world. Al-Hasa oasis in eastern **Saudi Arabia** is one of the largest date producers in the Peninsula, covering some 50,000 acres (20,000 hectares) with over 3 million date palms. The Arab world produces 3 million tons of dates per year, most of which come from Iraq and the Arabian Peninsula, with Tunisia, Algeria, and Morocco being the major other producers. Although it is a matter of personal taste which is the best, in the Arabian Peninsula and the Gulf most people agree that the *khalasah* from al-Hasa oasis is the best, although in the **Hijaz** the *'anbarah* is considered superior, and in the **Najd** *nubut al-sayf* and *sukkari* are considered the best from their region. Most date markets offer between 200 and 300 varieties as well as different stages of ripening from *balah*, or fully grown; *rutab*, or partially grown and ripe; *tamr*, or fully sugared; and *tamr yabis*, or dried and much of its sugar lost. *Hawhil* refers to the dates from a previous year that have become rough and have cracked skin, which, although edible, are most often fed to livestock.

Dates, coffee, and tea are elements of traditional hospitality in the Arab world. The host has spread a mat made from palm leaves outdoors in front of a traditional barasti house in Dubai. Courtesy of John A. Shoup.

FURTHER READING

Emirates Center for Strategic Studies and Research. *The Date Palm: From Traditional Resource to Green Wealth*. London: I.B.Tauris, 2004.

Hansen, Eric. "Carrying Dates to Hajar," *Saudi Aramco World* 55, no. 4 (2004): 9–15.

Hansen, Eric. "Looking for the Khalasah," *Saudi Aramco World* 55, no. 4 (2004): 2–8.

Al-Dawhah

John A. Shoup

Al-Dawhah (Doha) is the capital of **Qatar** and is located on the eastern side of the small peninsula that forms the country. The city has a population of 400,051 (based on 2005 census), which not only makes it the largest city in Qatar, but nearly eighty percent of the entire population of the country lives in it or in the immediate surrounding suburbs.

Al-Dawhah is a fairly "modern" city being founded in 1850 (the **Al Khalifah** and **Al Thani** families used the port/fort at Zubarah since they arrived in the eighteenth century). Dawhah was a small fishing village called al-Bida before it was renamed al-Dawhah, which means a tall tree with wide, spreading branches; local legend says the town was named for such a large tree that used to be at the heart of the original site. The town grew after *Shyakh* **Qasim** led local forces to victory over the Ottomans in 1883 and Al-Thani signed a treaty with the British that led to a protectorate status for the country—al-Dahwah was made the capital of the protectorate in 1916. Al-Dawhah remained the capital after Qatar gained its independence in 1971.

Qatar has embarked on an ambitious plan to make al-Dawhah rival its neighbor **Dubai** on the basis of the country's **oil** income. Al-Dawhah has some of the best medical centers and hospitals in the **Arabian Peninsula**, and the current ruler, *Shaykh* Hamad bin Khalifah, had invited six major American universities, including Georgetown and Northwestern, to open branch campuses as part of a development project called University City. In addition, al-Dawhah has branch campuses for two Canadian and one Dutch university as well as Qatari institutions of higher learning.

Al-Dawhah has several housing and commercial developments, and the skyline is dotted with a growing number of skyscrapers. Qatar allows non-nationals to buy and own property, which allows them to have renewable residency and work permits. The housing and development projects have caused land prices to increase and by 2007 land in al-Dawhah was the most expensive in the entire region.

Qatari nationals are a minority of the city's population, whereas expatriates form the vast majority. The largest numbers come from other Arab countries such as Egypt, Syria, Lebanon, Jordan, **Palestine**, and more recently Morocco. Others come from India, Pakistan, and Bangladesh, and smaller numbers of Europeans and North Americans live in al-Dawhah. The number of Christians in the city prompted *Shaykh* Hamad to allow the building of a Catholic church, which opened in March 2008 without any incident. *Shaykh* Hamad has allowed five more churches that will all be open soon.

Death Rites

Sebastian Maisel

For Muslims, death is considered the return of the soul to the creator. Death is inevitable, and life in the hereafter is something that is near and sought after. Therefore, the faithful keep their life and deeds in perspective and are prepared for the time to come and hopefully eternal life. According to the more puritanical or conservative religious views in **Saudi Arabia** and the other Gulf States, mourning should not be exaggerated, because the departed might join paradise soon.

In pre-Islamic Arabia as well as in Islam, Arabs believed in life after death. Therefore, distinctive rituals, or *janazah*, were practiced to worship the ancestors and their gravesites. The simplest form of a grave was a hollow in the ground with a marker or cairn on top. Among the **Bedouin**, special stones with cultic significance and sacred areas for the dead were found. The settled population used to bury their dead in caves, rock tombs, or cubic structures with several chambers. Grave goods were added, such as **jewelry**, amulets, ceramics, and figurines in addition to food and water.

Like their ancestors, Muslim Arabs bury the dead in the ground, rejecting other forms of funerals like cremations. According to general Islamic rules, the body is washed and sometimes scented with rose water, cedar tree oil, and camphor. After the washing, the body is wrapped in a seamless white cloth for burial called *kafan*. It is about fifteen meters long and made of soft cotton. Women can then be draped with an extra cover, usually a green cloth.

Relatives, friends, and others carry the bier to the mosque and later to the cemetery. It is considered a good deed to accompany the deceased on his last journey on earth. In front of the mosque or inside of it, the Imam will recite several funeral prayers. Only men escort the body to the cemetery, where the body is laid in a grave facing the Ka'bah in **Makkah**. In **Najd**, the grave is simply a hole in the ground, whereas in other areas small stone structures are erected. Because of hot and sometimes humid weather, it is recommended to bury the dead as soon as possible. At the gravesite, people are not allowed to erect elaborate grave markers, tombstones, or mausoleums or even put out flowers or candles. The best grave is one that can be washed away with one hand, according to the traditions of the Bedouin; this should also discourage relatives from excessive mourning or wailing. One of the most important doctrines of **Muhammad ibn 'Abd al-Wahhab's** reform movement was to eradicate those practices, which apparently had existed in Arabia at one point. Worshipping the dead distracts the faithful from concentrating on the one task of his short life on earth, worshipping God. It is also seen as showing discontent with God's wishes. Therefore, he should rather remember and pray to God and thank him for his mercy to take the deceased up to heaven.

After the burial, a three-day mourning period, *'azzah* in Arabic, is observed during which regular visits are paid to the family of the deceased. Between the two evening prayers, guests are received to offer condolences to the family. Typically, a senior family member meets the mourners, who then sit quietly together commemorating the deceased. In **Hijaz** and other areas, religious sheikhs read verses from the Qur'an. Public display of grief is, however, strongly discouraged, and in non-Wahhabi countries so is any display of decorative clothing or jewelry. Among **Shi'ite** communities in Arabia other forms of mourning are noted, for example, longer and multiple mourning periods, more elaborate tombstones, and additional readings and prayers. For widows, the mourning period, *'iddah* in Arabic, is extended to four months and ten days in accordance with Qur'anic rules. During this time she is not allowed to remarry or move from her home. The same clothing restrictions apply.

The burial of the late King Fahd of Saudi Arabia is seen as a typical example of how death rites are practiced in Saudi Arabia. Although Fahd was one of the wealthiest men in the world, his grave is very simple and unspectacular. The ceremony was very austere in contrast to the lifestyle of the former monarch. Members of the **Al Sa'ud** family carried the body wrapped in a brown robe, the last 'abayah (cloak) that he wore, on a wooden stretcher to the local mosque, where a simple and short prayer was held in his name before he was carried to the public cemetery and laid in an unmarked grave. Family members then began covering the body with soil brought to the site in wheelbarrows.

FURTHER READING

Hurreiz, Sayyid Hamid. *Folklore and Folklife in the United Arab Emirates.* London: Routledge, 2002.

Long, David. *Culture and Customs of Saudi Arabia.* Westport, CT: Greenwood Press, 2005.

Yamani, Mai. "The Rites of Passage III: Death—the Final Vindication," in *Cradle of Islam: The Hijaz and the Quest for an Arabian Identity,* edited by Mai Yamani. London: I.B. Tauris, 2006.

Deserts

John A. Shoup

The **Arabian Peninsula** is one of the most arid regions in the world, and by definition nearly the whole peninsula is "desert." However, within the peninsula are several sand deserts stretching from Wadi Sirhan in the north to the Arabian Sea in the south. These are among the driest places on earth, with yearly rainfalls of less than four inches (100 millimeters), and it is not unusual for as many as ten years to pass with no rainfall at all.

The Nafud sands are 280 miles (450 kilometers) at the widest and some 260 miles (418 kilometers) at the longest point lying between the cities of al-Jawf and Sakakah on the north and **Ha'il** in the south; the volcanic **mountain** ranges of Harrat al-'Uwayrid and Harrat Hutaym mark its western limits; and its eastern limit is the al-Labbah plateau, which extends toward the **Saudi Arabian** border with Iraq. The Nafud is an area of shifting dunes, and although a formidable barrier, it was crossed regularly by **Bedouin** in the past.

The Dahna' is a long finger of sand desert that connects the Nafud in the north with the Rub' al-Khali in the south. It runs much of the length of Saudi Arabia in a narrow arch some twenty miles (thirty-two kilometers) wide and 400 miles (643 kilometers) long between the central plateau of the **Najd** and the Gulf coast.

The Rub' al-Khali is the largest of the sand deserts in the Arabian Peninsula and can easily be called a sand sea. It stretches from the highlands of **Yemen** in the west to the salt flats of the Gulf coast in the east, covering nearly 500,000 square miles and taking up nearly one half of the total area of Saudi Arabia. It is nearly 900 miles (1,448 kilometers) wide and 500 miles (804 kilometers) long, or approximately the size of France. It was a major barrier to the movements of

Sunrise over the Empty Quarter, Saudi Arabia. Courtesy of Sebastian Maisel.

people and goods until recently, in the past being mainly crossed by Bedouin raiders who did not want to be seen. No Bedouin used it as part of their grazing lands, although the **Al Murrah**, **'Awamir, Bani Yas**, and **Rashid** included the fringe areas as part of their seasonal grazing lands. Although none of the Bedouin live in the Rub' al-Khali, it is well-known, and individual chains of dunes are named, such as the 'Uruq al-Shayba', which averages over 600 feet (180 meters) high. Different parts of the Rub' al-Khali are composed of recognizable different types of sand noted for color and grain size. The slopes along the northeastern edge of the great sand sea give rise to the small **oasis** of Liwa, where springs allow **date** cultivation in a scattered collection of small groves able to support a relatively small population even today. The eastern edge receives several small seasonal streams from the Western Hajar Mountains, which flow into the dangerous quicksands called Umm al-Samim. The far western side of the Rub' al-Khali is less forbidding; chains of sand dunes are not as high and there are broad stretches of flat gravel plains between them. It is also possible to find grazing for **camels** as well as for wild herds of oryx, a large desert antelope; in the recent past, even ostriches were found there until hunted to extinction at the turn of the twentieth century.

The first known European to cross the Rub' al-Khali was the British explorer Bertram Thomas, who in 1930–1931 was able to make the south-to-north journey with a group of Bedouin guides from the **Bayt Kathir** tribe. He was followed a year later by the British convert to Islam and advisor to King **'Abd al-'Aziz ibn Sa'ud, Harry St. John Philby**, who took a north-to-south route. Perhaps best known is the Englishman Wilfred Thesiger, who with Bedouin guides from the Bayt Kathir and Rashid tribes crossed it twice between 1946 and 1948.

The Wahibah Sands are not connected to the other great sand deserts and are located in **Oman** between the coastal plains and the uplands of Bani Bu 'Ali.

They are also much smaller than the other sand deserts, being less than 100 miles (160 kilometers) wide and about 100 miles (160 kilometers) long. They are named for the Bedouin **Wahibah** tribe, whose traditional grazing territories lie between the sands and the oasis cities of Adam and **Nizwa** to the north.

The Jiddat al-Harasis is the only desert noted here that is not composed of mainly sand, but of pebbles. It is a wide-open plain between the western slopes of Jabal al-Akhdar and **Dhufar**, stretching over 200 miles (320 kilometers) in length. The Jiddat takes its name from the Bedouin **al-Harasis** tribe, who are the only people to live year-round in the plains. Summer temperatures soar over 110°F (forty-three degrees Celsius) and with little seasonal rain the Jiddat has little natural pasture. It seems that the Harasis tribe was pushed out onto the plain as a result of conflicts with others in Dhufar and until their occupation the plains had no permanent population. It is perhaps because of this that the Jiddat was also home to the last wild herds of oryx. These large desert-dwelling antelope once inhabited the whole Arabian Peninsula into Jordan and Syria, and a hunting party in the Jiddat slaughtered the last wild herd in Oman in 1972. In 1979 the Omani government approved a project to reintroduce oryx to the Jiddat as an integrated project that included Harasis camel pastoralism. However, since 2003 hunting parties have again endangered the oryx.

See also **Oases**; **Travelers and Explorers**.

FURTHER READING

Beaumont, Peter, Gerald Blake, and Malcom Wagstaff. *The Middle East*. London: John Wiley & Sons, 1976.

Chatty, Dawn. *Mobile Pastoralists: Development Planning and Social Change in Oman*. New York: Columbia University Press, 1996.

Fisher, W.B. *The Middle East: A Physical, Social, and Regional Geography*. London: Methuen, 1971.

Thesiger, Wilfred. *Arabian Sands*. London: Readers Union Longmans, Green and Co., 1960.

Dhafir

Sebastian Maisel

Dhafir is a tribal confederation in Iraq, **Kuwait**, and **Saudi Arabia**. As a component tribe, it includes elements of different origin; for example, some groups claim *sharif* (descendant of the Prophet **Muhammad**) ancestry or some originating from other tribal groups such as the ʿ**Anazah**, **Bani Tamim**, or Subay. Today, the Dhafir claim a territory that stretches from al-Hajara to al-Zubayr in Iraq.

The tribe lived originally in the **Hijaz** Mountains under the loose leadership of the Al Suwayt. First mentioned in Washm and Sudayr in **Najd** at the end of the seventeenth century, the Dhafir fled the area to the north after heavy losses in the fighting with the rising **Wahhabi** power into the Ottoman-controlled Basrah Province. They merged with the Fudul tribe, another victim of the Wahhabi expansion. Caught between the powerful **Muntafiq** to the north and the expanding **Shammar** in the south, they were required to establish good relations with both of them; however, this created constant strife with the 'Anazah, the arch-enemy of the Shammar.

The long-lasting dependency on the Shammar and Muntafiq was thrown off in 1911 by Hamud bin Suwayt, who managed to significantly weaken the influence of the Muntafiq. After World War I, the tribe split into pro-Iraqi and pro-Saudi fractions. The entire tribe was sucked into the quarrels between the Hashemite Kingdom in Iraq and the **Al Sa'ud** state in Najd. Both countries claimed that the Dhafir belonged to them and therefore had to pay taxes to them. In the treaty of Muhammara in 1922, they were declared Iraqi citizens, but part of their tribal territory was converted into a neutral zone. However, this did not prevent the *Ikhwan* from occasionally raiding their camps. The pro-Wahhabi party settled in Najd in the *hijrah* (agricultural colony) al-Shu'aybah. The Al Sa'id began to move to Kuwait in the 1930s. A split in the supreme leadership of the tribe occurred during that period between 'Ajami ibn Suwayt, who swore allegiance to **'Abd al-'Aziz ibn Sa'ud**, and Jad'an ibn Suwayt, who led the Iraqi and Kuwaiti fractions. As shown above, the two main segments of the Dhafir, the Butun and the Samadah, are in permanent contrast to each other in terms of allegiance. The Butun include the Al Suwayt, Al Sa'id, and Bani Hussein, whereas the Samadah group was made of the 'Askar, Dhir'an, Zuwasim, 'Urayf, Ilijanat, and Ma'alim. In addition, the origin of both *shaykh*ly families is somehow nebulous. It is believed that the ibn Suwayt of the Butun were of Sulubi origin (as tinkers, hunters, and gatherers, the **Salubah** are on the bottom end of the social hierarchy) and the Aba Dra' are descendants of slaves. For themselves, they claim to be *ashraf* (singular *sharif*), or of **Qahtan** origin. Despite all this, contacts with relatives in Kuwait and Iraq were maintained as were transnational grazing and pasture search. Most tribe members gave up nomadism and **camel** breeding and switched to sheep because of market demand and convenience. With the help of trucks they were able to move the animals over a wider area than before.

FURTHER READING

Ingham, Bruce. "Notes on the Dialect of the Dhafir of North-Eastern Arabia," *Bulletin of the School of Oriental and African Studies, University of London* 45, no. 2 (1982): 245–259.
Ingham, Bruce. *Bedouin of Northern Arabia: Traditions of the Al-Dhafir*. New York: KPI, 1986.

Dhahirah

John A. Shoup

The Dhahirah is a region in **Oman** encompassing the area between the Hajar **Mountains** and the Rub' al-Khali and from the oasis of al-Buraymi on the north to Jabal al-Kawar on the south and is the home region of the **Duru'** tribe. There are two major dry streams along which most of the settled population live, Wadi

Dhank and Wadi al-'Ayn. Along Wadi Dhank lie the towns of Dhank, 'Ibri, and Yanqil, whereas Wadi al-'Ayn flows north into the **United Arab Emirates**, where the main settlements of al-Buraymi/al-'Ayn are located.

The region is a **desert** and has an average annual rainfall of between one inch (thirty millimeters) in the west and nearly fourteen inches (350 millimeters) in the east along the slopes of the Hajar Mountains. The Dhahirah region has been identified as the home of the ancient Majan culture referred to in Sumerian texts as an important source of copper although copper is not mined today. In the recent past sulfur and salt were mined by the Duru' and sold in market centers such as **Nizwa**. Duru' and other **Bedouin** tribes in the region raised sheep, goats, and **camels** and today the famous Duru' camels are primarily raised for racing. In addition, the many settlements along the main *wadis* support extensive cultivation of **date** palms, lemons, barley, corn, and even sugar cane. Many of these **oases** are fed by *aflaj* systems tapping water sources some distance from the fields.

Al-Dhahirah is a natural corridor between Oman and the Gulf coast formed by the Hajar Mountains and the Rub' al-Khali. As a result, there are many historical forts and walled towns in the region. Among the most spectacular is Qala'at al-Salif, which was built by *Sultan* ibn Sayf al-Ya'arubi in 1724 AD but is now abandoned. Other historical forts are Husn 'Ibri in 'Ibri and the numerous forts in al-Buraymi and al-'Ayn.

See also **Deserts**.

Dhahran

Sebastian Maisel

Dhahran is a large city in eastern **Saudi Arabia** and is headquarters of Saudi **Aramco**, one of the most important locations for the Saudi Arabian **oil industry**. As such it is part of the metropolitan area in the Eastern Province that includes **Dammam** and Khobar. Until the late 1980s the city was still recognizable, but since then has significantly grown closer toward the other two. The distance between Dhahran and Dammam is less than twelve miles (twenty kilometers). The size of the greater Dammam area, which includes Dhahran, is approximately 434 square miles (700 square kilometers), and the population exceeds 2 million. Dhahran also hosts King Fahd University of Petroleum and Minerals, founded in 1963 by Aramco, King Faysal University, and the new Dhahran International Airport, making it one of the busiest and fastest-growing communities in the kingdom. With the current presence of two public and several private universities and colleges, as well as private and public schools, Dhahran is also seen as an educational and cultural center of the region. In addition to schools, two museums attract large crowds of local and international visitors.

In the early 1930s, Standard Oil of California, now Chevron Texaco, began exploring the area around Dhahran Rock, the only notable hill in the area. The city developed on the site of an exploration camp of Aramco in 1935 and quickly witnessed the building of industrial facilities, administrative buildings, and housing complexes for the employees of the **oil** company. During World War II, after Italian planes bombed Dhahran on October 19, 1940, an American airbase was built where the first oil facilities had been. For a long time Dhahran was a gated community surrounded by fences and walls and guarded by checkpoints, sharply contrasting the "real" city of Khobar, which was built free from security and economical concerns. In between the two centers, the country's second largest airport and a university connected the cities. Generally, Dhahran has one of the best infrastructures in the country because of the oil industry. Highways, airports, and trains connect the city domestically and internationally. The city made headlines in recent years as the target of several terror attacks against foreigners and Saudi nationals, both civilians and **military**, and oil industry facilities.

Saudi author 'Abd al-Rahman Munif depicted the drastic changes in the life of the population since the discovery of oil in his classic 1989 novel *Cities of Salt*, in which the fictitious oil camp of Darran is widely believed to be Dhahran. In 1950, only 5,000 inhabitants, mostly foreigners working for Aramco, lived in the city.

FURTHER READING

Facey, William. *The Story of the Eastern Province of Saudi Arabia*. London: Stacey International, 1994.

Munif, Abd al-Rahman. *Cities of Salt*. New York: Vintage Books, 1989.

Parssinen, Jon, and Kaizir Talib. "A Traditional Community and Modernization: Saudi Camp, Dhahran," *Journal of Architectural Education* 35, no. 3 (1982): 14–17.

Stegner, Wallace. *Discovery! The Search for Arabian Oil*. Portola, CA: Selwa Press, 2007.

Symonds, Walter. *Jebel Dhahran and the New Saudi Generation: A Personal Encounter*. Houston: Brockton, 1993.

Dhows

John A. Shoup

The term *dhow* is not used in **Arabic** but seems to have been borrowed into English from the Persian/Indian term *daw*. The general term in Arabic for a sailing ship is *markab* or *safinah*, and generally speaking no one in the region uses the term *dhow* unless speaking in English. Instead, people refer to specific types of ships such as *bum* or *baghalah*.

There are some thirty terms used for specific types of sailing vessels depending on size, number of sails, and purpose. Among the sleekest of crafts is the *sambuq* used primarily in the past for **pearling**. It is built for quick maneuvering required in the pearl banks and has both sails (it has two masts) and oars. The upper deck runs the whole length of the ship, which provides the sailors and pearlers with an easy working space. The lower deck is used for storage. Similar to the *sambuq* is the smaller *shu'ai*, which lacks a carved stern and the stem is longer and more elegant, although not painted like that of a *sambuq*. Although the *sambuq* was only

A *baghalah* on the corniche in Sharjah. Dhows can pull up right next to the shore to off- and on-load their cargos. Most of the dhows working in and out of Sharjah are Iranian, whereas in Dubai ships from Somalia make up the majority. Courtesy of John A. Shoup.

used for pearling activities, the *shu'ai* is still used for fishing and in the past for pearling. A smaller craft used mainly for coastal fishing is called a *badan*, which is still the most common craft along the Omani coast, and those used in **Musandam** have highly decorated prows. There are several other small vessels; for example, the *jalbut*, which shows a good deal of European influence in its shape with a rather short, upright prow that was used in pearling and also coastal shipping. The *shashah* is a small fishing vessel made of palm fronds propelled by oars and one sail and is really not in the same category as those ships generally referred to as dhows.

The *batil* is larger than the *sambuq*, with fine lines making it the fastest of all large sailing vessels in the Gulf. Its speed made it the favorite for **military** use in the past, and its shallow draft allowed it to escape into shoals and the shallow waters of the Gulf coast. It was also the choice of the admiral of pearling fleets, being a large vessel that stood out among the others. A *batil* has several unusual characteristics. Its bow piece is made of a flat fiddle-shaped piece of wood, which British explorer Wilfred Thesiger noted he saw some in **Dubai** that had the Latin letters "IHS" carved on them, no doubt in imitation of Portuguese ships from the past. Its stern is a carved horse head with a wooden horse's tail that extends from the rudder just above the waterline. The *batil*, although large, has little storage space below deck and was not used for hauling cargo.

More common cargo vessels today are the *baghalah* (called *shabuf* in **Oman**) and the *bum*. The word *baghalah* means mule in Arabic, and the ship is the largest cargo ship built in the Gulf. It has a square stem and the stern has a cabinlike room lined with a row of windows that extends over the rudder. The rudder is connected to the steering wheel by a rope that runs through the room. Similar to the *baghalah* is the *ghanjah*, which has recently been motorized. The main difference between them is the decoration on the prow: *ghanjah* have a trefoil decoration. The *bum* is smaller but is considered the better vessel because its longer and pointed stem makes it a faster ship and better able to deal with open seas. Some argue the *bum*'s shape allows it to take on more cargo and today it is the main sailing vessel built in the Gulf.

Dhows play a major role transporting cargo around the Gulf region and there are still several places with active dhow-building harbors in Iraq, Iran, Pakistan, and India in addition to Oman, the **United Arab Emirates**, **Qatar**, **Bahrain**, and **Kuwait**. Dhows are also used for cargo shipments between the Gulf region and East Africa. In addition to sails (most crafts have two masts) and oars, most of the ocean-going dhows have had diesel engines installed. With the added speed the engines give them and with their shallow drafts allowing them to use natural harbors that are too shallow for other vessels, dhows are still used by pirates along the Somali coast.

See also **Travelers and Explorers.**

FURTHER READING

Aguis, Dionisius. *In the Wake of the Dhow: The Arabian Gulf Region.* London: Garnet Publishing, 2002.
Aguis, Dionisius. *Seafaring in the Arabian Gulf and Oman.* London: Kegan Paul, 2005.
Dickson, H.R.P. *The Arab of the Desert.* London: George Allen and Unwin, 1949.
Richardson, Neil, and Marcia Dorr. *Craft Heritage of Oman.* Dubai: Motivate Press, 2003.
Thesiger, Wilfred. *Arabian Sands.* London: Readers Union Longmans, Green & Co., 1960.

Dhufar
John A. Shoup

Dhufar is the southern region of **Oman** located some 285 miles (460 kilometers) from the capital **Masqat**. It is the single largest region in Oman, occupying 120,000 square kilometers or about one-third of the total area of the country. Today the area called Dhufar includes the coastal plain around the city of **Salalah**, which is the administrative capital of the whole region; the Qarah Mountains, which are home to the South Arabian Qarah and Mahrah people; and the **Najd**, or the **desert** plateau that stretches into **Yemen** and north to the Rub' al-Khali and **Saudi Arabia**, which is inhabited primarily by **Bedouin**.

Dhufar differs from the rest of Oman by receiving summer monsoon rains starting in June and lasting into September. Rainfalls vary between five inches

(127 millimeters) on the coast to over fifteen inches (381 mm) in the **mountains** turning the countryside green. Although the rest of the **Arabian Peninsula** suffers from the extreme heat of the summer, most of Dhufar receives mild southern breezes off of the Indian Ocean. Because of the summer monsoons, Dhufar supports forests that include the frankincense tree (*luban*), which has been exploited for its fragrant resins since ancient times.

Dhufar is the home of two of the Southern Arabic-speaking peoples generally called Ahl al-Hadarah by most Omanis: the Mahrah and the Qarah, who have maintained their own customs and languages. The Ahl al-Hadarah also include the **Harasis**, who live to the east of Dhufar on the Jiddat al-Harasis, and the Shihuh of the **Musandam** Peninsula. The differences between the Ahl al-Hadarah and other Omanis in custom and language have given rise to several popular folk beliefs about them, many of which center around their different eating habits. In addition, it seems that some of them also keep the pre-Islamic practice of animal totems. The Mahrah consider the Somalis to be closely related to them, and in the recent past a Mahrah family owned the Kuria and Muria Islands. Tribal lore states that one of the early Mahrah leaders escaped the massacre of his family and sought refuge with the leader of Socotra Island, possibly indicating connections to East Africa as well.

The economy in Dhufar traditionally rested on fishing, **farming**, and pastoralism, with each of the three areas providing different products. The discovery of **oil** in the Najd of Dhufar greatly changed local conditions after the Dhufar Rebellion ended. The Rebellion caused a good deal of the population to flee the fighting, with some seeking refuge in Yemen (then Marxist-led Southern Yemen) and others with the Harasis in Oman.

See also **Dhufar Liberation Front**.

FURTHER READING

Carter, J.R.L. *Tribes in Oman*. London: Peninsular Publishing, 1982.

Dhufar Liberation Front
Christopher Danbeck

The Dhufar Liberation Front (DLF—later the Popular Front for the Liberation of the Occupied Arab Gulf) was originally organized to challenge the central government of **Oman**'s control over the **Dhufar** region. Oman had annexed the region in 1879, but it was never fully integrated into the Sultanate because the people of Dhufar generally had greater historical ties to Northern **Yemen** rather than Oman. In 1962, Dhufari tribesmen started a rebellion against the control of the Omani *Sultan*, **Sa'id bin Taymur**. The rebel's main grievances revolved around the lack of attention paid to Dhufar by the central government in terms of infrastructural development and revenue sharing from **oil** profits. In 1964, three main rebel organizations (the Dhufar Benevolent Society, the Dhufar Soldiers Organization, and the local branch of the Arab Nationalists Movement) formed the DLF.

The *Sultan's* response to the DLF, however, was arguably weak because no **military** units were stationed in the Dhufar region and there were no local Dhufaris in the military forces. By 1965 the DLF held de facto control over most of the Dhufari countryside and issued a manifesto calling for the overthrow of the Sultan and the end to foreign influence (British) in Oman. Two years later, the DLF's efforts were aided by external support provided by the recently formed People's Democratic Republic of Yemen (PDRY). The PDRY government provided logistic support and safe havens inside Yemen to the DLF that eventually aided the DLF's ability to launch a major offensive in June 1970. This offensive resulted in the retreat of the *Sultan's* forces to several key coastal cities.

Great Britain, which had long supported the *Sultan* because of vital British holdings, became frustrated at his inability to combat the DLF. As a result, the British instigated a coup and successfully replaced the *Sultan* with his son, **Qabus bin Sa'id Al Bu Sa'id**, on July 23, 1970. The newly emplaced *Sultan* Qabus and his British backers developed a new counterinsurgency plan centered on resolving rebel grievances through reforms rather than relying solely on military force. Between 1971 and 1975, the government allocated twenty-five percent of the nation's development funds to Dhufar (a significant increase from previous years), which was aimed at improving the region's transportation, **education**, rural health, and religious facilities. The government also used propaganda to encourage defection of DLF forces and their subsequent reintegration into the *Sultan's* armed forces. Administratively, the government established networks along preexisting tribal structures with the *Sultan* paying tribal *shaykhs* a financial allowance in exchange for their loyalty.

In 1972, the DLF found itself pressured by two factors: the *Sultan's* counterinsurgency strategy had proved moderately successful in weakening the DLF's support base, and the demise of Arab nationalism in the region in the wake of Israel's victory over Nasir's Egypt in the 1967 Suez War. These factors forced the DLF to look elsewhere for support, and in February 1972 the group officially changed its ideology from nationalist to Marxist. Additionally, the DLF changed its name to the Popular Front for the Liberation of the Occupied Arab Gulf (PFLOAG) and expanded its goal from overthrowing the *Sultan* to ending the entire post-colonial structure established by the British in the region. Despite this change, the *Sultan's* strategy was still successful and in 1974 the PFLOAG split into the Popular Front for the Liberation of Oman and the People's Front in **Bahrain**. This final split is widely recognized as the end of the DLF's original movement.

Divorce

Sebastian Maisel

Divorce, *talaq* in Arabic, is an important aspect of rights of passage and family affairs in the societies of the Arab Gulf States. Although some alterations and modifications are observed, generally Islamic and cultural traditions govern the application of divorce.

Marriage is a legal institution in Islam; therefore, to annul that bond is strongly discouraged. However, quite paradoxically, divorce in the Arab Gulf States is common and simple, going back to pre-Islamic times when tribal societies made divorce an easy, straightforward act. With the implementation of *Shari'ah* guidelines, divorce was made more difficult in order to strengthen the position of women. *Shari'ah* law and the application of a specific legal school give explicit details of how to end a marital relationship and what to do with child custody, property claims, and the aspect of re-marrying.

Repudiation, as a one-sided form of divorce by the husband, is an essential principle of Islamic family law, which is maintained in **Saudi Arabia** and the Gulf States. It is recommended for a man to state three times to his wife, "I repudiate you." After the first two announcements, he should wait and reflect before issuing his third and final statement, after which a divorce is irreconcilable. Women can seek divorce also; however, the process is much more complicated and often requires sufficient funds. She needs the support of her legal guardian and on the basis of the agreements of the wedding contract can file for divorce in court if the husband did not fulfill his marital obligations. Another method for a woman to divorce her husband is to buy her way out of the wedding contract. This can be done by returning the dowry or paying him a certain amount of money. Otherwise, she can file for divorce in case the husband is impotent, insane, abusive, or negligent. In these cases, she has to go to court and there has to rely on the verdict of the judge.

No unilateral provisions for alimony are made in Islam; however, it is custom that the woman can keep the dowry, but will not receive any other compensation. She also has to return to her father's family. Custody over the children is split; boys to the age of six or seven and girls to the age of nine are supposed to live with their father. Oftentimes, girls remain with the mother. After the official divorce, women are required to wait for a specific period of time before getting re-married in order to find out if she is pregnant from the previous marriage.

Recently, concerns are growing over the increase of the divorce rate in the Gulf countries and Saudi Arabia, particularly on the basis of incompatibility. In the past, families selected the spouses and marriages were arranged by carefully choosing a matching partner. With the area's rapid modernization and **urbanization,** these practices tend to be less frequent. Nowadays, spouses are better educated, more worldly, and often from different regional and tribal backgrounds. The divorce rate in Saudi Arabia and other Gulf States is rising to an unprecedented fifty percent. In **Bahrain** the divorce rate is around twenty percent, and in **Qatar** it is around thirty percent. The highest number of divorces is recorded in the Eastern Province of Saudi Arabia and the capital **Riyadh**. Local experts explain this trend by pointing to changing attitudes toward marriage, the unwillingness to compromise (e.g., over the issue of working spouses), or not understanding the meaning of marriage. Women are also savvier about their rights and responsibilities, and many traditional men are unable to deal with modern women. The government of Qatar supports divorced women by giving a monthly allowance in addition to the grant of a house.

FURTHER READING

An-Na'im, Abdullahi A. *Islamic Family Law in a Changing World: A Global Resource Book*. New York: Palgrave, 2002.

El Alami, Dawoud. *Islamic Marriage and Divorce Laws of the Arab World*. London: Springer, 1996.

Long, David. *Culture and Customs of Saudi Arabia*. Westport, CT: Greenwood Press, 2005.

Vogel, Frank. *Islamic Law and Legal System: Studies of Saudi Arabia*. Leiden, The Netherlands: Brill, 2000.

Dress

Sebastian Maisel

Clothing protects the human body from the elements of the environment, such as weather, harmful animals, and hazardous materials or actions. However, clothing is not only worn for safety, but also to convey a message to the outside world about the status of the wearer. From what a person is wearing, society can place him in a social hierarchy or position and knows how to interact. Simply looking at what a person is wearing can help identify marital and social status, religious affiliation, or profession. Although often taken for granted, the process of making clothing used to be and still is in many parts of the world a substantial aspect of social origin and development.

The hot summer days and frosty winter nights of Arab countries require special attire that insulate from the cold and chilling winds, but in the summer let the air and cool breeze circulate underneath. Loose-fitting items seem to be most comfortable in these kinds of weather conditions, and not surprising long garments that loosely cover the body shape most traditional clothing in Arabia. This feature is considered the optimal adaptation to the climate as well as to Islamic morals and values, which require both sexes, but especially women, to hide their bodies in public. However, despite a uniform appearance, differentiations in style, color, pattern, or application can be noted. Clothing often gives away the social status of the wearer and information regarding the social, lifestyle, ethnic, confessional, or occupational group to which he belongs. Most clothing is worn by both sexes, but differences remain in the type of material used or in the pattern. From a functional point of view, five main components of Arabian clothing can be recognized.

UNDERGARMENTS

Because of the wide tailor, Arab undergarments are very different from Western styles, although they are worn directly on the body. They usually consist of pants, *sirwal*, and a type of shirt with openings for the head and on the front. A *sirwal* has a drawstring to secure the pants at the waist or hip level. A long type and a short type of *sirwal* are common in Arabia, whereas the short type is worn in the eastern and the long *sirwal* in the western parts of the peninsula. The original form of underwear was a simple rectangle loincloth, *izar*, which is wrapped around the waist. Some farmers in the **Tihamah, Asir, Yemen**, and **Oman** still wear the *izar* as their main piece of dress, whereas others prefer the *izar* to wear at night to modern types of pajamas.

OVERGARMENTS

The ankle-long dress that allows air to circulate freely, *thawb*, is a common piece worn by men and women alike. Sometimes it is held together by a belt or can be buttoned up; then it is called *qumbaz*. They are cut in a way that several dresses can be worn on top of each other. Women *thawbs* have distinct regional and tribal variations, including colored fabric appliqués, silk, or metal thread embroidery, or have silver coins sewn on to them. In areas of higher altitude, women wear *thawbs* with narrow sleeves and semi-fitted yokes to keep the body warm. The closer one gets to the warm areas of the **desert** and coast, the wider the sleeves and looser the garment gets. However, they all have in common the use of brightly colored embroidery to decorate them, which is in sharp contrast to the monochrome appearance of the stark environment.

OUTERGARMENTS

Both sexes wear obligatory outergarments, which are considered part of the traditional clothing. Worn outside the house in public, they should cover the entire body and therefore are very wide and reach down to the ankles. Two basic forms are the simple wrapper made from one piece and often not sewn together and a cloak with arms or at least armholes, *'abayah* or *bisht*. Another type is the knee-long, fur-lined jacket or *farwa* worn in the winter. An important accessory is the belt, which holds the overgarment in place and serves as decoration and storage for weapons and money. Made from leather, cotton, or wool, belts show a variety of forms.

HEADGEAR

Headgear in Arabia is rated higher than in Western societies, because modesty and custom require covering the head. For this reason, headgear throughout the Middle East has resisted change and Western influences. Type, form, and color of the headgear indicate social and ethnic affiliation. In addition to different types of caps, various forms of scarves are seen and wrapped around the head. In some areas with a more tropical and arid climate, straw hats are worn in the fields. A separate issue and distinct part of women's clothing is the facecover, which is connected to Islamic understandings of morals. Sometimes women wear larger wrappers not just over the shoulder, but also over the head as part of their headgear. A range of regional terms is used to describe veiling, which for most women in the area is not considered a burden but rather is seen to beautify the face by covering. The *hijab* is an ordinary headscarf that covers the head but leaves the face exposed, whereas the *bukhnuq* is a highly decorated hood worn by young girls. The *niqab* is a face veil that covers the entire face except the eyes and is worn with a headscarf. In Oman and the **United Arab Emirates** the *burqa'* is a piece of cloth worn like a mask that usually reaches to just below the nose and leaves the mouth free, whereas in Pakistan and Afghanistan it covers the entire face and body, leaving only a mesh screen to see through. *Shaylah* is a long, rectangular scarf popular in the Gulf region. It is wrapped around the head and tucked or pinned in place at the shoulders. The *chador* is a full-body cloak worn by Iranian women. Although there are few Iranians in the Gulf, the *chador* is seen in some places among the Persian population.

FOOTWEAR

Shoes are only considered a necessary accessory in the cities, but **Bedouin** and many people in the countryside go barefoot or only wear shoes on special occasions. Leather shoes are much less common than footwear or sandals made from palm fronds. Leather or wooden sandals (*na'l*) and slippers (*qabqab*) are common at home and in public. Because shoes are in direct contact with dirt and filth, they are regarded as a lower, despicable object in custom, traditions, and proverbs. For that reason, people have to take them off before entering a house or mosque.

In pre-Islamic times, Arabs of the peninsula were mostly Bedouin, farmers, or merchants with a common preference for loose wraps, with urban people wearing wraps of finer quality and decoration. Many objects that are still worn in Arabia, such as the *izar* or *shamlah*, have been mentioned in the poetry of the *Jahiliyah*. The fashion of dress among the early Muslim community was certainly an extension of the preceding *Jahiliyah* period; however, new religious components were added or restrictions imposed. Standard articles of clothing at the time of the Prophet **Muhammad** included underwear, a body shirt, a long overdress, a gown or tunic, and a coat or wrap in addition to head and footwear. Islam has a significant dress code with special rules for pilgrims and non-Muslims. The ritual dress for those making the **pilgrimage** to **Makkah** and **Madinah** was very similar to the dress of this time period, two sheets of unhemmed cloth wrapped around their waist and another draped over the shoulder. Women wear their regular modest dress, including a headscarf that covers their hair. Today, this is regarded as a sign of submission to God's message and a symbol of unity and equality among all pilgrims regardless of their place of origin and social status.

But the most important innovation was the transformation of the veil, which was commonly worn, and now turned into an obligatory part of women's clothing. Men were supposed to wear some type of headgear also, and the most popular form was the *'imamah* or turban, a strip of cloth wrapped around the head. Some religious reform movements such as the **Wahhabis** felt it necessary to clamp down on the urban elite, who wore luxurious clothes based on the *Hadith* of Muhammad, which forbade seven things: silver vessels, gold rings, silk, brocade, *qassi* (a striped fabric from Egypt containing silk), satin, and tanned hides. With the expansion of Islam, Arabs encountered a wide range of clothing styles from the Byzantine and Persian empires. Urban dress in the Umayyad and 'Abbasid capitals of Damascus and Baghdad showed the blending of cultures.

The **Arabian Peninsula** was marginalized, and its traditional dress changed little from that of the time of Muhammad. During the tenth and eleventh centuries, styles from Iran and Central Asia penetrated the Penisula when shirt styles and the *sirwal* were adopted. The Turkish Saljuqs and Ottomans introduced elements of Central Asian dress that were adopted mainly by the urban populations of the **Hijaz**.

Special colors were chosen to express grief and mourning—among the **Shi'ites** white, and **Sunnis** often wore dark blue. Because of different historical developments and influences, regional differences in clothing appeared. The Arabian Gulf region experienced Persian and Indo-Malayan influences, whereas the western region was exposed to Ottoman styles and many other international styles, which were introduced during the pilgrimage. With the beginning of the nineteenth century, far-reaching changes in the social life affected the entire Middle East. The Ottoman administration and particularly the urban population were now exposed to European fashion, and Western tailored clothes replaced gradually traditional loose-floating garments. With the increasing economical and political control, European and Indian manufactured goods and products were inundating the local market. New types of cheaper clothing were available. Market economy and textile industry became part of a new understanding of what to wear and where to buy. No longer was it necessary to make your own clothing; now everyone was able to buy the desired dress at the market. This led to the decline of an entire local industry, for example, in **al-Hasa**, where many families had produced *thawbs* and *bishts* for the entire region. Technological progress helped change the pace and quality of tailoring. Machine stitching replaced traditional hand embroidery and sewing machines became the first signs of modernization in Arabia.

Today Western fashion is very common in many Arab countries, except in the Arabian Peninsula, where people from all social classes prefer to wear an indigenous style that includes *thawb* and *abayas* as well as traditional headgear. This traditional attire is considered the national dress in many Arabian Gulf States; wearing Western clothing on the other hand is seen as a statement of **modernization** and belonging to the non-native section of the population. For example, in **Kuwait** or the **Emirates** it is possible to see that women dress more in Western ways than men. In the Gulf States with their high percentage of guestworkers from Southeast Asia, Indo-Malayan trends and fashions, like the sari or sarong, became common.

REGIONAL FORMS

The Hijaz used to be the most cosmopolitan area in the Arabian Peninsula because of the influx of international pilgrims during the Hajj. It also has been a center for trade and commerce with contacts to many other cultures. The long presence of Ottoman officials was also reflected. The typical dress for Hijazi women was the highly embellished *sidriyah* (vests) and *sirwal*, which are covered by elaborate *thawbs*. In public, women wore the '*abayah* to cover the body, and a long cloth called *jamah*. The traditional headgear had three parts of fabric wrapped around the head in a distinct cloud shape and had multiple holes to see through and allow ventilation. Rural women in the Hijaz used to wear *thawbs* heavily embroidered with distinct tribal motifs. In the past, Hijazi men were recognized by their traditional headgear: a high, brimless cap (*taqiyya*), around which a turban (*usbah*) was wrapped in a very specific way indicating a religious scholar, merchant, or even resident of a particular town. Today, however, most people prefer to wear the *kufiyah* usually called *ghutrah*, the red-checkered headscarf. As outer garments they wore the usual *thawb* tailored in bright, striped materials with embroidered front edges and two front pockets, called *jubbah*.

In **Najd**, the central region, the dress code resembled much of the Bedouin and early Islamic clothing with its simple forms and modest appearances. Najd was isolated from the rest of the peninsula for long times, and therefore was able to preserve its unique dress. Men usually wore the *thawb*, white in the summer and brown in the winter, over which they put a long-sleeved cloak as an outer garment. Women too wore the *thawb* as their basic garment with narrow sleeves and embroidered cuffs. As overdress they chose another thawb with an embroidered neckline cut in the center. The scarf or hood to cover their hair and neck was also embroidered and called *bukhnuq*. To protect the face, a black veil with slits to see through was worn over the face. Finally, an *'abayah* covered the entire body.

Along the Gulf coast, men wore a similar dress to those in Najd, but theirs had wider sleeves and was called *dishdashah*. In **Kuwait**, men of high status wore an additional section of gold braid on their outer cloak or *bisht*. Women's dresses from early on were imported, reflecting the extensive trade relations with India, Persia, and East Africa. Manufactured dresses and synthetic materials were common long before the **oil** era and bartered for local seed pearls. *'Abayahs* and *bukhnuqs* were worn as outergarments and when in public. Men in **Bahrain** commonly wore a simple garment called *awzar* (*izar*) over their *dishdashah*s, especially when working. The main Bahraini women's article is the *dirah gawan*, a waisted, scooped-neck, short-puffed-sleeve garment, and the *thawb nashal*, a gown with enormous sleeve openings. Although the national dress of **Qatar** and the **United Arab Emirates** is very similar to the Saudi fashion, a remarkable difference is noted in Oman with regard to the national headgear. The Omani turban, the *masar*, was for a long time exclusively made and imported from Kashmir. It is wrapped in a significant shape, which allows one to recognize Omanis from a distance.

Yemeni dress is distinctive from that of the rest of the Peninsula, and although there are numerous local variations, the styles from the capital Sana'a are the most influential. As a symbol of the natural abundance, men adorned their hair with aromatic herbs. A leather headband decorated with silver and colored ribbons held them in place. In addition, a long cotton cloth was wrapped around the head with a portion falling over the shoulders. Tribal chiefs and wealthy members of society wore decorated headbands. Other headwear included straw hats, *ghutrah* (the checkered headscarf), and the *'iqal*, which holds the *ghutrah* in place and is made from goat hair. Important men had their *'iqal* embroidered with metal threads. Undergarments included a cotton vest (*sidriyyah*), a *sirwal*, and the *wizrah*, the rectangular sarong wrapped around the waist. Over the ordinary *thawb* a cover or shawl was worn made from colored and striped cotton. In the winter, which sees occasional snowfall, long, wide, and heavy cloaks (*farwa*, *shamlah*) with tanned sheepskin on the inside and embroidery on the outside were thrown over the *thawb*. If shoes were worn, they were made either of leather or palm fronds.

Women's headgear included a colorful scarf worn underneath a straw hat. They usually placed herbs and flowers under this scarf. Other shawls and scarves were used to cover hair and rarely the face. *Sirwal* and *sidriyyah* were the common types of underwear. The dress is the most special item of **Asir** clothing because of distinct cuts, shapes, and patterns that indicate the tribal and regional affiliation of the wearer. It was custom to wear an *izar* over the dress to protect it while working. Capes covered the shoulders and back and provided protection from the elements. Belts and sandals made from leather were also commonly worn. Special clothes were made for occasions such as weddings or mourning. Wedding dresses usually were tailored from the best fabric and heavily decorated with embroidery and **jewelry**. During the mourning period, women normally wore a white dress with a black head cover and white headband.

RELIGIOUS/ISLAMIC CLOTHING

Performing the pilgrimage to Makkah and Madinah requires wearing specific ritual garments to reflect on the spiritual status of *ihram* and declaring the intention of making the pilgrimage. The pilgrim takes a bath and puts on two clean, unstitched, and seamless pieces of white cloth. The upper cloth (*rida*) is draped over the left shoulder leaving the right shoulder bare, and the lower one (*izar*) is wrapped around the waist. No headgear is permitted, except an umbrella. All male Muslims are required to wear the same and no other outfit during the *Hajj*. Only when the weather becomes very cold are the pilgrims allowed to cover up with a blanket. Women can dress in their regular clothes, but should not cover their faces. This type of religious dress has not changed since the implementation of the first pilgrimage rules by the Prophet Muhammad.

The Arabian Peninsula maintained the traditional clothing style successfully even in times of dramatic social and economical change. They still were very much the same clothes that people wore in pre-Islamic and early Islamic times. Only Westernized people gave up the old styles. Sophisticated urban women also wear Western fashion, but when they leave the house to go in public they have to cover their bodies under the common black *'abayah* and their faces under veil (*burqa'*, *bukhnuq*, *niqab*). The same law does not apply to foreign women, although they are required to dress modestly. Non-Saudi Muslim women usually wear a cloak and headscarf, but do not cover their faces, whereas non-Muslim women wear the *'abayah* and carry a headscarf in case they are approached by the religious police. Expatriates are not encouraged to dress in the distinct Arabian attire; however, they should wear professional clothes without exposing too much skin (i.e., shorts and t-shirts are not recommended). But very slowly, especially among the young generation, a shift is noticeably changing the traditional outfit for more Western clothing, such as t-shirts, baseball caps, and sweat pants.

FURTHER READING

Al-Bassam, Laila Saleh. "Traditional Costumes of Asir," *al-Ma'thurat al-Sha'biyah* 67 (2003): 8–29.

Lindisfarne, Nancy, and Bruce Ingham. *Languages of Dress in the Middle East.* Surrey, UK: Curzon, 1997.

Long, David. *Culture and Customs of Saudi Arabia.* Westport, CT: Greenwood Press, 2005.

Scarce, Jennifer. *Women's Costume of the Near and Middle East.* London: Routledge, 2003.

Stillman, Yedida Kalfon. *Arab Dress: A Short History, from the Dawn of Islam to Modern Times.* Leiden, The Netherlands: Brill, 2003.

Topham, John. *Traditional Crafts of Saudi Arabia.* London: Stacey International, 1981.

Yamani, Mai. *Cradle of Islam: The Hijaz and the Quest for an Arabian Identity.* London: I.B. Tauris, 2004.

Drugs

Sebastian Maisel

According to the teachings of Islam, any substance that alters the state of mind of the faithful or blurs his judgment is prohibited, as are those substances that create health problems. **Saudi Arabia** applies strict interpretations to the Islamic rule of banning alcohol and drugs. The other Gulf States follow different directions, allowing limited alcohol sale at hotels or licensed stores. However, drugs are officially banned, and their sale, production, and possession penalized. The countries signed all three international drug control treaties and are members of the United Nations Drug Control Program (UNDCP). Its drug enforcement personnel regularly participate in international training programs.

Currently no significant drug production is reported for Saudi Arabia. Since 1988, the Saudi government has imposed the death penalty for drug smuggling. High numbers of executions for drug trafficking suggest the existence of a drug abuse problem. Because of the lack of official data, it can only be assumed that the issue is not at an alarming level. Cultural and religious norms and restrictions, particularly the application of the harsh Saudi Islamic legal code, contribute to a low level of drug abuse.

However, drugs are available and addicted people are treated in the country's four hospitals specialized for curing drug-related cases in **Riyadh, Jiddah, Dammam,** and **Buraydah.** No such institutions exist to treat female addicts. Foreign nationals, on the other hand, are usually deported. Free counseling is available, but most drug abusers do not seek treatment, often because they are afraid of being treated in a psychiatric hospital as mentally ill.

The Ministry of Interior is the leading agency in the nationwide effort to fight drugs. Special training programs, units, and drug-control officers help prevent extensive drug abuse. They collaborate with the Presidency of Youth Welfare to raise early awareness among teenagers and to educate them about the dangers of illegal drugs. The country works closely on a bilateral level with countries from the **Gulf Cooperation Council** as well as neighboring states like Jordan and

Syria and lately with U.S. Customs advisory teams. In 2003, Saudi Arabia was rated third in the world in terms of its measures to combat drug trafficking and abuse according to the United Nations Office for Drug and Crime.

Among the most heavily consumed drugs in Saudi Arabia are hashish, heroin, cocaine, and amphetamines. Paint or glue inhalation and prescription drug abuse are also noted. In the southern regions of **Najran**, **Asir**, and Jizan, *qat*, a stimulant plant from **Yemen**, is often chewed. This traditional drug plant is very popular in Yemen, but illegal in Saudi Arabia. The culture of the region is very similar to Yemeni culture, and therefore, the plant and the custom of chewing it during the afternoon break became part of local tradition. An increase of drugs coming from Yemen, but also from **Bahrain** and Iraq, is a growing concern for the government.

Although not a drug-producing country, the **United Arab Emirates** are believed to be a major trans-shipment center for marijuana and opium from Pakistan, Afghanistan, and Iran. The country's laissez-faire policy of free ports and a heterogeneous population with large numbers of nationals from those countries contribute to a growing drug-related problem. The government battles this with harsh punishments for smuggling. However, capital punishment, although existent, was usually not applied. Other efforts include bilateral counternarcotics agreements with neighboring Iran and a crackdown on organized **crime**. Recently, the country has taken a tougher stand on illegal narcotics, which is reflected in imposing harsher punishment for possession of drugs, usually four years in prison, and a subsequently higher number of drug-related arrests.

The explanation for the growing number of arrests, confiscations, and addicts is usually the changing demographic structure of the countries. The population in all countries of the area is getting younger every year; in some cases over fifty percent are younger than eighteen years of age. Economically, they are well off or at least they have most of their needs provided for free. Because alcohol is not available, some affluent youth that are bored and feel disconnected from the traditional conservative and religious heritage of their parents turn to drugs as a way to pass their time. Frustration with current economic, social, and political developments adds to the willingness to take drugs in order to escape daily routine. Consumers and dealers are both nationals and foreigners, whereas couriers are easily found among the thousands of underpaid and underprivileged guestworkers. Clearly overrepresented, most of the arrested and convicted drug smugglers are from this social group.

FURTHER READING

Isralowitz, Richard, and Mohammed Afifi. *Drug Problems: Cross-Cultural Policy and Program Development*. Westport, CT: Auburn House, 2002.

Al-Mennaa, Fahad Nasser. "The Causes of Drug Usage, Distribution, and Smuggling in Saudi Arabia." PhD dissertation, Washington State University, 1995.

Sarhan, Hashim. "Drug Abuse in the United Arab Emirates." PhD dissertation, University of Newcastle upon Tyne, 1995.

United Nations. *Laws and Regulations Promulgated to Give Effect to the Provisions of the International Treaties on Narcotic Drugs and Psychotropic Substances: Qatar*. Vienna: United Nations, 1995.

Dubai
Carla Higgins

Dubai is a small emirate of approximately 3,900 square kilometers of **desert**, sea, and the enclave of Hatta, a mountainous area on the border of **Oman**. Dubai has an estimated population of 1,204,000 (2003 estimate). The emirate is primarily comprised of Dubai city and is a city-state. Dubai is characterized by sea and desert but with a somewhat unique geography—it straddles a creek that extends a considerable distance inland, providing a natural harbor and offering the opportunity of maritime trade.

It is thought that Dubai began as a small fishing village in the eighteenth century by members of the **Bani Yas** confederation, who were under **Abu Dhabi** rulers. Members of the Al Bu Falasah subsection of the Bani Yas settled in Dubai and seceded from Abu Dhabi in 1833. Maktum bin Buti, one of the co-rulers of Dubai at that time, established the **Al Maktum**s as the ruling family. **Pearling** and trade created wealth and connections to an outside world, and made Dubai an attractive destination for immigrants. By the turn of the twentieth century Dubai had approximately 10,000 residents that were divided into three quarters. The quarter of Shindaghah was probably the original fishing village and was to the west of the creek. The quarter of Dubai proper, now known as Bur Dubai, was further inland to the west of the creek and housed Al Fahidi Fort, the main mosque, and was the home of government. The quarter of Deira is located to the east of the creek and was home to Arabs, Persians, and Baluchis as well as the biggest *suq* (market) on the Trucial Coast. The population of Dubai was more multinational than any other on the Gulf coast at the beginning of the twentieth century.

Pearling was the major economic activity, and Dubai had a greater share of its population engaged in pearling than in any other emirate, although unlike Abu Dhabi, the population engaged in pearling were permanent residents—they did not leave Dubai when the pearling season was over. Pearling in Dubai brought in less revenue because the ruler exempted many boats from taxation, and this reluctance to tax most likely encouraged entrepreneurship; however, after the 1920s pearling declined.

Trade became a key component of the Dubai economy, and grew rapidly after a 1902 increase in customs dues on trade through Persian ports; entrepot trade then moved from the Persian coast to Dubai. Persians involved in entrepot trade also moved to Dubai, eventually with their families, along with craftsmen and other workers, although prominent merchants remained largely of Arab origin. Many Persians arrived from the Bastak region, settled in what is known today as the Bastakiyah district of Bur Dubai, and were **Sunni** Muslims from Arab tribes.

All of Dubai was organized into different tribal groups well into the 1960s, and because of this organization, neighborhoods had spokesmen or headmen to settle conflicts and bring problems to the ruler's attention. There was no state police, no government-sponsored educational system, no authority over land use, and little to no contact with the ruling *shaykhs*. The government was, however,

New high-rise buildings in Dubai's newly planned business district are the world's largest collection of postmodern buildings in the world. Courtesy of John A. Shoup.

engaged with business, worked to improve commerce on the banks of the creek, and contracted a merchant to collect customs duties. By 1955, however, customs duties for larger vessels were collected by the British Bank of the Middle East.

Dubai's prosperity was firmly based in trade abroad by the 1930s, as well as the international community that maintained it. When pearling failed, in conjunction with World War II and the resulting disruption of additional trade, many residents of Dubai became destitute and oral histories indicate that some Dubai residents starved. Local products such as **dates** and milk were not available to many without local tribal connections. Food supplied by the British was rationed. A black market trade also arose, but by the end of the war it was also depleted. Many former workmen on pearling boats became porters and indispensable to the movement of goods, and a small reform movement began to focus on their labor rights. When plans were being formulated to deepen the creek, prominent merchants suggested to the ruler that local labor should be used, thus furthering the idea that the needs of locals should be addressed as a priority in Dubai's multinational environment.

As the pearling industry and trade failed, the **oil** concessions and rents paid by the British for exploration and landing facilities began, going directly to the ruler and dramatically increasing his wealth. Persian merchants also had some means to fall back on. The ruler's cousins, who were merchants, suffered substantial loss and in 1938 were among those merchants calling for reform, as well as efforts to depose *Shaykh* Sa'id bin Maktum. *Shaykh* Sa'id was supported by the British, who valued him as a moderating force in the region. Dubai became divided into two armed camps. In this environment, an advisory *majlis* was set up with the stated power to veto decisions of the ruler, to set up budgets for the city and allocate resources, and whose members were proposed by leaders in the community. A Council of Merchants was set up as well as a municipal council that made proposals, initiated schools, and began attempting to run the city-state until disbanded in 1939 by tribesmen loyal to the ruler. This brief attempt to run an organized city, however, was appreciated by many, among them the ruler's son. When *Shaykh* Rashid became ruler in 1958, he initiated a Municipal Council, as well as the beginnings of a police force under a British police officer. Improvements to the creek also increased sustained traffic into the port, and the Dubai Port Committee was initiated by this time.

A system began by the late 1950s to offer community services by private **companies**, such as electricity and telephone, and the ruler owned substantial shares in each. In the late 1950s an airstrip was built, soon to be an airport in 1965. A bridge connecting Deira to Bur Dubai was built. Both of these projects were built for the future—they were far beyond immediate needs at the time. The ambition to develop Dubai rapidly was shown to be a success with the rapid influx of foreign companies and the growth of trade in later years.

Mention of Dubai's development must include the role of the British beyond that of signing truces in the nineteenth century. In 1954, the British created a political agency in Dubai, from which limited development and social services were organized, garnering the attention of rulers from other areas of the Trucial States, who replaced it in 1965 with the Development Office of the Trucial States Council, located in Dubai. The British sent foreign specialists, and Dubai residents observed changes in community services. Medical facilities and health services were initiated. Schools, began by the British in Sharjah in 1953, were built in the northern states by **Kuwait** from 1954, and expanded into Dubai in the 1960s. Emphasis was on technical **education**.

In 1969, the first oil exports left Dubai. Although oil wealth was to play a role in Dubai's development, it did not have near the impact of Abu Dhabi's mass reserves. Immediately after Dubai first began exporting oil, it began planning for a future without it and utilized its revenues toward building ports and in building trade and business opportunities.

Economic and population growth accelerated, as did determination to build a business community and attract new businesses with appropriate facilities and support. With the discovery and impending export of oil from the offshore field of Fath, efforts were made to create a deep-water harbor in 1967; by 1972 Port Rashid was opened and the population of Dubai had doubled to 120,000—and it doubled again by 1981. Port Rashid had been expanded from nine berths to thirty-five, and dray docks had been constructed. After the 1973 October war, and using rising oil revenues, Dubai began to industrialize and established Jabal 'Ali as its center. Another harbor was built with sixty-seven berths, and Jabal 'Ali became the Jabal 'Ali Free Zone with an initial clientele of 650 enterprises, including the aluminum smelter DUBAL, the largest in the Middle East.

Dubai's experiments have paid off, creating a city-state known worldwide for the fast pace of development, wealth, and cosmopolitan character. It has remained true to its roots, and is more a multinational city than ever. Business reigns supreme. The free zone experiment began at Jabal 'Ali has expanded into over twenty-four free zones in Dubai alone. Dubai is the leader in a $3-billion-a-year exhibit/conference industry. Housing has exploded and huge projects with luxury accommodations are visible features of the skyline, as are huge malls with high-end consumer goods. The world's tallest building is being built there, the Burj Dubai. A new metro system is underway. Sports arenas host a variety of sporting events, including horse racing, motor racing, tennis, rugby, cricket, sailing, soccer, and golf to attract tourists. Major international **music**/pop stars perform in Dubai. Efforts to build the arts and promote cultural events abound, beginning with the Heritage Village that features historical homes in Shindaghah. New developments, such as The World and Palm Island, offer luxury housing and entertainment venues. Concurrent to such development, Dubai leaders struggle to address issues of human and labor rights among its poor, imported laborers; the issue of how to provide social services to its huge expatriate population; and how to meet the high standards of its national citizens.

Dubai Media City
Carla Higgins

Dubai Media City (DMC) is one of the many free zones in **Dubai**. A free zone is an area, and usually a group of facilities, where national and international investors can locate and build businesses with 100% foreign ownership, with a corporate tax holiday, freedom to repatriate capital and profits, and no import duties. It is a widely held belief in Dubai that free zones bring jobs and expertise and boost the national economy, and free zones have now proliferated. The first free zone was that of Jabal 'Ali and was established in 1985. Currently, there appear to be approximately thirty free zones spread throughout the **United Arab Emirates**, and seventeen are in Dubai alone, two in **Sharjah**, one in **'Ajman**, one in **Umm al-Quwayn**, one in **Ra's al-Khaymah**, and one in **Fujayrah**; two are proposed for **Abu Dhabi**. These free zones host more than 3,000 **companies**.

DMC states in its mission statement the intent "to create and market world class enabling services for the **media** industry." Its vision is "to become an efficient and leading provider of services to foster the growth of Dubai's knowledge based economy." DMC, in large part because of its free zone status, has developed into a media community without equal, hosting advertising agencies, broadcasting, film, **leisure** and entertainment, news agencies, printing and publishing, online media and marketing services, and production and information agencies. Companies such as the Associated Press, Bertelsmann, BMG, CNBC, CNN, the international headquarters of Middle East Broadcasting Company (MBC), McGraw-Hill, Reuters, and Sony now occupy Media City, as do individual freelancers. Importantly, the Arabic news channel *Al-'Arabiyah* is also located at DMC. The Showtime network opened its headquarters there in 2004, and BMG MENA is now there, controlling a large music production library that is used by production companies and advertising agencies. The Voice of America is also based in DMC.

DMC promises that all businesses are given the freedom to create. It has initiated Dubai Studio City, which offers a single location to shoot a film from beginning to end. DMC has presented and organized the Dubai International Film Festival since 2004 to showcase excellence in Arab cinema and contribute to the development of the regional industry. A new International Media Production Zone (IMPZ), the first in the region, has created an "environment for media production companies … to interact and collaborate effectively." DMC launched the Ibda'a Media Student Awards to recognize and foster young media talent from the Arab world.

Other emirates have launched alternatives to DMC. The emirate of Fujayrah has launched Creative City with the intent to attract international broadcast television and radio providers to Fujayrah through providing a similar set of services as DMC. Ra's al-Khaymah Media Free Zone and Film City were initiated in January 2006 to compete with DMC, with the expectation that the high cost of living in Dubai will push media companies to the less expensive emirate.

FURTHER READING

"Dubai Media City." Available at http://www.dubaimediacity.com (last accessed October 8, 2008).
"UAE Free Zones." Available at http://www.uaefreezones.com (last accessed October 8, 2008).

Duru'

John A. Shoup

The Duru' tribe is one of the most important in **Oman**, being located in the **desert** to the west of **Nizwa** and Adam, the original home of the ruling **Al Bu Sa'idi** dynasty. The Duru' tribe belongs to the Ghafiri (northern) faction and had long-standing feuds with **'Awamir** and the **Wahibah** tribes that ended in the 1960s. The Duru' controlled the salt mines at Qarn al-Milh and also extracted salt from Wadi Umm al-Samim, which they marketed in **Nizwa** and 'Ibri. They also gained control over the sulfur mines at Qarn al-Kibrit, although this was contested by the Wahibah and the cause for their long conflict.

The Duru' had good relations for the most part with the Al Bu Sa'idi *sultan*s and frequently provided tribal troops when necessary. The tribe supported the **Imam of Nizwa** in the first part of the twentieth century, and Wilfred Thesiger noted that he and his companions were threatened by them during his last trip into Oman in 1949–1950. He was saved only by the protection extended by a *shaykh* of the Wahibah tribe. The Duru' formally submitted to the Omani *Sultan* **Sa'id bin Taymur** in 1954.

The first discovery of **oil** in Oman was within the traditional grazing area of the Duru' and the *Sultan* used this as a means to break the power of the tribe. He organized the labor supply so that rival *shaykhs* took their turn, which had the intended effect. The tribe was weakened and divided to such an extent that in the 1970s some 800 tribesmen left Oman for **Abu Dhabi** and **Dubai**, where it was easy for them to become citizens. This was a major loss of manpower when the total number of the tribe was estimated to be around 2,500.

Those who remain in Oman are still important to the government although much of the corporate action of the tribe has been minimized. Although their economy based on trade in salt and sulfur has suffered since the 1960s because of the improvements in transportation of goods from the coastal cities, some Duru' remain pastoral nomads and raise **camels**, sheep, and goats that they market in Nizwa. Duru' own the **date** groves at Tana'am as well as up to one half of the groves at 'Ibri and Adam. The **Bedouin** come in for the harvest in the summer;

otherwise, the date groves are left in the care of settled sections of the tribe, who are called "servants." The Duru', along with the Wahibah, own the best camels in Oman, which are famous for their speed and endurance. Camels bred for racing sell for hundreds of thousands of dollars each and are sought after by avid breeders and racers from the **United Arab Emirates**, **Saudi Arabia**, **Qatar**, and **Bahrain**.

See also **Travelers and Explorers**.

FURTHER READING

Carter, J.R.L. *Tribes in Oman*. London: Peninsular Publishing, 1982.

Chatty, Dawn. *Mobile Pastoralists: Development Planning and Social Change in Oman*. New York: Columbia University Press, 1996.

Thesiger, Wilfred. *Arabian Sands*. London: Readers Union Longmans, Green & Co., 1960.

E

Economic Structures

Jack Kalpakian

The economies of the **Gulf Cooperation Council** (GCC) states reflect the dynamics of **oil**-dependent development. Governments in the region used their vast oil reserves to fund the construction of modern economies that engage in international trade, finance, and manufacturing. Oil and gas are the central aspects of GCC economics, but it is what has been done outside the petroleum industry that deserves special attention, particularly since oil and gas represent limited, albeit vast, endowments. The GCC states have followed economic development strategies. These include moving into basic industries, manufacturing, finance, technology, entertainment, and services. All of these strategies represent state involvement in the economy at a level not experienced in other capitalist, free market economies. The key to understanding the economic structures of the GCC states is the proper appreciation of the role of the state in fostering local enterprises through contracting, special projects, and political facilitation. Aside from the state, commercial agencies, vast petrochemical outfits, and state-sponsored/owned industries dominate the region's economies. Sometimes, these operations are associated with international firms as a part of offsets programs linked to defense spending. In short, the state structures the economic game to benefit its backers, often the same persons as the local rulers, their families, and their clients.

There have been three broad routes taken by the **Arab Gulf** state in its pursuit of a post-oil future. The first method was pioneered by **Kuwait** through its Kuwait Investment Authority (KIA). Under this strategy, Kuwait invests in overseas economies, especially in profitable businesses and cash cows. The dividend stream generated by these investments is expected to replace oil revenues, if only partially, to enable Kuwait to enjoy a developed economy long after oil revenues have disappeared. A similar approach is also used by all of the other Gulf States, with significant variations in emphasis and application. The creation of sovereign wealth funds in the **United Arab Emirates**, Kuwait, **Bahrain**, and **Qatar** has its roots in the Kuwaiti experience. The GCC sovereign wealth funds represent a very vast reserve of cash and investment—the **Abu Dhabi** Sovereign wealth fund is slowly approaching $1 trillion. Other holding **companies** are controlled by leading individuals whose wealth cannot be said to be independent of the state, such as Al-Walid ibn Talal, a member of the Saudi Royal family and the key shareholder in the "Kingdom" Holding Company. Although these are not sovereign wealth funds per se, they share many features in common with them, including vast overseas investments and substantial revenue streams in dividends and capital appreciation.

The second approach was pioneered by **Saudi Arabia** through its Saudi Arabic Basic Industries Corporation (SABIC). Funded and owned by Saudi Arabia, SABIC represents an economic strategy that has sought to add value to petroleum products upstream rather than downstream. SABIC processes oil and gas into fertilizers, plastics, chemicals, and other economically useful substances in Saudi Arabia, thereby replacing expensive imports and moving a great deal of production of basic substances to the kingdom. **Yanbu'** and **Jubayl** owe their economic genesis to SABIC. Other firms producing steel, cement, construction materials, and supplies have also been established and capitalized by the Saudi government and its leading princes. There has also been a significant emphasis on consumer product production and replacement. There are Saudi companies producing milk, tomato paste, soap, shampoo, detergent, and all manner of consumer sundries. These firms are often allowed to function as monopolies or near-monopolies with substantial legal and political cover provided by the state.

To the extent that the GCC states still import many of their products, imports are handled by commercial agencies. Indeed, one of the main reasons that membership in the World Trade Organization (WTO) was initially feared by many local interests is the threat that many believed the WTO posed to the agency system. To sell products in the Gulf, foreign firms need to have local agents representing them, and this need is generally created by law. The agency system guarantees local importers substantial profits and bargaining power vis-à-vis their foreign suppliers and mentors. The agency system has survived the entry of these economies into the WTO and it shows no signs of abetting except in **Dubai** to some extent. Associated with the agency system are rules governing foreign investment and ownership in the GCC. Although actual practice varies in detail, all GCC members require the inclusion of a domestic partner for all foreign investors in the region, except in the economic free zones. Although the partnership percentage varies, it often represents fifty or fifty-one percent of the initial investment, thereby curtailing foreign access to the local economies and insuring a large degree of local control on foreign economic activities. Naturally, foreign firms prefer to work with well-connected individuals close to the centers of power in these countries to safeguard their interests, and this dynamic further cements the economic control of the ruling elites.

The third approach was implementing economic liberalization policies within specific areas and zones. For the UAE as a whole, this meant using Dubai as a liberal zone, especially the Jabal 'Ali Economic Free Zone, which entailed attracting manufacturing, services, and entertainment companies to the region. It also meant forays into high-skill, high-input services like higher education, banking, and health care. The policy was essentially to duplicate all of the amenities found in the industrialized world in Dubai. The policy was extremely successful, and oil accounts for only three percent of the Emirate's income today. Its success has led to attempts to duplicate it across the region in Saudi Arabia, Qatar, and Kuwait. In Bahrain, some elements of the policy were already in place with regard to attracting corporate headquarters and banks. Although the airline, Emirates, appears to be a very different kind of company than SABIC, the two companies share state involvement and the idea of "adding value" to oil by moving processing upstream. The two firms stem from an economic philosophy that combines the market with the state and attempts to move as much as possible of the value-addition process upstream on the oil and gas supply system.

All of the GCC states depend on foreign labor to some extent. At the lower end of the dependence are states like **Oman**, Saudi Arabia, and Bahrain, where foreign labor accounts for less than one-third of the population. At the higher levels of dependency, the Emirates, Qatar, and Kuwait have populations that are mostly composed of noncitizens. In all of the states, except Bahrain, citizens have generally been shying away from jobs and professions that require physical labor or contact with substances like grease, fertilizer, soil, and so forth. Many young GCC citizens aspire to white-collar work. As a result, there is **unemployment** among young men, even as these states import large numbers of workers. Instead of viewing these tasks as stepping stones toward better careers, or a transitional phase in life, they are often seen as demeaning and beneath the dignity of GCC citizens.

Many foreign workers are also mistreated by their employers, who often withhold wages or fail to pay the salaries or wages they promise. In some cases, foreign workers can be caught in a legal limbo, particularly because their employers often confiscate their passports upon arrival and refuse to return them after the contract expires or upon firing. As long as countries like the Philippines, Bangladesh, India, Pakistan, and Afghanistan suffered poverty, the workers often bore these indignities with little complaint. But as the Asian economies developed, labor supplies dwindled and strikes took place in 2006–2007 in the UAE. The UAE was taking steps such as publicizing the names of abusive firms and fining them, but it took a hard line toward the strike leaders, promising to deport them. The crisis outlined the squalid conditions of the vast majority of foreign workers and their grievances.

It is now clear that the rapid development of Asia will lead to fewer and fewer workers willing to work in the GCC states, but there is no current policy to educate local citizens about the need to accept what are seen as menial jobs. The focus is on replacing white-collar foreign workers with indigenous employees in Saudi Arabia under the **Saudization** policy. In practice, this meant the departure of Western, Palestinian, and Egyptian professionals from Saudi Arabia and their replacement with local personnel. Although that policy does make sense, it cannot by itself solve the problem of unemployment among local Saudis. The policy may increase friction within Saudi society for the better jobs and also may create further strains at the international level.

Compounding the problem is the emphasis placed on Islamic studies at the university level in Saudi Arabia. There are many unemployed graduates of Islamic universities vying for a relatively limited number of positions as judges and clerics. Many of these young men find themselves without the technical, communicative, or linguistic skills demanded by the job market. Although they are certainly learned and literate, their training and expectations render their experiences on the employment circuit difficult and harsh. Under their circumstances, militant Islamism can become a rather attractive alternative because it promises to replace the existing religious establishment—meaning that it promises to lead to changed circumstances under which they are more likely to be employed. The availability of oil revenues allows the state to pay these young men social and political rents, thereby probably restricting complete alienation to a minority.

Although petroleum wealth has been generally beneficial to these countries, it has come with a significant price—it has enabled the state to dominate the economic and social sphere while introducing a social form of the Dutch disease problem of international political economy. The vast availability of oil funds allowed the state to shape the economic structure of the region; development was not a bottom-up process—it came with Bechtel and its local equivalents. The funds also meant that other industries did not develop independently of oil, even when the latter became less important in some cases. Even independent, truly private local firms developed in the shadow of the state, feeding on contracts and depending on cheap, imported labor. Consequently, the local labor force did not develop in the familiar patterns seen in the developed world; employers simply did not employ locals in many of the manual and menial tasks, and thereby a form of misery-bringing growth took place. Although jobs were created, they did not, for a wide variety of reasons including the vast availability of oil funds, go to locals—at least not in the main. The Saudization program was an attempt to correct this problem, but it has not been as successful as its promoters hoped, because the Saudi educational system has not been producing the cadres needed to replace the foreign professionals. A more thoughtful approach is being followed in the UAE and Qatar with the development of new universities.

The state dominates the economic structures of the GCC states. Private firms as well as the attempts to diversify the local economies have been defined by state policies to that effect. Private industry and markets have not been independent. Economic development is often defined in terms of planning for a post-oil world in which the region will have to depend on other industries and investments—again under plans generated and implemented by the various states. Labor is largely imported with dramatic social, political, and economic consequences, and attempts to break free from foreign labor have been thwarted by the abundance of oil and powerful local preferences for white-collar work instead of manual labor. In the classic descriptions of Dutch Disease, the Netherlands experienced growth when it began to sell gas on the world market. As a result of these sales, the guilder gained in value and the Netherlands was able to import many products more cheaply than they could produce; the imports damaged Dutch industry and joblessness grew. In the case of the GCC, the oil wealth simply facilitated the importation of labor, which damaged the bargaining position of local labor and delayed its development.

See also **Education**.

FURTHER READING

Kapiszewski, Andrzej. "Arab versus Asian Migrant Workers in the GCC Countries." Paper presented at the United Nations Expert Group Meeting on International Migration and Development in the Arab Region, Population Division, Department of Economic and Social Affairs, United Nations Secretariat, Beirut, Lebanon, May 15–17, 2006.

Kingdom Holding Company. "About Us, Executive Chairman." Available at http://www.kingdom.com.sa/index.asp?id=40 (last accessed February 27, 2008).

Kuwait Investment Authority. "Objectives and Strategy." Available at http://www.kia.gov.kw/KIA/About+KIA/Objective+and+Strategy/ObjectivesandStrategy.htm (last accessed February 20, 2008).

Looney, Robert. "Saudization and Sound Economic Reforms: Are the Two Compatible?" *Strategic Insights* 3, no. 2 (2004). Available at http://www.ccc.nps.navy.mil/si/2004/feb/looneyFeb04.asp (last accessed February 28, 2008).

Metz, Helen Chapin (ed.). *Persian Gulf States: A Country Study.* Washington, D.C.: Government Printing Office for the Library of Congress, 1993.

Pepper, William. "Foreign Capital Investment in Member States of the Gulf Cooperation Council: Considerations, Issues and Concerns for Investors, Part 1," *Arab Law Quarterly* 6, no. 3 (1991): 231–266.

Pepper, William. "Foreign Capital Investment in Member States of the Gulf Cooperation Council: Considerations, Issues and Concerns for Investors, Part 2," *Arab Law Quarterly* 6, no. 4 (1991): 331–343.

Pepper, William. "Foreign Capital Investment in Member States of the Gulf Cooperation Council: Considerations, Issues and Concerns for Investors, Part 3," *Arab Law Quarterly* 7, no. 1 (1991): 33–63.

Saudi Arabian Basic Industries Corporation. "Corporate Profile." Available at http://www.sabic.com/corporate/en/ourcompany/corporateprofile/default.aspx (last accessed February 27, 2008).

"Sovereign Wealth Funds: Asset Backed Insecurity," *The Economist*, January 17, 2008. Available at http://www.economist.com/finance/displaystory.cfm?story_id=10533428 (last accessed February 28, 2008).

Walters, Timothy N., Alma Kadragic, and Lynne M. Walters. "Miracle or Mirage: Is Development Sustainable in the United Arab Emirates," *Middle East Review of International Affairs* 10, no. 3 (2006): 71–99.

Economies, Traditional

John A. Shoup

The Arabs of the Peninsula have been engaged in a wide range of economic activities since ancient times. As the **Arabian Peninsula** slowly dried up toward the end of the Neolithic period, farming was concentrated near water sources and **pastoralism** became more developed. Long-distance trade with its neighbors in Asia and Africa was also developed, and mercantile states emerged at an early period. Other forms of economic activity were also encouraged including mining, fishing, shipbuilding, **pearling**, sailing/navigation, and fine craftsmanship. Certain cities in **Yemen**, **Oman**, and **Bahrain** became well-known for fine crafts in silver, copper, brass, wood, cloth, and clay.

HUNTING AND GATHERING

Hunting and gathering did not play a major role in the overall economy of the Peninsula but was supplemental to both settled agriculturalists and pastoral nomads. **Bedouin** hunted gazelles, oryx, and wild goats as well as a wide variety of local birds such as ostrich, bustard, grouse, and quail. In the northern part of the Peninsula, near Iraq and Syria waterfowl such as ducks and geese arrived in large numbers migrating from Europe to Africa. The introduction of the gun spelled the doom of many of the wild species that used to inhabit the Peninsula. Hunting is still an important **sport** for the elite using trained falcons and the Arabian greyhound or *Saluki*, and although falconing is still done, there is little to no game to hunt today. Oman developed a project for integrated use of the Jaddat al-Harasis by Bedouin pastoralists and the last wild herds of oryx, but unlimited hunting was allowed by the government and the herds have been greatly decimated.

Gathering activities included collecting a range of seasonal plants such as mushrooms and truffles that emerge in the winter. Women collected aromatic plants and wild spices, including sage, which are used in cooking and in traditional medicines. Wild honey is also used in traditional medicine and as a sweetener for pastries. Honey is also collected from domesticated bees kept in the **oases**.

Salt and sulfur were mined from natural sources particularly by the **Duruʻ** tribe, whose area includes both Qarn al-Milh and Qarn al-Kabrit near Wadi Umm al-Samim. The **Wahibah** tribe especially contested control over the salt mines at Qarn al-Milh and the two fought a long conflict over the control. The Duruʻ were eventually able to establish firm control over these sources in the 1940s.

PASTORALISM

Pastoralism has been one of the most important economic activities in the Arabian Peninsula for millennia. Domestication of small stock began during the Neolithic era, with goats being first domesticated some 10,000 years ago in the Zagros Mountains of Iran and sheep being domesticated between 9,000 and 11,000 years ago in Iraq. With the growing desertification of the Peninsula some 5,800 years ago, pastoralism was concentrated in areas where water sources were available. Use of the deep **desert** was not possible except for during the winter season when rains made it possible to move flocks into it. The domestication of the **camel** in southern Arabia sometime between 2000 and 1500 BC allowed greater mobility, and pastoralists were able to use the desert even in the summer months. Domestication of the camel also allowed for more trade between the northern and southern parts of the Peninsula because of the camel's ability to go up to twenty-one days without water and its ability to carry heavy loads of 440 pounds (200 kilograms)—twice the weight a bull cart can carry. Improved camel saddles and harnessing developed in north Arabia some time after 500 BC allowed camels to carry heavy loads over long distances and gave the Arab Bedouin both **military** and economic dominance. A fully loaded camel can walk at a speed of three miles an hour (four to five kilometers an hour), whereas a camel carrying only a rider can cover up to 100 miles in a day (150 kilometers).

Domestication of the camel gave rise to the Bedouin culture, which by the time of the Prophet emerged as one of the most dominant cultures of the

Peninsula. Camel pastoralists took the top position in social ranking, considering themselves to be the most "noble" of Arabs or *asil*. Those who raised small stock, mainly sheep and goats, and thus had restricted migration patterns were referred to as *shawiyah* or "small," and those who combined some agriculture with raising livestock were referred to as *ru'a'* or simply "herders." Until the early twentieth century the *asil* tribes were able to militarily dominate much of the Arabian Peninsula because of the high mobility camel pastoralism gave them. Camels also gave the important means to play influential roles in the economy, providing both transport and skilled guides for commercial and **pilgrimage** caravans.

Pastoralism provided both settled and pastoral populations with important items. Sheep, goats, and camels were all milked and even today many people prefer the taste of sheep or camel milk to cow's milk. Milk and milk products such as sour milk, butter, cheese, and yogurt were traded or sold in the towns and cities for nonpastoral products. Pastoralists did not consume much meat but sold unwanted male sheep, goats, and even camels in urban markets. Pastoralists also sold wool and hair (goat and camel) in urban **markets** where they were processed into numerous finished products. Goat hair was woven by Bedouin women to make the black tents they lived in.

AGRICULTURE

Traditional agriculture was confined to mainly the oases and occasional use of seasonal streams. Intensive production systems based on irrigation technologies made even small oases highly productive. Multilayering of plant species and multicropping allowed a small plot of land to not only support a family but also provide surplus for sale. Many of the settled communities had long-term contacts with pastoralists and in many instances pastoralists owned property in oases. Various types of agreements were worked out whereby pastoralists took care of livestock owned by settled people whereas settled farmers took care of farms owned by pastoralists. The **date** harvest was one of the few times many pastoralists would come into the oases.

Seasonal streams were dammed by both pastoralists and settled farmers, and water collected behind them during the wet season could be used to water livestock or for irrigation. As the water dried up, the newly exposed land was green with grasses and other natural plants—or could be farmed as small plots of dryland wheat and barley. Control mechanisms such as *hima*, or protected status, were used to ensure that the crops or meadows were for those who have usufruct rights to them.

The main traditional system of irrigation in most of the Peninsula was underground canals or *aflaj*. *Aflaj* tapped both groundwater and surface water sources depending on which was available, and in some places both sources were used. Water distribution was managed by a person called an *'arif* (plural *'urafa'*), meaning someone with knowledge. The *'arif* knew how many shares any one farmer owned, which translates into the number of hours water can flow into a particular field. Shares were inherited and could be bought and sold. Those who gave money for the upkeep and repair of the *aflaj* were entitled to a larger share of the water. This money, called *masha*, in most of the region was collected by the *'arif*, who along with his helpers were entitled to a share of the sum as salaries.

Among the most important agricultural crops were dates. Some 600 date varieties are grown in the Arab world, and most are found in the Peninsula. In the recent past, dates were among the most important agricultural products of the Peninsula, and even today the Arab world exports over 3 million tons of dates a year. Other agricultural products include wheat, barley, citrus fruits, pomegranates, figs, and vegetables.

SHIPBUILDING AND PEARLING

The Gulf States and Oman have long histories of shipbuilding, sailing, and pearling. **Kuwait**, Bahrain, the **United Arab Emirates**, and Oman have shipbuilding yards that still turn out **dhows**. Much of the wood is imported from the mangrove stands along the East African coast or from India. Dhows also were (and still are) made in southern Iraq and in Iranian port cities. Dhow building made little use of nails but planks were lashed together by ropes, making the ship better able to take rough weather. The inside surface was sealed with layers of tar. Little was made from locally available materials, and even the ropes were often made in East Africa. The canvas for the sails was made mainly in Bahrain (which has an active cloth industry) or Kuwait. Dhow-building yards did not turn out many new ships per year; yards in the United Arab Emirates produced from ten to twenty ships a year. Then the only craft made from local palm wood was the small, one-man fishing craft called a *shashah*.

Pearling was one of the most important traditional sources of income for much of the Gulf and the eastern part of Saudi Arabia. Pearling supplemented both agricultural and pastoral production, and both settled farmer and pastoral nomads participated in the major pearling season. Pearls became more important in the world market in the nineteenth century and into the early twentieth century before the invention of cultured pearls in Japan. The main pearling season was in the summer, from June to September, when other forms of income were not as viable.

Pearls were marketed through brokers located in the Gulf cities, and during the nineteenth century many brokers moved from Iranian ports to those along the Arab side of the Gulf to escape high taxes. As the Iranian government tried to impose more control and taxes on the merchants, the rulers of the Arab states offered better conditions, including land. Most of the pearl merchants were ethnic Arabs and **Sunnis** and many moved, sparking much of the subsequent development of the Gulf. Bahrain controlled large pearl banks where the conditions were best for the oysters and Bahrain also attracted several Indian merchants, mainly from Bombay. Bombay was the largest market for pearls, supplying the British Empire and via London most of Europe. New York was the second largest market for Gulf pearls, and some of the large **jewelry** houses had agents in **al-Manamah**.

FISHING

Fishing was restricted to the coastal communities, and many of the Peninsula communities located away from the coast did not eat fish. In the northern desert, Bedouin dislike those who eat fish, and to be called an eater of fish, or *samamkah*, is an insult. Fish are eaten from Iraq to Oman and today fishing is an important activity, although most of the fishermen are Pakistani or Indian. Fishing in the Gulf was and for the most part still is done by setting large wire traps or nets. Nets are both small-cast or are large and require crews from several ships to lay them and then bring them inland, where women with baskets wait to catch the fish.

Dried fish is an important part of the diet in much of the southern region of the Peninsula, especially in Oman. Dried fish is eaten by humans and is fed as a fodder to livestock, even to camels. Dried sardines are used as fertilizer and in the pre-**oil** period dried sardines were among the yearly exports from the United Arab Emirates (then called the Trucial States). When possible, fishing was often combined with other activities such as date farming and/or pastoralism; for example, groups of the **Bani Yas** settled along the coast from **Abu Dhabi** to **Dubai** and relied on multiple sources of income, including fishing.

TRADE

Trade has been an important economic activity in the Arabian Peninsula for millennia. Trade along land routes was greatly improved with the domestication of the camel, and ancient states such as those of Yemen, the **Nabateans** in the **Hijaz** and Jordan, and Palmyra or Tadmur in the Syrian Desert were built on controlling the trade between the Indian Ocean and India on one side and the Mediterranean on the other. The **Quraysh** tribe of **Makkah** became wealthy because of their control of water between **Yemen** and Syria and their contacts with Bedouin tribes that provided camels. With the rise of Islam many of the Bedouin in the northern desert provided camels, guides, and/or protection for the pilgrims. Governments paid tribal leaders subsidies to make sure pilgrims arrived safely and continued to do so even after the **Hijaz Railway** was completed in 1908.

Long-distance ocean trade also predates the rise of Islam. Bahrain figures in Sumerian texts as the Land of Dilmun, and Oman's **Musandam** and **Dhahirah** were called Majan. Both were sources of items such as copper traded to Mesopotamia. People from the Arabian Peninsula established colonies and trading posts along the East African coast, in India and Indonesia, and as far east as China. Basrah in Iraq, Kuwait, Bahrain, **Suhar**, **Salalah**, and other ports along the coast of **Yemen** were heavily involved in sea trade. Today many families in Kuwait and Bahrain have close ties with India and Pakistan, whereas Omanis have ties to Zanzibar and coastal cities such as Mombassa.

CRAFTS

Traditional crafts include working in metal, jewelry making, pottery, and weaving. Towns such as **Bahla** and **Nizwa** in Oman have long traditions of fine copper work and many items have become collector or museum pieces. Trays, coffee pots, spice containers, and other kitchen utensils from Nizwa were exported to the Gulf coast. In the northern part of the Peninsula, copper and brass were often imported from Syria and Iraq. Oman and Yemen in particular are famous for the high quality of their silver work not only in fine jewelry for women but also in making silver-mounted weapons such as swords, daggers, and even rifles. Smiths from Nizwa and Bahla were the best known and produced distinctive items with embossed floral designs. Silversmiths in other parts of the Peninsula such as in the Hijaz often made items for Bedouin women in the interior.

Weaving was a village craft in Bahrain and **al-Hasa**, where men wove cloth for clothes and for trade. In Bahrain certain **Shi'ite** villages still carry on the craft and make cotton cloth worn as an undergarment or as an apron by agriculturalists. Bedouin women weave a wide variety of useful items from tents to bags from wool and hair. In most of the Peninsula Bedouin weaving is being lost, but in Kuwait the government has opened a special center called *al-Sadu* to keep the art alive, and Oman has attempted to encourage weaving as a national heritage. In Oman men as well as women weave bags and other items associated with Bedouin life. In the United Arab Emirates various women's associations are trying to keep the art alive, but they have begun to use industrial cotton yarn rather than wool.

An important craft that is not in danger is the fine metal thread embroidery called *talli*. Women in many of the Gulf countries still make metal thread by hand. The thread is then used to embroider traditional dresses worn at weddings and other celebrations and national holidays. Young girls wear an embroidered hood called a *bakhnuq*, whereas older girls and women wear huge heavily embroidered dresses and cloaks.

FURTHER READING

Agius, Dionisius. *In the Wake of the Dhow: The Arabian Gulf and Oman*. London: Garnet, 2002.

Altorki, Soraya, and Donald Cole. *Arabian Oasis City: Transformation of 'Unayzah*. Austin: University of Texas Press, 1989.

Bulliet, Richard. *The Camel and the Wheel*. New York: Columbia University Press, 1990.

Chatty, Dawn. *Mobile Pastoralists: Development Planning and Social Change in Oman*. New York: Columbia University Press, 1996.

Ferdinand, Klaus, and Ida Nicolaisen. *Bedouins of Qatar*. London: Thames and Hudson, 1993.

Heard-Bey, Frauke. *From Trucial States to United Arab Emirates*. Dubai: Motivate Publishing, 2004.

Insoll, Timothy. *Land of Enki in the Islamic Era: Pearls, Palms, and Religious Identity in Bahrain*. London: Kegan Paul International, 2005.

Al-Shamlan, Saif Marzooq. *Pearling in the Arabian Gulf: A Kuwaiti Memoir*. Translated by Peter Clark. London: London Center of Arab Studies, 2001.

Education

Rachel Sondheimer

Education has long been an integral part of the society and culture of the Gulf States, albeit in various forms. For centuries, the mainstay of traditional schooling took place in the *kuttab*, where children met in mosques or private houses to learn recitations of the Qur'an. Despite some efforts by missionaries and others, modern forms of education did not take hold in the Gulf States until the middle of the twentieth century. Vast government resources, the result of increases in **oil** revenues, encouraged the expansion of state-sponsored educational systems across the region. As a result, education is dominated by state-financed and -operated institutions with low to no tuition fees.

The past six decades witnessed a proliferation of all types of schooling, ranging from pre-primary classes to institutions of higher learning, across the Gulf States. Concurrent to the spread of formal schooling is the commensurate increase in the adult literacy rate, which averages approximately eighty percent across the region. No modern colleges or universities existed in **Bahrain, Kuwait, Oman, Qatar, Saudi Arabia,** or the **United Arab Emirates** (UAE) before 1950; as of 2003, there were twenty-three across the region, including at least one in each nation.

Quantitative data on education rates in the Gulf region are compiled by the United Nations Educational, Scientific and Cultural Organization (UNESCO). Recent data suggest a wide disparity in education rates across age groups and nations. Pre-primary education for children older than three is not compulsory in any of the Gulf States, prompting wide variations in enrollment rates across the region. In 2004, less than ten percent of pre-primary-aged children attended formal schooling in Oman and Saudi Arabia, whereas over half of similarly aged children attended in Kuwait and the UAE. In most of the region, primary education is compulsory, resulting in markedly higher enrollment rates. Despite these requirements, differences in enrollment rates persist, with Bahrain and Qatar approaching near-universal primary school attendance and Saudi Arabia posting enrollment of only fifty-nine percent in 2004. This trend continues into secondary education with Bahrain and Qatar posting enrollment rates over ninety percent and Saudi Arabia posting a sixty-six percent enrollment rate. A steep dropoff occurs when progressing to levels of higher education with Qatar posting the highest gross enrollment rate of nearly seventeen percent in 1996. Oman maintains the lowest rates of higher education with a gross enrollment of just eight percent in the same year.

The number of children exposed to formal education is on the rise in the region, but questions relating to the quality of education students are receiving in the Gulf States are increasing in salience. Like other facets of society in the region, educational administrators, faculty, and students face difficulties in reconciling the move toward modernization with the region's traditional Islamic values. This tension is evident in three main areas: curriculum development, pedagogical methods, and gender parity of the student population. Traditional culture permeates throughout the primary and secondary schooling experience in the region because of the dominance of Arabic and Islamic studies. The salience of these subjects undercuts the time available to provide students with a strong core of vocational training. Many outside observers argue that the traditional emphasis on language, religion, and regional history fails to prepare students for the realities of joining the modern workforce. As such, some suggest increased focus on science, technical, and English and/or French language instruction.

The tension between traditional and modern cultures exhibits itself in pedagogical methods as well. As an extension of the *kuttab*, there is a tendency to focus on rote memorization as a means of learning material. This method results in students with a strong knowledge base but few skills applicable to the modern work environment. Educational reformers call for more emphasis on the development of critical-thinking and communication skills through problem-solving and reasoning activities rather than rote memorization.

Another concern fostered by the tension between traditional and modern cultures centers on the education of women in the Gulf States. Although girls learned the Qu'ran through the *kuttab*, additional forms of education for women were not encouraged until recently. Views toward the role of women within contemporary Gulf society are changing, accompanied by and allowing for increasing female access to formal schooling at all levels. Expansion of educational opportunities for girls is evident in the gender parity of enrollment ratios in primary schools throughout the Gulf region. Most of the Gulf States also maintain gender parity in secondary schooling, except for Saudi Arabia where approximately eighty-eight females attended for every 100 males in 2004. Somewhat surprisingly, female enrollment outstrips male enrollment in post-secondary educational institutions in many countries in the region.

Discussions concerning the core curricula and methods of instruction represent a shift in the designation of key problems confronting education in the Gulf States. In past decades, concerns are centered on providing education for all children in the region. Although work remains to be done in this area, recent emphasis is shifting to improving the quality of education to produce graduates competitive in the global marketplace.

See also **Universities and Higher Education**.

FURTHER READING

Bahgat, Gawdat. "Education in the Gulf Monarchies: Retrospect and Prospect," *International Review of Education* 45, no. 2 (1999): 127–136.

Bashshur, Munir. *Higher Education in the Arab States*. Beirut: UNESCO Regional Bureau for Education in the Arab States, 2004.

Education for All Global Monitoring Report. *Regional Overview: Arab States*. Paris: UNESCO, 2007.

Mazawi, Andre Elias. "The Contested Terrains of Education in the Arab States: An Appraisal of Major Research Trends," *Comparative Economics Review* 43, no. 3 (1999): 332–352.

Rugh, William A. "Arab Education: Tradition, Growth and Reform," *The Middle East Journal* 56, no. 3 (2002): 396–414.

Rugh, William A. "Education in Saudi Arabia: Choices and Constraints." *Middle East Policy* 9, no. 2 (2002): 40–55.

Emir

Sebastian Maisel

The word emir (*amir*) is derived from Arabic, translating as commander, governor, or prince, and describes an honorary or hereditary title of an independent tribal leader. During the early Islamic period, the same title was used for the commander-in-chief and the provincial governors. The Prophet **Muhammad** was named *amir*, as were his successors, the *khulifa'* or caliphs, who were called *amir al-mu'minin* (commander of the faithful).

Today, *amir* is used as the title of the head of state among several ruling families in **Saudi Arabia** and the Gulf States. The area governed by an *amir* is called *imarah* (emirate), and some emirates are sovereign, independent countries, such as **Kuwait** or the **United Arab Emirates**.

In Saudi Arabia, the title *amir* is also used to describe different political and social positions. The rulers of the second Saudi state elected the title *amir* over the title *imam* (religious leader of the Muslim community), which was used by their predecessors. Other Arab tribal "dynasties" such as the **Al Rashid** of the **Shammar** tribe adopted the same title. Only **'Abd al-'Aziz bin 'Abd al-Rahman**, the founder of the third Saudi state, chose the more secular title *sultan* and later king. In the newly established kingdom, and until today, the title of *amir* is bestowed on the governors of the fifteen provinces. In addition, members of the royal Saudi family are called *amir*, indicating the male and female (*amirah*) offspring of the Saudi king. An *amir* belonging to the immediate lineage of a Saudi king is referred to as His Royal Highness, whereas others are addressed with His Highness.

FURTHER READING

Long, David E. *Culture and Customs of Saudi Arabia*. Westport, CT: Greenwood Press, 2005.

Ethnic Groups
John A. Shoup

Saudi Arabia and the Gulf States are mainly inhabited by Arabs but there are significant numbers of non-Arabs who have lived in the **Arabian Peninsula** for centuries if not millennia. These populations have not assimilated fully into Arab culture, but have retained aspects of their original identity including language. These are not to be confused with those non-Arab populations who have been attracted to the region as a result of the **oil** economies, who usually cannot become citizens and who are considered to be guest workers. The older ethnic minorities have citizenship and in some instances represent an older, indigenous population such as the *Baharnah* of **Bahrain**.

The *Baharnah* in Bahrain are Indo-European, Persian-speaking, and represent some seventy percent of the islands' population. They consider themselves to be the original people of the island and the descendants of the ancient civilization of Dilmun, although most likely they are a mix of Arab, Persian, and Indian peoples who have lived on the island since the pre-Islamic period. The *Baharnah* are concentrated in the agricultural villages in the north of the main island of Bahrain and in **Muharraq** where they still engage in **date** cultivation as well as in fishing, weaving, and pottery production. They are nearly 100% **Shi'ites**, belonging to the 12er Shi'ite rite dominant in Iran. Their Persian differs somewhat from that spoken in Iran and although they consider themselves to be Persians, they do not necessarily consider themselves to be Iranian. Although they are the majority of the population in Bahrain, they were politically and economically marginalized, which gave rise to several acts of violence and support for radical Shi'ite organizations such as the Bahrain Hizballah. King Hamad bin 'Isa Al Khalifah has included them in his new political and economic reforms, and they are now represented in the country's elected parliament.

*Farasi*s, or *'Ajam*, or Persians are the second Indo-European Persian-speaking group in the Gulf, and like the *Baharnah* are one of the oldest in the region. Iran borders the northern limit of the **Persian Gulf**, and historically states based in Iran have exercised a good deal of influence and even direct control over the whole Gulf. Persian speakers have had a long presence in Gulf towns on the southern shore and in Iraq, often being important urban merchants. In the recent past, some of the Gulf's Arab emirates have included both shores of the Gulf, and as a result Iranians were encouraged to settle in their towns such as **Dubai** and **Sharjah**. The Iranians brought with them several technologies including the *barjil*, or wind tower, a traditional form of air conditioning that has become a symbol of the Gulf. Dubai's historic Bastakiyah District is the Iranian quarter of the town that was built in the early twentieth century. Like the *Baharnah*, they tend to be 12er Shi'ites for the most part and have preserved not only their language, but also several customs that differ from those of their Arab neighbors. Nonetheless, the *Farasi*s have been able to integrate into mainstream Gulf society, especially in the **United Arab Emirates** and **Kuwait**, where many have risen to important positions in business.

The Baluch originally are from Baluchistan, a large region that lies mostly inside the modern state of Pakistan though the western part is in Iran. Baluchistan touches the northern shore of the Gulf and several of its port cities were under Arab control until the nineteenth and twentieth centuries. Omani control of some ports ended only in the 1950s. Baluch are Indo-Europeans and their language is a distant relative of Persian (classified as East Iranian, whereas Persian is a West Iranian language). Baluch are **Sunni** Muslims who are both tribally and non-tribally organized. They have been heavily recruited into the militaries by several Arab Gulf rulers for the past several centuries. In many instances the Baluch served in the militaries and as palace guards and then returned to Baluchistan to live out their lives. Others have stayed, particularly in **Oman** and in the United Arab Emirates where they have brought wives from Baluchistan, although some have married local women. Baluch form an important yet small Sunni bloc in Bahrain where they have forged close ties to the ruling family through both **military** and household service.

Oman's overseas empire included not only parts of Pakistan and India, but also much of the East African coast from Somalia to Tanzania. The coastal area had been part of an Arab and Islamic sphere of influence for centuries. Arab, Persian, and Indian Muslims established trade centers as far south as Mozambique, and from this contact the Swahili culture and language emerged. By the time of Oman's expansion in the early nineteenth century, much of the coastal areas and the islands of Lamu, Pemba, and Zanzibar were Muslim and greatly Arabized. African slaves had been sent to the Arabian Peninsula and beyond since the first contacts, and it must be remembered that among the close companions of the

Prophet **Muhammad** was the former slave Bilal. Many of African descent in the Arabian Peninsula, the Gulf, and beyond in the Islamic world identify with Bilal (often called *Sidna Bilal* or Our Master Bilal) as their direct ancestor.

Africans in the Peninsula and Gulf are mainly Arabized today and some have been brought into the families of their former owners, although often as a second lineage and not considered to be of equal status with the full Arab lineage. In nearly all instances, they have Arabized to the degree that they no longer consider themselves or are considered by others to be Africans, but are Arabs. Close connections are often maintained with former owners, and in many of the Gulf States such as Bahrain former slaves are an important core in both the military and the police. In the past freed slaves found work on **pearling** ships or other such occupations.

Swahili is still spoken by both Africans and Arabs in many places in Oman. Some of the Swahili speakers are from families who escaped the bloody uprising in Zanzibar in 1964. Others are descendants of African slaves who although greatly Arabized have preserved their language. Swahili is the language of certain types of **music** in the Gulf region such as al-Liwa and is used in some popular religious practices performed mainly by former slave families such as al-Riwa (a trance dance for curing illnesses that is rarely done today). Swahili remains an important second or third language for many Omanis, and Omani investment in Zanzibar is beginning to return.

The *Hawalah* are another of the ethnic groups in the Gulf region and take their name from the fact that over the centuries they have switched back and forth between the southern and northern shores of the Gulf. Although many have Persian origins they have greatly Arabized, which is helped by the fact that they are Sunnis usually following the Shafi'i school of law. Most of them came back to the southern shore of the Gulf in the nineteenth and early twentieth centuries when the center of the pearl trade also moved to places such as Bahrain and the United Arab Emirates, whereas others arrived after the discovery of oil in the twentieth century. They are a thoroughly urban population and are an important economic bloc, often very supportive of the Sunni leaders in Gulf States. They are easily recognized as most have family names that connect them to places in southern Iran such as Kanu, Fakhru, and Khunji.

The *Bukhari* are Turkish-speaking people, most of whom are Uzbeks from Central Asia. The general term *Bukhari* comes from the fact that many carry al-Bukhari as a last name although al-Andajani and al-Samarqandi are also common last names. The *Bukhari* are Sunni Muslims, and most of them came following the 1918 Bolshevik Revolution when Muslim religious leaders and scholars began being persecuted. As a result of repressive measures by the Bolsheviks, those who could escaped, and many found final refuge in **Saudi Arabia**. They have settled in several towns and cities in Saudi Arabia, although **Makkah** and **Madinah** were where most wanted to live. They have been able to maintain use of their own language at home, and some younger people have been able to study at universities in Turkey as a result. They are an educated urban population and are active in business as well as in fine crafts such as making the gold thread embroidery pieces for the *kiswah* or cover for the Ka'abah in Makkah.

There are several other very small ethnic minorities in the Gulf and Saudi Arabia, some numbering only in the hundreds. The Khojah are a very small

145

population living in several Gulf port cities who are descendants of Hindu merchants who converted to Islam. The word Khojah is Turkish and means "a gentleman" or "an educated man" and perhaps was used originally because the community was (and still is) composed of merchants. The largest Khojah population lives in **Musqat** in Oman, although they are found in nearly every port city of the Gulf. In addition to the Khojah are small numbers of Indian Hindus whose ancestors arrived in the pre-oil days and have citizenship. The largest of this Hindu population are in Bahrain where they are an important part of the local economy. Their ancestors moved from cities such as Bombay to Bahrain, where they set up shops dealing with international pearl buyers.

See also **Madhhab**.

FURTHER READING

Coles, Anne, and Peter Jackson. *Windtower*. London: Stacey International, 2007.
Dubai Municipality. *Folk Songs and Dances. The United Arab Emirates*. Dubai: Dubai Municipality, 1996.
Heard-Bey, Frauke. *From Trucial States to United Arab Emirates*. Dubai: Motivate Publishing, 2004.
Insoll, Timothy. *The Archaeology of Islam in Sub-Saharan Africa*. Cambridge, UK: Cambridge University Press, 2003.
Khuri, Fuad. "From Tribe to State in Bahrain," in *Arab Society. Social Science Perspective*, edited by Nicholas Hopkins and Saad Eddin Ibrahim. Cairo: American University in Cairo Press, 1987.

Ethnicity

Sebastian Maisel

The ethnic composition of **Saudi Arabia** and the Gulf States is heterogenic and includes a variety of ethnic elements, both indigenous and foreign. Citizenship of those states is based on the concept of ethnicity. A major criterion for defining citizenship is for the individual to prove belonging to or descent from one of the recognized **ethnic groups**. Originally, the population of the **Arabian Peninsula** was Arab with small Persian, Turkish, and Indian communities. With the establishment of nation states and the area's transformation in the wake of the **oil** boom, new ethnic groups migrated to the region and a selection had to be made on who is considered a citizen and who is only a resident. Only citizens fully enjoy all of the social and economic benefits. However, with the exception of Saudi Arabia and **Oman**, in all other Gulf States, citizens are in the minority, in some cases as little as twenty-five percent.

The influential notion of pan-Arabism under Egyptian president Gamal 'Abd al-Nasir in the 1950s and 1960s never really picked up in the Gulf area, mainly because of the closeness of the tribal society and its efforts to maintain the homogenous character and access to resources as well as because of the rivalries between the Egyptian and Saudi ruler over the leadership of the pan-Arab movement. As Arabs, all of the countries support the struggle of the Palestinians with **military**, economic, and financial help. Of particular importance was the issue of refugees. Gulf States willingly accepted and welcomed them. Many of the Palestinians had higher **education** levels than most of the nationals, but rarely were they granted citizenship.

The Iranian Revolution also had a tremendous impact on the development of ethnic identities in the area. Although primarily a religious movement, it also represented an Iranian element in conjunction with **Shi'ite** Islam, a combination that all of the rulers of the Gulf States, and all those who were **Sunni** Arabs, were very concerned with. To maintain stability and to legitimize their rule of the countries and resources, a fragile network of ethnic interaction was formed. Under the leadership of a ruling family, all citizens participated in and benefited from the oil boom. The status quo was to be maintained in order to guarantee stable oil production. Unfortunately for the local rulers, most of the people living in the area of the oil fields (although of Arab origin) were Shi'ites, and flags were raised over alleged collaboration between them and their brothers in religion from Iran. Tensions were high, and Shi'ite uprisings in the Eastern Province of Saudi Arabia and demonstrations and clashes in **Makkah** during the **pilgrimage** clearly showed the necessity of finding an ethnic and religious middle ground. The governments, however, chose to side with Iraq in its war with Iran, supplying unlimited amounts of money and weapons to the Iraqi (Sunni and Arab) government in order to be protected from Iranian exports of revolution and destabilization. During the following 1990–1991 war between Iraq and an international alliance of troops over the occupation of **Kuwait**, Palestinians expressed their support for Saddam Hussein, which in return led to the expulsion of hundreds of thousands of Palestinians from the Gulf States. The same happened in Saudi Arabia and other Gulf States to the **Yemeni** community when political leaders and the public cheered for the occupier of Kuwait and possible aggressor against Saudi Arabia. Only in this case was the number of expelled Yemeni guest-workers much higher, reaching almost 1 million.

Less than half of Kuwait's population, according to the status of citizenship, is actually indigenous (i.e., was granted citizenship). They are mostly Arabs. Arabs from other Arabic countries, such as **Palestine**, Egypt and Iraq, form another important block in the Arab identity of the country; but most people in Kuwait are expatriates, coming mainly from Southeast Asian countries such as India, Pakistan, and the Philippines. A large Persian community is found because of the proximity of Iran. Kurds from Iraq who fled from Saddam Hussein's regime add to the Indo-European feature of Kuwait, and so do several thousand Europeans and Americans.

Bahrain faces a similar problem, where a small religious minority rules over a majority that is different in terms of their religious and often ethnic background. The ruling Sunni group is of Arab descent, whereas the Shi'ites are split between ethnic Arabs (*Baharnah*) and Persians (*'Ajam*). Still two-thirds of the population are Bahraini nationals, but the other third are again from Southeast Asia. Some Indian families (*Bunyan*) have lived in Bahrain for many generations and have been nationalized and distinguished from recent guestworkers. Among the Bahraini citizens, the majority is Shi'ite and usually underrepresented and less privileged than Sunnis in Bahrain.

Saudi Arabia has a very homogenous population excluding the guestworkers that make up twenty percent of the overall population. Almost all Saudis are Arabs. A small ethnic minority are black Saudis, descendants of former slaves from Africa. Another ethnic group comes from central Asia: families of pilgrims who decided to stay in the **Hijaz**. Other Arabs come from Egypt, Yemen, and Sudan, but they do not have citizenship. People from Southeast Asia, Pakistan, India, Sri Lanka, and the Philippines form the largest non-Arab community.

A rather controversial division is seen in **Qatar**, where forty percent of the population is Arab, followed by a combined thirty-five percent of Pakistanis, Indians, and others from Southeast Asia, as well as a significant ten percent Iranian minority. Qatari natives originated from tribes that migrated to the area from **Najd** and **al-Hasa**, whereas others descended from Omani tribes.

The **United Arab Emirates** are predominantly Sunni Arab, but have a fifteen percent Shi'ite minority, many of them of Iranian or Baluchi descent. **Dubai** established good business relations with neighboring Iran. They earned big revenues from the first Gulf War but maintained their contacts with Iran, even allowing local Persians to participate in Iranian presidential elections. More than fifty percent of the population in the Emirates comes from South and Southeast Asia (India, Afghanistan, Bangladesh, Pakistan, etc.). National Emiratis form only twenty-five percent of the country's population.

Sultan Qabus of Oman follows a moderate and successful political attempt to control the ethnic and religious pluralism of his country. The majority of the population are ethnic Arabs, but of mixed background. Still many southern Arabs live in the **Dhufar** region, which unsuccessfully tried to break away from the central government in **Musqat**. Although northern and southern Arabs are both Semitic, they speak distinct variants of Arabic. The diverse religious setup of the country helps to stabilize ethnic conflicts. Most people in Oman are *Ibadi Kharaji*, but because of the presence of many Sunni Arabs and non-Muslims from India and Pakistan as well as Shi'ites, a balance of co-existence is maintained by the government.

FURTHER READING

Brand, Laurie. *Citizens Abroad: Emigration and the State in the Middle East and North Africa.* Cambridge, UK: Cambridge University Press, 2006.

Kapiszewski, Andrzej. *Nationals and Expatriates: Population and Labour Dilemmas of the Gulf Cooperation Council States.* Reading, UK: Garnet, 2001.

Metz, Helen (ed.). *Persian Gulf States: Country Studies.* Washington, D.C.: Federal Research Division, Library of Congress, 1994.

Al-Ostad, Ameer. "An Ethnic Geography of Kuwait: A Study of Eight Ethnic Groups." PhD dissertation, Kent State University, 1986.

Yamani, Mai. *Cradle of Islam: The Hijaz and the Quest for an Arabian Identity.* London: I.B. Tauris, 2004.

F

Fahd bin 'Abd al-'Aziz (1922–2005)

Sebastian Maisel

The fifth king of **Saudi Arabia**, Fahd bin 'Abd al-'Aziz Al Sa'ud, was born in 1922. Following the regular succession to the throne, he became king in 1982 after his half-brother Khalid died. Fahd is one of the Sudayri Seven, a sibling group of seven full brothers, sons of Hussa al-Sudayri, who maintain crucial positions within the inner circle of power. They include current crown Prince Sultan, minister of interior Prince Nayif, and governor of **Riyadh** Prince Salman. Before his enthronement, Fahd held various political posts including Minister of Education (1953), Minister of Interior (1962–1975), second Deputy Prime Minister (1968–1975), first Deputy Prime Minister (1975–1982), and Crown Prince (1975–1982). As King of **Saudi Arabia** he automatically resumed the title of Prime Minister in 1982. Because of King Khalid's poor health, Fahd was unofficially acting prime minister and regent.

Fahd continued the same **foreign policies** of his predecessors that included close ties with the United States, suspicion of **Shi'ite** Iran, and support of the Palestinians. He showed his commitment to Islam by adopting the title "Custodian of the Two Holy Places" instead of "His Majesty the King," and spent large amounts on extending the mosques in **Makkah** and **Madinah** as well as other religious institutions abroad. Saddam Hussein challenged his authority during the **Gulf War**; and after stationing American and other foreign troops in Saudi Arabia to protect the country, Islamic militant opposition groups objected to the fact that infidels defend the Holy Places. However, in the early 1990s he initiated political reforms culminating in the introduction of a codified system of governance or basic law of Saudi Arabia in 1992. Other domestic policies were concerned with economical change after the country suffered massive losses and huge budget deficits with the fall of **oil** prices in the 1980s. His development plans called for diversification, foreign investment, and adjustments to the global economy.

In 1995 he suffered a stroke that forced him to delegate most of the official business to his half-brother and Crown Prince 'Abdallah; however, 'Abdallah was still restricted by Fahd in his decision-making for over a decade, thus creating a long period of stagnation. This era was further shattered by an increase in violence and fighting with militant Islamic opposition groups, including **al-Qa'idah**, who has attacked government institutions, citizens, foreigners, Muslims, and non-Muslims alike since 2003 in their struggle to bring down the **Al Sa'ud** government.

Fahd reacted with strong security measurements and crackdowns on opposition groups in general.

FURTHER READING

Farsy, Fouad. *Custodian of the Two Holy Mosques, King Fahd bin Abdul Aziz*. Guernsey, UK: Knight Communications, 2001.

Reed, Jennifer. *The Saudi Royal Family*. New York: Chelsea House, 2006.

Reich, Bernard (ed.). *Political Leaders of the Contemporary Middle East and North Africa*. Westport, CT: Greenwood Press, 1990.

Family Life
Sebastian Maisel

The extended family is the most important social unit in Arabia. Every Arab in **Saudi Arabia** and the Gulf States belongs to this extended group of close relatives, which provides the core layer of identification and loyalty. Some families are larger than others, whereas other families choose to live in alliance with other related families and form tribes. This concept has not changed for more than 2,000 years despite the rapid **modernization** and upheaval in society and culture.

Families in Arabia have been described as patriarchal, patrilinear, patrilocal, endogamous, and occasionally polygamous. Patriarchal refers to the authority within the family being in the hands of the elder male members. Patrilinear alludes to the origin and descent of the group through the male bloodline. Patrilocal means that adult sons and their families live with their father. Endogamous refers to the preference of marrying within the same kin group, which can be polygamous, although Islamic law has injunctions on the degree of closeness of kin for related co-wives.

The living and working conditions in Arabia required families to work and stick together. This sense of togetherness or solidarity has survived among all tribally organized groups. The extended family is kept together by sharing the same morals and values as well as material interests. Single family members usually remained with the family, and couples live with the husband's family. If they choose to live in their own house, they would not give up their ties to the extended family. Widows can return to their families and bring back children up to a certain age. Divorcees are taken in under the premise that they remarry quickly. If family members visit each other, the rules of hospitality apply: relatives are always protected and receive special treatment.

In addition to the intellectual strengthening of the family, they also work on the material improvement and view children as the best investment in the future, because sons and even single daughters can take care of their parents. Social acceptance and reputation increase with the number of children, especially boys, in a family. A large number of children can prevent a **divorce**, because of the moral standards of the community. Family planning is very uncommon in Arabia, although governments of some Gulf States promote family planning through sex **education** programs or prescription of contraceptives. For birth control, Islam allows the method of *'azl, coitus interuptus* but specifically prohibits the killing of female infants, which was custom in pre-Islamic Arabia because of concerns for the economy and reputation. Abortion is permitted until the fourth month and only if the pregnancy is a risk for the mother. Islam requires parents to treat all children fairly and justly. Equality is required in polygamous relationships, which occur very rarely. The husband is allowed to marry four women at the same time, if he can provide for them equally. He is responsible for their living and expenses (i.e., not only for his wife and children, but also for other family members without income such as unmarried siblings or old relatives, uncles, aunts, etc.). He is also concerned about the reputation of his family and represents them in legal matters. His **honor** and the honor of his family depend upon the moral behavior of the female members of the group. He expects faithfulness from his wife, chastity from his unmarried female siblings, and a reclusive life of widows in the family. Sons, brothers, and cousins protect the honor and morality of their female relatives. They are allowed to check on them and force them to obey. Men are usually busy with all of the things around the house, whereas women take care of the housework. Their shares include taking care of the children, taking care of the house, and helping with agriculture. Women with jobs outside the house normally get support with taking care of the children from other members of the tribal network. Girls are usually tied to the house, just like their mothers and aunts. They have to help with the chores such as cooking, cleaning, or childcare. Boys are subordinated to the authority of the father and often play and work outside the house. The structure of an extended family is shown through a variety of legal norms such as **marriage**, divorce, and inheritance as well as through a certain dress code. According to the Qur'an, men do have authority over women, and in reality fathers, brothers, uncles, or cousins exercise their power. Despite the separation of sexes as required in some countries, mothers always had a highly esteemed position and reputation in Arab society. Mothers exercise their influence in the family and contribute to the decision-making process at home. According to tradition, elder people are highly respected and enjoy a hierarchical eminence. It is them who ultimately decide the fate of the family and are in charge of most customs and traditions, such as circumcision, marriage, games, socialization, and death.

FURTHER READING

Bowen, Donna Lee, and Evelyn A. Early. *Everyday Life in the Muslim Middle East.* Bloomington: Indiana University Press, 2002.

Ismael, Jacqueline S., and Nancy Walstrom. *Turbulent Times and Family Life in the Contemporary Middle East.* Calgary: University of Calgary Press, 2004.

Long, David E. *Culture and Customs of Saudi Arabia.* Westport, CT: Greenwood Press, 2005.

Shechter, Relli. *Transitions in Domestic Consumption and Family Life.* New York: Palgrave MacMillan, 2003.

Faysal bin Abd al-Aziz (1905–1975)

Sebastian Maisel

The third king of **Saudi Arabia**, Faysal bin 'Abd al-'Aziz Al Sa'ud, was born in 1905. He began ruling the kingdom as king in 1964; concurrently as *Imam* he led the **Wahhabi** authority. His father was the founder of the kingdom, and through his mother Tarfah he is related to the other influential family, the Al al-Shaykh, who trace their origin back to the founder of the reform movement in the eighteenth century, **Muhammad bin 'Abd al-Wahhab**. If **'Abd al-'Aziz** is considered the creator of the kingdom, Faysal was beyond a doubt the architect of the modern Kingdom of Saudi Arabia.

From 1926 until 1960 he was Vice Regent for the **Hijaz**. Other important positions in the leadership and government of Saudi Arabia included Crown Prince (1953–1964), Prime Minister (1958–1960, 1960, and 1962–1975), and Foreign Minister (1953–1960 and 1962–1975). After a long power struggle with his brother, King Sa'ud bin 'Abd al-'Aziz, he finally succeeded in forcing his abdication in 1964, and Faysal was chosen as king by the **Al Sa'ud** family council. In both his domestic and **foreign policy**, he followed pan-Islamic principles and enforced an opening of the country and the society toward the West. The growing **oil** revenues were used to modernize the kingdom gradually while maintaining its Islamic character and values. During his rule, many universities and schools, including those for girls, were founded. He abolished slavery by royal decree and introduced **television** in the late 1960s. In order to extend central rule of all social groups in the country, he announced a national policy to settle the remaining nomadic **Bedouin**. During the **Yemeni** civil war, he supported the Royalists against his main regional political rival, Egypt's president Jamal 'Abd al-Nasir. His pan-Islamic policies were seen as an attempt to counter Nasr's pan-Arabism. Although a close ally of the United States and an anti-communist, he strongly supported the Palestinian struggle for independence and in 1973 during the October War he proclaimed an oil embargo against several Western nations who supported Israel financially and militarily against previous declarations and agreements. On March 25, 1975, he was killed during a public meeting by his nephew Faysal bin Musa'id bin 'Abd al-'Aziz, an act that is widely believed to be in retaliation for the shooting of Faysal bin Musa'id's brother Khalid in a demonstration against the introduction of television. Faysal was succeeded by his half-brother Khalid bin 'Abd al-'Aziz. Many of his sons, including Sa'ud, Khalid, and Turki, hold high-ranking positions in the Saudi government.

See also **Education**.

FURTHER READING

de Gaury, Gerald. *Faysal: King of Saudi Arabia*. New York: Praeger, 1966.
"King Faisal: Oil, Wealth and Power," *Time*, April 7, 1975.

Reich, Bernard (ed.). *Political Leaders of the Contemporary Middle East and North Africa*. Westport, CT: Greenwood Press, 1990.

Festivals in the United Arab Emirates

Carla Higgins

Festivals and conferences play a key role in the efforts of the **United Arab Emirates** (UAE) to raise its profile as a tourist destination, promote itself as a business hub, encourage commerce, and create public discourse about local issues. This $3.27 billion industry is being consolidated into a corporation, the UAE Exhibitions and Conferences Authority, and organized under the UAE Ministry of Economy and Planning, as well as the Chambers of Commerce from each emirate.

Sharjah initiated conferences in 1977 when it opened its Expo Center. Since 1982, it has hosted an international book fair designed to promote reading among youth, as well as to make a variety of books available and affordable to Emirati citizens. The Sharjah World Book Fair is a direct result of the ruler, *Shaykh* Dr. Sultan bin Muhammad **al Qasimi**, and his vision of promoting **education** within Sharjah and beyond.

The National Careers Exhibition is another annual education-related event aimed at Emirati citizens interested in banking and finance. Sharjah also hosts TEXPO, an international exhibition for trade in the garments industry; Mideast Watch and **Jewelry** Shows; and an Arab Asia Trade Fair. In 2002 it inaugurated Expo City, a multipurpose facility with four exhibition halls.

Dubai has become the leader in the conference/exhibitions industry. In the 1980s, Dubai built the Dubai World Trade Center as part of a huge exhibition complex and began hosting a wide array of exhibitions—early examples focus on electronics, fashion, health, and engineering. Dubai launched the concept of festivals in 1996 with the Dubai Shopping Festival, now an international hit that brings citizens from all over the Middle East to shop. Dubai Summer Surprises emerged in 2003 as the second annual shopping festival, with an emphasis on entertaining children while school is out.

Examples of conferences that Dubai hosts now include the Gulf Information Technology Exhibition, known as GITEX; the Arabian Travel Market; Gulfood; the Bride Show, Cable, Satellite; Careers UAE; Dubai 200 (Aerospace Exhibition); Dubai: The City That Cares; Leaders in Dubai; the WOIBEX Forum on Women; the Dubai International Film Festival; the Dubai International Music Festival; and the Philips Dubai International Jazz Festival.

Abu Dhabi is becoming a player in event hosting. In 1998 it created the General Exhibitions Corporation (GEC), which later became the Abu Dhabi National Exhibition Company in 2005. Abu Dhabi boasts a new Abu Dhabi

International Exhibitions Center (ADIEC), a 500,000 square meter conference facility. The new the Emirates Palace hotel provides luxurious and state-of-the-art facilities needed to host any and all conferences. Future plans are to build an Abu Dhabi World Trade Center.

Examples of Abu Dhabi conferences include the Abu Dhabi International Petroleum Exhibition & Conference (ADIPEC), the International Defense Exhibition and Conference (IDEX), and the Festival of Thinkers.

The three Emirates of 'Ajman, Ra's al-Khaymah, and Fujayrah have all developed exhibition facilities to host seasonal fairs for the general public, such as Summer Festivals, Back to School Exhibits, and *Ramadan* festivals.

FURTHER READING

"Exhibitions and Events," in *United Arab Emirates Yearbook*. Abu Dhabi: United Arab Emirates Ministry of Information and Culture, 2006.

Film Industry
Sebastian Maisel

In comparison to other Middle Eastern areas, particularly Egypt and the Maghrib, the film industry of **Saudi Arabia** and the Gulf States is less vibrant and developed. However, when the industry in Egypt experienced serious funding issues starting in the 1970s because of governmental budget cutbacks, sponsors from the **Arabian Gulf** helped produce and finance many film projects, including *The Message* (1976 by Mustafa Akkad) and *Rana's Wedding* (2002 by Hany Abu Assad).

The film industry of the Gulf States started in the 1930s with short documentaries about social life in the Gulf area, but it took nearly four decades before the first feature film, *The Storm*, was made in **Kuwait** and the entire Arabian Gulf in 1965 by Muhammad al-Sanusi. Other short films (e.g., by Khalid al-Sadiq) and documentaries followed soon afterward. Sadiq's first feature film, *Bas Ya Bahr* (Dangerous Sea) from 1972, was also the first film to cast exclusively Kuwaiti actors and staff. The experiment worked, and the film enjoyed Arab and international success. His second feature film, *The Wedding of Zain* (1977), was based on the novel of the same name by Sudanese author al-Tayib Salih. For his 1995 short film *Shahin*, he used for the first time an international work of literature as a model for his film. Sadiq was both producer and director and managed to get international support from India and Italy. Unfortunately, the film has not been shown yet because some reels went missing. Although small in number, all Kuwaiti films are described by their sense of realism with themes of life before the discovery of **oil** in Kuwait. They help to bridge the gap between the past and present, where the traditional reality has vanished and lives on in the memory of the film director. Newer productions include *Cool Youth* (2004) by Muhammad al-Shammari and *Midnight* (2005) by Abdallah al-Salman.

In **Bahrain**, the origins of the film industry go back to the mid-1970s, when the first attempts were made to produce a local feature film. In 1975, Bassam al-Thawadi introduced first his short documentary and then the feature film *al-Hajiz* (The Barrier). It took until 2003 to come up with his second film, *Visitor*, which turned out to be successful mostly because Thawadi chose topics that were popular in the audience. Another film by Thawadi was made in 2006 called *A Bahraini Tale*. More films are likely to come out of Bahrain after the establishment of the Bahrain Film Production Company. Movie theaters are found all over the country showing Western and Indian productions. During the annual film festival, feature films from other Arab countries are shown.

Although public movie theaters are banned in Saudi Arabia, in recent years it has witnessed small steps to bring back films to the audience. It started in the more liberal areas of the kingdom, the Eastern Province and **Jiddah**, with private and semi-private viewings and film festivals in 2005 and continued with the country's first feature film *Kayf al-Hal?* (How are you?), which was produced by Ayman al-Halawani and directed by Palestinian-Canadian Izidore Mussalam and shown at the Cannes Film Festival. The film is almost entirely in Saudi **Arabic** dialect and aims at discussing cultural issues in the kingdom, particularly **women's rights**. Prince al-Walid bin Talal, owner of market leader Rotana, produced the film, which cannot be shown in the kingdom. However, it reaches the audience through DVDs, pay-per-view TV, and the Rotana movie channel. In the feature-length documentary *Cinema 500km*, the story of a young Saudi cinema lover is told, who travels all the way to Bahrain to watch his first movie in a cinema. The Ministry of Culture and Information granted permission to produce the film in the kingdom, although it cannot be shown there. The film directed by 'Abdallah al-Iyaf premiered at the Emirates Film Competition in 2006. The film industry in Saudi Arabia lacks professional schools and training, production **companies**, and usually official support. But individuals like al-Iyaf or filmmaker Haifa Mansoor with her 2006 award-winning documentary *Nissa bila dhill* (Women without Shadows) began challenging those difficulties and developing a small sector of both feature and documentary films. The supportive role of Prince al-Walid cannot be underestimated, especially for future projects.

Although there are many movie theaters in the **United Arab Emirates**, they predominantly show Western and Indian films. Only on rare occasions, such as the annual Dubai Film Festival or the Emirates Film Competition, are local and regional productions shown. Only one feature film, *al-Hilm* (The Dream), came out from the Emirates in 2007; however, there is an active scene of short filmmakers called the Emerging Emirates that produced some twenty short films over the last few years that includes Nayla Al Khaja (the first female director), 'Abdullah Ahmad, and Jasim al-Salty. They cover issues of social conflict and problems between the generations. As part of official investments in the **media** and arts, Dubai Studio City was created to provide for the various film production needs.

The film industry in **Oman** is almost nonexistent with only one feature film released by 2007, called *al-Bum* (type of **dhow**), directed by Khalid al-Zajali. The drama talks about a personal conflict between a modernist and a traditionalist placed in the setting of an old fishing village. Although there is an annual film festival, the local market is not developed and relies mainly on Indian films. Very few cinemas exist.

FURTHER READING

Leaman, Oliver. *The Companion Encyclopedia of Middle Eastern and North African Films.* New York: Routledge, 2001.

Shafik, Viola. *Arab History: History and Culture.* Cairo: American University of Cairo Press, 2007.

Fine Arts

Sebastian Maisel

Plastic arts in Arabia have never been able to step out of the overwhelming shadow of the various forms of literary expression. The dictum of not depicting human forms was upheld in the Peninsula in contrast to other Muslim areas such as Persia or India. However, economic development brought rapid and distinct cultural change, which is reflected in the evolution of vibrant modern arts scenes throughout the Gulf area. Concurrently with the development of a modern and post-modern art scene, Islamic art continued growing. Some artists combined religious tradition with modern techniques.

The first modern art exhibit in the **Arabian Gulf** was opened in 1959 in **Kuwait**. A year later, the Free Atelier began offering art courses, supplies, and venues. This model, which also includes state-funded full-time artists, was introduced in **Qatar**, **Oman**, and the **United Arab Emirates**. **Saudi Arabia** was the first Gulf State to offer art **education** for male students at the university level since 1965. In 1969, the Modern Art Society of **Bahrain** was founded as the first of its kind in the area. With the growing development of the countries, additional outlets for the arts and artists became necessary and resulted in the formation of the Kuwaiti National Council for Culture, Arts, and Letters and the Saudi Arabian Society for Culture and Arts, with the goal to channel, supervise, and support the fast-growing art scene. Additional free ateliers and art societies throughout the peninsula were established, which all enjoyed financial support from **oil** revenues.

This support is extended in Oman to the country's contemporary art movement, where the Atelier for Fine Arts in **Masqat** was established to provide art education and patronage. From this institution, the Omani sisters Nadira bint Mahmud and Rabha bint Mahmud emerged as the region's most prolific abstractionists. Today, the contemporary art scene is slowly attempting to introduce new mediums and venues to move beyond the label of national art. Since 2000 the gallery Bayt Muzna has been a pioneer in bringing in Omani and international artists who push the boundaries of modern art.

However, the art scene of the area not only drew from petrol-related sources, it also relied on the long tradition and history of civilization and interaction with other cultures. In particular, the small but active art scene in Bahrain draws from the ancient heritage of Dilmun, and today three leading galleries exhibit national and international artists who reflect on these themes. The goals of the Bahraini Art Society, established in 1982, were to create an independent, non-for-profit institution that enabled its members to participate in the development of the art scene in the Arabian Gulf. The Ministry of Information in Bahrain became a major patron of the local arts, organizing solo and group exhibitions and granting awards to successful artists. The annual art exhibition of fine arts in conjunction with the National Museum is the culminating event of the Bahraini art scene.

Over the years, the government of Kuwait has sponsored the development of fine art through scholarships, funds, and educational institutions. In 1960, the "Free Studio" was founded to encourage art students and to provide professional instruction and technical help. Several galleries exhibit the works of local and foreign artists. In 1983 the Kuwait National Museum opened to the public, exhibiting among other things contemporary Kuwaiti art from the **Al Sabah** collection.

In the **Shariqah** (**Sharjah**) Emirate, the Art Museum was inaugurated to house artwork from the Sharjah International Art Biennial, which opened in 1993 and by 2003 started to bring international artists to the Gulf. With bold and controversial themes, it stands out and attracts large crowds of participants and spectators every year. Sharjah is also home to the oldest art association in the Emirates, which started around 1987. Its rich and huge catalogues indicate how the art scene has matured and diversified over the last three decades.

Although Qatar promotes its artistic scene as predominantly Islamic, there are nevertheless significant contributions to the field of art education, especially through the School of Arts at Virginia Commonwealth University in Qatar, which was founded in 2001. The Fine Arts Society of Qatar focuses on exhibiting local artists in some galleries in the capital **Doha**. The governmental National Council for Culture, Arts, and Heritage sponsors and organizes art-related events in order to promote **tourism**.

In the region's fastest-growing city, **Dubai**, more than twenty art galleries help to create and preserve the city's multicultural identity on the basis of a combination of creativity and economical development that attracts foreign and local visitors alike. In neighboring **Abu Dhabi**, the former slower pace of growth has caught up and competes with Dubai. It began with the opening of the Abu Dhabi Culture and Heritage Authority and its Cultural Foundation, the main concern of which was to offer space and support for artists and collectors. In addition, they worked on bringing world-class museums to the Emirate, including the Guggenheim, which is scheduled to open in 2012.

The art scene in Saudi Arabia is a reflection of the country's cultural development, which is based on modernization and preservation of Islamic and traditional forms and values. Although modern and contemporary art needs artists, it also requires an educated class of art lovers and space to exhibit. The kingdom is gradually offering more room for artists to express themselves in public galleries and art shows. Talented young artists are now able to create and exhibit art as long as they follow the country's strict moral guidelines. The Mansouriyah

Foundation in **Jiddah** facilitates the growing bond between artist and audience with exhibitions, publications, and the kingdom's first collection of contemporary Saudi art. Other patrons of the arts include Prince Khalid bin Faysal, himself a renowned artist and painter, and the city of Jiddah, which commissioned sculptors to create some 300 large plastics and statues along the roundabouts on the Corniche representing aspects of modern technology and traditional **cultural heritage**. They represent the city's strife for civic beauty in a hostile, arid environment. Jiddah stands out among the Saudi cities as a patron of the arts with its many galleries, artists, and art centers. The Darah Binzagr, home, studio, and gallery of one of Saudi Arabia's most prolific and acclaimed painters, Safeya Binzagr, is only one of them. The government maintains its influence over the art scene through the Saudi Arabian Society for Culture and Arts, which sponsors and supports artists, facilitates exhibitions, and raises the level of artistic awareness in the society.

FURTHER READING

Ball-Lechgar, Lisa. "Fresh Gulf Currents," *Saudi Aramco World* 58, no. 6 (2007): 2–13.
Fullerton, Arlene, and Géza Fehérvári. *Kuwait: Arts and Architecture*. Kuwait: No publisher stated, 1995.
Long, David. *Culture and Customs of Saudi Arabia*. Westport, CT: Greenwood Press, 2005.
Rajab, Tareq Sayid. *Tareq Sayid Rajab and the Development of Fine Art in Kuwait*. Kuwait: No publisher stated, 2001.
Al-Salem, Mohammad, and Saad al-Obaied. *Fine Arts: Exhibition of Riyadh Yesterday and Today*. Riyadh: Saudi Arabian Cultural and Arts Society, 1986.

Fiqh

Sebastian Maisel

The Arabic meaning of *fiqh* is knowledge or comprehension and it is defined as Islamic jurisprudence. It combines the doctrines of the sources (*usul al-fiqh*, i.e., the Qur'an and *Hadith*), and the doctrine of its practical regulations (*furu' al-fiqh*). Both are part of a wide array of literature; however, a codified and comprehensive set of rules that applies to all Islamic groups does not exist. In contrast to the **Shari'ah**, which is part of the divine Islamic law, *fiqh* is based on human interpretation of the sources.

The legal scholars, *faqih* (plural *fuqaha'*) in Arabic, refer in their ruling to selected sources and books, which are interpreted in a way to find legal "tricks," *hiyal*, to avoid the harsh regulations of Islamic law. These tricks are often used in trade and property law, but are also found in the area of ritual regulations. Important bases for all **Sunni** scholars are adjudications by scholars from al-Azhar University in Cairo, where all four schools of law are present. **Shi'ite** scholars prefer adjudications from the Islamic university in Najaf in Iraq and Qum in Iran. For example, Islam prohibits earning interest; however, the rule can be avoided by purchasing shares and earning a dividend (i.e., part of the overall profit), which is legal. In this way, an entire banking system evolved that did not violate *Shari'ah*.

Prior to **Muhammad**'s revelations, law was a matter of knowledge of local traditions; however, experts had no authority, and law was enforced through oath and bails or other means of guaranties. Muhammad became the first Islamic arbitrator, and was succeeded by the caliphs. Under the Umayyads, for the first time independent judges were appointed who used reasoning and local customs to come to their conclusions. Formal schools of legal thought were established after the eighth century under the rule of 'Abbasid. Until the tenth century, Islamic law was codified by using *ijtihad*, or independent reasoning; however, later the more dogmatic trend of *taqlid*, or imitation, gained importance within the Sunni schools of law. With the establishment and consolidation of contemporary Islamic countries in the nineteenth and twentieth centuries, legal norms based on Western concepts of jurisprudence began to limit the spheres of Islamic regulations. In addition, calls for updating and abolishing outdated regulations became louder. However, in the 1970s during a time of Islamic revival, some Arab countries tried to re-establish the older ethic and moral values expressed in the Islamic law.

Islamic jurisprudence is based on four sources. The first source is the Qur'an, which has approximately 500 verses relating to legal issues. The second is the ***sunnah***, or traditions, which describe the sayings and deeds of the Prophet Muhammad that were narrated in the *Hadith*. The *Hadith* have been collected and cited since the early decades of Islam. Six *Hadith* collections are considered to be authentic, that is, containing sayings that can be verified through an unbroken *isnad*, or chain of narrators of undisputed good authority. The two most influential of these collections are by al-Bukhari and ibn Muslim. The third source is *ijma'* or consensus of the Muslim community (although this can be interpreted as the community of scholars rather than all Muslims). The fourth main source is *qiyas* or reasoned analogy although Hanbali jurists usually reject both *qiyas* and *ijma'* because they depend on man rather than on the divine word of God. Other secondary sources generally not included in decisions today include *'urf* (custom), *ra'i* (opinion), and *ijtihad* (reasoning) although *ijtihad* is still used by *Kharaji* and *Shi'i* scholars. *Ijtihad* has been replaced by *taqlid* for the four major schools of Sunni Islam.

Four main schools of interpreting Islamic law and applying Islamic jurisprudence developed over time: Hanafi, Maliki, Shafi'i, and Hanbali, each named for their founders. **Saudi Arabia**'s dominant school is Hanbali and the teachings of **Muhammad ibn 'Abd al-Wahhab** are based on this school. In the **Hijaz**, the Shafi'i School prevailed until the region was incorporated into Saudi Arabia in the 1920s. In the eastern part of the **Arabian Peninsula**, particularly in **Kuwait** and **Bahrain**, the Maliki School is the most widespread. Shi'ites in Saudi Arabia and other Gulf States follow the Ja'afari School, whereas the Ibadis of **Oman** have their own school, but both are often regarded as semi-official by the Sunni schools.

The practical application of Islamic Law is called *furu' al-fiqh*, or branches of the jurisdiction, which is based on a collection of cases and rules. Every scholar can give a legal opinion in any given case called a *fatwa*. A *fatwa* requires the use of all of the accepted sources of Islamic law to solve a case or give a ruling on an issue. *Fatwas* are usually binding when given by a *mufti* in service of a state, but are not binding on individuals and can be contradicted by a ruling by another religious scholar. Human actions are usually classified as obligatory, commendable, indifferent, objectionable, and forbidden, and punishments for infractions are given out accordingly.

The regulation of individual cases is described in thematic books by authors from all different schools of law. They usually start with their interpretations of the rituals followed by marital, criminal, political, procedural, and economical cases and finish with regulations for inheritance. Most of the schools of law emphasize reconciliation between the parties before taking a suit to court. In most of the Arab Gulf States, the ruler is the final court of appeal; however, his interpretation and ruling must be consistent with the usual legal consensus of the leading Islamic legal scholars. For this, the ruler is subject to the law and can be sued in court and punished.

Most Islamic countries experienced transitional periods in their legal system over the last century, usually at the instigation of colonial powers. This led to restricting application of Islamic law to mainly family law. In contrast, Saudi Arabia and the Gulf States continue to regard *Shari'ah* as the main source of law and apply *fiqh* for all types of law.

See also **Education**; **Madhhab**.

FURTHER READING

Ballantyne, William M. *Essays and Addresses on Arab Laws*. Richmond, Surrey, UK: Curzon, 2000.

Heer, Nicholas (ed.). *Islamic Law and Jurisprudence. Studies in Honor of Farhat J. Ziadeh*. Seattle: University of Washington Press, 1990.

Motzki, Harald. *The Origins of Islamic Jurisprudence: Meccan Fiqh before the Classical Schools*. Leiden, The Netherlands: Brill, 2002.

Nafisa, Motleb Abdullah. "Law and Social Change in Muslim Countries: The Concept of Islamic Law Held by the Hanbali School and the Saudi Arabian Legal System," SJD thesis, Harvard Law School, 1975.

Shoup, John. *Culture and Customs of Syria*. Westport, CT: Greenwood, 2008.

Vogel, Frank. *Islamic Law and Legal System: Studies of Saudi Arabia*. Leiden, The Netherlands: Brill, 2000.

Flora and Fauna

Sebastian Maisel

The arid **climate** and **desert** appearance of many parts of the **Arabian Peninsula** belie the existence of a rich biodiversity in all geographical areas ranging from the mountaintops of **Asir** via the large sand desert of the Empty Quarter to the shallow waters of the Gulf. Everywhere life is abundant, and many plants and

Dhub, a spiny-tailed lizard (*uromastix*), Saudi Arabia. Courtesy of Sebastian Maisel.

animals continue to live in their natural habitat. However, human development, especially the industry and urban sector, infringes on the wildlife, which in turn has to retreat or will become extinct if it cannot adapt to the new conditions.

In the ancient past, the Arabian Peninsula was connected to Africa, creating a land bridge that facilitated biological exchange. Only after the formation of the Red Sea and the **Arabian Gulf** was the Peninsula isolated from the other landmasses. Climatic change during and after the Ice Age also left its mark on the flora and fauna. The Arabian Peninsula was much more fertile with permanent rivers and lakes, thus it had a greater diversity than it can support today. An arid climate has since been the characteristic condition with subsequent large deserts and steppes. The types of animals and plants in Arabia today are a direct reflection of the changing terrain and climate.

Generally, vegetation is sparse because of climate and soil conditions. Some trees and bushes are better fit to live in this kind of weather, such as the tamarisk, the **date** palm, acacias, and mangroves along the coastal wetlands. Forests are rare and only found in higher altitudes such as the Asir and **Hijaz** Mountains in **Saudi Arabia** or the **Jabal al-Akhdar** in **Oman**. The most common varieties, including acacia, juniper, *sidr*, and tamarind supply firewood and fencing material for rural communities. Special varieties in Oman include coconut palms and frankincense trees. Large state-run projects to reforest the more mountainous areas of Saudi Arabia help stem ongoing desertification. After the rainy season in the northern and central parts of the Peninsula (from December to March), most plants blossom and produce seeds. Annuals have larger leaves and no sharp thorns, whereas perennials are larger in size and have deep, extensive root systems. Sometimes, leaves are hispid or covered with felt to prevent transpiration. Seeds can survive long periods of drought and wait years before sprouting. Plants develop other survival strategies. Some appear to die off completely but start to grow with the first rain. Others have green leaves in the spring and hard, prickly ones in the summer. Many perennials are poisonous to animals; acacia seeds can destroy other seedlings by excreting a substance. All plants of Arabia have adapted in one way or another to the harsh conditions of their environment.

Animals have also found ways to live in areas with sparse water and an abundance of direct sunlight and little nourishment. Similar to plants, they developed specific skills or features that enable them to survive in Arabia's arid climate and desert terrain.

In the **oases** of the Gulf, many insects, caterpillars, dragonflies, beetles, ants, and grasshoppers are found. Small permanent water sources are sufficient for their survival. Dragonflies are fast, long-distance flyers and eat mosquito larvae. Grasshoppers are found in nearly all areas of the Peninsula. They have the ability to jump farther than any other insect. After good rain, the local grasshopper populations can explode and swarms of locust cover the countryside, destroying crops and other plants. Today swarms can be controlled with modern technology. Some **Bedouin** consider locust a delicacy and eat them either by quick-frying them in a bit of butter or oil or after they have been left to sun dry. Dried locusts were fed to livestock in the past.

A very large variety of beetles are found in the desert. In addition, scorpions are common, both the large black and yellow types, as are spiders. The *shabath*, or camel spider, is the most "notorious" because local belief is that its bite is fatal. However, it is not poisonous, but its size gives it the bad reputation.

Snakes live in every type of terrain, even in the sea. Poisonous varieties of sea snakes are very common in the shallow, warm waters along the coast of the Arabian Gulf. Many different members of the lizard family are found in Arabia, including geckos, skinks (sand fish), agamas, *warals* (desert monitor), chameleons, and the spiny-tailed lizard called *dhub* in Arabic. Bedouin eat the *dhub* and it seems that its consumption is legal in the **Shari'ah**. The Caspian Pond Turtle frequently inhabits irrigation channels of the eastern part of the Peninsula, as do types of small fish.

Fish, snakes, turtles, and other maritime reptiles are found in abundance in the waters of the Red Sea, the Arabian Sea, and the Gulf. Sea life is more plentiful and varied, with coral reefs and deep-sea fish, such as sharks, groupers, and swordfish. Offshore, whales and dolphins can be spotted. It is believed that the waters of the Gulf were heavily polluted and their wildlife was almost completely destroyed. Indeed, the **1991 Gulf War** significantly polluted the Gulf environment. Crude **oil** flowed from damaged wells and entered marine ecosystems of the Northern Arabian Gulf, killing many plants and animals. **Military** construction and minefields furthered the destruction of the already fragile ecosystem. Particularly damaged were the maritime wildlife and coral reefs, although they have began to regenerate recently. Marine turtles, virtually extinct after the war, started to show up again and began nesting. Other areas in the south near the **United Arab Emirates** and **Qatar** remained untouched, and many species survived.

Jerboas with their long and powerful hind-legs are common in the stony desert with pockets of sandy soil. Gerbils and mice inhabit all parts of the Peninsula.

The hedgehog is adapted to living in the desert with large ears to detect movements from far distances. Its ears are also wide and round to dissipate heat. It does not need water because it has the ability to extract liquids from food such as insects and plants. Two types of mongoose live in Arabia, the Indian Grey Mongoose in the eastern part and the white-tailed African species in the coastal plain of the southwest. The *wabar*, or rock hyrax, is a shy shrewmouse in the rocky terrain in the Hijaz and Asir Mountains. Arabia's largest rodent is the Arabian Porcupine, which lives in the Asir Mountains and is almost three feet (one meter) in length. Its distinct black and white quills are used in Bedouin ornaments.

The honey badger, or *ratil*, belongs to the weasel family; similar to skunks, it can produce a nauseating secretion from its anal glands. It receives its name from its passion for honey, and its thick hide prevents bee stings and even snakebites. However, the honey badger has a bad reputation because Bedouin claim it digs up graves and eats the dead. More than fifteen species of bat have been recorded in the Peninsula. Among them is the large pallid desert big-eared bat. Bats are more common in tropical areas but are still abundant in most parts of Arabia.

The striped type of hyena is found in the mountainous area of the west and southwest. Because it preys on livestock, Bedouin and farmers have hunted the animal almost to extinction. The same region is also home to the only baboon species of Arabia, the Arabian or sacred baboon. They live and travel in troops of fifty or more members. They are omnivorous and often live close to human settlements. They are frequently seen along the streets and outskirts of villages and towns. Foxes are well known throughout Arabia as a popular game. The desert fox of central and eastern Arabia is smaller and slighter than those living in the **mountains** of Hijaz and Asir. The desert fox has larger ears and has the ability to go without water for long periods of time. Wolves used to be found all over the Peninsula with the exception of the Empty Quarter and Nafud Desert. Wolves rely on small permanent springs and pools of water, which also attract prey. Many folk tales are attached to the wolf, and Bedouin believe in his ability to cure persons possessed by the devil. Live wolves were captured to frighten away evil spirits that can cause women to be infertile. Because wolves prefer the easy prey of domesticated livestock to trying to pursue wild animals, Bedouin shoot them when possible.

The Arabian caracal lives in the remotest areas of the southwestern mountains, but its numbers are greatly reduced, and it is rarely seen. In the past, local hunters trained young caracals to hunt other animals. In central and eastern Arabia the secretive sand cat is found. Its existence was discovered only some fifty years ago by the British desert traveler Wilfred Thesiger. It is closely related to the equally shy wild cat. The largest cat of Arabia, the Arabian leopard, used to live in the mountains of western Arabia from Asir to al-'Ulah and preyed on baboons, birds, and gazelles. Today the species is critically endangered because of pest control and hunting. Gazelles and oryx antelopes have been common in the past, but became extinct in the wild after the introduction of modern firearms and excessive hunting.

The Arabian Peninsula is also home to several domesticated animals such as **camels, horses,** sheep, goats, cattle, and donkeys. None of these animals exist in the wild today, although there are still small herds of wild ibex in some of the mountains. Camels are one of the few species of domesticated livestock that are indigenous to the Peninsula, whereas horses were first domesticated in Central Asia. The **Arabian horse** was developed in the Peninsula and the northern deserts of Syria, but cannot exist in the wild in the desert. It, like most of the domesticated species, is heavily dependent on man for its survival. Cattle were imported from India, and although the variety of zebu found in Oman is a hardy animal, cattle require water at least once a day.

The abundance of numerous insect species, shade, seeds, and occasional water sustain the life of many birds. Most are found in the oases, wadis, and other vegetated areas, but some birds live in the desert, steppes, and mountains. The geographical position of the Peninsula makes it a four-way bridge with African birds present in the southwest, Asian birds in the southeast, European birds in the northwest, and two major migratory routes in the east. In addition, along the entire coastline, large varieties of gulls, terns, and waders are found, and cormorants and flamingoes can be seen. Common birds in Arabia are sparrows, pigeons, warblers, and wagtails. In the desert areas larks, hoopoes, and hawks are common. Weaverbirds nest in the Asir where there are also large eagles and vultures. Cultivation and irrigation provide additional food and shelter and attract more birds, some of which breed while in the Peninsula. The houbara bustard is the most important quarry for falcons, a traditional type of **sport** that almost led to the extinction of the former. At the National Avian Research Center in Abu Dhabi, houbaras are bred to reintroduce them into the wild and to reconcile with the age-old tradition of falconry.

Another successful example of reintroducing species after many decades of extinction is the Arabian oryx antelope. In the past often hunted by Bedouin and the upper class, it vanished shortly after World War II. The same people who contributed to its original loss are now working on preserving the remaining animals and protecting their grazing grounds through fenced-off and patrolled nature reserves. Other species were less fortunate and are now considered endangered, threatened, or already extinct because of a rapid process of habitat degradation in the entire Peninsula.

See also **Travelers and Explorers**.

FURTHER READING

Larsen, Torben. *Butterflies of Saudi Arabia and its Neighbors*. London: Stacey International, 1984.

Miller, Anthony, Thomas A. Cope, and J.A. Nyberg (eds.). *Flora of the Arabian Peninsula and Socotra*. Edinburgh: Edinburgh University Press, 1996.

Silsby, Jill. *Inland Birds of Saudi Arabia*. London: Immel Publishing, 1980.

Vincett, Betty. *Animal Life in Saudi Arabia*. Cernusco, Italy: Garzanti Editore, 1982.

Vincett, Betty. *Wild Flowers of Central Saudi Arabia*. Milan: PIME Editrice, 1977.

Vine, Peter. *Natural Emirates: Wildlife and Environment of the United Arab Emirates*. Bangor, Australia: Trident Press, 1996.

Wittmer, Walter, and Willi Buettiker (eds.). *Fauna of Saudi Arabia*. Basel, Switzerland: Pro Entomogogia, 1979–1999.

Folklore

Sebastian Maisel

Within the cultures of the **Arabian Peninsula** all forms of folklore are existent and enjoy popularity. Today folklore in the form of songs, **dance**, stories, and such is connected to the period before the **oil** boom and has become part of the local **cultural heritage** that was in danger of being totally lost. Local cultural heritage has found a new political and social platform to combat the effects of modernization and Westernization, although more often than not it is through a nostalgic glimpse with a strong sense of national pride. Because so much of daily life has changed, people cling to the few remnants that connect them with previous generations.

The **material culture** of the Arabian Peninsula is classified along regional lines and according to the lifestyle of the people who used the object: city dwellers, **oasis** farmers, or **Bedouin**. Significant items include **dress** and textiles, **jewelry**, tools and household equipment, and **architecture**. Only a few artifacts have survived the extensive transition that region has undergone since the 1950s. Arguably the most profound changes have occurred in the field of material objects, things that have been replaced with modern equipment and no one thought then worthy of preservation except for a few museums and private collections, many of which are outside of the region. Old things were associated with the past of poverty and backwardness, and anything new was in high demand. The only resistance was over items that might interfere with religion such as radios or **television**. People were quick to adapt to new technologies and innovations that made life easier for them. Perhaps the one area of material culture that successfully withstood a good deal of transformation is clothing. What is called the "national dress" of **Saudi Arabia** and the Arabian Gulf States is much the same as it was although still impacted by the fashion tastes of each generation. It is easy to guess the decade if not the year from the specific forms of national dress.

Although most material objects are gone, stories and other oral traditions have been preserved and they are an active feature of Arab culture. The oral character of Arab society gives the spoken word superiority over the written one. Folkloristic study of the oral traditions of the region includes poetry, especially *Nabati*, which is used for the narratives of tribal history; folktales; songs; and most other artistic forms or oral expression. Even the young generations are able to recite popular phrases, poems, and stories. Furthermore, much of what is known about the history of Arabia has been recorded orally, thus making the oral narratives and stories a valuable source. The legal traditions and practices, although generally written, may also be part of the oral heritage.

Folk practices may be difficult to classify into specific categories because they are often very close to public standards and orthodox norms. Such aspects as language, religion, medicine, and artistic expression (literature, **music**) may exist in written forms and only vary slightly from accepted norms of "high culture." These may be codified and regulated by official Islam and classical Arabic literary and grammatical forms. They can include "folk" expressions as popular Islam or by using local dialect.

Today it is difficult to find forms of popular **Islamic practices** because of the efforts of the reformer **Muhammad 'Abd al-Wahhab**. However, popular Islam was once spread throughout the Peninsula. From his writings and those of casual observers it is clear that many people in the Peninsula followed folk customs such as venerating saints and their tombs, trees, or rocks. Sufi *Turuq* (singular *Tariqah*) had followers in the cities and towns but they lost popularity not only because of the anti-Sufi stance of Muhammad 'Abd al-Wahhab, but also because of the forces of modernization. Shi'ite practices are considered heretical to Wahhabis and were subject to official disfavor, but the revival of Shi'ite identity and power over the past several decades allows them to be openly observed. The same can be said about the use of local dialects of Arabic. The Qur'an was revealed in a perfect form of Arabic. Although Classical Arabic is promoted as the language of God and religion, nobody uses it for daily interactions. Local dialects such as *Khaliji*, *Hijazi*, and *Najdi* are the main means of normal communication, although television and radio promote the use of Classical Arabic as much as they can. Folk medicine has been almost completely eradicated because it is associated with magic and sorcery. Pre-Islamic religion in the Arabian Peninsula made use of soothsayers and sorcery, which are condemned in the Qur'an. In Saudi Arabia practicing folk medicine is considered a **crime** and can be brought to court. However, this is different from what is called *al-Tibb al-Nabawi*, or the Prophet's medicine, which makes use of herbal-based medicines. It is somewhat like homeopathic medicine and includes proper diet and preventative practices.

Folklore is also expressed through certain types of behavior. How an Arab from the Peninsula acts and reacts depends on his cultural background, and the values that he considers important. A very specific code of behavior is expressed in the social values of tribes. Virtually every Arab belongs to an extended group of relatives, sometimes as big as a tribe with up to 1 million members. The social interaction between tribal members is regulated by ancient rules often transmitted through oral narratives. Their main characteristic is the common responsibility and solidarity within the kin group. Relatives should stick together. Added to that is the concept of right or wrong, **honor**, and shame, which also reflects on non-tribal members. Other values such as hospitality, chivalry, bravery, and generosity are integral parts of what broadly is defined as the area's behavior pattern. Behavior is furthermore exhibited through rituals and customs; for example, the rites of passage, holidays, the *majlis*, or the **pilgrimage**. They all combine traditional folkloristic aspects with regulations from the authorities.

Although folklore developed from the bottom of the society, heritage has been prescribed from above. This is shown in fine detail by domestic policies of all Arabian Gulf States that are concerned with the preservation of a national heritage or what the authorities consider of national importance. Projects and programs are funded to collect, preserve, and demonstrate an official look of what is worth saving from the past. Open-air museums, restored buildings, and heritage festivals are used to convey this message to the people. With the ongoing and increasing centralization of power and unification of culture, some aspects of the rich and diverse folklore of Arabia will disappear or assimilate into a larger, national folklore.

FURTHER READING

Hariri-Rifai, Wahbi, and Mokhless Hariri-Rifai. *The Heritage of the Kingdom of Saudi Arabia*. Washington, D.C.: GDG Publications, 1990.

Hurreiz, Sayyid H. *Folklore and Folklife in the United Arab Emirates*. London: Routledge, Curzon, 2002.

Jenner, Michael. *Bahrain, Gulf Heritage in Transition*. New York: Longman, 1984.

Kurpershoek, P. Marcel. *Oral Poetry and Narratives from Central Arabia*, 5 vols. Leiden, The Netherlands: Brill, 1993–2005.

al-Mutawa, Mohammed, John W. Fox, and Nada Mourtada-Sabbah (eds.). *Globalization and the Gulf*. London: Routledge, 2006.

Foreign Policies
Tom Landsford

The foreign policies of the Gulf States and **Saudi Arabia** reflect the history and traditions of the individual countries. Their diplomacy has also been shaped by the region's colonial legacy and the lingering impact of the Cold War, as well as the ongoing Arab-Israeli conflict, the Iran-Iraq conflicts, and the global **War on Terror** of the United States. In general, the states have pursued moderate, pro-Western foreign policies and endeavored to contain both Iraq and Iran from becoming regional hegemons.

BAHRAIN

Bahrain is one of only two of the Arab Gulf states with a representative assembly. However, the conduct of the nation's foreign policy remains the domain of the monarchy. Bahrain's foreign policy can best be described as one of engagement, both regionally and globally. The country has sought to integrate itself into international bodies and develop close relations with neighboring states, including Iran. However, a failed Iranian-backed coup in 1981 continues to affect relations between the two states, and tensions have increased since the 1990s, when Iran was discovered to be supporting radical, anti-government elements in the country. In 1986, a causeway was constructed from the island nation to Saudi Arabia. A long-standing border dispute between Bahrain and **Qatar** was settled by the International Court of Justice in 2001, with both countries receiving some areas that were in dispute. The settlement removed the country's main source of tension with surrounding states.

The country has had close relations with the United States since independence in 1971 and has been used as an American naval base since 1947. During the

Cold War, ties to the United States were perceived as the optimum means to counter Soviet influence in the region. After the end of the Cold War, Bahrain continued a close **military** relationship with the United States to counter potential Iranian or Iraqi influence and ensure regional stability. When Iraq invaded **Kuwait** in 1990, Bahrain joined the U.S.-led coalition of nations that opposed the regime of Saddam Hussein. The country also became a major hub for coalition operations, and Bahraini air units participated in the liberation of Kuwait in 1991. After the war, the United States pre-positioned military equipment in Bahrain, and the UN-sponsored naval patrols used the countries facilities to enforce the weapons and economic sanctions against the Saddam Hussein government. U.S. basing rights were guaranteed through a 1991 accord between the two countries. Bahrain subsequently provided the use of bases and airspace during the invasion of Afghanistan in 2001 and the invasion of Iraq in 2003. It also increased intelligence and law enforcement cooperation with the United States in the aftermath of the September 2001 terrorist attacks on the United States. In 2001, the administration of George W. Bush designated Bahrain a major non-NATO ally. This allowed the sale and transfer of more sophisticated weaponry and increased intelligence collaboration. From 2000 to 2007, U.S. military sales to Bahrain totaled $608.9 million. Bahrain's monarch, King Hamad, has made three visits to the United States since ascending the throne in 1999. Bahrain also has strong economic ties to the United States, and the 2004 U.S.-Bahrain Free Trade Agreement took effect in 2006. Trade between the two countries exceeded $1 billion in 2006.

Bahrain joined the **Gulf Cooperation Council** (GCC) in 1981. The following year, the organization provided the country with $1.7 billion to modernize its military and **security** infrastructure. Bahrain has advocated expanded economic and security cooperation within the GCC and stronger commercial ties with the European Union (EU), including a proposed free trade agreement between the GCC and the EU. In 1994, Bahrain, along with the other GCC states, ended some boycotts of Israel. In 2005, the government eliminated its official economic embargo on Israel, a move that was strongly opposed by the nation's parliament, but was a condition of the country's free trade accord with the United States.

KUWAIT

Kuwait's foreign policy remains profoundly affected by the country's 1990 conquest by Iraq. Since its independence in 1961, Kuwait was subject to territorial claims by Iraq that argued that the country had been artificially separated from Baghdad by the colonial powers. Relations between the United States and Iraq improved significantly in 1987 when the United States began to re-flag Kuwaiti **oil** tankers during the **Iran-Iraq war** to ensure their safety. In 1990, the regime of Saddam Hussein invaded and quickly overran Kuwait. A U.S.-led multinational coalition was formed under the auspices of a UN Security Council resolution. Coalition forces liberated Kuwait in 1991.

Kuwait's post-liberation foreign policy has sought to expand security alliances and bolster relations with countries that supported the anti-Saddam coalition.

Tensions remained high with countries that did not join the coalition or that supported Iraq during the conflict, including Cuba, Jordan, Sudan, and **Yemen**. However, in 1999, Kuwait launched a diplomatic initiative to improve relations with Jordan and Yemen. Kuwait was one of the main financial backers of the Palestine Liberation Organization (PLO), but the group's support for the Saddam regime reduced Kuwaiti backing of the PLO leadership. In 1993, the government ended some aspects of its embargo on Israel.

Kuwait has the world's fifth largest proven oil reserves and it provides substantial foreign aid for states such as Egypt and Syria. The government also gave Lebanon $800 million following the 2006 war in south Lebanon between Israel and Hezbollah. Established in 1961, the Kuwait Fund for Arab Economic Development (KFAED) now also disburses aid to non-Arab states. KFAED has granted more than $37 billion in economic development and humanitarian grants and loans, including a $50 million grant to the United States following Hurricane Katrina.

Following the war, Kuwait signed a series of bilateral defense agreements with France, Russia, the United Kingdom, and the United States. In 1994, Iraq agreed to a UN-mandated border settlement with Kuwait; however, the maritime boundary between the two states remains in dispute. Kuwait and Saudi Arabia also dispute control of the Qaruh and Umm al Maradim islands in the Persian Gulf. Kuwait was a founding member of the GCC in 1981. It supported greater defense capabilities for the member states, and Kuwait's GCC partners participated in the 1990–1991 anti-Saddam coalition. After the war, Kuwait endorsed greater economic integration and a common market among the GCC countries.

The alliance with the United States emerged as the cornerstone of Kuwaiti foreign policy. Kuwait purchased $81 million in U.S. military equipment in the first year following the invasion and signed a ten-year security agreement in which the United States guaranteed Kuwaiti sovereignty in exchange for pre-positioning equipment and providing funding for joint military exercises. From 2003 to 2007, the country's currency, the *dinar*, was pegged to the U.S. dollar. By 2007, Kuwait had purchased more than $8.1 billion in arms and weaponry. Furthermore, American firms were given priority in Kuwait's reconstruction projects and energy development programs. The country imports more than $2.1 billion in U.S. goods each year, not including military sales.

Kuwait was one of the staunchest supporters of the U.S.-led invasion of Iraq in 2003. The country served as the base for the campaign and provided technical and logistical support for the U.S.-led coalition government. In 2003, Kuwait pledged $1.5 billion in economic assistance for the Iraqi government and has supported the political reconciliation process, including the country's elections in 2005. The result has been dramatic improvement in relations between the two countries.

OMAN

Since independence, **Oman** has sought to improve relations with neighboring states and ensure regional stability. After *Sultan* **Qabus bin Sa'id Al Bu Sa'id** came to power in 1970, he undertook an aggressive foreign policy to end the nation's relative isolation and become integrated into **international relations**. More than any other Gulf State, Oman has pursued relations with a wide range of countries. Although it was a member of the Non-Aligned Movement during the Cold War, the country has strengthened ties with the United States, although not to the degree of Bahrain or Kuwait. Instead, Oman has pursued close ties with the EU, its main trade partner, and Asian countries such as China, India, and Pakistan. It has also been involved in Central Asia and initiated joint economic projects with several countries in the region, including a pipeline project with Kazakhstan. The United Kingdom remains Oman's closest Western ally and continues to provide economic, technical, and security assistance to the sultanate. This relationship is based on the long-standing historical connection between the two countries and a series of treaties.

The country is a member of a range of international organizations and was a founding member of the GCC in 1981 and the Indian Ocean Rim Association (IORA) in 1997. Oman supported a more robust GCC and in 1991 unsuccessfully called for the organization's military component to be expanded to 100,000 troops. It was one of the driving forces in the GCC for the creation of a common market and the initiation of discussions with the EU to establish a free trade agreement between the two organizations. Oman perceived the IORA as a means to attract more investment into the Gulf region from Asia and to enhance trade relations. It supported the expansion of the IORA from its original fourteen countries to nineteen members in 2001. Oman joined the World Trade Organization in 2000, and in 2005, Oman and the United States concluded a free trade agreement.

In the 1980s, Oman endeavored unsuccessfully to mediate the Iran-Iraq War. It maintains better relations with Iran than any of the other Gulf States, with the possible exception of Qatar. Throughout the 1990s, Oman concentrated on settling several outstanding border disputes with neighboring states. In 1990, Oman and Saudi Arabia finalized a series of border agreements that resolved their mutual boundary questions. The accords went into effect two years later. In 1995, Oman settled its remaining border issues with Yemen. The two countries subsequently agreed to construct a major highway from southern Yemen to Oman and initiate negotiations on a bilateral free trade agreement. Finally, in 1999, Oman and the **United Arab Emirates** signed an accord to finalize their borders.

Oman has officially supported the Arab-Israeli peace process and participated in several rounds of negotiations. In addition, the *Sultan* invited Israeli participation in a regional water desalination conference in 1994, when the other GCC states still did not have official relations with Israel, and he invited Prime Minister Yitzak Rabin to come to Oman in the first visit of an Israeli leader to a Gulf state. The government opened reciprocal trade offices with Israel in 1996, but was forced to close the Israeli office in 2000 because of public demonstrations in support of the second *intifadah*. Oman endorsed the creation of a Palestinian state and provided funding for the Palestinian Authority.

The government condemned the 1990 Iraqi invasion of Kuwait, and Omani troops were part of the coalition of nations that liberated Kuwait. This marked the first time that Oman abandoned its non-aligned principle, and the *Sultan* renewed and expanded a 1980 facilities agreement with the United States that allowed the pre-positioning of military equipment and the American use of Omani military facilities. However, Oman subsequently condemned the UN-sponsored economic sanctions against Iraq. It asserted that the sanctions had little impact on the regime and instead unfairly hurt the Iraqi people. Oman also opposed the 1998 Anglo-American airstrikes on Iraq that were undertaken after Saddam forced UN weapons inspectors to leave the country. Oman offered intelligence and financial cooperation to the United States and the EU in the wake of the 2001 terrorist strikes. Although it opposed military action against Iraq in 2003, Oman did allow the United States to use its airspace and military facilities to support the invasion and the subsequent occupation. Omani officials did criticize the U.S. response to the Iraqi insurgency and contend that the ongoing violence has increased radical Islamic terrorism. Oman did provide aid and technical support for the post-Saddam Iraqi government.

QATAR

Like Oman, Qatar has maintained close relations with the United Kingdom since it gained full independence in 1971. Qatar has generally pursued a moderate, pro-Western foreign policy and was a founding member of the GCC. Its relations with neighboring states have been complicated by a series of border disputes. For instance, a boundary dispute with Saudi Arabia turned bloody in 1992 when troops from both countries engaged in a series of border skirmishes. Since then, the two countries have engaged in continued negotiations over the contested area, but have been unable to finalize a settlement. In 1995, Qatar even boycotted the GCC in response to the selection of a Saudi citizen as the organization's secretary-general. Qatar also had a long-standing dispute with Bahrain over the Hawar island chain in the Persian Gulf. In 1986, when Bahrain attempted to construct a coast guard facility on one of the islets, Qatari forces took the Bahraini workers prisoner. They were later released. In 1994, the conflict was submitted to the International Court of Justice for arbitration. The Court ruled in 2001 that the main islands belonged to Bahrain, but other areas of the disputed territory were restored to Qatar.

During the **Gulf War**, Qatari troops participated in the liberation of Kuwait along with other GCC forces. In 1992, Qatar signed a bilateral security accord with the United States and then similar agreements with France and the United Kingdom. **Emir** Hamad bin Khalifa **Al Thani** seized power in Qatar in 1995 from his father. The United States quickly granted recognition to the new regime, and in return, Hamad drew Qatar even closer to the United States. As part of a broader liberalization program, Hamad ordered elections in 1999 for a municipal council. The United States and other Western powers provided technical assistance for the balloting, and the American Congress enacted a resolution congratulating Qatar for its democratic progress and advancement in **women's rights**.

After the September 2001 terrorist attacks, Qatar offered closer cooperation with the administration of George W. Bush, including use of bases and facilities during the invasion of Afghanistan. The U.S. Central Command established a forward headquarters at Camp Al Sayliyah prior to the invasion of Iraq. The command oversaw the 2003 invasion of Iraq. When the United States withdrew from Prince Sultan Air Base in Saudi Arabia, it moved its main airbase in the region to the al-'Udayd air field in Qatar, which has the longest runway in the region (15,000 ft.). The base also became home to some 5,000 U.S. service personnel who transferred from Saudi Arabia. Bush visited Qatar in 2003, and Hamad reciprocated with a trip to Washington, D.C. the following year and again in 2005.

One area of tension, both with the United States and with surrounding states, is the presence of the **Al Jazeera** ("the Peninsula") satellite **television** network in Qatar. Considered the freest news source in the Arab world, Al Jazeera has been critical of Western nations and the neighboring Gulf countries. For instance, Bahrain banned the network from 2002 to 2004 because of charges of bias against the country and Israel.

UNITED ARAB EMIRATES

The foreign policy of the United Arab Emirates (UAE) is based on global engagement and Arab unity. Leaders have repeated called for closer cooperation and collaboration among Arab states, and supported efforts to strengthen organizations such as the Arab League and the GCC. It has participated in a variety of international bodies, and, like neighboring Gulf States, the UAE has used its energy wealth to support humanitarian causes. The **Abu Dhabi** Fund for Development (ADFD) was created in 1971 to provide loans, grants, and technical assistance to Muslim and developing nations. The ADFD also coordinates the aid programs of the UAE government. The UAE has provided significant aid to the Palestinian Authority, and granted Lebanon $50 million for demining programs.

In 1974, the UAE and Saudi Arabia negotiated a border accord, but the Emirates later refused to ratify the agreement and called for it to be renegotiated. The dispute remains unresolved. The UAE and Oman signed a framework agreement in 1999 to delineate their border. There are also territorial disputes with Iran. The UAE claims two islands, the Lesser and Greater Tunbs, that are controlled by Tehran. In addition, both countries claim the island of Abu Musa. In 1992, Iran deployed military forces to ensure control of the territory.

The GCC is one of the cornerstones of UAE foreign policy. The UAE has been one of the staunchest supporters of the organization and endorsed proposals to strengthen the GCC and enhance its military capabilities. For instance, the Emirates established the UAE Air Warfare Center, the largest air training facility in the Gulf, to provide joint training and exercise means for the GCC states and allies. The UAE was part of the anti-Saddam coalition following the Iraqi invasion of Kuwait. Like other Gulf nations, the UAE endeavored to increase its security through stronger bilateral ties with countries such as the United Kingdom. The UAE became the site of the second largest deployment of British forces outside of North Atlantic Treaty Organization (NATO; the UAE is also the United Kingdom's main trade partner in the region).

The UAE supported the NATO-led campaign against Serbia in Kosovo in 1999. The Emirates provided troops for the NATO-sponsored peacekeeping force in Kosovo. The UAE was one of the few countries with diplomatic ties to the Taliban, but the Emirates' government condemned the 2001 terrorist attacks on the United States and broke off relations with the Afghan regime. It also offered a range of support to the United States. It worked closely with the Bush administration to reduce terrorist financing networks by enacting new legislation and increasing cooperation with international bodies. The UAE further provided logistical and military support for Operation Enduring Freedom, the U.S.-led invasion of Afghanistan. The UAE was the first country to join the U.S. Container Security Initiative, in which American customs officials are stationed in host nations to provide pre-inspection of seaborne goods delivered to the United States. It also became part of the U.S. Department of Energy's Megaports Initiative, which implements programs designed to reduce the potential for smuggling nuclear materials. The Emirates donated $100 million to the United States in the aftermath of Hurricane Katrina in 2005. However, relations between the two countries were strained in 2006 when it emerged that a company owned by the UAE government, **Dubai** Ports World, was going to take over the management of commercial operations at American ports. Of particular concern to many congressional leaders was the continuing support of the UAE for groups linked to Hamas and other Palestinian groups with ties to terrorist activity. Domestic opposition in the United States caused the UAE government to withdraw from the agreement.

The UAE supported efforts to strengthen international law, including the creation of the International Criminal Court. The Emirates have also called for debt relief for developing African nations and international efforts to increase development on the continent. To promote regional stability, the UAE has supported the post-Saddam government in Iraq and provided more than $215 million between 2004 and 2007.

SAUDI ARABIA

Saudi Arabia has pursued a moderate foreign policy based primarily on the promotion of regional stability. It has further endeavored to maintain and project a role as the leading **Sunni** power in the Gulf. Saudi Arabia has also used its wealth to support a range of Arab and Islamic causes while generally favoring multilateralism. Saudi Arabia was a founding member of the **Arab League**, the **Organization of Petroleum Exporting Countries** (OPEC), and the GCC. Within the Arab League, the kingdom has backed a range of Arab and Islamic causes, including support for Israel's withdrawal to the pre-1967 borders and the creation of a Palestinian state. Saudi Arabia has long been a dominant member within OPEC and often been able to forge consensus on production levels and output in line with the broad goal of maintaining a stable global energy market. However, it has resisted calls to develop the GCC into a more robust collective security organization, and the kingdom has specifically rejected efforts to give the organization a domestic mandate. Saudi Arabia continues to have several border disputes with neighboring states, including Kuwait, the UAE, and Yemen.

Although generally considered to be pro-Western, the kingdom has pursued policies in line with its strategic interests, often placing it at odds with the United

States and Europe. For instance, Saudi Arabia condemned the 1978 Camp David Accords (it also broke diplomatic relations with Egypt until 1987) and maintained a boycott on Israel. Although Saudi Arabia did not participate in U.S.-sponsored efforts to resolve the Arab-Israeli conflict in the 1990s, the kingdom did exert diplomatic pressure on Syria to take part in the peace initiatives. This support marked a change in Saudi policy as a result of the Palestinian refusal to support the anti-Saddam coalition during the Persian Gulf War. By the late 1990s, Saudi support for the Palestinian Authority was restored to previous levels.

Saudi Arabia has allied itself with Western powers when it was necessary or convenient in its pursuit of national interests. Saudi Arabia worked with U.S. intelligence services to provide funding for the anti-Soviet *Mujahidin* in Afghanistan. The kingdom and the United States also worked to support the Bosnians during the civil wars in the former Yugoslavia. When Kuwait was invaded, the kingdom strengthened ties with the United States and other European countries. **Riyadh** provided the United States some $15 billion to defray the costs of the war, and the kingdom provided another $40 billion to other allies and to provide humanitarian support for refugees. Saudi Arabia served as the main base for the coalition strike to liberate Kuwait, and it allowed the United States to build several military facilities. The largest would become Prince Sultan Air Base. Following terrorist strikes on American military personnel in 1995, the majority of U.S. forces were moved to Prince Sultan Air Base. The base served as the main air facility during the operations to enforce the UN-mandated no-fly zones over Iraq. Following the 2001 terrorist attacks, the base also played an important role in Operation Enduring Freedom. About 5,000 American service personnel remained at the base until 2003 when relations between Riyadh and Washington D.C. deteriorated because of the Iraq War. The main U.S. air facility in the region was subsequently relocated to Qatar.

In 1997, Saudi Arabia became one of three countries to offer diplomatic recognition to the Taliban regime in Afghanistan. The kingdom officially provided $2 million per year in assistance, whereas private Saudi sources donated substantially larger funds for the regime. After the September 11, 2001 attacks, the Saudi government broke off diplomatic relations with the Taliban and provided intelligence and logistics support to the U.S.-led Coalition that overthrew the regime. Because fifteen of the nineteen hijackers involved in the terrorist strikes were Saudi, the regime launched an expensive and multifaceted public relations campaign to emphasize its ties with the United States.

The kingdom's foreign policy has also adroitly changed alliances and relationships in response to external factors. When the U.S. Congress blocked sales of advanced aircraft to Saudi Arabia, the kingdom turned to the United Kingdom and negotiated a series of arms deals known collectively as Al-Yamamah. The first arms sales and weapons transfers were sold in 1985, and new contracts were signed as recently as 2006. The deals represented the largest arms sales in the history of the United Kingdom, worth more than $80 billion (Saudi Arabia paid for the purchases through oil exports). The multibillion-dollar sales were demonstrative of the kingdom's efforts to counter regional threats from Iraq or Iran with advanced weaponry. The ability of Saudi Arabia to shift alliances underscores the interest-driven nature of the kingdom's foreign policy and underscores Riyadh's continuing efforts toward regional stability and Arab leadership.

FURTHER READING

Cordesman, Anthony. *Saudi Arabia Enters the Twenty-First Century.* Westport, CT: Praeger, 2003.

Korany, Bahgar, and Ali E. Hillal Dessouki (eds.). *The Foreign Policies of Arab States.* Boulder, CO: Westview Press, 1984.

Long, David E., and Christian Koch (eds.). *Gulf Security in the Twenty-First Century.* New York: British Academic Press, 1997.

Owen, Roger. *State, Power and Politics in the Making of the Modern Middle East*, 2nd ed. London: Routledge, 2000.

Peterson, Erik R. *The Gulf Cooperation Council: Search for Unity in a Dynamic Region.* Boulder, CO: Westview Press, 1988.

Peterson, J.E. *Saudi Arabia and the Illusion of Security.* London: Oxford University Press, 2002.

Rubin, Barry (ed.). *Crises in the Contemporary Persian Gulf.* London: Frank Cass, 2002.

Zahlan, Rosemary Said. *The Making of the Modern Gulf States: Kuwait, Bahrain, Qatar, the United Arab Emirates and Oman.* Reading, UK: Ithaca Press, 1998.

Fujayrah

John A. Shoup

Fujayrah is the youngest of the states that make up the **United Arab Emirates**, and the region was ruled mainly by **Sharjah** (al-Shariqah) until the nineteenth century. In 1879 the tribal leader Hamad ibn 'Abdallah of the Hafaytat lineage of the Sharqiyin tribe was able to assert his independent authority over a good part of the eastern shore. The British did not recognize Fujayrah as its own entity until 1952 but considered it to still be under the Qawasim rulers of Sharjah. Fujayrah separates the **Musandam Peninsula** of **Oman** from the main body of the country. The Arabian Sea coast is a patchwork of different ownerships with several small enclaves (**oases**) being part of Oman, other regions belonging to Sharjah, and Sharjah and Fujayrah jointly administering some of the others. This patchwork is mainly due to the tribal nature of the coast and to whom tribal peoples gave allegiance during the eighteenth and nineteenth centuries. Some of the communities are **Ibadi Kharaji** and support the *Sultan* of Oman, whereas others are **Sunni** and give their allegiance to one of the Gulf *shaykhs*.

The region was relatively poor with **pearling**, **agriculture**, and pastoralism the mainstay of the economy into the 1970s. Because the economic conditions are difficult, many of the people were pastoral nomads and moved part of the year out of Fujayrah into Oman, Sharjah, or other *shayhkdom*s to make a living. Fujayrah is greatly supported by the **oil** wealth of its neighbors, **Abu Dhabi** and **Dubai**, and has little oil of its own. Fujayrah's *shaykh*s have tried to improve the conditions for their people by building new residential quarters, but it remains a pale shadow of the massive building projects in Abu Dhabi, Dubai, or Sharjah.

See also **Al Qasimi**.

FURTHER READING

Heard-Bey, Frauke. *From Trucial States to United Arab Emirates.* Dubai: Motivate Publishing, 2004.

G

Gender and Gender Relations
John A. Shoup

Saudi Arabia and the Gulf States are part of a wide region of the world referred to as the Patriarchal Belt that includes the Mediterranean and the Middle East stretching into Central and Southeast Asia. It is called the Patriarchal Belt because of the power men have over women, especially in the public sphere; in the private sphere women exercise a good deal of power. It is also a region where concepts of **honor** and shame are important in the relationships between men and women. Individual behavior, especially of a woman, is a measure of the honor (or shame) for an entire family. There is an Arabic saying that states that "honor rides on the skirts of women," and women are held more responsible for upholding family honor than men. Unni Wikan quotes the Omani, saying "the bride should be a virgin, the groom should be a man" to indicate the high importance women's honor holds for the region as a whole.

Men and women in Saudi Arabia and the Gulf States live greatly segregated lives, Saudi Arabia being the most extreme case. As a symbol of this segregation, women wear both an outer modesty garb (it is not the same garment throughout the Peninsula), which is worn whenever she leaves the confines of the home, and often a face veil (again, it varies greatly in the Peninsula). In **Oman** the modesty garment can be highly colorful cotton prints woven locally or imported from India made for the East African trade. In most of the region the garment is dark in color, usually black, and worn over the top of the head, hanging down to below the ankles. In some regions it is often an adapted form of the large outer cloak worn by men called a *bisht* or *'abayah*. Until recently many of the **Bedouin** women from the northern part of the Peninsula wore the same black crepe cloth called a *shambar* that is worn by Bedouin women in Jordan and Syria. The *shambar* covers the hair and neck and is held in place by a brocade or flower print headband. The face is uncovered for ease of work but the cloth can be quickly brought up over the nose and mouth should a strange man approach. Since the 1950s this form of **dress** has been changed to the full-face veil, or *burqa'*, worn by urban women in Saudi Arabia and some of the Gulf States.

Girls in much of the Gulf region wore a heavily embroidered headpiece or hood called a *bukhnuq* that allowed the face to be seen but covered the head, hair, neck, and shoulders. In the northern **Hijaz** and some of the other areas closer to Jordan and Syria, Bedouin girls wore an embroidered hood with a long tail that ends in silk floss tassels "to wipe away her steps." In other parts of the Hijaz and in the **Tihamah** girls wore heavily beaded hoods. Girls were allowed to interact and play with boys until they reached near puberty, when they were withdrawn from male company outside of the house. Starting to wear the face veil marked a girl's transition to womanhood. In much of the Gulf region the face veil is more of a visor made of stiffened material worn as a mask. In the **United Arab Emirates** some of them have openings for the eyes and cover the nose but expose the mouth and chin, making it a far more practical piece to wear.

Depending on the region, women have had a wide range of individual freedoms, with Bedouin women able to exercise the most freedom and urban women the least. Bedouin women own and often manage their own property (flocks and herds) independent of their husbands, including marketing them to urban merchants. Today in **Nizwa** it is possible to interact with Bedouin women from the **Wahibah**, **Duru'**, and **Harasis** tribes at the weekly livestock market. Honor is maintained by discreet distances between the parties or the presence of a male, even if he is a small child.

Women in the Gulf have a wide range of job possibilities today and in **Bahrain** have a wide range of political rights as well. Women are interested in pursuing careers as professionals and are well able to compete with men in the United Arab Emirates, Oman, **Qatar**, Bahrain, and **Kuwait**. In Saudi Arabia restrictions on driving and the requirement of total separation from men have made it more difficult for women, but there are more and more all-female **companies** and even banks where all of the employees are women catering only to women clients.

Total separation of the genders in the Peninsula has given rise to a "third" gender called *khanith*, although only Oman allows any form of public recognition of them. *Khanith* are usually young unmarried men who for a time take on the "role" of women, establishing relationships with other young unmarried men; they are considered transsexual rather than transvestites because they rarely wear women's clothes. Most of the men who belong to the third gender affect feminine behavior, mannerisms, and gestures and are allowed access to the otherwise closed women's part of segregated activities. They are often sexually active as male prostitutes, although prostitution is illegal and homosexual prostitution is considered a major sin in Islam. Their activities are generally tolerated (a blind eye to the activities of young unmarried men), and they are expected to eventually become "men" again and marry a woman, although researchers have noted that they never behave fully masculine. Third-gender behavior is expected of any male servant and of former slaves. The British traveler Wilfred Thesiger noted that in his many journeys with Omani Bedouin such behavior was never practiced, and his companions drew it to his attention when they pointed out two well-known *khanith* in **Dubai**, one a former slave. Wikan noted that transvestism and the recognition of a third gender were also found among the Marsh Arabs of southern Iraq.

See also **Sex Trade**; **Travelers and Explorers**.

FURTHER READING

Dickson, H.R.P. *Arab of the Desert*. London: George Allen and Unwin, 1983.

Haddad, Yvonne Yazbek, and John Esposito. *Islam, Gender, and Social Change*. New York: Oxford University Press, 1998.

Thesiger, Wilfred. *Arabian Sands*. London: Readers Union Longmans, Green & Co., 1960.

Wikan, Unni. *Behind the Veil in Arabia: Women in Oman*. Chicago: University of Chicago Press, 1982.

Gulf Cooperation Council
Tom Lansford

The Cooperation Council for the Arab States of the Gulf, commonly known as the Gulf Cooperation Council (GCC), is a regional security and economic organization that was formed as a collective defense body in 1981. Concerned over the potential spillover of the **Iran-Iraq War**, especially an increase in Iranian-backed **Shi'a** fundamentalist groups, **Bahrain**, **Kuwait**, **Oman**, **Qatar**, **Saudi Arabia**, and the **United Arab Emirates** created the GCC on May 25, 1981 during a summit in **Riyadh**, Saudi Arabia. The six countries proclaimed that the new organization would reflect their shared values and interests. Saudi Arabia emerged as the principle force behind the creation of the body, and the GCC headquarters was established in Riyadh. The presidency of the GCC rotates annually among the member states in alphabetical order. A secretary general of the organization is appointed for a three-year term by the Supreme Council, made up of the heads of state of the members. The Supreme Council is the highest decision-making body in the GCC. **Yemen** has sought membership in the organization on several occasions, but its bids have been rejected because of its weak economy.

After the GCC was established, defense ministers from its member states met to initiate plans for collective defense plans, including the creation of a joint command system and integrated **military** units. One operational problem the GCC members confronted was that the six countries had different weapons systems purchased from the United States, France, the United Kingdom, and Russia. Consequently, their armaments and communications systems often were not interoperational. The more wealthy states of Saudi Arabia and Kuwait began to provide military aid to the other GCC states so they could enhance their capabilities. Bahrain received funding to purchase new fighter aircraft and to modernize its main airbase. Oman also secured military support. Efforts were undertaken to integrate command-and-control structures, standardize equipment, and ensure that early warning systems and communications were standardized.

In 1984, the GCC approved the creation of integrated military unit, Peninsula Shield Force. The proposed structure consisted of two brigades of 5,000 troops each with forces from all six GCC members. One brigade would serve on a permanent basis, whereas the other could be activated in response to a specific crisis. The permanent force was stationed in Saudi Arabia, under the command of a Saudi officer. The GCC states held a series of regular military exercises, dubbed Peninsula Shield. GCC units also participated in exercises with the United States and the United Kingdom.

In 1991, during the Persian Gulf War, the Peninsula Shield force was reinforced; however, the unit did not take part in the combat operations in the conflict. Instead it remained as a reserve force. Following the War, the GCC members pledged to expand security cooperation and further increase military capabilities. It initially offered to station a joint deterrent force in Kuwait, but members were unable to agree on the size and funding of that mission. Nonetheless, the United States supported the enhanced GCC with additional arms sales and weapons transfers (there were also increases in defense procurements from other states such as France and the United Kingdom). The United States also pre-positioned some military equipment in the GCC members in case of future conflict in the region. In 1997, the GCC launched a new initiative to improve communications between the militaries of the member states to link the early warning systems of the respective states. One continuing contentious issue among GCC members was the role and size of the joint military unit. Originally envisioned as a collective defense force, there were unsuccessful calls throughout the 1990s to expand the size of the unit. For instance, in 1991, Oman made a failed proposal that the force be increased to 100,000. In addition, some member states advocated that the unit should be authorized to operate against domestic groups, something opposed by the majority of members. In 2004, the GCC states did sign a new intelligence cooperation agreement that was designed to counter domestic terrorist groups and suppress financing of international terrorist organizations.

Meanwhile, the GCC also endeavored to enhance economic integration. In November 1982, the GCC established the Gulf Standards Organization in an effort to coordinate standardization in data and measurements. Subsequently, in 1984, the GCC created Gulf Investment Corporation as a vehicle to support economic development and fund multilateral projects in the region. The GCC members also pledged themselves to the creation of a common market through the removal of tariffs and other trade barriers. In 1988, the organization signed a cooperation agreement with the European Community, now the European Union (EU). The goals of the accord were expanded economic interaction and strengthened political ties between the two bodies. Under the agreement, ministers from the GCC and the EU meet at an annual summit and there is a standing joint committee comprised of representatives from both organizations. There are also working groups on energy and environmental issues. A range of technical and cooperative programs has been undertaken in areas such as finance, agriculture, fisheries, and technological development. One result was an increase in direct investment by the GCC states in the EU. Between 2001 and 2006, GCC investments in the EU member states increased from $150 million to $1.3 billion.

In 1990, the GCC and the EU launched negotiations over a free trade agreement. However, the EU sought the formation of a GCC customs union before substantial agreements were finalized. This led to a halt in negotiations, which were resumed in 2002 after the GCC announced its intention to finalize its customs union. The customs agreement came into force in 2003 and removed the major remaining trade barriers amongst the nations. The GCC has also held talks with China and Turkey over free trade agreements. Further negotiations among the GCC states were then started on the possible creation of a common market, and 2010 was set as the initial deadline for the establishment of a monetary union. Decisions by Bahrain and Oman to seek bilateral free trade accords with the United States have slowed the process of integration.

See also **War on Terror.**

FURTHER READING

Korany, Bahgar, and Ali E. Hillal Dessouki (eds.). *The Foreign Policies of Arab States.* Boulder, CO: Westview Press, 1984.

Long, David E., and Christian Koch (eds.). *Gulf Security in the Twenty-First Century.* New York: British Academic Press, 1997.

Nakhleh, Emile A. *The Gulf Cooperation Council: Policies, Problems, and Prospects.* New York: Praeger, 1986.

Owen, Roger. *State, Power and Politics in the Making of the Modern Middle East,* 2nd ed. London: Routledge, 2000.

Peterson, Erik R. *The Gulf Cooperation Council: Search for Unity in a Dynamic Region.* Boulder, CO: Westview Press, 1988.

Sandwick, John A. (ed.). *The Gulf Cooperation Council: Moderation and Stability in an Interdependent World.* Boulder, CO: Westview Press, 1987.

Zahlan, Rosemary Said. *The Making of the Modern Gulf States: Kuwait, Bahrain, Qatar, the United Arab Emirates and Oman.* Reading, UK: Ithaca Press, 1998.

1990–1991 Gulf War

Audra Grant

On August 2, 1990, Iraq invaded and occupied **Kuwait**, touching off an international crisis that would escalate into the Gulf War. The invasion of Kuwait caught many observers by surprise. Iraq had just emerged from an eight-year war with Iran from 1980 to 1988, exhausted from the near-decade long conflagration. The conflict meant for some that Iraqi President Saddam Hussein would have to limit his more pan-Arab ambitions to more nationalist aims. However, Saddam Hussein's bold aggression against Kuwait suggested that the authoritarian leader had aspirations that could potentially alter the strategic configuration of the Middle East.

BACKGROUND TO THE WAR: THE KUWAIT CRISIS

The Iraqi invasion of Kuwait was the culmination of a long-standing conflict and grievance between the countries. Several political and economic factors fueled arguments for Iraqi invasion. To begin, Iraq was convinced that Kuwait was nothing more than a product of boundaries created by the British during the Mandate period (1920–1932). The two countries had been engaged in territorial dispute since 1938. Iraq argued that Kuwait originally was a part of Iraq and existed as a former district located in the province of Basrah. In addition, the *shaykh*dom of Kuwait was anathema to Saddam Hussein's goal to create an Arab nation. Kuwait and its elites were criticized for their wealth and passivity. Historic claims to land notwithstanding, economic factors are the more likely reason for the invasion. With an economy crippled by the war with Iran and burdened by ensuing debt and plunging **oil** prices during the 1980s, Saddam Hussein was desperate for revenue to rebuild his state and resuscitate the Iraqi economy that was also beleaguered by inflation. So he began a series of assertive moves to force Arab and particularly Gulf countries to compensate Iraq for its economic losses. First, in 1990 Hussein asked Gulf States to forgive his debt and provide a substantial grant amounting to $30 billion. Second, in an apparent effort to galvanize Arab support and justify potential future aggression against Kuwait, Hussein accused Kuwait and the **United Arab Emirates** (UAE) of exceeding their **Organization of Petroleum Exporting Countries** (OPEC) quotas, thereby causing the price of oil to drop at the expense of the Iraqi economy. He also said Kuwait was siphoning oil from Iraqi fields and demanded financial compensation. Each of these moves evoked outrage and intransigence from Kuwait. Iraq, perceiving this continued course of "economic sabotage" as an act of war, used Kuwait's refusal to cooperate as grounds for aggression. Facing a discontented, restive public, the Iraqi solution to its domestic ills laid with invading Kuwait, its neighbor to the east—a strategy intended to divert public attention away from problems at home while accessing critical oil reserves.

Iraq began to assemble troops in the vicinity of the Kuwaiti border around July 1990, starting a flurry of crisis negotiations involving the United States, Egypt, and the **Arab League**. Although efforts to dissuade Hussein from withdrawing his troops proved futile, few observers expected Hussein to invade beyond Kuwait's northern border. Hussein, however, defied those expectations with a full invasion of the country, heightening fears that Iraq would not only control Kuwait—and twenty percent of the world's oil production—but also push south toward **Saudi Arabia** and the rest of the Gulf, putting the region's vast oil reserves and financial resources in the hands of Hussein. Iraq was also suspected of having aspirations to produce nuclear, chemical, and biological weapons. Thus, the potential impact on the geopolitics of the region was far-reaching.

The international community, with the United States at the helm, responded with several political and economic measures intended to isolate Iraq. The United States looked to the United Nations to condemn the invasion of Kuwait, and also invoked a full battery of sanctions that included the freezing of Iraqi assets abroad. UN Resolution 678, passed in 1990, gave Iraq until January 15, 1991 to withdraw from Kuwaiti soil and authorized members to use whatever means necessary to uphold UN resolution 660, which condemned the invasion of Kuwait, and called for immediate troop withdrawal to be followed by a peaceful resolution of the dispute. With Hussein still undeterred, the United States prepared for a **military** response to the crisis. To stop Hussein and force Iraq's retreat in Kuwait, the cooperation of the United States with key European, and even more critically, Arab allies was essential. In the spirit of UN Resolution 660, fourteen of twenty-one states in the Arab League passed a similar resolution condemning the Iraqi invasion of Kuwait. If, however, a U.S.-led Coalition was to take effective military action, the use of Saudi Arabian bases was required for military deployment. With grave concerns about the imminent threat from Iraq widespread in the kingdom, Saudi Arabia's **Fahd bin 'Abd al-'Aziz** gave the United States access to Saudi soil.

Efforts to build an Arab coalition against Iraq revealed deep fissures between countries. Jordan, with its large Palestinian population resentful of the U.S. role in the Middle East, sided against the United States, as did the Palestine Liberation Organization and Algeria. Egypt, Saudi Arabia, Morocco, and a host of other Arab states joined the anti-Saddam Coalition.

On January 17, 1991, U.S.-led military action against Iraq began supported by UN resolutions authorizing the use of force and an international coalition of thirty-four countries. In addition to the United States, the following countries were involved: Afghanistan, Argentina, Australia, **Bahrain**, Bangladesh, Belgium, Canada, Czechoslovakia, Denmark, Egypt, France, Greece, Italy, Hungary, Kuwait, Morocco, the Netherlands, New Zealand, Niger, Norway, **Oman**, Pakistan, Philippines, Poland, **Qatar**, Romania, Republic of Korea, Saudi Arabia, Senegal, Sierra Leone, Singapore, Spain, Sweden, Syria, UAE, and the United Kingdom.

In addition to resolving the Kuwait crisis, however, the United States declared on August 4, 1990 that a broader aim of the crisis resolution was to create a stable Middle East, a proclamation reinforced at the Helsinki Summit in 1990, just before the Iraqi invasion of Kuwait. The Gulf War was followed by domestic upheaval in Iraq. Saddam Hussein quickly crushed **Shi'a** revolts in the south, and to the north the Kurds established a local self-governing administration that was supported by the West. No-fly zones were created in northern and southern Iraq to protect these populations. Furthermore, Iraq was subjected to UN weapons inspections to eliminate the threat it posed to the region.

See also **2003 Gulf War; Iran-Iraq War**.

FURTHER READING

Pimlott, John, and Stephen Badsey (eds). *The Gulf War Assessed*. London: Arms and Amour Press, 1992.

2003 Gulf War
Audra Grant

The 2003 Gulf War was brief, lasting twenty-one days from March 20 to April 9, 2003. Perhaps the greatest controversy leading up to the war was determining the legal justification for military action against Iraq. Supporters of military action against Iraq cited Saddam Hussein's refusal to cooperate with the UN weapons inspectors after more than a decade-long suspension of monitoring mandated after the **1990–1991 Gulf War**. As in that conflict, Saddam Hussein was suspected of trying to produce nuclear, biological, and chemical weapons.

What was striking was that Saddam Hussein, backed by an army of 400,000, went to battle confronting a Coalition force half its size, yet Iraqi forces barely demonstrated any response. The bellicose Iraqi leader did not defend any frontiers, and despite an eleventh-hour effort to hold Baghdad, the move did not culminate in significant street warfare at that time, an outcome that was expected by many observers. Even more striking, however, is the difficulty with bringing stability and democracy to Iraq, a Coalition goal that has been both elusive and costly.

BACKGROUND TO THE WAR: CRISIS IN 2002–2003

The September 11, 2001 attacks on New York and Washington, D.C. triggered a significant redirection of U.S. **foreign policy** as the United States began to identify enemies that lay outside of the traditional lens of the Cold War, which came to an end about a decade before. This new U.S. strategy culminated in the **War on Terror**, which sought to eliminate terrorist threats to American and global **security**. Thus, with the defeat of the Taliban in Afghanistan soon after the 9/11 attacks, the United States turned its attention toward Iraq, long seen as a threat to the Middle East because of its attempts to acquire and produce weapons of mass destruction (WMDs). Saddam Hussein, after all, used chemical weapons against Iran during the Iraq-Iran War (1980–1988), and against Iraq's own Kurdish population. Human rights abuses also continued, and Saddam Hussein is also believed to have orchestrated an assassination attempt against former U.S. President George Bush, who created the Gulf War Coalition against Saddam in 1990–1991. Furthermore and more controversially, the Iraqi leader was allegedly linked to the global terrorist group, **Al-Qa'idah**, held responsible for the 9/11 attacks. The U.S. ability to build a broad international coalition supported by the full force of the United Nations as in the 1990–1991 Gulf War proved elusive for efforts to launch **military** action against Iraq in the aftermath of the 9/11 assault. The impressive Arab support evident in the war just ten years earlier virtually evaporated against the backdrop of weak justification for military action against Saddam Hussein and the subsequent elimination of his oppressive regime. The signs, in fact, were ominous, beginning with **Saudi Arabia's** refusal to allow the United States access to its bases to deploy troops. Turkey was also uncooperative, and Jordan went with the tide of Arab opinion on the matter as well. In sharp contrast, **Kuwait**, risking isolation, agreed to allow the United States access to its bases. Aside from more solid support from Britain, a U.S. ally in 1990–1991, and Spain and Australia, the United States had a dearth of allies. Even the United States' European partners balked at the prospects of war against Iraq. France, usually more supportive of Arab causes, opposed a military solution to the Iraqi threat, as did Germany. The Coalition that prevailed in 2003 was a mere shadow of the one that dominated the 1990–1991 Gulf conflict.

To strengthen its position, the United States sought to build support within the United Nations. The United States set about at proving that Saddam Hussein was in violation of UN resolution 678, required Iraq to prove that it was not producing WMDs, and threatened serious consequences if Iraq resisted. The prospect of military measures under these circumstances evoked protest and opposition from many European capitals and their publics. Perhaps of greatest consternation to Washington D.C. was the opposition among two of its historically strongest allies, France and Germany. Anti-war movements soon emerged as publics launched large-scale demonstrations. Countries questioned the legal *casus belli* for the conflict, which rested on dubious supporting intelligence. In fact, the credibility of the intelligence was widely criticized. The coalition that emerged was dubbed "the Coalition of the Willing," and in addition to the United States it included the following countries: United Kingdom, Australia, Poland, South Korea, Romania, El Salvador, Czech Republic, Azerbaijan, Georgia, Denmark, Albania, Mongolia, Bosnia-Herzegovina, Ukraine, Estonia, Macedonia, Kazakhstan, Moldova, Bulgaria, Armenia, Latvia, Italy, Netherlands, Spain, Japan, Thailand, Honduras, Dominican Republic, Hungary, Nicaragua, Singapore, Norway, Portugal, New Zealand, Philippines, Tonga, and Iceland. The United States and the United Kingdom ultimately accounted for the vast majority of the deployed troops.

Iraq, responding to UN demands, submitted papers to UNMOVIC, although there were U.S. doubts that inspections would produce any tangible evidence either way. U.S. President George W. Bush accused Iraq of violating UN requirements, paving the way for a military confrontation despite lack of international consensus. On March 20, 2003, a U.S.-led military force invaded Iraq, marking the beginning of "Operation Iraqi Freedom." As in 1990–1991, Coalition forces were met with little Iraqi resistance. The Republican Guard numbering 60,000, the regular army numbering between 150,000 and 200,000, and irregular units were no match for the smaller but well-equipped invasion force. Iraqi forces were also saddled with poor equipment that was in low supply, further hampering their defensive capability. On April 9, 2003, the United States declared victory in Iraq. Saddam Hussein was captured in December 2003 and later executed in 2006.

As the invasion transitioned to occupation, the victory appeared hollow, for the U.S.-led coalition quickly found the goals of establishing a stable democracy in Iraq challenged by a formidable insurgency. Sectarian conflict between **Sunni** and **Shi'a** groups, Al-Qa'idah terrorism, multifaceted violent opposition forces, and Iranian-supported Shi'a militias have created an environment of violence and instability. With the death tolls ranging from 150,000 to 1 million amid continued insurgency, Coalition support has substantially waned.

FURTHER READING

Graham-Brown, Sarah. *Sanctioning Saddam Hussein: The Politics of International Intervention.* London: Tauris Books, 1999.
Keegan, John. *The Iraq War.* New York: Knopf, 2004.

H

Ha'il

Sebastian Maisel

Ha'il is a large **oasis** settlement in northern **Saudi Arabia** with approximately 400,000 inhabitants located on the southern edge of the Nafud Desert and the old **pilgrimage** route from Baghdad via Kufah to **Makkah**. It is surrounded by several **mountain** ranges, including the Jabal **Shammar**, Jabal Aja, and Jabal Salma. For over five decades from the middle of the nineteenth century, Ha'il was the center and capital of the **Al Rashid** Emirate, who governed and taxed most of central Arabia from here. However, during World War I and the concurrent political and economical changes it lost its status and independence to the **Riyadh**-based **Al Sa'ud**. With British help, **'Abd al-'Aziz ibn Sa'ud** defeated the Al Rashid and conquered Ha'il in 1921, incorporating the area into his newly established realm.

The population of Ha'il belongs to two main tribes, the Shammar and **Bani Tamim**. Although the Shammar claim the entire region as their territory, including the city, the Bani Tamim are settled farmers and city dwellers who have coexisted with the Shammar for centuries. Today the city's demographics have changed and Saudi nationals of different tribal origins as well as foreign guestworkers populate the city. Although in the past most people in Ha'il lived off of some form of **agriculture**, either farming or animal husbandry, today Ha'il is a developed and industrialized city. It serves as the administrative capital of the Ha'il province, which largely overlaps with the traditional territory of the Shammar tribe. The province is 125,000 square kilometers large and has approximately 500,000 inhabitants.

Historically, Ha'il became an important settlement of the region in the early nineteenth century when it superseded the former center of Fayd. The leading families of the Shammar tribe, the Al 'Ali and Al Rashid, made Ha'il their tribal capital, which attracted other social and economic groups to settle, including merchants and artisans. In the middle of the city is a large fortress, Barzan Palace, and the city itself was fortified with walls and towers. At the height of Al Rashid power between 1873 and 1902, Ha'il was the capital of an area that covered most of central Arabia, including Riyadh, parts of **Kuwait**, al-Jawf, **Tabuk**, and Tayma. However, the main power base of the Al Rashid were nomadic groups belonging to the Shammar confederation, who were a less reliable fighting force than those from settled forces loyal to the Al Sa'ud. With continuing

European involvement and the construction of the **Hijaz Railroad**, the dominant economic activities of Ha'il began to decline, most notably the caravan trade.

After World War I, Ibn Sa'ud amassed sufficient support, including some rival Shammar groups, and took Ha'il after a short siege. Most members of the Al Rashid were exiled to Riyadh, and a loyal Saudi governor was installed in their place. The city fell into decline. The fortifications and central buildings were torn down and many loyal followers of the Al Rashid left to neighboring Iraq, where other Shammar groups were well established. Many European travelers of the nineteenth and early twentieth centuries visited the city because of its less rigid attitude toward foreigners than the Wahhabi capital of Riyadh. Among those who left detailed accounts about the life in Ha'il at this time period were Georg Wallin (1854), William Palgrave (1865), Lady Anne Blunt (1881), Charles Doughty (1888), Julius Euting (1896), Gertrude Bell (1907), and Eldon Rutter (1931).

Today Ha'il is surrounded by large irrigation projects, making the area one of the Saudi Arabian breadbaskets. The Saudi government invests in and subsidizes large-scale agricultural projects as well as initial investments to establish a tourist industry.

FURTHER READING

Al Rasheed, Madawi. *Politics in an Arabian Oasis. The Rashidis of Saudi Arabia*. New York: I.B. Tauris, 1991.

Al Rasheed, Madawi. "Durable and Non-Durable Dynasties: The Rashidies and Sa'udis in Central Arabia," *British Journal of Middle Eastern Studies* 19, no. 2 (1992): 144–158.

Vassiliev, Alexei. *The History of Saudi Arabia*. London: Saqi Books, 1998.

Ward, Philip. *Ha'il—Oasis City of Saudi Arabia*. New York: Oleander Press, 1983.

Handicrafts
Sebastian Maisel

Prior to the **oil** boom, the **Arabian Peninsula** had little industry other than traditional crafts that have a long tradition in the *suq* (market) economy. Craft producers and sellers were always an integral part of the local economy, with many of the skills going back to the earliest craft of the late Neolithic period. People used the local resources available to them, such as leather, stone, hair, or plants. Other materials were obtained through trade relations with other areas, for example, wood and metals. Specific patterns, shapes, and colors were applied to give an object a distinct regional identity.

The traditional organization and function of crafts have changed very little since the Classical Islamic period until the oil boom of the 1950s. Crafts provided needed items, tools, and equipment for the population, settled or nomadic. However, in addition to useful tools, some objects were produced to be sold to outside markets such as spices and fragrances. Extensive trade routes emerged to

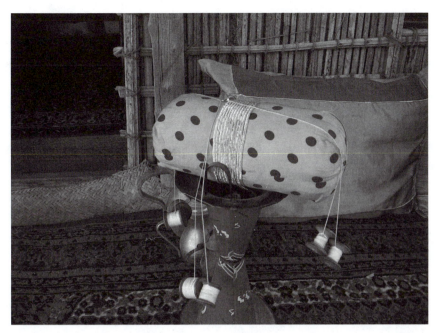

Traditional women's clothes in the Gulf and Oman make liberal use of embroidery in metal threads called *talli*. *Talli* **is made by first braiding metal and silk or cotton thread to make a strip. The strips are embroidered onto cuffs, sleeves, collars, and other parts of clothes.** Courtesy of John A. Shoup.

bring these items to international markets. Artisans depended on the macroeconomics of international trade and were able to compete effectively because their products were of higher quality. During the rapid and drastic economic transformations in Arabia during the mid-twentieth century, much of the local micro-economy of the craft industry was shattered.

The traditional structures of organizing artisans and small-scale businesses were very different from those of today. In larger trade centers of the larger cities and towns, wholesale dealers controlled the market and prices. Individual artisans were often organized into guilds. Most of the local producers were self-employed such as tinkers, tanners, goldsmiths, carpenters, weavers, builders, or wood-workers. They usually belonged to settled, non-tribal populations. Their clients included **Bedouin**, who although they despised the artisans needed their products. All of their metal and most of their wooden equipment were purchased from the market, such as **coffee** pots, tools, weapons, and saddles. The craft industry of Arabia also produced boats for fishing and **pearling**, rugs, tents, cooking utensils, **jewelry**, and clothes.

STONE AND CLAY PRODUCTS

Pottery is an ancient craft of Arabia, where clay objects date back to the end of the Neolithic period. Pottery is still alive, particularly in the **oases** along the

Few traditional handicrafts are still practiced in the Gulf States and Saudi Arabia following the exploitation of oil. In recent years, the governments in most of the Gulf States have tried to keep the traditions alive by bringing craftsmen such as this blacksmith to Heritage Villages such as this one in Dubai, where they are a living museum of the country's past. The craftsmen can sell their wares to locals trying to reconnect with their past and to tourists. This blacksmith makes a variety of tools and daggers for sale. Courtesy of John A. Shoup.

Gulf coast, **Bahrain**, and **Oman.** The techniques and styles have not changed much. Pots and jars were usually thrown on a wheel, often unglazed, and had little decoration. They were used for storing and refrigerating water and other produce. In addition, stones and adobe bricks were used as a building material for houses, towers, and storages. Sometimes theses buildings were covered with mud plaster and had their walls decorated or painted.

GRASS, LEAVES, AND WOOD

Palm fronds and some types of grass were woven into a variety of baskets, mats, and other products. Mats of different sizes formed simple huts called *barasti* or could be woven finer into types of food trays or mats to sit on. Baskets were used by farmers for storage containers or for winnowing wheat. In Oman Bedouin women of the **Wahibah** tribe still weave baskets that are so tight they can be used as milk bowls. Other palm frond or grass products included hand fans and wide-brimmed hats. Because of its scarcity, wood was collected for heating; tamarisk and acacia trees were the most common. Only a few items were manufactured from it, such as small bowls, looms, saddles, and litters. Wood as a building material was usually imported from India. Sometimes it was supplemented with the wood from palm trees, which could only be used for construction.

WEAVING

Weaving was a popular craft among sedentary as well as nomadic people, with several techniques applied such as twill weaving or pile weaving. Pile weaving is a recent development that required further skills such as extra warp twining. Often, many techniques were in a single item. It indicates the high technical and esthetic level of weaving in Arabia, but also influences from the outside brought to the area via **pilgrimage** or as gifts from rulers such as the Ottomans. Both settled and nomadic peoples used similar designs; however, the woven products of settled areas were produced on more complex looms. Bedouin weavers use a ground loom with no movable parts that allows for it to be moved during migrations. Tribal and regional affiliations were shown in distinct symbols or colors. A predominantly geometrical pattern symbolized the typical Arabian weaving. In addition, tribal brands/markers called *wasm* were sometimes included. Colors are usually bright, and synthetic dyes became widely popular following their introduction in the late 1940s and early 1950s. Natural dyes made from indigo, onions, pomegranates, iron, and copper ores were used, but the colors are muted in comparison to the synthetic dyes. Undyed wool from sheep or hair from **camels** and goats is used to provide brown, black, gray, and white tones. Typical weaving products included tents, rugs, curtains, blankets, saddlebags, and other camel and horse equipment. Today much of the local weaving has been greatly affected by the importation of inexpensive manufactured textiles.

LEATHER

Skins from camels, goats, and sheep were transformed into bags to carry water or milk as well as footwear such as sandals. Bedouins made large watering troughs from a wooden frame and a leather basin. As experienced tanners they were able to shape leather into various useful objects, such as water pulleys, udder bags, saddlebags, butter churners, or baby cradles.

JEWELRY

Silver jewelry is an important adornment for women all over Arabia. As part of their wedding dowry or simple adornment, jewelry shows a woman's social status and is worn every day. Certain pieces carry protective charms and are considered amulets and talismans against misfortune and the evil eye. Men usually do not wear jewelry, but use metal decoration on their weapons and sometimes their animals. One of the original centers of silversmithing was **Najran**—the other was **Yemen**. Clear distinctions in style, quality, and design can be made between jewelry worn by urban, rural, or nomadic women. City-women wear gold jewelry with more sophisticated designs. Blue and red semiprecious stones, such as turquoise and coral, amber, and glass insets are frequently found in urban jewelry. A woman's wealth was in her jewelry, personal property her husband had no right to touch and reflected her own status. Women adorn themselves with jewelry ranging from headpieces to necklaces, bracelets, anklets, earrings, nose rings, fingerings, toe rings, and belts. During the past several decades, most rural women have sold off their silver jewelry and replaced it with gold items that were imported from India and Italy.

Other metalwork included vessels, bowls, and pots that made of copper, brass, and tin. Manufactures for these items were found all over Arabia, but despite their importance and skills, tinkers belong to the lowest social class according to most Bedouins. They make even coffee pots, or *dallah*, an important symbol of Arab culture. Every family has a set of multiple pots that are used in the formal coffee ceremony. One of the main areas to manufacture those hourglass-shaped coffee pots is **al-Hasa**. Other places such as **Nizwa** in Oman are well-known for the quality of their metal work. In the southern area of the Peninsula, and predominantly in Yemen, highly decorated daggers and swords were locally produced and maintained their ceremonial importance as a symbol of status and virility. The curved daggers were normally made from embossed metal and ornamented with silver work. Special handles were made from imported or smuggled rhinoceros horns.

Today little of the local handicrafts are still found, although some effort is being made to keep aspects of them alive. *Saddu* House in Kuwait attempts to keep the art of Bedouin weaving alive by offering a place where the craft can be learned as well as items sold. Bahrain's potters and cloth weavers still have a ready market for the items they make, and in Oman the government policy is to provide both a pride in local crafts as well as a guaranteed market for craft items. Traditional handicrafts such as embroidery or woven items for camels are part of the growing sense of the need for a local identity.

See also **Dress**.

FURTHER READING

Faroqhi, Suraiya, and Randi Deguilhem (eds.). *Crafts and Craftsmen of the Middle East. Fashioning the Individual in the Muslim Mediterranean.* London: I.B. Tauris, 2005.

Richardson, Neil, and Marcia Dorr. *The Craft Heritage of Oman.* London: Motivate Publishing, 2003.

Topham, John, Anthony N. Landreau, and William E. Mulligan. *Traditional Crafts of Saudi Arabia.* London: Stacey International, 1981.

Topham, John. "Skilled Hands, Designing Hearts," *Saudi Aramco World* 38, no. 5 (1987): 30–36.

Harasis

John A. Shoup

The Harasis tribe is one of the groups that make up the Southern Arabian-speaking peoples generally referred to as the *Ahl al-Hadarah* in **Oman**. The Harasis occupy the Jiddat al-Harasis, a large pebble plain that separates **Dhufar** in the south from northern Oman. The Jiddat is a harsh region that historically was not permanently occupied until the arrival of the Harasis tribe, perhaps in the late nineteenth century. The tribes' right to use the Jiddat was recognized in the 1930s by *Sultan* **Sa'id bin Taymur**.

The Harasis are Hinawi (southern) and claim to have originated in the Hadaramawt. Unlike nearly all other tribal peoples in the **Arabian Peninsula**, the Harasis have maintained the pre-Islamic custom of a tribal totem of a fox. Despite being linguistically close to the Qarah and Mahrah peoples in Dhufar, the Harasis speak a dialect of Mahrah; they belong to the Arab **Bedouin** *suff* or confederation of the **'Awamir**, **Wahibah**, and **Bayt Kathir**; and until recently they considered both the Qarah and Mahrah as enemies. There seems to have been a degree of integration between the Bayt Kathir and the Harasis, and some of the Harasis lineages seem to be of Kathiri origin. When *Sultan* Sa'id ended tribal raiding in the 1950s, the Harasis and the Mahrah developed friendships, and during the Dhufar Rebellion several Mahrah families sought refuge with them.

The Harasis along with the **Duru'** and Wahibah are famous for their excellent **camel**s. Their camels are sought after by racing enthusiasts, and individual animals can cost hundreds of thousands of dollars. Some of the Harasis are still pastoral nomads, and the government development plan instituted for the Jiddat included integrated usage for pastoral nomads and herds of oryx. The plan brought Bedouin into the scheme by making them responsible for protecting the oryx.

Although some of the Harasis have opted to remain pastoral nomads, others have settled in the new towns and settlements that have grown up as a result of **oil** exploration such as Haima, Yaluni, and al-Ajaiz. Men found work with the oil **companies** as drivers and guides, whereas others have used new wealth from jobs to open shops and buy pickup trucks to bring supplies from Adam or **Nizwa**. They also help ship camels and small stock to northern markets, especially to Nizwa. Dawn Chatty notes that some families have been able to take advantage of a wide range of economic strategies with different brothers specializing in different fields.

See also **Dhufar Liberation Front.**

FURTHER READING

Carter, J.R.L. *Tribes in Oman*. London: Peninsular Publishing, 1982.
Chatty, Dawn. *Mobile Pastoralists: Development Planning and Social Change in Oman*. New York: Columbia University Press, 1996.

Al-Hasa

Sebastian Maisel

Al-Hasa (or al-Ahsa) is a region and administrative province in the eastern part of **Saudi Arabia** along the **Persian Gulf** that stretches over 60,000 square kilometers and includes more than 1 million inhabitants, many of them being **Shi'ite**

Large palm grove in al-Hasa oasis near Jabal Qara. Courtesy of Sebastian Maisel.

in contrast to the country's majority that is predominantly **Sunni** Hanbali. Major tribal groups in the region include the **Bani Khalid, al-Murrah, 'Ajman,** Manasir, Bani Hajir, and **'Awamir.** Often al-Hasa is equated with the Eastern Province of Saudi Arabia, but one has to dissociate the two. Historically, al-Hasa and al-Qatif formed a cultural and political unit. After administrative reforms, the newly created governorate of the Eastern Province includes not only them but also other areas and cities that developed later. The two main urban centers are Hufuf and Mubarraz, both **agricultural** and administrative centers and home for many **oil** workers. Al-Hasa is also considered among the largest **oases** in the world with more than 200 square kilometers of farmland and over 2 million **date** palms surrounded by dunes and salt marshes. To the southeast, the sand **desert** al-Jafurah borders the region, and to the west are the Summan plateau and the Dahna desert. Sand is blown into the oasis from the deserts, which covers and sometimes damages the irrigation system. To counter this problem, a large windbreak of trees was planted. The oasis is supplied by several karsts springs that provide warm groundwater that is distributed through pipelines and canals to the settlements and fields. The word *Ahsa* means the sound of underground water in Arabic. Caves made from sandstone are found throughout the area.

Al-Hasa is the ancient al-Hajar, an independent kingdom that originated around 1800 BC. Old Semitic inscriptions dating back to 300 BC have been discovered in the region. Al-Hasa was on the caravan route connecting **Yemen** with Mesopotamia, and the radical Shi'ite sect of the Qaramitah founded a settlement in the oasis. From their base in the Eastern Peninsula, they launched an attack on **Makkah** in 930 and stole the Black Stone of the Ka'abah, which they kept for twenty-two years in the Jawathah Mosque, which some believe to be the second oldest mosque in Islam. Between the sixteenth and eighteenth centuries several attempts were made by the Ottoman Empire to incorporate the area, but the local Bani Khalid tribe successfully drove them out. In 1793, the **Al Sa'ud** and their **Wahhabi** movement from central Arabia occupied it for the first time. After the first Saudi State was crushed by Muhammad 'Ali of Egypt, the area fell back under Ottoman control until **'Abd al-'Aziz ibn Sa'ud** finally subjugated the area to Wahhabi control in 1913. He annexed it to his realm of **Najd** and dependencies. The fortress Qasr Ibrahim in Hufuf is the most important remain of the Turkish period in eastern Arabia. The Bin Jiluwi branch of the ruling Al Sa'ud family was made governors of the area and virtually turned it into their own domain that they still rule today. The current governor, Badr bin Muhammad bin Jiluwi, is a member of the region's ruling family. In 1932, al-Hasa was officially incorporated into the Kingdom of Saudi Arabia. In the late 1930s huge oil deposits were discovered. The world's largest oil field, the Ghawar field, is located in al-Hasa. **Aramco**, the main exploring company, invested largely in the area's infrastructure and oil facilities, providing jobs, **education**, and other services to the population without discriminating between different religious groups. However, many Shi'ites were eager to work in the **oil industry** and received training. Unlike most of the **Bedouin**, they were willing to work with their hands and therefore became the core of the workforce in the oil industry. The entire area boomed when oil was found in sufficient quantities and revenues were invested in the infrastructure. Roads, schools, mosques, hospitals, and other facilities were built, including a railroad in 1953 that connected the **Damman** and al-Hasa with the capital **Riyadh**. In November 1979, the Shi'ite minority rioted, demanding religious and political concessions similar to those in neighboring Iran after the Islamic Revolution. King Faysal University has its largest campus in Hufuf as well as a campus for female students. The private Arab Open University also opened a campus in Hufuf.

FURTHER READING

Burkholder, Grace. *An Arabian Collection: Artifacts from the Eastern Province*. Boulder City, NV: GB Publications, 1984.

Facey, William J. *The Story of the Eastern Province of Saudi Arabia*. London: Stacey International, 1994.

Mandaville, Jon E. "The Ottoman Province of al-Hasa in the Sixteenth and Seventeenth Centuries," *Journal of the American Oriental Society* 90, no. 3 (1970): 486–513.

Nicholson, Eleanor. *In the Footsteps of the Camel: A Portrait of the Bedouins of Eastern Saudi Arabia in Mid-Century*. Riyadh: Transworld Arabian Library, 1983.

Vidal, Federico. "Date Culture in the Oasis of al-Hasa," *Middle East Journal* 8 (1954): 417–428.

Vidal, Federico. *The Oasis of al-Hasa*. Dhahran, Saudi Arabia: Arabian American Oil Co., Local Government Relations, Arabian Research Division, 1956.

Hashemites

Sebastian Maisel

The Banu Hashim, or Hashemites, are the ruling dynasty of Jordan but previously controlled much of northern Arabia, including the **Hijaz** and Iraq. They take their name from the great-grandfather of the Prophet **Muhammad**, Hashim bin 'Abd al-Manaf, who died around 540. The Banu Hashim is a clan of the **Quraysh** tribe of **Makkah** and gave Muhammad protection when the main ruling familes of the city were persecuting the young Muslim community. The Banu Hashim faced economic sanctions but did not give Muhammad up to the others. Muhammad's parents died when he was still very young, and it was his uncle Abu Talib and the extended Hashemite family that raised and protected him. The leadership of the Bani Hashim fell to 'Ali ibn Abi Talib, the cousin of the Prophet, and then to his two sons Hassan and Hussein. Claims for the Bani Hashim as the clan of the Prophet to rule the *ummah*, or entire Islamic community, were pressed by the followers of what is called the 'Alid cause until the 'Abbasids led a successful revolt against the Umayyads, establishing a ruling family of Hashemite origin (the 'Abbasids took their name from al-'Abbas, another uncle of the Prophet).

The dynasty of the **Sharif**s of Makkah who governed the Holy City from the tenth century to 1924 traces its origin back to the Bani Hashim. Because of their close descent from the family of the Prophet, they became masters of the two holiest places in Islam. The descendants of Hussein governed in **Madinah**, and those of Hassan in Makkah. The chief of the Hassanides in Makkah was known as the Grand Sharif of Makkah and was in charge of organizing the annual **pilgrimage** and the protection of caravans. After the collapse of the 'Abbasids in 1258 they had to acknowledge the sovereignty of other governments, but they never lost their privileged position in the Hijaz. The last Grand *Sharif* of Makkah was **Hussein bin 'Ali** (1916–1924). He was influenced by the growing Arab nationalist sentiment even while under house arrest in Istanbul. He was released after the Young Turks seized power from the *Sultan* 'Abd al-Hamid II, but resented the Young Turks' policy favoring Turks over other peoples of the empire. He entered into an exchange of letters with the British in Egypt even before World War I began, and once hostilities began he pressed the British to promise the creation of an independent Arab kingdom in exchange for his support. In 1916 he declared the **Arab Revolt**, which was supported by tribal fighters initially from the Hijaz. His son Faysal led the Arab Revolt against the Turks, and after World War I he tried to establish a Hashemite kingdom in Syria. Faysal was defeated by the French in 1920 at the Battle of Maysalun outside of Damascus and was forced to retreat into British Mandate territory. Later he was awarded with the throne of Iraq by Britain. Hashemite rule in Iraq ended on July 14, 1958 with the revolution and abolition of the monarchy. Some members escaped the subsequent massacres to Jordan, where another son of Hussein, 'Abdallah, was able to build a separate country. In 1922 Jordan was detached from the British Mandate of Palestine and 'Abdallah was given the region, then called the Transjordan. Jordan became fully independent in 1948 as the Hashemite Kingdom of Jordan, which is ruled today by King 'Abdallah II.

In the Hijaz, the Hashemites remained in power after World War I, first under *Sharif* Hussein bin 'Ali and then under his son, 'Ali ibn Hussein. They gradually lost the support of Great Britain. In 1924 Kamal Attaturk abolished the position of *khalifah*, or caliph, and *Sharif* Hussein bin 'Ali tried to seize the opportunity to claim the title for himself. This provocative move created immediate tensions with his biggest regional rival, **'Abd al-'Aziz ibn Al Sa'ud**, *Sultan* of **Najd**, who started a **military** campaign with the goal to incorporate the Hijaz into his realm. Although highly ambitions, without military and financial backing of Great Britain his attempt was short lived. To save the Hijaz for his family, he abdicated in 1924 for his oldest son 'Ali and renounced his claims to the caliphate. However, 'Ali was quickly defeated and lost all major cities in the Hijaz, including **Ta'if**, Makkah, and finally **Jiddah**. The heartland of Bani Hashim was lost to the **Al Sa'ud** and became an integral part of the Kingdom of **Saudi Arabia**.

The Bani Hashim remained the most dangerous opponent to the Al Sa'ud in the Middle East and continued challenging Saudi hegemony by supporting Hijazi opposition groups such as the Hijazi Liberal Party and the Ibn Rifada rebellion in 1931. It took another twenty-five years before the two hostile dynasties reconciled in 1957 in the wake of the creation of the Baghdad Pact, the propagation of the Eisenhower Doctrine, and a common anti-Nasrist policy. Today, the ruling Hashemite family of Jordan is well respected in the Middle East and enjoys good relations with the West.

FURTHER READING

Paris, Timothy. *Britain the Hashemites and Arab Rule, 1920–1925.* London: Routledge, 2003.

Susser, Asher, and Aryeh Shmuelevitz (eds.). *The Hashemites in the Modern Arab World. Essays in Honor of the Late Professor Uriel Dann.* London: Frank Cass, 1995.

Teitelbaum, Joshua. *The Rise and Fall of the Hashemite Kingdom of Arabia.* New York: New York University Press, 2001.

Wilson, Mary C. *King Abdullah, Britain and the Making of Jordan.* Cambridge: Cambridge University Press, 1987.

Wilson, Mary C. "The Hashemites, the Arab Revolt, and Arab Nationalism," in *The Origins of Arab Nationalism*, edited by Rashid Khalidi et al. New York: Columbia University Press, 1991.

Health Care Systems

Sebastian Maisel

The Arab Gulf States enjoy one of the best and sophisticated medical systems in the Middle East. With the revenues from the **oil industry**, large-scale medical complexes and hospitals have been built in the region providing the most up-to-date, state-of-the-art technologies and practices. Most of these services are available at low or no cost at all.

Health care is the domain of the government, usually the Ministry of Health, which provides preventative, curative, and rehabilitative care through a network of medical institutions such as local health care centers, regular hospitals, and specialized clinics. Care is also provided by other state agencies such as the **military** and public **companies** that have their own medical centers. Citizens and expatriates working in the public sector receive free health care. There is a growing sector of private health care providers with state-of-the-art hospitals who provide extensive treatment for a fee. Many prefer this to public health care, which, although free, does not have the same quality of care. Additionally, the Red Crescent provides emergency care through ambulances and first aid centers. The Red Crescent plays a pivotal role for maintaining health care and first aid to millions of pilgrims during the *Hajj* season.

Modern health care and hygiene systems were introduced to **Saudi Arabia** in the late nineteenth century to improve the sanitation needs of the **pilgrimage** to **Makkah**. The *Hajj* brought together several hundreds of thousands pilgrims from all over the world and diseases spread quickly, particularly cholera. The first quarantine stations were built in **Jiddah** in the 1880s.

In 1913, the Saudi ruler **'Abd al-'Aziz ibn Sa'ud** invited missionary doctors from the American Mission in **Bahrain** to provide medical service for his people. Their services were initially rejected by the local population, which relied on traditional medical practices. However, soon the service proved to be successful and was extended to various communities in central Arabia as well as along the Gulf coast from **Kuwait** to **Oman**. The American Mission contributed enormously to the improvement of medical and hygiene conditions in Arabia. The American Mission was financed and staffed by members of the Reformed Church of America, and their services were greatly appreciated despite the fact that it was a Christian mission. The doctors and nurses made progressive changes to the understanding and application of modern medicine.

Another major contributor to improving medical and health conditions in eastern Arabia was **Aramco**. From its beginning in the 1930s, they provided Western medical facilities not only to their Western workers, but also to the local staff and population. However, it took until the 1970s for adequate service to reach more remote areas of the kingdom. The new medical services replaced the more traditional profession of healers, who often relied on amulets to cure diseases. Another traditional practice was the exhortation of evil spirits, which required the services of an experienced specialist in spirit possession. Elder, experienced women in the family usually treated simple illnesses.

The benefits of the new state-supported health care can be observed in a very low rate of infant mortality as well as an extended life span of the older generation. Both issues contribute much to a significant demographic change in the Gulf society. Arab Gulf States have a higher birth rate as well as longer lifespans than most other Middle Eastern countries.

There is substantial variation in the quality of Saudi primary care services. To improve quality, there is a need to improve the management and organization of primary care services. Professional development strategies are also needed to improve the knowledge and skills of staff. Until recently, almost the entire medical staff were expatriates, with doctors mostly coming from Western nations and nurses from the Philippines and the West. Although it is one of the few permissible occupations for local women, their percentage in the medical workforce is marginal because of constant interaction with unrelated men. Only a few Saudi and Gulf women proceed with medical careers; however, Saudi and Gulf doctors are more common.

Population growth and longer life expectations have created a major demand for change in the health care system of **Qatar**, where Hamad Medical Corporation (HMC), the public provider, is trying to cope and the private sector is not yet ready to step in. Since 1979 HMC has provided free services to Qataris, but it is largely inefficient. With the formation of the National Health Authority in 2005, the government is attempting to reform the system by investing in new infrastructure, health awareness campaigns, and modern technology. In Bahrain, similar policies have been introduced. The country's largest hospital, Salmaniyah Medical Complex, carries the maximum load of patients, which should be shifted to primary health care centers or the private sector. In addition, it is hoped that modernization in the health care sector will bring in medical tourists and keep Bahrainis from going abroad for critical operations. Kuwait is facing the same demographic problems in which higher birth rates and a larger number of elderly people require more services.

Lifestyle and eating habits of most Gulf people have changed and demand additional health care to deal with new problems such as obesity. The public health sector needs to expand, whereas the private sector needs to be more involved. To address the shortage in medical personnel, the government of Saudi Arabia expects to hire more non-nationals. However, hiring more non-foreigners will negatively affect the country's policy of nationalizing the workforce. Although other Gulf States talk about modernizing their health sector, the **Emirates** started with it and invested large sums in a concept of unifying health care policies across the country. All nationals and residents are compelled to have medical insurance.

Before 1970 Oman had only one hospital run by American missionaries. After **Sultan Qabus** came to power, he invested largely in health care and hygiene. Today, the country has several modern hospitals; however, most of the professional staff is still foreign. The government encourages health care workers to move to the countryside to help improve the low standards of living and to improve the general health care standards. Mass immunization campaigns helped to significantly decrease infant mortality and raised the life expectancy.

FURTHER READING

al-Ahmadi, Hanan, and Martin Roland. "Quality of Primary Health Care in Saudi Arabia: A Comprehensive Review," *International Journal for Quality in Health Care* 17, no. 4 (2005): 1–16.

Amerding, Paul L. *Doctors for the Kingdom: The Work of the American Mission Hospital in the Kingdom of Saudi Arabia, 1913–1955.* Grand Rapids, MI: Eerdmans, 2003.

Conrad, Peter, and Eugene Gallagher. *Health and Health Care in Developing Countries.* Philadelphia: Temple University Press, 1993.

Doumato, Eleanor Abdella. *Getting God's Ear: Women, Islam, and Healing in Saudi Arabia and the Gulf.* New York: Columbia University Press, 1999.

Mufti, Muhammad H. *Health Care Development Strategies in the Kingdom of Saudi Arabia.* New York: Kluwer Publisher, 2000.

Pierre-Louis, Anne Maryse, Francisca A. Akala, and Hadia S. Karam. *Public Health in the Middle East and North Africa: Meeting the Challenges of the Twenty-First Century.* Washington, D.C.: World Bank Publications, 2004.

Hijaz

Sebastian Maisel

The Hijaz ("barrier" in English) is a mountainous region in northwest **Saudi Arabia** between the Midian **Mountains** in the north and the **Asir** Mountains to the south, stretching over an area of more than 500,000 square kilometers and including 2.5 million inhabitants. It separates the heartland of Arabia, **Najd**, from the coastal plains of the **Tihamah**. Important urban centers in the Hijaz include **Jiddah**, **Makkah**, **Madinah**, **Ta'if**, **Yanbu'**, and **Tabuk**.

The Hijaz consists of an arid, **desert**-like highland that reaches an altitude of over 8,202 feet (2,500 meters) south of Ta'if. In the west it sharply drops in an escarpment to Tihamah. Steep **wadis** run toward the Red Sea coast and cut the escarpment. The largest of these is Wadi al-Hamdh, which reaches the Tihamah south of al-Wajh. Basaltic volcanic fields called *harrah* in Arabic cover large areas of the Hijaz. The mountains receive higher amounts of precipitation, making the area attractive for farming. Intensive agriculture and caravan trade were the two most important sources of income until after World War II.

In pre-Islamic times, the area was inhabited by Arab tribes, some of which settled along the caravan routes and established centers for trade and commerce. During the early Islamic period under the Prophet **Muhammad** and his immediate successors, the Hijaz was the core of the Islamic Empire. Makkah and Madinah as holy sanctuaries were closed to non-Muslims. After the rise of the Umayyad dynasty, the center of the empire shifted to Damascus, and under the 'Abbasids to Baghdad. However, Makkah and Madinah remained the focal point of Muslim worship and the yearly **pilgrimage**. Some of the **Bedouin** tribes from other parts of the Peninsula migrated into the Hijaz during the early Islamic period, such as the Banu Harb. Despite the Hijaz's peripherial position in the politics and economics of the Islamic empires, control over the two Holy Cities and the Hijaz in general was an important asset in legitimizing Islamic rule. The Ayyubids, the Mamluks, and later the Ottomans all strove to include the area within their areas of control. The Ottomans created a new administrative province with Makkah as its capital. Three *sanjaks*, or administrative subdivisions, were formed around the cities of Makkah, Madinah, and Jiddah. Nonetheless, the Ottomans did not disturb the local forms of self-government that remained intact.

The religious reform movement of **Muhammad 'Abd al-Wahhab** that started in central Arabia spread quickly through the Hijaz, and several times the two Holy Places were occupied by **Wahhabi** forces. Their strict interpretation of Islamic law was considered offensive to the cosmopolitan people of the Hijaz as well as for the Ottoman *Sultan*. The *Sultan* sent his vassal Muhammad 'Ali of Egypt to expel the Wahhabis and reinstate the authority of the *Sharif*s of Makkah.

The **Hashemites** sided with Great Britain and in 1916 declared the **Arab Revolt**. Bedouin tribes from the Hijaz joined the fight for an independent Arab kingdom to be established in the former Arab provinces of the empire. The Hashemites continued to govern the Hijaz until 1924, when Wahhabi Saudis finally overthrew them. The last King of the Hijaz, 'Ali ibn Hussein, surrendered to **'Abd al-'Aziz ibn Al Sa'ud**, who declared the Hijaz part of his realm but granted special political privileges to the **Bani Hashim**. **Faysal ibn 'Abd al-'Aziz** was made viceroy, who consulted with a body of local representatives in political matters. In 1932 the Hijaz was officially incorporated into the newly established Kingdom of Saudi Arabia. The Hijaz at this time was economically the most advanced region of country with an economy based on the yearly pilgrimage and subsequent trade. Not only did the Saudi state depend on *Hajj* revenues, but also many local merchant families were wealthy and influential due to providing *Hajj* services. Until the beginning of the **oil**-based economy, the Hijaz continued to dictate the country's development and progress. Today, some of the old rivalries between the Hijaz and other regions, particularly Najd, are still present with complaints about discrimination against the former Hijazi elite.

FURTHER READING

Baker, Randall. *King Husain and the Kingdom of Hejaz*. New York: Oleander Press, 1979.
Hogarth, David. *Hejaz before World War One*. Cambridge, UK: Oleander Press, 1978.
Ochsenwald, William. *Religion, Society, and the State in Arabia: The Hijaz under Ottoman Control, 1840–1908*. Columbus: Ohio State University Press, 1984.
Rotter, Eldon. "The Hejaz," *The Geographical Journal* 77, no. 2 (1931): 97–108.
Yamani, Mai. *Cradle of Islam: The Hijaz and the Quest for an Arabian Identity*. London: I.B. Tauris, 2004.

Hijaz Railway
Sebastian Maisel

The Hijaz Railway, built between 1900 and 1908, was one of the most important railroads of the Ottoman Empire. Commissioned by *Sultan* Abd al-Hamid II, the German engineer Heinrich August Meissner Pasha supervised the construction. The railway was initially planned to connect Damascus with **Makkah** to facilitate the **pilgrimage** to the Holy Places in the **Hijaz**. Meissner, who previously participated in the construction of the Baghdad Railway, was charged with the planning of the railway. Over 800 miles (1,300 kilometers) of narrow-gauge (41 inch or 1,050 millimeter) monotracks were built by Turkish workers and soldiers with German assistance. The completed railway included 1,532 bridges, two tunnels, and ninety-six stations. However, the final destination was **Madinah** rather than

Makkah. A side branch was added to connect Dara'ah in Syria with the Mediterranean port of Haifa to bring in building materials and other supplies. Engines, wagons, and specialized staff were brought in from Germany. The stations were built with a German-like style following the tastes of what is called Ottoman rococo. Officially aimed to transport pilgrims, the construction was mainly financed by donations from Muslims from all over the world. The Hijaz Railway had strategic importance for the Ottoman state to enable better economic control of Syria and **Palestine**, which then included Lebanon and Jordan, as well as for improved **military** control of the Arab provinces. Regular service was provided for seven years.

During the **Arab Revolt** in World War I, the Arab army under **Lawrence of Arabia** made great efforts to cut and destroy the railway by blowing up tracks, stations, and bridges. The Hijaz Railway was a vital tool to bring in reinforcements. After its destruction, Turkish forces were no longer able to keep the area under their control. Attempts were made to revive the railway after the war, but the last regular train was recorded in 1924. After the conquest of the Hijaz by Saudi Arabia and several destructive heavy rains, the section between Ma'an in Jordan and Madinah was closed. According to the Locarno Treaties in 1925, the fleet engines and other equipment were split between Syria and Transjordan.

Several unsuccessful attempts were made to repair the tracks and get the trains running again. In 1935, during the Conference of Haifa, a restart of the service was discussed; however, the plan was dismissed because of financial problems. The destruction of the Yarmuk Bridge in 1946 finally ended the direct connection between Damascus and Haifa. Only those sections in Syria and Jordan (307 miles, or 495 kilometers) were fixed and kept operational. In the 1950s the last pilgrim trains brought Muslim pilgrims from Damascus to Ra's al-Naqab in Jordan, from where they had to change to buses. Occasionally, plans are drawn to open up the section from Ma'an to Madinah and eventually extend the network all the way to **Jiddah** or **Riyadh**, from where a connection to **Dammam** on the Persian Gulf exists. In 1977, after Jordan and Syria purchased new engines, new talks with Saudi Arabia began to reconstruct the entire railway; however, because of strained bilateral relations they were abandoned in 1983. In 1999 passenger trains started to run again between Damascus and 'Amman.

FURTHER READING

Nicolson, James. *The Hijaz Railway.* London: Stacey International Publishers, 2005.

Ochsenwald, William. *The Hijaz Railroad.* Charlottesville: University Press of Virginia, 1980.

Tourret, R. *The Hedjaz Railway.* Abingdon, UK: Tourret Publishing, 1989.

Holidays and Festivals: Islamic

John A. Shoup

There are two major festivals celebrated by all Muslims: *'Id al-Adha*, or Feast of Sacrifice, on the tenth of *Dhu al-Hajj* toward the end of the *Haj* or **pilgrimage** to **Makkah**, and *'Id al-Fitr*, or Feast of Breaking Fast, which marks the end of the month of *Ramadan* and is celebrated during the first three days of *Shawwal*. These are the only two religious festivals fully sanctioned in Islam; however, there are other festivals that have arisen over the centuries that are seen by many in the Islamic world as religious. These include *'Ashurah* on the tenth day of *Muharram*, which marks the death of *Imam* Hussein ibn 'Ali at the hands of the Umayyads; *al-Isra' wa al-Mi'raj* on the twenty-seventh of *Rajab*, which is the night the Prophet **Muhammad** had his mystical journey to Jerusalem and then to heaven; and *Mawlid al-Nabi*, or the Birthday of the Prophet Muhammad on the twelfth of *Rabi' al-Awwal*.

'Id al-Fitr is also referred to as the *al-'Id al-Saghir*, or the Lesser Festival. It marks the end of the month of *Ramadan* when all Muslims of a certain age are to fast: not eating, drinking, smoking, or allowing anything to pass the lips from dawn to dusk. When the new moon of the next Islamic month is sighted, an official announcement is made (today using **television** and radio) stating that the *'Id* has begun. The Islamic **calendar**, similar to the Jewish calendar, starts the day at dusk and runs to the following dusk. A special type of cake/cookie called *ka'k* is prepared and forms an important part of the breakfast eaten the next morning. In many of the Gulf States families used to give the *musahir*, or the person who walked the neighborhood beating a drum to make sure all are awake for the pre-dawn meal (*suhur*), gifts of money, rice, and wheat. Children are given new clothes to wear. In **Bahrain** on the first day of the *'Id*, women of the house perform a special **dance** called *muraddah*, which is accompanied only by clapping and stamping. In Bahrain, **Qatar**, and other central Gulf areas the *'Id* includes performances of other dances in public with men wearing horse costumes. The dancers' upper body is dressed as a rider, and from the waist down they wear horse costumes. The dancers imitate the gaits of horses, prancing and parading to the beat of a chorus of drums. Traditionally in much of the Gulf, the *'Id* lasted a full week, with people visiting each other and bringing gifts of sweets and dried fruits, but today the *'Id* normally lasts three days.

A unique part of *Ramadan* in the Gulf was the custom that on the night of the fourteenth and fifteenth of the month, children went from house to house with large cloth collection bags playing drums. They were given coins, sweets, and a mix of dried figs and nuts called *girga'*. Older children formed into groups that also went from house to house but performed dances to the beat of drums. They too were given *girga'* as a reward. Such customs are rarely practiced anywhere in the Gulf today.

The pilgrimage to Makkah is an obligation of all Muslims who can afford to make the journey, and the ninth day of the pilgrimage is marked by prayer at 'Arafat. On the same day children in Bahrain and Qatar celebrate what is called *hiya biya*. Children collect green sprouts of wheat, wheat or barley grain, and sweets in a basket called a *nanun* that they take to the sea singing the *hiya biya* song. When they reach the shore the baskets are thrown into the sea. A similar custom used to be done to mark the stages of a child's life, including the first step, first tooth, and so forth. Today this is rarely done.

The tenth day of the pilgrimage is marked by *'Id al-Adha*, which is also called *al-'Id al-Kabir* or the Great Festival. In the morning a lamb or sheep is slaughtered in imitation of both the Prophet Ibrahim (Abraham), whose hand was stayed by an angel when he was about to sacrifice his son Isma'il (Ishmael in the Muslim tradition), and of the Prophet Muhammad, who first sacrificed a lamb on that day. The Prophet Muhammad gave the meat to the poor, and following his example part of the animal killed that morning is to be distributed to those who are in need, the family consumes a portion, and part is dried to eat at other times of the year. The *'Id* usually lasts two to three days depending on the country.

An important part of both holidays are the *'Id* prayers. For both *'Id al-Fitr* and *'Id al-Adha*, the morning prayer is an important time for all males of the community to pray together, and although this can be held in a local mosque, the numbers may be too great to accommodate everyone. As a result, a large outdoor place marked with the direction of prayer called a *musallah* is used instead. Men wear their best or new clothes to attend the prayer, and fathers bring their sons as an important part of being socialized into the community of believers.

'Ashurah is celebrated mainly by **Shi'ites** as a day of intense mourning for the death of *Imam* Hussein ibn 'Ali at Karbala in Iraq in 680. Some Shi'ite practices such as self-mutilation are highly discouraged by the **Sunni** governments in the Gulf and **Saudi Arabia** to the point that in some countries the celebration is banned. Where the Shi'ites form a large minority (**Kuwait**) or the majority (Bahrain), governments have been willing to turn a blind eye to much of the outpouring of grief. The day is not an official holiday in any of the Gulf countries. *'Ashurah* is not generally a celebration for Sunnis in the Gulf, although in much of the rest of the Sunni world it is a children's holiday: a cross between trick-or-treating and Christmas caroling. Children dress up and in the evening go from door to door singing and in return are given money, sweets, and dried fruit or nuts.

The *Mawlid al-Nabi* is not an official holiday in many of the Gulf States or in Saudi Arabia. The celebration of the Prophet's birthday is seen by many conservative Islamic scholars as *bid'*, or innovation, and therefore not legal. Historically the celebration appears to have started in Egypt under the Shi'ite Fatamids and was accepted by the subsequent Sunni dynasties of Egypt and Syria. The Sunni Ottoman Turks embraced it and made it an official holiday. In the Gulf region it was a day when religious poems in praise of the Prophet were read or sung, but little is done for it today. Kuwait, with its long historical connection to Iraq, does include the Prophet's birthday as an official holiday, as do **Oman** and the **United Arab Emirates**. The *Isra' wa al-Mi'raj* celebrates the mystical journey of the Prophet to Jerusalem and then to the seven spheres of heaven. It is not officially recognized as a holiday in the Gulf and Saudi Arabia except in Kuwait.

Holidays and Festivals: National

John A. Shoup

Saudi Arabia and the Gulf States have several national days and celebrations that are not part of the **Islamic practice**. Some of these are official holidays and all government offices are closed, whereas others, although there is official recognition of them, are not days when government offices close.

New Year's Day, both for the Western calendar and the Islamic **calendar**, is a holiday in several Gulf States and is considered to be a secular, nonreligious holiday. Islamic practice has not made any special difference for the first day of the Islamic year, and it is not a holiday in **Saudi Arabia**. **Qatar** includes only Islamic New Year as an official holiday, whereas **Bahrain**, **Kuwait**, **Oman**, and the **United Arab Emirates** all close government offices for both Western and Islamic New Year. Although nothing is done for the New Year's celebrations, expatriates from the countries where Western New Year's is a holiday organize parties as do many of the large hotels. Most of the Gulf States allow hotels and shops to display Christmas decorations as well, although none give Christmas any official recognition.

All of the countries have official National Days at different times of the year. For many the day celebrates the country's full independence from Britain, as is the case for Kuwait, Bahrain, Qatar, and the United Arab Emirates. In Oman the National Day and the *Sultan's* birthday are only one day apart, November 18 and 19, and both are celebrated. National Days throughout the region are celebrated with displays of national culture, **music**, **dance**, and foods. In some countries such as Oman and Saudi Arabia, massive parades and pageants are staged in large outdoor stadiums with **military** and civilian participation. National and satellite **television** channels carry the events live. In Saudi Arabia the National Day has taken on greater importance after the celebration of 100 years after the founding of the current state (2002 marking the century of the state according to the *Hijari* calendar) and after recent terrorist activities. National Day has come to be a means by which the Saudi government is trying to instill feelings of greater integration of the different regions of the country.

Bahrain's National Day each year has had special themes and frequently the National Museum sets the theme. Each year a different part of the culture is the focal point for cultural and book displays as well as activities, including performances of traditional music and dance. These have included the social importance of the **Arabian horse**, for example, as well as on **pearling**, **dates**, and the art of Arabic calligraphy. Bahrain's National Day has served as the launching idea for several subsequent festivals in other Gulf countries, especially in the United Arab Emirates.

See also **Holidays and Festivals: Islamic**.

Honor

Sebastian Maisel

Honor has an important meaning in the culture of the **Arabian Peninsula**. A person who demonstrates bravery, hospitality, generosity and respect for others and is helpful has "honor" and is a prominent member of society. Living according to these attributes brings both a good reputation and honor. It is possible to lose both good reputation and honor through what is deemed publicly as "bad" behavior. To win them back a person may have to submit to socially sanctioned punishment. Reputation and status, both good and bad, are linked to wider considerations of family and can be passed on to the next generations. Neither honor nor reputation is measured by material possessions, and a person's wealth does not bring honor; respectable behavior of the individual brings honor.

The concept of honor is closely related to shame, *'ayb* in Arabic or *haram* in a religious context. Honor is found in interpersonal relations between relatives as well as other members of society, pointing to the existence of individual and collective forms of honor. The honor of the group is called *sharaf*, whereas for the individual honor is called *wajh*, meaning face in Arabic. Special attention is given to the honor of women with regard to their sexual conduct and reputation. According to the tribal concept of collective responsibility, honor of the entire group is dependent on the chastity of its female members of childbearing age. Misconduct affects not only the woman, but also her male relatives. The honor of women is called *'irdh* in Arabic and it plays an important part in the definition of *sharaf*. To keep good reputations and maintain honor, women should avoid contact with men other than relatives and show restraint when this cannot be avoided; that is, dress modestly; avoid eye contact, and not make what would be judged as unnecessary communications and improper movements. Honor must be defended when it is questioned or violated. It is not possible to live in Arab society with a damaged reputation or tainted honor. A person who cannot or will not protect his personal honor and the honor of his kin group is considered weak, and others avoid contact with him and his group.

The main focus of identity within Arab society is still on the extended family and the code of personal and collective honor. The code can be seen as a guideline of how to interact on personal, communal, and even economic levels. It is most imperative to guarantee that everyone involved with the group respects the code and makes sure that no one will "lose face."

In the Gulf societies these values are often mixed with religious values, although other Muslim societies interpret them more liberally. For example, modest **dress** is required for Muslim women, which usually includes covering the body and hair. In **Saudi Arabia** women are also required to cover their faces and sometimes their hands. This is explained with religious arguments, but is mainly an extension of the concept of female honor and the social rule of not bringing shame to the family. The traditional custom of gender segregation and its application to virtually every aspect of public life have to be seen in the same light.

Because of the strict application of Islamic law, which embedded many pre-Islamic legal norms of honor and shame, **crimes** related to honor cases are very rare. Honor killings are not usually noted in the legal system in Saudi Arabia, although they are for some of the other countries in the Middle East such as Jordan, Syria, and Iraq. However, issues related to honor such as personal offenses and more serious crimes do exist and are often dealt with by the families rather than furthering the family shame by bringing them to court.

There are two ways to harm someone's honor. The first is sexual violation, that is, adultery or rape. However, because every woman is a member of a larger extended kin group, the honor of the group is also violated and therefore requires legal actions to restore honor to all. The second is when a person is harmed and therefore is seen to have lost face—honor must be restored. In Arabic such an action has "blackened" the face, meaning it has been shamed. Should this matter be brought to a court, rulings often include two penalties: a compensation for any material loss, and another one for the restoration of the victim's honor. The victim's face has again been "whitened."

See also **Crime**.

FURTHER READING

Abu Lughod, Lila. *Veiled Sentiments: Honor and Poetry in a Bedouin Society*. Berkeley: University of California Press, 2000.

Bowen, Donna Lee, and Evelyn Early. *Everyday Life in the Muslim Middle East*. Bloomington: Indiana University Press, 2000.

Meeker, Michael E. *Literature and Violence in North Arabia*. Cambridge, UK: Cambridge University Press, 1979.

Stewart, Frank Henderson. *Honor*. Chicago: University of Chicago Press, 1994.

Human Rights in Saudi Arabia
James Sater

Human rights are commonly understood as being protected if the legal framework in a given country protects basic rights of the individual, such as the freedom of speech and religion. A mechanism through which this is achieved connects these civic rights with basic political rights on the basis of choosing political representatives, and establishing a system of political accountability checks and balances. Some of these legal principles have been enshrined as the rule of law (i.e., a **judicial system** based on guaranteeing rights of the accused by minimizing arbitrary legal procedures).

In **international relations**, some of these principles have been codified in the International Covenant on Political and Civil Rights (ICPCR). Although many mostly liberal democratic states are signatories to the ICPCR, Saudi Arabia and other Gulf monarchies have not signed it, thereby officially stating their resistance to the normative dimension of human rights as understood by the ICPCR. Numerous human rights violations comprise inhuman capital punishments such as stoning, public beheadings, and mutilations; the absence of defense lawyers in secret trials; the widespread use of torture and intimidation by unchecked police forces; the lack of religious rights of the country's large **Shi'a** minority (five to fifteen percent depending on sources); and especially the complete social and legal disenfranchisement of women.

Saudi human rights activists tried to take Saudi Arabia's particular tribal-religious ethos into account: after all, Saudi Arabia was created by the tribal expansion of **'Abd al-'Aziz ibn Al Sa'ud** supported by the particularly orthodox **Wahhabi** sect founded by **Muhammad ibn 'Abd al-Wahhab** in the eighteenth century. Thereby a tribal state was created based on the promise to establish the Wahhabi vision of Islam. The only human rights group that was ever created on Saudi territory (in May 1993) was named (in English) Committee for the Defense of *Shari'ah* Law. Its charter stated that "all men are brothers in Islam" and "it is an obligation upon Muslims to support the oppressed, eliminate injustices, and defend the rights prescribed by the *Shari'ah* for man." One signatory to the charter of the committee, 'Abdallah ibn 'Abd al-Rahman al-Jabrin, declared that "legitimate rights" are not rights applied to everybody, but rather are to be allocated according to religious (i.e., Wahhabi) criteria.

Despite the committee's "tamed" and religious character, the government dismissed four of the committee's founding members from their university positions; it closed the offices of two lawyers; and the spokesman for the committee, Muhammad al Mas'ari, was arrested and detained without charges before being imprisoned for six months. The history of the committee not only illustrates how severely basic civil liberties are restricted, but also how the Saudi state uses Islam to counter attempts that try to carve out political space with reference to the legitimacy of Islam. The head of the government-financed Council of Senior Muslim Scholars, *Shaykh* 'Abd al-'Aziz ibn Baz, called the committee "illegitimate" and "superfluous," "because the kingdom is already ruled by the *shari'ah* and therefore the rights of everybody is already protected by the law."

Given that the Saudi family controls all political decisions and institutions and relies on the country's orthodox *'ulama'* for legitimacy and support, no real changes have occurred in recent years. One notable exception is the controlled electoral process in 2006 to the country's formerly uniquely appointed consultative *shura* council, in which only men were allowed to participate. The council has no power to hold the government accountable for its actions. As long as critics are banned from publicly expressing themselves, such as King Saud University Professor Khalid al-Dakhil's frequent calls for more reform, these changes will remain cosmetic and only respond to the country's increasing subjection, especially to U.S. criticism.

See also **Education.**

FURTHER READING

Doumato, Eleanor Abdella Doumato. "The Ambiguity of *Shari'a* and the Politics of 'Rights' in Saudi Arabia," in *Faith and Freedom; Women's Human Rights in the Muslim World*, edited by Mahnaz Afkhami. Syracuse, NY: Syracuse University Press, 1995.

Niblock, Tim. *Saudi Arabia: Power, Legitmacy, Survival.* New York: Routledge, 2007.
Simons, Geoff. *Saudi Arabia: The Shape of a Client Feudalism.* London: Basingstoke, 1998.
Al Rajhi, Ahmed et al. *Economic Development in Saudi Arabia.* New York: Routledge, 2003.

Huwaytat

Sebastian Maisel

The Huwaytat are a former nomadic but now mostly settled **Bedouin** tribe spread over several countries, but predominantly in southern Jordan, northwest **Saudi Arabia**, and Egypt. Two main branches dominated the northern division of the Huwaytat: Abu Tayy and ibn Jazi. During the last decades of the nineteenth and first decades of the twentieth century, their two main *shaykhs*, 'Awadah Abu Tayy and Hamad ibn Jazi, fought over leadership of the entire tribe. 'Awdah sided with the **Arab Revolt** and fought alongside the legendary **Lawrence of Arabia** and Amir Faysal ibn Hussein ibn 'Ali, but after 'Awdah's death, leadership has reverted to the ibn Jazi. Most of the Huwaytat were nomadic **camel** and sheep herders, although a few lived in the scattered villages of southern Jordan, where they engaged in **agriculture** and animal husbandry.

The origin of the Huwaytat is controversial. During the sixteenth century they belonged to the Bani 'Atiyah Confederation in the area of the Gulf of 'Aqabah, but they split off a century later. The Huwaytat expanded north and east, establishing their tribal area or *dirah* from Wadi Sirhan to Karak south to the Gulf of 'Aqabah. In the nineteenth century the ibn Jazi Huwaytat emerged as tribal leaders in southern Jordan. The Huwaytat became one of the most powerful of Jordanian tribes, and under the leadership of 'Awdah Abu Tayy the Huwaytat provided fighters during the Arab Revolt. They participated in the capture of 'Aqabah in 1917 as well as major battles near Petra, Tafilah, Irbid, and the capture of Damascus.

After World War I, some sections of the ibn Jazi gave their allegiance to **'Abd al-'Aziz ibn Al Sa'ud**, and some even joined the *Ikhwan*. However, most of the tribe chose to continue their close support for Amir 'Abdallah ibn Hussein and raided their traditional enemies both inside Jordan and across the border into what would become Saudi Arabia until Jordanian **military** forces stopped all raiding in the 1920s. The Huwaytat on the Jordanian side were often raided by the *Ikhwan*, which was also compounded by the issue of tribal territory that existed on both sides of the borders drawn up by British colonial officials in 1920 in Cairo. In 1925 Saudi Arabia and Jordan signed the Hadda Agreement over a dispute related to the Wadi Sirhan, which was an important grazing area for several Jordanian Bedouin, including the Huwaytat. Despite the treaty, raiding continued into the 1930s.

Saudi officials often tried to entice tribal groups from the Jordanian side of the border to settle in Saudi Arabia. An example of this is the close contacts between the Saudi king and *Shaykh* Muhammad Abu Tayy, son of 'Awdah. To prevent him from switching his loyalty to the **Al Sa'ud**, the Jordanians decided to offer him financial support. Today many Jordanian Bedouin have numerous passports, and it is a common feature for Jordanian Bedouin to serve in the National Guard in Saudi Arabia and the regular Jordanian military at the same time. Jordanian Bedouin often serve in the palace guard or other branches of the military in many Gulf States.

Since the 1950s, many of the sections of the tribe in Jordan have given up camel nomadism and switched to seminomadic animal husbandry with sheep and goats. Since the 1960s, there has been a growing trend to move to government-built settlement projects or to migrate to urban centers in search of wage labor. The Jordanian government encourages eventual settlement of Bedouin, and *Shaykh* Faysal ibn Jazi built the settlement of al-Husayniyah on the main 'Amman to 'Aqabah road, which now houses over 100,000 Huwaytat tribesmen. During drought years the move is more pronounced but studies by the University of Jordan have shown that the trend is reversed when the rains return. Most still invest in livestock when at all possible. The Huwaytat were among the first to be enlisted in the newly created Jordanian Desert Patrol Force, or *Quwwat al-Badiyah*, created in 1930 by Major John B. Glubb, known as Glubb Pasha. The military has proven to be one of the most important employers for Jordanian Bedouin.

The Huwaytat al-Tihamah live in northwestern Saudi Arabia on the coast of the Red Sea between Dub and Muwailih. They participated in an anti-Saudi rebellion in 1932 together with the **Hashemites** and the Billi tribe. They are mainly seminomadic or completely settled but maintain agriculture through farming and animal husbandry. The current leader of this tribal group is Shaykh 'Awn 'Abdallah Abu Takikah.

FURTHER READING

Abu Athera, Said Salman. *Tribal Poetry of the Tarabin and Huwaytat Tribes and Its Relationship to That of Neighboring Tribes.* PhD dissertation, University of Glasgow, 1995.

Abu Jabir, Kamil, and Fawzi Gharaibeh. *Bedouins of Jordan: A People in Transition.* Amman, Jordan: Royal Scientific Society Press, 1978.

Alon, Yoav. "The Tribal System in the Face of the State Formation Process: Mandatory Transjordan, 1921–46," *International Journal of Middle East Studies* 37, no. 2 (2005): 213–240.

Rutter, Eldon. "The Hejaz," *The Geographical Journal* 77, no. 2 (1931): 97–108.

Shoup, John. *Culture and Customs of Jordan.* Westport, CT: Greenwood, 2007.

Trench, R. (ed.). *Gazetteer of Arabian Tribes.* Slough, UK: Archive Editions, 1996.

I

Ibadi Kharaji Islam

John A. Shoup

Oman is the only country in the **Arabian Peninsula** where the majority of the people follow *Kharaji* Islam. *Kharaji* Islam developed as a result of the conflict between 'Ali ibn Abi Talib and Mu'awiyah ibn Abi Sufyan over succession to the position of *Khalifah*, or Caliph, following the assassination of 'Uthman in 656. The *Khawarij* (plural of *Kharaji*) were originally adherents of 'Ali but when he agreed to negotiations with Mu'awiyah they left, thus their designation from the Arabic verb *kharaja* for those who left or withdrew from the main body of Muslims. The *Khawarij* saw themselves as the only ones maintaining the purity of the religion as taught by the Prophet **Muhammad**, whereas the rest of the Muslims had departed from the real spirit and meaning of Islam and thus are referred to as *kuffar*, or infidels.

Several different groups of *Khawarij* emerged shortly after their break with 'Ali, but among the most successful of them is the *Idadiyah*, named for Abu 'Abdallah ibn Ibad al-Murri al-Tamimi, who is credited for founding the *Idabiyah* around 684 in Basrah, Iraq. *Ibadi* scholars were well-known and attracted a good number of students even from among the **Sunni**s, and for a time had good relations with the Umayyads in Damascus. However, they eventually fell out with the Umayyads and with their successors, the 'Abbasids. Nonetheless, under the leadership of Abu 'Ubaydah Muslim ibn Abi Karim al-Tamimi, *Ibadi* missionaries reached a wide area within the Islamic world, including Oman, where *Kharaji* doctrines had already taken root. In Oman, the town of **Nizwa** emerged as the main center for the sect, and since the year 793 elections of *Imam*s have been held in Nizwa's main mosque.

Oman was able to become independent from the central government in 750, when al-Julanda ibn Mas'ud was elected the first *Imam* for Oman. The 'Abbasids attempted to assert their authority over Oman, but starting in the 800s the *Ibadi* were able to shake off their control and defeated every attempt to force them back under the 'Abbasid *Khilafah* (Caliphate). Oman remains independent and the only place where the majority of people adhere to *Kharajism* of any kind. *Ibadi Kharajism* remains the dominant religion in Oman, but there are *Ibadi* communities scattered in India, the Gulf States, **Yemen**, East Africa, and North Africa.

Ibadi doctrines are moderate and are close to those of the Sunni Maliki **madhhab**. It is because of its moderate stance on many issues that *Ibadism* has been able to survive whereas other more radical versions of *Kharajism* have died away.

The *mihrab* of the mosque at Jabrin in Oman dates from the seventeenth century and was restored in the late twentieth century. Courtesy of John A. Shoup.

Although the *Ibadi* believe that the most qualified person is the one who should be elected as the *Imam*, they recognize that the position can be held by more than one tribe or even by one family. Because from an early time the *Ibadi* community was scattered over a wide area from North Africa to India, they allowed there to be more than one *Imam* at the same time. Unlike the more radical versions of *Kharajism*, the *Ibadi* also refer to their *Imam* as *Amir* or Prince and give him other titles such as *Amir al-Mu'minin* (Commander of the Faithful) and *Amir al-Muslimin* (Commander of the Muslims), titles associated with kings and monarchies that are condemned by most *Khawarij*. For the *Ibadi* the *Imam* is an absolute ruler, a leader in times of war, and the ultimate judge. He must be an authority on religion, well versed in the Qur'an, the *sunnah* of the Prophet Muhammad, and the examples set by the early *Imams*. *Ibadi* doctrines are tolerant of non-*Kharaji*s and allow marriage with non-*Kharaji* Muslims, although they refer to non-*Kharaji* Muslims as *kuffar*, or unbelievers, *Ibadi* doctrine allows for members of the community to live secretly among non-*Kharaji*s pretending to belong to the Sunni Maliki *madhahb*.

Ikhwan

Sebastian Maisel

Ikhwan is a short designation for the organization of mainly **Bedouin**, who starting in 1910 formed the military force for the ruler of central Arabia, **'Abd al-'Aziz ibn Sa'ud**. The *Ikhwan* settled in newly established settlements and were encouraged to take up farming to replace pastoral nomadism. Preachers and scholars were sent to instruct them in the teaching of **Muhammad bin 'Abd al-Wahhab** of the **Wahhabi** movement, a puritanical reform movement of the mid-eighteenth century. The goal of the movement was to purify Islam and return to the lifestyle of the ideal Islamic community, that of the Prophet **Muhammad** and his early followers. Following the example of the *hijrah* of the Prophet, the *Ikhwan* had to leave their tribal affiliation behind and immigrate to a new settlement. This was an enormous step because they were giving up their social and economical network, but the incentives were big enough to attract them.

For Ibn Sa'ud, this meant a significant improvement and strengthening of his position. Concurrently, the power and cohesion of nomadic tribes in Arabia were weakened, and through his powerful army, he was able to conquer large areas on the Peninsula. Members from all major tribes joined the *Ikhwan*, sometimes as entire sections. By 1912, over 11,000 *Ikhwan* were listed and lived in the newly established agricultural settlements. Farming was hard in the arid conditions, and most were unsuccessful; therefore, they had to rely on subsidies from ibn Sa'ud. Within the settlements, members of the different tribes did not like to mingle with those from other tribes. As a result, each settlement was assigned to a specific tribe. The *Ikhwan* participated in all major battles during the war of unification, starting with the conquest of **al-Hasa** in 1913. The *Ikhawan* defeated the **Al Rashid** and the **Shammar** in 1921 and the **Hashemites** of the **Hijaz**, taking the cities of **Ta'if**, **Makkah**, and **Jiddah** in 1924–1925 and participating in the various smaller campaigns against **Yemen**. For many years, the alliances between the *Ikhwan*, Ibn Sa'ud, and the religious establishment were excellent. Success was achieved through raiding the area of the enemy, a well-known strategy for the *Ikhwan*, who practiced this in their nomadic days.

However, with the establishment of permanent borders, restrictions were imposed on them. The *Ikhwan* grew more and more belligerent and objected to ibn Sa'ud's growing good relations with the British, who they considered infidels and possible colonizers. They could not comprehend ibn Sa'ud's political pragmatism to ensure the survival of his realm. Some sections of the *Ikhwan* under Faysal al-Duwaysh, Ibn Bijad, and Ibn Hithlayn openly revolted against ibn Sa'ud and in 1929 were finally defeated in the Battle of Sibilla. Their rebellion was not only a religious rebellion against someone they considered to be a corrupted Muslim leader, but also an expression of tribal opposition to the claims of hegemony by the **Al Sa'ud**. Defeating the *Ikhwan* was a major step in the formation of a centralized state in 1932 with the foundation of the Kingdom of Saudi Arabia.

The *Ikhwan* did not cease to exist, but as an official organization it was disbanded. They continued living in agricultural communities and took wage jobs and positions in the new administration, especially the military. In 1956, tribal forces were again organized into a para-military unit called the Saudi Arabian National Guard. Tribal groups who seized the Grand Mosque in Makkah in 1979 claimed to be descendants of the first *Ikhwan* movement.

FURTHER READING

Al-Azma, Talal. "The Role of the Ikhwan under Abdul Aziz Al Saud, 1916–34." PhD dissertation, University of Durham, 1999.

Habib, John S. *Ibn Saud's Warriors of Islam: The Ikhwan and Their Role in the Creation of the Sa'udi Kingdom, 1910–1930*. Leiden, The Netherlands: Brill, 1978.

Kostiner, Joseph. "On Instruments and Their Designers: The Ikhwan of Najd and the Emergence of the Saudi State," *Middle Eastern Studies* 21, no. 3 (1985): 298–323.

Al Rasheed, Madawi. *A History of Saudi Arabia*. New York: Cambridge University Press, 2002.

Vassiliev, Alexei. *The History of Saudi Arabia*. London: Saqi Books, 1998.

Zaid, Abdulla S. "The Ikhwan Movement of Najd, Saudi Arabia, 1908–1930." PhD dissertation, University of Chicago, 1989.

Imamate of Nizwa

John A. Shoup

Selection of the *Imam*, or religious head of the **Ibadi Kharaji** community, traditionally takes place in the main mosque of **Nizwa**, and generally the *Imamate* and the *Sultanate* have been in the hands of the same person throughout most of **Oman**'s history. However, the split between the two positions of *Sultan* and *Imam* began in 1913, when most of the tribes from the interior of Oman refused to recognize the succession of Taymur bin Faysal of the **Al Bu Sa'idi** family to both positions. Instead they recognized Salim bin Rashid al-Kharusi as the *Imam* of the *Ibadi Kharaji* community and refused to acknowledge Taymur's authority over them. In 1915 a tribal army tried to take **Masqat**, the *Sultan*'s capital, but were defeated and pushed back with British assistance. In 1920 Salim bin Rashid was killed and Muhammad ibn 'Abdallah al-Khalili was elected as the new *Imam*. In the same year, 1920, a truce was signed at Sib (Seeb) where the new *Imam* recognized the *Sultan*'s "authority," whereas the *Sultan* recognized the spiritual and temporal authority of the *Imam* over most of the interior centered on Rustaq and Nizwa, which became the capital of the Imamate.

When Taymur resigned as *Sultan* in 1932, his son and successor **Sa'id** was not content to let matters lie as they were and was determined, with British assistance, to regain his position of both *Imam* and *Sultan*. Sa'id began laying the foundations for his renewed attempt to bring the whole of Oman under his control by trying to win over support from individual tribal leaders, particularly from the important Harith tribe of Izki, a major community that protects the entrance to Nizwa from Masqat. Sa'id was not successful in winning over support from the Harith, but had some success with other tribal groups in the **Dhahirah** region because of his success in forcing the Saudis to withdraw from al-Buraymi in 1952.

The *Imamate* had passed to Ghalib bin 'Ali al-Hina'i, who realized that Sa'id had been able to outmaneuver him and had successfully regained the loyalty of several tribes in the Dhahirah. The *Imam* decided to try to outwit the *Sultan* at his own game and in 1954 applied to the **Arab League** to be admitted as an independent state. He sent the able leader of the Harith to negotiate and had strong support from both **Saudi Arabia** and Egypt. In 1955 *Sultan* Sa'id marched with Omani and British troops to Nizwa, which he was able to occupy, and forced *Imam* Ghalib into internal exile in his home village outside of Nizwa.

Ghalib's brother Talib was able to escape and briefly took refuge in Cairo. A little over a year later he came back to lead an armed rebellion against the Sultan. Ghalib joined his brother and from their bases in Jabal al-Akhdar among the Bani Riyam tribe who had not yet submitted to Sa'id put up a stiff resistance to the *Sultan's* army. The conflict is referred to as the **Jabal War**, and the rebels were defeated only after Sa'id called in support from the British Royal Air Force, which bombed several towns and villages to rubble. Tanuf and Birkat al-Mawz, both located a short distance from Nizwa, were destroyed, and Tanuf remains a ruin today. Unable to get material support from either the Arab nationalists in Cairo or from Saudi Arabia, the rebels acknowledged defeat and the *Imamate* ended in 1959. From that time on, the two offices of *Sultan* and *Imam* have again been held in the hands of Oman's head of state.

Incense

Carla Higgins

Aesthetics are of high value in the Gulf. Gulf citizens are well dressed and groomed and smell nice. Traditionally they incensed their clothes and hair. Good grooming and fragrance are considered essential to well-being, to the maintenance of social roles, and to health. Both women and men use incense. Incense refers to a variety of substances used to perfume the body, clothes, and home, and is used in both private and public social and religious ritual. The primary types of incense are aloewood, *dukhun*, and frankincense. Aloewood (*'ud*) is a dark, fragrant wood from India and is just one of many products that made up the economic and cultural relationship between the Gulf and India. It is considered the most important and valuable of the incenses. *Dukhun* refers to a mixture of perfumed incense that may be created in the home or purchased in the market. It is sold as small, round, dense disks of compacted granules.

Frankincense (*luban*) is a gold tree resin produced in **Oman** and **Yemen** and has had a profound historical and economic impact on the region as a prized commodity in ancient and contemporary trade. The Gulf played a central role in an ancient global economy because of the production of frankincense and the control of trade routes that distributed it as far as India. Till the sixth century AD, the Gulf was home to sophisticated civilizations that flourished as a result of this trade. Both frankincense and myrrh were used in court and temple ceremonies and in the spice markets and perfume industries of the Near East and Mediterranean worlds.

The inside of a traditional house made of *barasti* in Dubai shows the use of space in the one-room building. Most items are stored away by being hung on the wall or on rods. The stand in the right-hand corner is used to incense clothes. The burner is placed underneath and the clothes are placed over the frame, or alternatively, the person stands over the frame, allowing the smoke to circulate inside. Courtesy of John A. Shoup.

Frankincense is sold in small, hard drops and nodules. Unlike aloewood and *dukhun*, frankincense is used mainly for religious purposes, after the daily evening prayer and during religious occasions and holidays—traditionally it was used to counter bad spirits and the evil eye. This is an example of using scent for protection.

Appropriate social rituals for women may include offering perfumes/incense to guests, and good guests use scent liberally. Incense is used liberally during major public events such as weddings. Public areas of buildings may be scented with incense. Regardless of whether one is in a traditional market or a modern mall with high-end retailers, there are incense and perfume shops in abundance. Shops may burn incense to display their products, to attract customers, and to offer wonderful scent.

Intellectuals, Secular

Sebastian Maisel

The ancient culture of Arabia, embedded with Islam and transformed over centuries, has produced scores of people who contributed to social, political, and economic development of the area. While recognizing there are different fields of expertise, several individuals stand out in Gulf States. They can be distinguished by their **education** and/or achievements for the greater good of society.

Because of the late start of secular education in most of the countries in the **Arabian Peninsula**, the number of those who obtained higher degrees is remarkably lower than in the rest of the Middle East. Those who have continued their education often go on to become social, economic, and political leaders. However, there are examples of bright, self-educated individuals who have huge influence on public opinion such as the late 'Abd al-'Aziz al-Tuwaijri or Hamad al-Jasir. These two men greatly influenced the scholarly and intellectual life of central Arabia outside the religious arena.

Saudi Arabia emphasizes combining modernity with tradition and produces representatives of both genres in the arts as well as in public discourse. Among those intellectuals turned politicians are Ghazi Qosaibi, poet and labor minister, and Faysal bin Mu'ammar, director of the King 'Abd al-'Aziz Public Library and Secretary General of the National Dialogue series. Recently tribal values have become part of a larger national identity that has given tribal intellectuals a strong push into the spotlight. Tribal poets, just like in the days of the *Jahiliyah* and early Islam, still are highly respected and considered the living memory of Saudi tribal identity. Scholars on the history and culture of the kingdom find their position on the stage of public recognition; for example, Fahd al-Semmari, the director of the King 'Abd al-'Aziz Historical Center, and Sa'ad Sowayan, eminent authority on **Bedouin** poetry and customs. Novelists, however, find it is harder to get public recognition in Saudi Arabia. First, because the literary scene is still small, most of them write on sociopolitical affairs. This forces them to position themselves on a fine line between mainstream acceptance and elite criticism. Writers like 'Abd al-Rahman Munif or Turki al-Hamad paid for their critical remarks with continual repressions by state and religious authorities. Other authors faced death threats issued as *fatwa*s or physical violence, a fate that they share with other Saudi intellectuals in the fields of media and religion. However, when seriously threatened many of Saudi Arabia's intellectuals unite and act together to support colleagues or to defend/denounce government policies on civil liberties.

Bound by religious and traditional limitations, Saudi women are increasingly finding their way into the public domain, creating extraordinary pieces of artwork, inventions, or other contributions. The famous painter and intellectual Safia bin Zagr from **Jiddah** pioneered the role of other women writers such as Raja Alam, Raja'a al-Sanee, or Ni'mah Isma'il Nawwab. Private salons are the main venues for intellectual exchange and debate as well as for literature clubs. Attending *majlis* sessions and publishing in the mass media are other outlets for dialog and constructive criticism that are frequently used by activists and intellectuals throughout the Arabian Peninsula.

Saudi intellectuals are involved with local and international events, which they struggle to influence against the power of the Saudi political and religious establishment. Joining forces with other groups such as women, Shi'ites, and reformists, they challenge the status quo by constantly sharing ideas that cross religious, ethnic, and gender borders. Occasionally they do achieve recognition and change. However, more often they face tremendous public pressure and sometimes persecution or legal prosecution. The role of the intellectual as a symbol of the country's moral elite is still in its early stages.

In the other Arab Gulf States, intellectuals are similarly engaged in the public debate over politics, culture, and identity. In **Kuwait**, both secular and religious intellectuals joined forces in their struggle to return to parliamentary representation. Another field of action is defending the Arabic nature of those countries that are under threat of being assimilated by foreign cultures because of the large number of guestworkers. Protecting and promoting the **Arabic language** is one tool being exploited by Gulf intellectuals. Because of their continual pressure, the government of the **United Arab Emirates** endorsed Arabic as the country's official language. Gulf intellectuals often link the issues of Arabic culture and language with the area's lack of cultural development, particularly the inability to create a culture of knowledge or innovation like the Muslim world had been in the past during the Golden Age. Today, intellectuals, scholars, researchers, and other educated people leave the area to find work abroad. The "brain drain" became a serious issue that has been discussed largely in academic circles in the Gulf region. Khalaf al-Habtur, one of the world's 500 leading intellectuals, stands as a counterexample to this trend. A self-made businessman, he started his company, Al-Habtoor Group, and concurrently continued to invest in public and private education, founding international schools throughout the Emirates.

Intellectuals in the Gulf States have an easier life than do their counterparts in Saudi Arabia. Although they face opposition and occasional discrimination, very rarely are they attacked based on religion, although they experience difficulties when debating political and social issues. Recently Gulf intellectuals recognized globalization as the main threat to Arab identity, which is based on the state (*dawlah*), the nation (*ummah*), and the fatherland (*watan*). On the other hand, they realize that globalization can help reform their regimes by setting up international standards and values.

FURTHER READING

Abul, Ahmed Jafar. "The Participation of Kuwaiti Intellectuals in the Development Process, 1961–1985." PhD dissertation, University of Essex, 1992.

Anonymous. *Letter to the West: A Saudi View.* Riyadh: Ghainaa Publications, 2005.

Blankenhorn, David (ed.). *The Islam/West Debate: Documents from a Global Debate on Terrorism, US Policy, and the Middle East.* Lanham, MD: Rowman & Littlefield, 2005.

Perthes, Volker (ed.). *Arab Elites: Negotiating the Politics of Change.* Boulder, CO: Lynne Rienner, 2004.

International Relations

Tom Landsford

Saudi Arabia and the Persian Gulf continue to be among the most important regions in international relations. The area's strategic importance is based on its geographic location on major trade routes and its abundance of energy resources. Saudi Arabia and the Gulf States (**Bahrain**, **Kuwait**, **Oman, Qatar**, and the **United Arab Emirates**) have also successfully managed to develop alliances with powerful outside actors, such as the United States or the United Kingdom, as a means to protect their national interests and prevent domination by regional states such as Iran or Iraq. However, those alliances with Western powers have undermined the standing of the regimes among domestic audiences and other Muslim states and reduced the influence of the countries in the Arab world.

The energy resources of the region attracted outside interest even before World War II; for instance, the United States signed a commerce treaty with Oman in 1833. Nonetheless, it was the conclusion of that global conflict that elevated the geostrategic value of the area amid the escalating Cold War. Tensions between the United States and the Soviet Union over the latter's occupation of northern Iran contributed to the onset of the superpower conflict and reinforced the centrality of the Persian Gulf in the superpower conflict. U.S., British, and other European national interests in the region, through the early days of the Cold War, were based on the maintenance of regional stability, access to inexpensive **oil**, and the protection of Israel. In 1951, the United States implemented the Mutual Security Doctrine, which was designed to provide weapons and training to anti-communist regimes in the Middle East. In 1956, the Baghdad Pact was created in an effort to develop a broad, anti-Soviet alliance in the region. Meanwhile, the Soviets endeavored to gain influence through support for Arab nationalism. With independence and the withdrawal of British military forces in the 1970s, the United States assumed an increasingly significant role, despite animosity generated by Washington, D.C.'s support for Israel. That relationship with Israel was counterbalanced for the Gulf States by the threat to the existing monarchial systems posed by communism or even Arab socialism.

Saudi Arabia and the Gulf States demonstrated their economic might during the 1973 oil embargo when along with other Arab states they stopped supplying oil to states that supported Israel during the October War. This caused the price of oil to quadruple, but it also led Western nations to adopt a variety of conservation efforts, including the use of alternative energy sources, especially in the aftermath of the subsequent 1979 energy crisis. One result was a global oil glut in the 1980s and serious economic problems for the region. In response, the countries of the region endeavored, with mixed success, to diversify their economies and invest the proceeds of their energy wealth. On the other hand, the embargo is generally credited with leading European states to adopt increasingly pro-Arab policies in place of their former pro-Israel stance. At the time, western Europe imported eighty percent of its oil from the Middle East, whereas the region only supplied the United States with twelve percent of its imported oil.

The Soviet invasion of Afghanistan in 1979 prompted closer relations with the West, including a series of military cooperation agreements between the Gulf States and the United States and United Kingdom. Saudi Arabia led the region in funding the anti-Soviet resistance in Afghanistan. During the **Iran-Iraq War**, Saudi Arabia and its Gulf neighbors further increased ties with the United States and other world powers in an effort to secure regional stability and to protect their borders and interests. By the early 1980s, Saudi Arabia had become the largest purchaser of U.S. arms and weaponry outside of western Europe, and it annually acquired more than five times the American arms and weapons systems that Israel received. Kuwait approached both the United States and the Soviet Union to re-flag the country's oil tankers in an effort to protect them from attacks in the Persian Gulf.

The Soviet withdrawal from Afghanistan and the end of the Cold War reinforced relations between the states of the Gulf and the United States. The Iraqi invasion of Kuwait, and the subsequent liberation of the country by the U.S.-led Coalition, further accelerated the increasingly close relations with Washington, D.C. In the aftermath of the conflict, the Gulf nations signed new military cooperation agreements with the United States, increased weapons purchases, and welcomed an expanded U.S. military presence in the region. The regimes also supported, overtly or tacitly, the dual containment policy of the United States, which was designed to restrain both Iran and Iraq. However, domestic opinion increasingly opposed the UN economic sanctions on Iraq.

The patterns of official cooperation continued following the September 11, 2001 terrorist attacks on the United States. Saudi Arabia and the Gulf States undertook a range of efforts to increase intelligence and law enforcement cooperation with the West and to suppress radical, anti-Western Islamists (who were also seen as a threat to the regimes). The governments also faced pressure from Washington, D.C. to liberalize domestic regimes, including enacting democratic reforms. Relations with the United States began to deteriorate as Washington, D.C. moved closer to war with Iraq in 2003. Gulf leaders, with the notable exception of the emir of Kuwait, warned that any war with Iraq could destabilize the Persian Gulf and remove an effective counterbalance to Iran. The U.S.-led occupation of Iraq was roundly criticized for its failure to deal with the post-invasion insurgency and the impact of the conflict in Iraq on regional stability. Gulf States also continued to criticize the U.S.-Israeli relationship, especially during the 2006 war in south Lebanon. Nonetheless, the Iranian nuclear program and Tehran's efforts to increase its regional influence combined to prompt the Gulf States to continue their **security** relationships with the United States as outside interest in the area continued to reflect the region's significance.

See also **Foreign Relations**.

FURTHER READING

Korany, Bahgar, and Ali E. Hillal Dessouki (eds.). *The Foreign Policies of Arab States*. Boulder, CO: Westview Press, 1984.

Long, David E., and Christian Koch (eds.). *Gulf Security in the Twenty-First Century.* New York: British Academic Press, 1997.

Owen, Roger. *State, Power and Politics in the Making of the Modern Middle East,* 2nd ed. London: Routledge, 2000.

Peterson, Erik R. *The Gulf Cooperation Council: Search for Unity in a Dynamic Region.* Boulder, CO: Westview Press, 1988.

Rubin, Barry (ed.). *Crises in the Contemporary Persian Gulf.* London: Frank Cass, 2002.

Internet

Sebastian Maisel

Modernization brought drastic and rapid changes to the societies of the **Arabian Peninsula**. The introduction of new technologies, such as radio, television, mobile phones, and the Internet, transformed and broadened the means of personal and mass communication. The Internet is seen as a useful tool to maintain interpersonal communication with other family members, but it also offers for the first time free access to information and entertainment. Although limited and censored, access to the Internet is now a basic technological asset.

Internet access has been available at Saudi universities and other research institutions since 1994, and individuals were allowed to purchase hardware and modems to access the Net through foreign providers. Because the Internet was greatly demanded, in 1999 **Saudi Arabia** began registration of the first public providers. However, before the entire population was allowed to go online, specific guidelines were required in order to protect religion, nation, and culture from negative and immoral sites such as those with pornography, gambling, or anything that threatened the social, political, and religious values of the people. Local Internet providers are connected to a single, government-controlled proxy housed in Riyadh at the King 'Abd al-'Aziz City for Science and Technology (KAACST). It controls and blocks inappropriate and undesired Web content. For example, access to Yahoo and other sites offering private clubs was banned by the authorities. Saudi authorities, like those in other Gulf States, try to censor everything that seems offensive to the country's values or **security**. Banned sites and topics include pornography, political opposition groups, Israel, homosexuality, **drugs**, alcohol, or women's rights. They maintain an updated and sophisticated control system to block these sites; however, ways to surpass the system exist and are exploited by sophisticated computer users. For a higher charge, individual users can have unrestricted Web access by calling an Internet service provider outside of the kingdom, for example, in **Bahrain**.

The Internet was introduced in the Gulf States at an earlier stage with **Kuwait** pioneering in the early 1990s. Following the Iraqi occupation of 1990–1991, Kuwait was assisted by U.S. institutions to access the Internet, and by 1993 Kuwait University and the National Science Foundation were connected, making Kuwait one of the first countries in the Middle East with Internet. Shortly after Internet service was transferred to the private sector, which offered access to the public. **Oman** joined the Internet community in 1997. The official General Telecommunications

Organization provides Internet access. Currently, the government of Oman is establishing the Information Technology Authority, an online government e-service that digitizes many administrative functions and forms. The **United Arab Emirates** claim to be the most wired country in the area. Through the country's official and sole provider, Etisalat, censorship is maintained mostly on pornographic sites. Bahrain, on the other hand, is trying to become the telecommunications hub of the Gulf region, thus investing largely in information technology and mass communication. Nonetheless, control of access and information is still blocked to some sites, especially those belonging to groups in opposition to the ruling **Al Khalifah** family.

Particularly popular in the Gulf are Internet blogs, which allow free expression of political and cultural ideas and opinions away from government and social control. Contesting the strong grip on official media, bloggers from Saudi Arabia and the Gulf States often discuss issues of social and political taboos, such as the role of women in society, political participation, or the religious police in Saudi Arabia. Although the authorities constantly work on shutting down these sites, and even arresting bloggers, Internet activities develop so rapidly that they can easily challenge technological and administrative hurdles.

Governments also began to use the Internet for their purposes. In Saudi Arabia, where the authorities currently struggle with Islamic opposition groups who use the Internet to attack the ruling family, the government launched their own Islamic websites where religious authorities explain and interpret Islamic law and doctrine and issue *fatwas* regarding important religious questions about *Jihad* and Islamic values.

The Gulf States experience a rising demand from the public for computers and Internet access. Polls suggest that Internet use and computer ownership have grown tenfold over the last four years. A ration of 121 users per 100 computers is one of the highest in the Middle East and indicates a high level of computer literacy. More than forty percent of all Internet users in the Arab world are from the **Gulf Cooperation Council** region, although it accounts for only eleven percent of the total Arab population.

Internet cafes enjoy great popularity for several reasons. In Saudi Arabia, unrelated men and women are not allowed to mingle in public places; therefore, special Internet cafes for women only were introduced, similar to women-only restaurants, banks, and shops. The majority of Internet users are young people; for example, in Kuwait they constitute sixty-three percent of all Internet users. Their use of and interest in the Internet will stimulate significant social change in the future.

See also **Education**.

FURTHER READING

Al-Zubaidi, Abeer. "Critical Assessment of the Internet Development in Oman." Undergraduate research paper, University of Leeds, 2001.

Hafez, Kai. *Mass Media, Politics, and Society in the Middle East*. Cresskill, NJ: Hampton Press, 2001.

Rugh, William. *Arab Mass Media: Newspapers, Radio, and Television in Arab Politics*. Westport, CT: Greenwood Press, 2004.

Wheeler, Deborah. *The Internet in the Middle East: Global Expectations and Local Imaginations in Kuwait*. New York: State University of New York Press, 2005.

Iran-Iraq War

James Sater

On September 22, 1980, Iraqi troops crossed the Iranian border in a front from near Baghdad to the Shatt al-'Arab. A month later, Iraq controlled much of the Iranian **oil-**rich and ethnically Arab province of Khuzistan, which borders the Persian Gulf and Iraq. Because of the Islamic revolution in Iran the year earlier, Iran was in turmoil and many observers predicted a swift victory for Iraqi troops. They were proven wrong, and the eight-year-long Iran-Iraq war became one of the longest conventional wars of the twentieth century, destroying much of the economy in both countries while keeping both political systems and territory intact.

Conflicts between these two countries existed since the early 1970s, when both struggled with their heterogeneous population and border control—a legacy of British colonialism and oil interests in the Middle East. Iraqi Kurds in the north of the country sought support from Iran in their struggle against the central government for autonomy or full independence. In turn, Iran supported this movement in an attempt to gain a stronger position in Iran's border dispute with Iraq over the Shatt al-'Arab—a strategic water access to the Persian Gulf.

Although the Algiers Agreement was signed in 1975 and officially ended the border dispute and Iran's support for the Kurds, tensions resurfaced with Iran's 1979 revolution, which saw the rise of Ayatollah Ruhollah Khomeini (1902–1989) in the same year as Saddam Hussein's (1937–2006) rise to power in Iraq. Tensions between both rulers were due to ideological differences, which had led to Khomeini's expulsion from Iraq—the Shah of Iran exiled him there—the previous year by Hussein, who was then in charge of Iraq's Ministry of Interior. With Ayatollah Khomeini in power, the new revolutionary Islamic Republic of Iran aimed at exporting its **Shi'a** revolution to neighboring Iraq in an attempt to liberate Iraq's sixty percent Shi'a population from Iraq's secular and **Sunni-**dominated regime. Partly responding to this threat, and partly attempting to claim a swift military victory over Iran, thereby creating Iraq's regional, pan-Arab leadership after Egypt's expulsion from the **Arab League** in 1979 in the Baghdad Summit, Hussein invaded Iran, hoping to rally the ethnic Arab majority of Khuzistan to Arab Iraq rather than to Persian Iran. The Shatt al-'Arab agreement of 1975, which officially shared Iraqi and Iranian access to the Persian Gulf, served Saddam Hussein as a pretext.

After the Iranian army's successful defense, the initial Iraqi attack was stopped, and starting in 1982, the Iraqi army retreated into Iraqi territory where the main remaining battles were fought. Iranian military advances were paid with a very high human toll and caused increasing international concern that Iran may be able to inflict a military defeat on Iraq and install a second Shi'a-dominated Islamic republic on Iraqi territory. Because of the Iranian leadership's anti-Western rhetoric and ideology, Hussein's turning to the West for aid fell on receptive ears, especially in the United States. As other conservative Gulf monarchies also feared an Iranian victory and its implications for its own heterogeneous populations (especially **Saudi Arabia**, with its own very important Shi'a minority), Gulf countries poured billions of U.S. dollars in aid into Iraq to prevent an Iranian victory and potential political instability in their own countries.

The war itself included attacking oil tankers; rocket attacks on civilian targets in Tehran and Baghdad; and decisively, the Iraqi use of chemical weapons against Iranian forces, which outnumbered Iraqi troops. Iraq thereby breached the 1925 Geneva agreement banning the use of these weapons. Although the international community condemned the use of chemical weapons by Iraq, it did not stop its aid to the Iraqi leadership because of the threat that Iran posed to Western geopolitical interests, especially its continued access to oil in the **Arabian Gulf** area.

With no party gaining military superiority—Iran profited from higher troop numbers and strong ideological commitment, whereas Iraq benefited from superior technology and the ruthless use of chemical weapons—both warring parties found it increasingly in their interest to look for a peaceful settlement. On August 20, 1988, the final ceasefire took effect. The war left both economies in shambles, led to an increased U.S. military presence in the Persian Gulf to protect oil tankers, and led a heavily indebted Iraq to further seek financial compensation from other Gulf countries in return for its protecting them from the Iranian threat. Whereas Iran was able to change its revolutionary foreign policy with the death of Ayatollah Khomeini in 1989, under Hussein Iraq continued its expansionist foreign policy in August 1990 with the occupation and annexation of **Kuwait**.

'Isa bin Salman Al Khalifah (1933–1999)

John A. Shoup

Shaykh 'Isa bin Salman **Al Khalifah** (1933–1999) was the first independent ruler of the modern state of **Bahrain** and ruled as **Emir** from 1961 to 1999. He was educated by a series of private British and Arab tutors and first entered the political arena in 1956 when he became President of the **al-Manamah** Municipal Council. The 1950s were a stormy period in Bahraini history because of the interference of the British Resident Charles Belgrave, who was forced to retire in 1956. The rise of Arab nationalism and Egypt's challenge to the old colonial powers of Britain and France not only caused a degree of anti-British feelings in Bahrain, but also split the Bahrainis with many of the **Shi'ites** and other lower-income groups supporting Arab nationalism and the mainly **Sunni** more affluent groups supporting more a conservative stance. In 1958 there were open elections for the al-Manamah Municipal Council and *Shaykh* 'Isa was also named the heir to the throne. He headed the Bahraini side in negotiations with **Saudi Arabia** to set the maritime boundaries and settle the claims to offshore **oil** fields.

In 1961 'Isa became the *Shaykh* following his father's death. 'Isa proved to be a vigorous leader and spent a good deal of effort in improving the infrastructure of the country, including schools. He also gained Iranian recognition and in 1970 Iran renounced any claims to the islands that comprise Bahrain. In 1971 Bahrain and **Qatar** decided to not join the **United Arab Emirates** when Britain pulled out and 'Isa was declared the first *Emir*. He allowed a constitution in 1973 as well as an elected parliament, which sat till 1975 when he decided to dissolve it on the grounds that it was not dealing with the issues of the country but only engaged in political grandstanding.

The last decades of his life were difficult as he faced a growing opposition from the Shi'ite majority. In 1994 there were street protests calling for the restoration of parliament. Things came to a head in 1996 when he ordered the arrests of several prominent Shi'ite leaders. A low-level rebellion began that simmered until after *Shaykh* 'Isa's death in 1999. His son, *Shaykh* Hamad, who has been able to solve many of the political problems inherited from his father, succeeded him.

Islamic Doctrines
John A. Shoup

Islam's doctrines are based on a specific set of legal practices and sources of legal knowledge. These include first and foremost the Qur'an as the revealed word of God; the *Sunnah*, or actions of the Prophet **Muhammad** as passed on by reliable sources back to the lifetime of the Prophet; the *Hadith*, or sayings of the Prophet that have also been passed on by reliable sources back to his lifetime; *ijma'*, or consensus of Muslim scholars on the basis of texts; and *qiyas*, or analogy using a similar (but not the same) incident from the time of the Prophet and looking at his judgment. For the **Shi'ites** there are two other sources not generally recognized by Sunnis. The first are the sayings of 'Ali ibn Abi Talib that, like those of the Prophet Muhammad, have been passed down by reliable sources. The second is what is called *ijtihad*, or individual analysis based on close readings of legal and religious texts. For Sunnis "the gate of *ijtihad*" was closed by the scholar ibn Taymiyah, whose texts have strong influence over mainly Hanbali jurists, including **Muhammad ibn 'Abd al-Wahhab**, founder of what in the West is called **Wahhabi** Islam.

Many Sunnis in the Gulf belong to the Maliki School of Islam (see **madhhab**), which was founded by the jurist Malik ibn Anas (716–796). Malik produced the first written text of Islamic law following the traditions of his native **Madinah**. He drew heavily on the local traditions and precedents set by the Prophet and the first Caliphs as well as on Qur'anic texts. He nonetheless gave highest priority to the use of consensus of the local community; reasoning could override traditions and practices, even those of the Prophet. Malik's major work did not cover a wide range of legal issues and did not address the different legal practices that continued in the former Roman and Persian provinces of the empire. Nonetheless, those who have followed the works of Malik have generally taken a moderate path, making it easy for the **Khawarij** to adopt Maliki identity when politically necessary.

The Shafi'i School is not widely practiced in the Gulf or the **Arabian Peninsula**, although it is the main Islamic school in Syria and Jordan. Shafi'i legal thought and the methods established by the founder Muhammad al-Shafi'i have greatly influenced all of the Sunni schools of law. Muhammad ibn Idris al-Shafi'i (767–820) incorporated the legal traditions in the main centers of Islamic law during the eighth century, drawing upon Roman, Persian, and Arab sources; a synthesis of the two main poles of his day, Kufah and the legal traditions of Abu Hanifa (700–796), and Madinah and Malik ibn Anas. Al-Shafi'i helped standardize legal methods, set the four main sources noted above, and gave first importance to the Qur'an as the word of God. The second source was the Prophet's actions and words following the Qur'anic injunction to "obey God and His Prophet." Any contradictions are to be settled by the Qur'an for the Qur'an and the *sunnah* for the *sunnah*; that is, the later revelation or tradition supersedes the earlier one and all contradictions are satisfied by either a Qur'anic verse or a *sunnah*. Consensus is the third source of law, and in Shafi'i legal texts consensus would come to mean a consensus of legal scholars, not the community itself. The fourth source is analogy, but in a limited format, trying to reduce the possibility of too many varied opinions by scholars. Analogy cannot contradict any rule established by any of the first three principles.

The Hanbali School of law was established as the main school in much of the Arabian Peninsula as a result of the Wahhabi reforming movement of the eighteenth century. Hanbali Islam was founded by the jurist Ahmad ibn Hanbal (780–855), who rejected any form of human reasoning as a source of law. Only the Qur'an and the *sunnah* of the Prophet could serve as the basis for Islamic legal decisions. The Syrian Hanbali jurist ibn Taymiyah (1263–1328) has been one of the most influential figures for Islamic doctrine in the much of the Sunni world. Ibn Taymiyah wrote at a time when Syria was under threat from both the Mongols in the east (who had recently converted to Islam) and the Christian Crusaders from the west. He took a more militant stance and divided the world into two main parts: *Dar al-Islam*, or the "Abode of Islam," and the *Dar al-Kufr*, or "Abode of Unbelief." For him, these two were in a hostile relationship. Ibn Taymiyah differed from the other jurists of his day and sought legal precedent in the writings of the more militant *Kharaji* scholars. Ibn Taymiyah stated that a bad Muslim ruler (he was referring to the Mongols in Iran) was as bad as a non-Muslim ruler and should be resisted. Words and actions of a good Muslim leader must be consistent with Islamic principles, and it was the duty of a good Muslim ruler to combat unbelief wherever it was found whether inside *Dar al-Islam* or in *Dar al-Kufr*. Thus he legitimized the conflict between the Mamluks of Egypt and Syria with both the Crusaders and the Mongols and gave it the status of *Jihad*. He advocated it as a duty to overthrow bad Muslim governments rather than to follow the opinion of other Muslim scholars of his day that a bad Muslim ruler was at least a Muslim and his rule should be obeyed. Ibn Taymiyah should be seen in his own historical circumstances, but he had a strong influence on Muhammad ibn 'Abd al-Wahhab and contemporary Muslim thinkers such as Sayyid Qutb and even men such as **Usamah bin Ladin**.

See also **Madhhab**.

FURTHER READING

Coulson, N.J. *A History of Islamic Law.* Edinburgh: Edinburgh University Press, 1999.
Delong-Bas, Natana. *Wahhabi Islam: From Revival and Reform to Global Jihad.* London: I.B. Tauris, 2004.

Islamic Fundamentalism— Salafiyah

Sebastian Maisel

Secular trends in Egypt and other Middle Eastern countries in the late nineteenth century caused Islamic reformist movements to emerge with the objective to end the degeneration of Islamic societies, which resulted in their "backwardness" and dependency on non-Muslim countries. For them Islam itself was not the reason for their "backwardness," but deviation from the true spirit and meaning of Islam and the power of traditions rather than understanding the true message of the religion were the causes. They advocated returning to the origins of Islam, the Islam of the "pious ancestors" or *al-salaf al-salih*, to first reform and then strengthen Islam. The way of living and thinking of the early Muslim community under the Prophet **Muhammad** and the four rightly guided caliphs was declared the only historical realization of Islam, and any deviation from this model led to degeneration. The movement takes its name, *salafiyah*, from looking back at the ancestors. They were greatly influenced by earlier fundamentalist movements and thinkers, such as ibn Taymiyah and **Muhammad ibn 'Abd al-Wahhab**, and discouraged traditions such as venerating saints and visiting shrines and tombs. They also rejected *taqlid*, or imitation of former rulings, which is an important part of Sunni legal rulings yet today. In political and economical terms, *Salafi*s consider the Islamic system superior to capitalism and communism. If understood correctly, Islam can be the base for the building of modern, prosperous, and progressive nations. True Islam, therefore, is different than the form of Islam that is represented by traditional Islamic law and current governments. Prominent thinkers who developed the *Salafi* reformist movement were Jamal al-Din al-Afghani, Muhammad 'Abduh, and Rashid Rida, who all lived at the end of the nineteenth and the beginning of the twentieth century. The first organizations that followed the doctrines of *salafi* Islam were the *Ikhawan al-Muslimin*, or Muslim Brotherhood, founded in 1929 by Hasan al-Banna' in Egypt. Today, many movements and organizations use the idea of cultural self-assertion as laid out by the *salafi* thinkers for their inspiration and ideology.

The main religious movement in **Saudi Arabia**, called **Wahhabiyah** after its founder, has often been equated with *salafi* Islam. However, the *salafi* movement originated some 150 years later but both refer to the first community of Islam as a period of near perfection. Although the *salafiyah* is a general Islamic reform movement, the Wahhabiyah is the reform movement in Saudi Arabia and adjunct areas. The Wahhabi movement originated in the mid-eighteenth century in central Arabia with the teachings of Muhammad ibn 'Abd al-Wahhab. He was frustrated with the state of Islam and the moral decline of the population that he believed had deviated significantly from the "straight path" of the forefathers. He began preaching to return to the fundamentals of Islam as embodied in the Qur'an and *Sunnah*. When the political leader of the area, Muhammad bin Sa'ud, started to use his teachings to legitimize his rule, a pact of mutual support and recognition was made between the two sides, thus combining religious with political authority and providing the means to create a pure Islamic state. The partnership lasts up to this day, and the Wahhabi version of the Hanbali School is the official form of Islam in the Kingdom of Saudi Arabia, **Qatar**, and the **United Arab Emirates**.

Wahhabis show no tolerance toward what they consider to be deviations, including celebrating the Prophet's birthday, Sufi mysticism, and certain modern technologies. Cultural expressions of this fundamental interpretation of Islam as practiced in Saudi Arabia include strongly enforced gender segregation, the prohibition of alcohol and **drugs** (and sometimes cigarettes), and a ban on women driving cars. It is also reflected in strained relations with non-Wahhabi groups, in particular **Shi'ites** and Christians. Many Wahhabis in Saudi Arabia prefer to call themselves *salafis* or *muwahhidi* (Unitarians) because they believe they follow the Prophet's example as staunch monotheists. They insist on the inerrancy of the scripture (Qur'an) and interpret it literally. Among the features that are applied is the prohibition of rebellion against an Islamic ruler, even in the case that he is corrupt or unjust. The **Al Sa'ud**, as the ruling family of Saudi Arabia, still receive support and recognition from the mainstream religious establishment of the country. On the basis of the historical pact between the two groups, *salafi* scholars and authorities like Muhammad bin Salih al-'Uthaymin and 'Abd al-'Aziz bin Baz support the Saudi government as custodians of the "Two Holy Places" and promoters of Islam worldwide. Religious institutions such as the **Committee for the Promotion of Virtue and Prevention of Vice** and the Grand Mufti of the Kingdom are used in a similar fashion.

There are other, smaller groups of *salafi* scholars in Saudi Arabia who disagree with the mainstream interpretation and accuse the Al Sa'ud of being corrupt. Following the injunctions of ibn Taymiyah, who advocated rebellion against unjust and corrupt Muslim rulers, they call for an end of Saudi rule. The reform *salafis* openly denounce the state's failures, including the violation of Islamic values and the subservience to foreign powers. They focus on broad social and political issues that touch the everyday lives of all Muslims, not only Saudis.

A rejectionist group called neo-*salafis* focus more on individual faith, morals, and practices. They withdrew from society to live a puritan lifestyle. They also claim that the Saudi state is illegitimate. In 1979, a group under the leadership of Juhayman al-'Utaybi seized the Great Mosque in **Makkah**. Another group of *salafis* in Saudi Arabia called the *Jihadists* emerged in the global holy war against the West beginning in 1980 in Afghanistan and continuing in Bosnia, Kosovo, Chechnya, and Iraq. Their resistance to the Saudi establishment is further shaped by the presence of foreign troops on sacred Islamic ground. During the **1990–1991 Gulf War**, American troops were stationed in Saudi Arabia to protect the country from a possible Iraqi attack. Using "infidel" troops to protect the Holy Places is another complaint and example of deviation in the eyes of many *salafis*. Following the stationing of non-Muslim troops in Saudi Arabia, some went further in their opposition and started to openly attack the representatives of "deviated" regimes. Among these new *Jihadist* organizations is **Al-Qa'idah**. Today the debate over the use of violence is probably the most significant sign of diversity within the *salafi* movement. Although Al Qa'idah and other groups advocate the overthrow of un-Islamic regimes, many *salafis* believe that violence should be the last resort. Mainstream Wahhabi and *salafi* groups are currently under attack by the more violent form of interpretation.

See also **Holidays and Festivals: Islamic; Islamic Doctrines; Madhhab.**

FURTHER READING

Al Rasheed, Madawi. *Contesting the Saudi State: Islamic Voices from a New Generation*. New York: Cambridge University Press, 2007.

Commins, David. *The Wahhabi Mission and Saudi Arabia*. London: I.B. Tauris, 2005.

DeLong-Bas, Natana J. *Wahhabi Islam: From Revival and Reform to Global Jihad*. New York: Oxford University Press, 2004.

Hegghammer, Thomas, and Stephan Lacroix. "Rejectionist Islamism in Saudi Arabia: The Story of Juhayman al-Utaybi Revisited," *International Journal of Middle East Studies* 39, no. 1 (2007): 103–122.

Kerr, Malcolm H. *Islamic Reform: The Political and Legal Theories of Muhammad Abduh and Rashid Rida*. Berkeley: University of California Press, 1966.

Islamic Practices

John A. Shoup

Islam requires that all believers perform five major acts that demonstrate belonging to the community. These Five Pillars of Faith are: (1) Declaration of Faith, or the *shahadah*; (2) Prayer, or *salat*, at five prescribed times during the day; (3) Fasting, or *siyam*, from dawn to dusk during the month of *Ramadan*; (4) Giving Alms, or *zakat*, usually at the end of *Ramadan*; and (5) **Pilgrimage**, or *haj*, to **Makkah** once during a lifetime, if it is possible. These are required of all Muslims no matter if they are **Sunni, Shi'ite,** or **Kharaji.**

The Declaration of Faith is a requirement of all Muslims and it is by saying it that a non-Muslim enters the community of believers. The Declaration states that there is no god but God and that **Muhammad** is the Messenger of God. To say this simple phrase in front of witnesses is to declare allegiance to Islam, and in this short, simple phrase two the most fundamental elements of Islam are stated. The unity of God is a fundamental point in Islam and in *Surat al-Ikhlas* it is clarified that for Muslims God has no partner and is eternal; neither begotten nor does he beget. When Muslims make the pilgrimage to Makkah they recite a line that says there is no god but God and he has no partners (*la Sharika lak*).

Old mosque in Shandaghah District of Dubai shows the traditional minaret design in the Gulf region. Gulf mosques tended to be small and modest until the arrival of oil monies, when more elaborate styles from Egypt or India became popular. Courtesy of John A. Shoup.

The second part of the Declaration of Faith is to acknowledge that Muhammad is the Prophet of God. Muhammad is referred to as the Seal of the Prophets or *Khatam al-Anbiya'*, meaning that there is no prophet after him; he is the last in the long line of prophets God has sent to guide man.

Shi'ites add another line to the Declaration of Faith, stating the 'Ali is the friend of God, or *wa 'Ali Wali Allah*. This addition separates Shi'ites from Sunnis because for Sunnis 'Ali ibn Abi Talib is one of the Rightly Guided Khalifahs elected by the council of Muslims and an exemplary man but no more than this. 'Ali was one of the closest companions of the Prophet and among the first converts to Islam; he was also the Prophet's cousin and his son-in-law. 'Ali married the Prophet's daughter, Fatimah Zahirah, and by her fathered Hasan and Hussein, who for the Shi'ites are the rightful heirs of the Prophet's political and religious authority. 'Ali was willing to give his life in place of the Prophet when the Quraysh plotted Muhammad's death prior to the *Hijrah* to **Madinah**. For some Shi'ites 'Ali takes on a greater role than that of even Muhammad with popular tales about the angel Gabriel mistaking Muhammad for 'Ali when the first *Surah* of the Qur'an was revealed.

Muslims are expected to pray five times a day in the direction of Makkah. Originally Muhammad told his followers to pray facing Jerusalem, but in a revelation found in *Surat al-Baqarah* the direction was changed to Makkah and the

Ka'abah. It is believed that the first Ka'abah was built by Ibrahim (Abraham) and his son Isma'il (Ishmael) following God's command to sacrifice Isma'il. God sent an angel to stop Ibrahim's hand, and a lamb was substituted for the boy. Following the sacrifice of the lamb, the two men set about building the first house of worship to the one God. Muslims believe that God set the five times for prayer: dawn, or *fajar*; noon, or *dhuhur*; mid-afternoon, or *'asr*; dusk, or *maghrib*; and nighttime, or *'ishiyah*. Prayer time is announced by the *adhan*, called out by the *mu'adhdhin* from a minaret or from the roof of the mosque. It is held that once the first mosque in Madinah was completed, it was debated how to announce prayer times. Different suggestions were made—a drum (but it was associated too much with war), a horn (like the Jews), and a bell (like the Christians)—but all were rejected. It was then suggested the human voice should be used as was in a dream by the companion of the Prophet, 'Umar ibn al-Khattab, and Bilal, one of the first companions of the Prophet, was asked to use his beautiful voice to announce prayer time. Bilal devised the words of the *adhan*. The call to prayer states "God is Great. I witness that there is no god but God and I witness that Muhammad is the Messenger of God. Come to prayer. Come to success. God is Great. I witness there is no god but God."

Each of the prayers is composed of several prostrations or *ruka'*, which vary according to the time of day. Each of these is composed of nine attitudes of prayer: from standing straight with the arms usually folded across the chest, bending at the waist, kneeling on the ground, placing the forehead on the ground with the palms of the hands flat, rising back up to the kneeling position with the feet folded underneath, and standing again. The different schools in Sunni Islam teach slightly different ways of doing these movements, and Shi'ites place their foreheads on a round, flat ceramic disk that contains dirt from Najaf or Karbala, where *Imams* 'Ali ibn Abi Talib and his son Hussein are buried. When prayer is completed the angels sitting on the right and left shoulders are greeted and then people shake hands and greet each other in brotherhood in a public display of what the Prophet said: "All people are like the teeth of a comb before God."

Fasting is done during the month of *Ramadan* from dawn to dusk by all Muslims that have reached a certain age and who are able. Pregnant women, the sick, injured, travelers, and others are exempted from fasting although many fast anyway. During the daytime it is not lawful to eat, drink, smoke, or allow anything to pass the lips. In **Saudi Arabia** the fast is imposed on everyone in all public places, whereas in much of the Gulf fasting is not required of non-Muslims, but anyone not fasting must find a secluded place where no Muslims can see them breaking the fast.

The fast is traditionally broken at the *maghrib* call to prayer with milk and **dates** or a drink made of water, dates, dried fruit, and nuts. Most Muslims then pray the *maghrib* prayer before eating. In some parts of the Gulf and Saudi Arabia this first meal is small following the *sunnah* of the Prophet and a larger meal is eaten after the *'ishiyah* prayer. However, today most people indulge in a major feast shortly after the *maghrib* prayer. A last meal called *suhur* is eaten before the *fajar* prayer. In the past a person called a *masharti or musahir* was hired to walk around playing a drum to wake people up for the meal, although this is rarely done today. *Suhur* needs to be finished some fifteen to twenty minutes before the call to prayer and this time is called *msak*, meaning to grab up and put away anything that is still uneaten.

At the end of *Ramadan* those who can are expected to give one-tenth of their wealth to the poor, called *zakat*. This is to be done in such a way as to not know who specifically is giving or who is receiving in order to preserve the **honor** and dignity of all. Those giving should not become proud and boastful of their actions, and those receiving should not be made to feel indebted. Today, in many countries, **companies** or governments include a monthly deduction from employees' salaries that is given to a division within the Ministries of Religious Affairs.

The last required practice is the pilgrimage to Makkah. This is an obligation but with the stipulation for those who can, meaning both financially and physically. There are two different types of pilgrimage. The *'umrah*, or small pilgrimage, can be done at any time of year, and the person performing it does not do all of the steps required in the *haj*, or main pilgrimage that is to be done over the first ten days of the month of *Dhu al-Hijjah*, or the Month of Pilgrimage, which is the last month of the Muslim **calendar**. Most of the steps in the *haj* take place during the first nine days and follow those first set out by the Prophet Muhammad. On the tenth day, the main Islamic holiday *'Id al-Adha*, or Feast of Sacrifice, takes place where Muslims follow the example of Ibrahim and sacrifice a sheep.

All Muslim males are circumcised following the example of Ibrahim and the Abrahamic traditions. Circumcision is considered an act of purification, and although *khitan* is the Arabic word for circumcision, the word *mudhahir*, or purified, is often used instead. It is held that for a male to open and read the Qur'an, he should already be circumcised. As a result, the general practice is that boys should be circumcised while they are still very young. Female circumcision seems to have been introduced to the **Arabian Peninsula** from the Horn of Africa or the Sudan, where the practice is widespread among all religions. Female circumcision is not part of Islamic practice and is not endorsed by Islamic scholars, yet it remains a practice perpetuated by women in some parts of the Peninsula.

See also **Holidays and Festivals: Islamic**.

J

Jabal al-Akhdar War

John A. Shoup

The Jabal al-Akhdar War, or Jabal War, was fought between the *Sultan* of **Oman**, **Sa'id bin Taymur**, and the *Imam* of **Nizwa**, Ghalib bin 'Ali al-Hina'i, from 1954 to 1959. The *Imamate* based in Nizwa had been able to exercise independent authority over much of the Omani interior starting in 1913, when most of the tribes refused to recognize *Sultan* Taymur bin Faysal and elected Salim bin Rashid al-Kharusi as the *Imam*. In 1920, an agreement was signed that established a modus vivendi between the two. When Sa'id bin Taymur became *Sultan* in 1932 he began trying to re-establish ties with tribes in the interior, and following his successful bid to oust the Saudis from al-Buraymi in 1952 he was able to win over several of the major tribes that had been loyal to the *Imam*.

Feeling increasingly under pressure from the *Sultan*, the *Imam* tried to establish ties with the **Arab League** and be recognized as an independent state in 1954. The *Imam* had strong support from both the Saudis and the Arab nationalists who viewed the *Sultan* as a puppet of the British. Despite strong political support, neither the Saudis nor the Arab nationalists were able to send much material support to the *Imam*. The bid to be recognized as an independent state prompted the *Sultan* to march with his forces and occupy Nizwa, the *Imam's* capital, in 1955. The *Imam's* brother, Talib, fled to Cairo, where he was able to obtain a degree of help from the Arab nationalists, whereas the *Imam* himself was sent to internal exile in his home village. The feelings of anger against the *Sultan* continued, especially among the Bani Riyam tribe whose traditional lands are in Jabal al-Akhdar, which rises up behind Nizwa. Talib returned in 1957 and with his brother Ghalib escaped into the **mountains**. The leaders of the Bani Riyam tribe took the side of the *Imam*, as did several other tribes from Jabal al-Akhdar.

The *Imam's* troops were able to hold out against attacks by the *Sultan's* army and inflicted several defeats on it as well. When the *Sultan's* army would try to attack rebel positions the tribesmen would disappear into the mountains, making them nearly impossible to fight. The situation was stalemated until reluctantly the *Sultan* called on British assistance (Sa'id had been trying to distance himself from the British as much as possible). The British ground troops and artillery were equally ineffective in fighting tribesmen loyal to the *Imam*. In the end Royal Air Force squads were called in to bomb rebel towns and villages. Several were destroyed, including the Bani Riyam tribal capitals of Birkat al-Mawz and Tanuf. As a result of the aerial bombings, the *Imam*, his brother, and the Bani Riyam *shaykhs* surrendered, ending the war in 1959.

FURTHER READING

Owtran, Francis. *Modern History of Oman: Formation of the State since 1920*. London: I.B. Tauris, 2004.
Peterson, J.E. *Oman at War: The Sultanate's Struggle for Supremacy*. London: Saqi Books, 2008.
Rabi, Uzi. *The Emergence of State in a Tribal Society: Oman under Saʿid bin Taymur, 1932–1970*. London: Sussex Academic Press, 2005.

Jahiliyah
Sebastian Maisel

According to Islamic historiography, the time of ignorance, in Arabic *jahiliyah*, is the period between the creation of the world and the proclamation of Islam by **Muhammad**. During the time of the *jahiliyah*, people did not accept divine revelations or only partly accepted those and therefore must be considered ignorant toward the true and final message of Islam. Generally, Muslims evaluate the culture and life of their predecessors negatively, except with regard to literature and some legal customs. In pre-Islamic Arabia, poetry was considered the highest form of artistic expression, a status that was preserved during the early years of Islamic development. The works of poets of the *jahiliyah*, such as ʿAntarah ibn Shaddad, Imruʾ al-Qays, or Tarafah ibn al-ʿAbd, still maintain a superior position in Arabic literature. Collections of their poems in the famous *muʿallaqat*, or suspended odes, are fine examples of pre-Islamic poetry that are still revered today. Much can be identified from the knowledge of pre-Islamic poetry, for example, detailed information on customs and the lifestyle of the people. Other *jahiliyah* qualities of the people of Arabia before Islam that are still held in high esteem include **honor**, bravery, hospitality, and chivalry. Poets traveled around the land reciting famous poems of tribal war and love and also served as messengers of political news and rainfall. Every year at the marketplace al-ʿUkaz near **Makkah**, the best poets competed in a contest for the best poem, which was then stitched on the cover of the Kaʿabah and hung onto it, visible for all, *muʿallaq* in Arabic.

For many Islamic historians *jahiliyah* was a time period to ignore. The distinct culture of Arabia developed many centuries ago and continued to influence even the Prophet Muhammad. Constant tribal warfare and raids between settled farmers in the **oases** and nomadic groups in the adjunct areas characterized life in Arabia before Islam. Although central Arabia did not develop states, Arabs in Syria, Iraq, the Gulf coast, **Oman**, and **Yemen** have long histories of kingdoms in the pre-Islamic period. These kingdoms were prosperous and attracted foreign invaders such as the Romans, Abyssinians, and Persians. In central Arabia, settled life centered on the oases of Khaybar, Yathrib (later called **al-Madinah**), and **Makkah**. In those settlements, Jewish and Christian groups gained strong support and eventually the majority. Ethnically, the inhabitants were Arabs speaking more or less the same language with dialect varieties. Their society was organized along tribal lines with collective rights and duties. Loyalty to the kin-group was imperative, because the extended family provided protection and access to the resources. The economy was based on small-scale farming, usually tending the **date** palm groves, animal husbandry, crafts, or trade. Makkah enjoyed special privileges as the place of the annual pilgrimage to worship their polytheistic idols in the Ka'abah. Since it was also an important trading point on the caravan route, it soon turned into the main urban center in central Arabia. Masters of Makkah were the Quraysh, who monopolized control of the Ka'abah and many trading privileges. When Muhammad brought Islam, he abolished many *jahiliyah* practices, such as the custom to bury infant girls or the lawlessness regarding women, but most importantly he cleansed the Ka'abah from objects of worship other than to God. Other customs he continued; however, the polytheistic, tribal society reached its end and was actively transformed and incorporated into the new Islamic community.

See also **Arabic Language**; **Madinah**.

FURTHER READING

Hitti, Philip. *History of the Arabs: From the Earliest Times to the Present.* London: Macmillan, 1956.

Hoyland, Robert. *Arabia and the Arabs: From the Bronze Age to the Coming of Islam.* London: Routledge, 2001.

Peters, F.E. *The Arabs and Arabia on the Eve of Islam.* Brookfield, VT: Ashgate, 1999.

Philby, Harry St. John Bridger. *The Background of Islam: Being a Sketch of Arabian History in Pre-Islamic Times.* London: Whitehead, Morris, 1947.

Shahid, Irfan. "Pre-Islamic Arabia," in *The Cambridge History of Islam*, edited by P.M. Holt et al. Cambridge, UK: Cambridge University Press, 1978.

Janadiriyah Heritage Festival
Sebastian Maisel

The various activities to preserve the traditional **Saudi Arabia**n culture culminate in the annual *Janadiriyah* Festival, which is organized by the Saudi Arabian National Guard under the direct leadership of King 'Abdallah. The venue is an open-air museum and arena with pavilions and showcases for every region in the kingdom, where cultural exhibits are shown. During the two-week-long event, every region introduces its cultural treasures, including **dance** and **music** shows, readings, poetry competitions, traditional markets for crafts and artifacts, food displays, and the like.

Visitors to the Janadiriyah Festival, Saudi Arabia. Courtesy of Sebastian Maisel.

Some decades ago, Janadiriyah was a small, quiet village in the Qasim province and the proximity of Riyadh, which was visited occasionally by some **Bedouin** tribes during the dry summer season. Today, the same place has turned into a magnet for thousands of visitors of the festival. One of the main attractions is the annual **camel** race, with more than 2,000 participating camels and jockeys. Even the King and Crown Prince attend the races and dedicate valuable cash and other prizes for the winners. It was the initiative of the then Crown Prince and now King 'Abdallah, who as the commander of the National Guard, a military unit based on tribal forces, to extend the small-scale event and turn it into a national event with the objective to depict and preserve the changing culture of the kingdom.

Among the festival's other goals are the confirmation of the country's religious and social values, the reactivation of customs and traditions, the combination of the country's **cultural heritage** with the achievements of a modern society, and the showing of the rapid change of daily life. In the meantime, the festival became a spectacle of significant size that required adequate organization and financing. Over 1 million visitors attended in 2006 and 2007, and the number is predicted to grow. New exhibitions, products, and ideas were added to the program; for example, a musical (a huge innovation for a country that does not have any theaters, operas, or other public showplaces), art and book exhibits, a competition to recite the Qur'an, international workshops, and special events for women only and families. In 2008, for the first time, a foreign country (Turkey) was presented as one of the festival's themes in order to reach out to international and domestic tourists.

Janadariyah became the space in Saudi Arabia where local and regional aspects blend into a national Saudi culture, a process that is not always smooth and stirs some controversy given the attempts of **Najd**, the central province, to homogenize culture and tradition. But despite occasional complaints about unfair treatment of non-Najdi participants from the **Asir**, **Hijaz**, or the Eastern Province, the festival has secured a solid position in the process of preserving Saudi heritage. The festival attracts a large number of Saudis, including the youth, because of the wide variety of entertainment, exhibits, food stalls, etc. The wide appeal of the festival to Saudi nationals should not be a surprise given the usual lack of public entertainment or activities other than going to shopping malls. The festival is broadcasted on Saudi **television** and local newspapers, providing a rare platform to discuss cultural development in public.

FURTHER READING

Campbell, Kay L. "Folk Music and Dance in the Arabian Gulf and Saudi Arabia," in *Images of Enchantment: Visual and Performing Arts of the Middle East*, edited by Sherifa Zuhur, 57–69. Cairo: American University of Cairo Press, 1998.
Clark, Arthur. "A Festival at Janadriyah," *Saudi Aramco World* 36, no. 5 (1985): 2–7.
Long, David. *Culture and Customs of Saudi Arabia*. Westport, CT: Greenwood Press, 2005.

Jannabah
John A. Shoup

The Jannabah tribe is one of the largest and most important in the Sharqiyah or eastern region of **Oman**, numbering over 5,000 people. The tribe has historically supported the Ghafiri (northern) bloc politically but does not have a Ghafiri origin itself. In the past they dominated the town of Sur and the whole coast stretching far to the south. They played an important role in Oman's overseas empire and made Sur the major port for the importation of slaves from East Africa. Jannabah were important in the Omani settlements in East Africa, and many are bilingual in Arabic and Swahili. During the height of the East African trade most of the *shaykh*s of the various lineages that compose the Jannabah established residences along the coast. Following the end of the slave trade by the British in the second half of the nineteenth century and Oman's split into Zanzibar and mainland Oman, the Jannabah turned their attention inland and moved their tribal capital from Sur to 'Izz. **Pastoral nomadism** and **oasis date** production replaced ocean trade as the main activities of the tribesmen.

The Jannabah did not have exclusive control over much of the inland areas used for pastoralism but shared them with both the **Wahibah** and the **Duru'**. Conflict over grazing lands claimed by the different tribes was a frequent occurrence well into the twentieth century, and tribal warfare ended only with the unification of the entire country in the 1950s under *Sultan* **Sa'id**. The Jannabah are known for absorbing numerous other tribes and lineages into their tribal organization through adoption. Not only have they brought in Arabs from the Harith and Al Bu 'Ali tribes, but many Baluch have also been fully absorbed into

Jannabah lineages. The process is swift, and within a few generations those absorbed have been fully incorporated into the Jannabah with no distinctions being made with those of "pure" Jannabah origin. This may help explain why the tribe follows the general politics of the Ghafiri bloc yet is of Hinawi origin.

The Jannabah have maintained several customs, perhaps pre-Islamic, that are unique to them. Jannabah brides run away from their grooms and it is the responsibility of the groom to find her and bring her back. There are stories of this hide-and-seek game between brides and grooms taking months, and even of grooms coming back empty-handed in disgust and frustration. Through hiding from the groom, Jannabah women demonstrate their abilities to manage **camels** and live in the **desert** unassisted by a man, perhaps as a warning to her potential husband of her independence. Similar customs around kidnapping or capturing brides were recorded in other parts of pre-Islamic Arabia. The other custom is that the Jannabah lineages near Jazir along the coast hold the sea turtle in special regard, what some have called a tribal totem. They are among the few tribal people in Arabia that still hold to totemism.

*See also **Jahiliyah**.*

FURTHER READING

Carter, J.R.L. *Tribes in Oman*. London: Peninsular Publishing, 1982.
Richardson, Niel, and Marcia Dorr. *The Craft Heritage of Oman*. Dubai: Motivate Publishing, 2003.
Thesiger, Wilfred. *Crossing the Sands*. Dubai: Motivate Publishing, 2006.

Al Jazeera
Bouziane Zaid

Al Jazeera, initially an international 24-hour Arab-language news and current affairs channel, was launched in 1996. Headquartered in **al-Dawhah**, **Qatar**, Al Jazeera started with a $150 million grant from the **Emir** of Qatar, *Shaykh* Hamad bin Khalifah. It has since then expanded into a network that includes the **Internet** and specialty television channels with broadcasting centers based in major world capitals. Al Jazeera's Web-based English and Arabic news services are editorially independent, with their own selection of news and commentary. Al Jazeera **television** network includes two **Arabic-language** sports channels, Al Jazeera Sports +1 and Al Jazeera Sports +2, launched respectively in 2003 and 2004; Al Jazeera Mubashir, modeled after C-Span and BBC Parliament, was launched in 2005 and broadcasts conferences in real time without editing or commentary; Al Jazeera Children's Channel was launched in 2005; Al Jazeera English was launched in 2006 and is a 24-hour English-language global news channel; and Al Jazeera Documentary Channel is an Arabic-language documentary channel that was launched in 2007. The stations' major sources of income include advertising, cable subscription fees, broadcasting deals with other **companies**, and sales of footage.

When launched in 1996, the Al Jazeera Arabic news channel was said to have changed the television landscape of the Middle East. Unlike the state-owned and state-censored national television stations of the Middle East, Al Jazeera presented controversial views about the governments of many Arab states. Al Jazeera exposed unethical, immoral, and illegal behavior by individuals, businesses, and governments in the Middle East. This level of freedom and independence in news reporting was previously unheard of in many of these countries. For the first time, people in the region had access to a free and independent source of news and comment that was neither under the control of dictatorial regimes nor Western states or corporations. The main slogans that Al Jazeera uses are *"al-Rai wa rai al akhar"* (the opinion and the other opinion) and *"minbaru man la minbara lah"* (the platform of whoever does not have a platform). Al Jazeera gave an Arab world hungry for information and debate the means to talk to itself and possibly shape its future.

Al Jazeera's broadcasts have therefore resulted in controversies involving many countries such as **Saudi Arabia**, Iraq, **Bahrain**, and Algeria. For example, on January 27, 1999, the Algerian government cut the electricity supplies to large parts of its capital to prevent television audiences from watching Al Jazeera's program *al-Itijah al-Muakass* ("The Opposite Direction"), in which critics of the Algerian government were speaking live. In general, since Al Jazeera started broadcasting in 1996, Arab countries have imposed and lifted bans on the station because it had aired a program that was deemed insulting to the Arab regimes.

When Al Jazeera was launched in 1996, it was praised by the United States as a brave step toward liberalization of the Middle Eastern media, but that all changed after September 2001 and the U.S. invasions of Afghanistan and Iraq. The station first gained widespread attention following the September 11, 2001 attacks when it broadcasted videos in which **Usamah bin Ladin** and other **Al Qa'idah** members defended and justified the attacks. This led the U.S. government to accuse Al Jazeera of engaging in propaganda on behalf of terrorists. Al Jazeera responded by stating that the station was merely sharing information and that they did not comment on the footage.

Al Jazeera's coverage of the 2001 invasion of Afghanistan and the 2003 invasion of Iraq also triggered strong protests from U.K. and U.S. officials. They both claimed that Al Jazeera's news coverage was biased against the United States and the West. Al Jazeera's response was that their coverage of the war made it more difficult for the United States and the United Kingdom to control the way the war was being reported.

Al Jazeera's offices in Kabul and Baghdad were bombed by the United States; its Baghdad correspondent, Tariq Ayyub, was killed, and its Kabul correspondent, Taysir Alluni, was arrested in Spain in 2003 and charged with terrorism. Al Jazeera cameraman Sami Al Hajj has been imprisoned as an "enemy combatant" at the U.S. naval base at Guantánamo Bay, Cuba, for five years. Pakistani police arrested him in December 2001 while he was on his way to a news assignment in Afghanistan.

Critics and scholars accuse Al Jazeera of sensationalism, and they use the notion of contextual objectivity to describe the station's controversial yet popular news approach. Critics claim that Al Jazeera aims to increase its audience share by striking a balance between audience appeal and objectivity.

See also **Jiddah.**

Jewelry
Carla Higgins

Traditionally, almost all jewelry in the Gulf was made of silver. Jewelry was frequently worn as an amulet to protect against the evil eye and misfortune. A common amulet throughout the Gulf was the *hirz*, a small, decorated, rectangular or cylindrical silver container that held verses of the Qur'an, or sometimes a spell, and was worn around the neck as a pendant on a leather cloth or string cord. Jewelry may include stones of red or blue, because these two colors have protective qualities, regardless of whether they are of glass, a stone such as carnelian, a discarded bead, or a red reflector—the color of the object was important, not the material. Another example of an amuletic use of jewelry was a beltlike silver chain (*manjad* in **Oman**) worn under clothing, draped from one shoulder across the chest.

Jewelry is a sign of wealth, security, and status. Jewelry is gifted to women as part of the marriage price (*mahr*), women receive jewelry throughout their lives, and jewelry is a wearable investment. Jewelry is and was women's currency. In the case of **divorce**, women keep all jewelry. When women have extra cash, they purchase jewelry for themselves. When a husband shows his regard, he gifts his wife with jewelry.

Jewelry is worn as personal adornment, and in a society that places a high value on aesthetics and traditionally had few material possessions, jewelry is and was an important component of the female aesthetic. Women wore jewelry all of the time and everywhere. They might wear toe rings, rings on every finger, bracelets, necklaces, and hair ornaments, and this jewelry could be attached to their clothing, under their clothing, and on headdresses and hats. On special occasions they wear more as a status display and to celebrate. Women also wear jewelry while performing ordinary daily tasks.

Sources of silver were primarily the Maria Theresa dollar or thaler and other coinage. Because custom is that a woman's jewelry upon her death is melted down and recast or reworked, much of the silver in use today has been used and re-used for many, many years and may represent, in some cases, ancient silver.

Silversmithing is done by men and women—this varies from region to region. Silversmiths were located in many larger towns, especially those with ports. **Yemen** is known for its superb silverwork prior to the 1950s, when silversmiths, who were primarily Jewish, left for Israel. **Oman** is known for the quality of its silver jewelry in terms of workmanship and high silver content. Craft centers such as **Nizwa** and **Bahla** provided a great deal of jewelry for the Gulf region.

Silversmith in the Omani town of Bahla works on a new piece of jewelry. Bahla is well-known for a number of crafts, including pottery, weaving, and silver work. The smith here makes use of older, traditional methods of making jewelry and more modern elements such as a gas torch. Courtesy of John A. Shoup.

Today gold is preferred and is easily affordable. Gold jewelry is available in traditional, Gulf, and Middle Eastern styles, and a considerable amount of jewelry from India is available. Huge amounts of gold are purchased in the Gulf; for example, shoppers in the **United Arab Emirates** spend thirty times more on gold than the rest of the world, and **Dubai** imported 522 tons of gold in 2005.

FURTHER READING

Richardson, Neil, and Marcia Dorr. *The Craft Heritage of Oman*. Dubai: Motivate Publishing, 2003.

Ross, Heather Colyer. *Bedouin Jewelry of Saudi Arabia*. London: Stacey International, 1983.

Topham, John et al. *Traditional Crafts of Saudi Arabia*. London: Stacey International, 2005.

Jiddah

Sebastian Maisel

Jiddah (Jeddah), a seaport on the Red Sea, is the largest city in western Arabia and the **Hijaz**. The coastline of the Red Sea is filled with coral reefs, and only at the location of Jiddah is it possible to find a natural harbor. From this the city benefited in pre-Islamic times, and over time the city developed a distinct urban culture similar to those in **Makkah** and **Madinah**. In 646, the third caliph, 'Uthman, developed Jiddah to become the seaport for pilgrims from Egypt and other places of the Islamic Empire. Later other ruling dynasties of the Islamic Empire took control of the city, such as the Ayyubids and Mamluks. After the conquest of large territories in **Yemen**, the Ottoman Empire took over the city in 1532 and fortified it with walls and towers; however, continual resistance of local tribes forced the Ottomans out a century later, and the city enjoyed semi-independence.

In the beginning of the nineteenth century, Jiddah was drawn into the conflict between Muhammad 'Ali, the ruler of Egypt, and the **Wahhabi**s of central Arabia, who at one point extended their emirate all the way to Makkah and Jiddah. Until its destruction by Wahhabis, a huge shrine for Eve existed outside of the city walls. The name Jiddah comes from the Arabic for grandmother, referring to Eve's grave, which was a regional shrine and place of worship and pilgrimage. But because Wahhabism denounces worshipping saints and tombs, the place was destroyed. In 1840, the city once again was occupied by Ottoman and Egyptian forces and remained under nominal Ottoman control until World War I. The real rulers of Jiddah were the Grand *Sharif*s of Makkah, whose main occupation was to ensure a safe and smooth *Hajj*-season every year. The city was visited and frequented by Europeans, and Western banks and trade houses were well established. In 1916 it was incorporated into the Kingdom of Hijaz, and in 1925 it was conquered by **'Abd al-'Aziz ibn Sa'ud**, *Sultan* of **Najd** and later King of **Saudi Arabia**.

Because the Hijaz in general and Jiddah in particular were accustomed to foreigners, 'Abd al-'Aziz made Jiddah the seat of the government and foreign embassies, starting a long-lasting rivalry with the official capital, Riyadh. In 1970, Jiddah was still larger in population than Riyadh with approximately 250,000 inhabitants. Today the city is part of a triangle conglomerate that connects with the Holy City of Makkah and the resort town **Ta'if** in the **mountains**. The city alone has a population of 3.5 million.

As the largest and most open city in the Hijaz, Jiddah developed a special cosmopolitan taste and style with regard to **architecture**, food, and clothing. In addition, the lifestyle of people in Jiddah was faster and more Western-oriented than of those in the central region. As such, the first newspapers (1946) and radio station (1948) of Saudi Arabia were introduced in Jiddah. An active and vibrant art scene in painting, sculpture, and literature make the city an intellectual center in the kingdom. Most visible is a series of open-air sculptures depicting features of modern and traditional life along the corniche road. The traditional architecture of Jiddah is represented by large multistory buildings made of coral rock or stone and decorated with enclosed wooden balconies. More than 500 of those houses are currently under reconstruction in order to preserve the ambience of the old city.

Several **wadis** from the Hijaz Mountains drain out into the plains of Jiddah, most important among them the Wadi Fatimah, which in the past provided potable water to the city until desalination plants were built in the 1960s. Jiddah is the most important center for trade and transportation in the western region of Saudi Arabia and a notable industrial location that includes refineries, power plants, assembly plants, and steel and cement factories. The port of Jiddah is the largest in the kingdom. The international airport built in 1981 has a special terminal for pilgrims that during *Hajj* season is the busiest in the world and frequented annually by several million passengers who arrive in Jiddah by plane, ferry, or bus. From Jiddah to Makkah, their ultimate destination spans a multilane highway connecting the two major cities in a relatively short time.

Jiddah is home to the King **'Abd al-'Aziz ibn Al Sa'ud al-'Aziz** University with some 80,000 students, several colleges (Prince Sultan College for Tourism, Effat College, Dar al-Hikmah), and newspapers (*Arab News, al-Madinah, al-Bilad*), but it has no library of national significance. Other significant international organizations headquartering in Jiddah are the **Organization of Islamic Countries** and the International Association of Islamic Banks. Domestic **companies** and institutions include Saudi Arabian Airlines and the Jiddah Economic Forum.

FURTHER READING

Buchan, James. *Jeddah—Old and New*. London: Stacey International, 1982.
Farsi, Hani M.S. *Jeddah, City of Art: The Sculptures and Monuments*. London: Stacey International, 1991.
Pesce, Angelo. *Jiddah—Portrait of an Arabian City*. London: Falcon Press, 1976.
Tarabulsi, Mohammed Yosuf. *Jeddah: A Story of a City*. Riyadh: King Fahd National Library, 2006.

Jihad
Jack Kalpakian

Jihad has become one of the most hotly contested and controversial words in international affairs. In traditional forms of Islam, both **Sunni** and **Shi'ite**, there have been at least two forms of *Jihad*: the inner or greater, and the outer or lesser. The inner form of *Jihad* concerns the resistance believers have to put up within themselves against the temptations of life and the forces of evil. It is primarily focused on self-restraint rather than the projection of force outward. The lesser or outer forms of *Jihad* are not necessarily violent. Under *Sunni* classification schemes, the lesser *Jihad* is divided into three forms: tongue, hand, and sword. The *Jihad* of the tongue is to speak out against evil and take a clear stance in confrontation to it. The *Jihad* of the hand concerns taking action against evil, and this need not be violent. The final form, the *Jihad* of the sword, is the form that has been most recently identified as *Jihad* writ large. Under this last form, the believer is exhorted to engage in combat to defend his religious community or country against an external attack. This military action is governed by an Islamic law of war that strictly limited the targets of military action and the consequences for civilian noncombatants, but it did allow for slavetaking.

The rise of Islamism as a political force in the twentieth century led to renewed emphasis on this small part of the tradition of *Jihad*. For some Islamist thinkers like Sayyid Qutb, *Jihad* was seen as warfare to establish global Muslim hegemony. Restraint for him came only as a result of tactical necessity and not principle. The *Jihad* of the sword came to contain the whole meaning of the word with the other forms ignored or forgotten. Within the context of **Saudi Arabia** and the **Gulf Cooperation Council** states, this last form of *Jihad* historically took place between the **Wahhabi** community and other Muslim communities in the **Arabian Peninsula**, but it also was used to justify wars within the Wahhabi community. The raids conducted by Saudi forces against Ottoman-controlled cities in the **Hijaz** during the nineteenth century were justified as *Jihad*, as were the wars that gave the Saudi family control over most of the Arabian Peninsula in the twentieth century, concluding with the conquest of the Hijaz in 1925. The ***Ikhwan*** movement used by **'Abd al-'Aziz ibn Sa'ud** to conquer the vast majority of the Arabian Peninsula believed itself to be fighting a *Jihad* to purify Islam from negative and pagan influences. Many of the people involved with violent movements like Al Qa'idah believe themselves to be on a *Jihad* to protect Islam against the encroachment of infidels and against the defilement of Muslim lands by nonbelievers. Although the interpretation of *Jihad* as warfare is currently dominant, Islamic history has shown that the word has many different meanings and it could morph back to its "greater" definition again, perhaps as the futility of warfare begins to be felt more strongly by the *Jihadists* themselves.

See also **Islamic Fundamentalism—Salafiyah**; **Al Sa'ud**.

FURTHER READING

Ahmed, Irfan. "The Destruction of the Holy Places," *Islamica Magazine* 15, (2006). Available at http://www.islamicamagazine.com/Issue-15/The-Destruction-of-Holy-Sites-in-Mecca-and-Medina.html (last accessed October 13, 2008).

Esposito, John. *Islam: The Straight Path*. Oxford, UK: Oxford University Press, 1998.

Lewis, Bernard. *The Crisis of Islam*. New York: Random House, 2004.

Metz, Helen Chapin (ed.). *Saudi Arabia: A Country Study*. Washington, D.C.: Government Printing Office for the Library of Congress, 1992.

Qutb, Sayyid. *Milestones*. Kazi Press, 1964. Available at http://www.kalamullah.com/Books/MILESTONES.pdf (last accessed October 13, 2008).

Jubayl
Sebastian Maisel

Jubayl, or Jubayl al-Bahri, is a port city in eastern **Saudi Arabia** on the **Arabian Gulf**. It is located sixty-two miles (100 kilometers) to the north of the urban center and tri-cities of **Dammam**, **Dhahran**, and Khobar, and has some 250,000 inhabitants. The climate is characterized by high humidity and occasional fog and mist. Winter weather is mildly cold, but the summer days are humid and hot. The area has less extensive **oases** and gardens than neighboring Qatif and **al-Hasa**. Historically, the area was long inhabited and maintained sea trade relations with the maritime center in Dilmun. People live mostly of fishing, trading, and **pearling**, their port being the port of entry for the capital city in Riyadh. The **Bani Khalid** tribe was the most influential in the city's vicinity. In 1933, the city became the landing spot for the first foreign **oil** exploration team. In the late 1960s Jubayl was a quiet fishing town with a small harbor and a base for the Royal Saudi Navy as the only outside employer.

In 1974, the former stretch of barren land, sand dunes, and salt flats was turned into a planned twin industrial city with **Yanbu'** on the Red Sea, and as such is part of an ambitious industrial development project with refineries, petrochemical, and other heavy industrial manufacturing, such as a steel mill, based on using excessive natural gas. Most of the city's traditional **architecture**, including several historical mosques, was demolished. A newly planned city in Western style and layout was to replace the old fishing village. According to the master plan of 1973, over the next three decades more than twenty industrial complexes, two deep-sea ports, and an international airport were supposed to be built. The project is coordinated by the Royal Commission for Yanbu' and Jubayl. A pipeline brings freshwater from the world's largest desalination plant to the capital in Riyadh. In 1982, a 727 mile (1,170 kilometer) long east-west double pipeline was constructed connecting Jubayl with Yanbu' and supplying energy for the many industrial projects in the twin city. Saudi Arabia Basic Industry Cooperation (SABIC) supervises most of the industrial facilities. The King Fahd Industrial Port of Jubayl is one of the biggest and busiest in the kingdom. An international consortium plans on building the first polysilicon plant using solar energy in Jubayl. In 1990, over 22,000 people were employed in the different industries, fifty-two percent of which were foreign guestworkers. An additional 15,000 people worked in the service and construction sector. The number of inhabitants grew subsequently, as did the infrastructural network of roads, housing, and industrial areas. The spread of urbanization will soon connect Jubayl with the already existing strip of urban settlement along the coastline stretching all the way down to Khobar.

FURTHER READING

Al-Shayeb, Abdallah A. *Al-Jubail: Saudi Village (Architectural Survey)*. Doha, Qatar: Arab Gulf States Folklore Center, 1985.

"Foundations," *Saudi Aramco World* 33, no. 6 (1982): 30–40.

King, Geoffrey. "Notes on Some Mosques in Eastern and Western Saudi Arabia," *Bulletin of the School of Oriental and African Studies* 43, no. 2 (1980): 251–276.

Pampanini, Andrea H. *Cities from the Arabian Desert: The Building of Jubail and Yanbu in Saudi Arabia*. Westport, CT: Praeger, 1997.

Judicial System

Sebastian Maisel

The judicial system of **Saudi Arabia** and the Arab Gulf States is based on the assumption that Islam and the Holy Qur'an are the primary source for the judiciary. Four major schools of interpreting the legal aspects of the Qur'an and the other legal sources in Islamic Law are the Maliki, Hanafi, Shafi'i, and Hanbali. The different branches of *Shi'ism* have their own schools of law, with the Ja 'afari School being the most widespread.

In Saudi Arabia, before the unification of the country under King **'Abd al- 'Aziz ibn Sa'ud**, individual judges derived their rulings from the school to which they belonged. In the western **Hijaz** Region, the Shafi'i and Hanafi Schools were dominant, whereas the central region saw the Hanbali School as the only major form of legal interpretation. The very personal way of dealing with legal issues gave religious legal scholars special importance, because the outcome of a trial was very much dependent on the individual's training and opinion. Another legal system existed far away from the urban settlements among the nomadic tribes, which applied their ancient code of **customary law** in front of tribal judges and notables. 'Abd al-'Aziz ibn Al Sa'ud combined the different judicial systems (tribal, Hijazi, and Najdi) and created a new form of judiciary that bases its rulings solemnly on the Qur'an and *Sunnah* without being limited to a specific school of thought or law. In 1927, a Royal decree was issued reorganizing the judicial system in three levels, expeditious courts, *Shari'ah* courts, and the High Commission of Judicial Supervision as the highest legal authority in the kingdom. *Shari'ah* courts have jurisdiction over any case that has no special assignment. The four levels of *Shari'ah* courts include minor, general, and cassation courts as well as the Supreme Judicial Council. The final appellate tribunal is the Board of Grievances under direct responsibility of the King. However, in reality, room for judicial interpretation is still given, and considering the dominance of scholars and judges from central Arabia, in **Najd** a tendency to apply Hanbali law can still be observed. Although slightly modified and extended, this original classification still exists. Because the country has no official constitution, in 1992 King **Fahd** decreed the Basic Law of Government, which defined the role of Islamic Law as well as the relationship between the executive, legislative, and judiciary branches. The legal system is administered by the Ministry of Justice; however, judges are most and foremost bound by the *Shari'ah*.

Kuwait has a constitution and after gaining independence in 1961 went on to codify its laws and regulations. Islam is the state religion and *Shari'ah* is the main source of legislation. This process continued in the 1980s with the codification of the Civil Code and Kuwaiti Code of Personal Status. The main Islamic school of law in Kuwait is the Maliki School, although the significant Shi'ite minority follows the Ja'afari interpretation. Three levels of courts hear all of the cases related to personal, civil, and criminal matters: the courts of first instance, high courts, and the Supreme Court.

Bahrain has long been exposed to the British legal tradition and therefore has a mixed system that includes important aspects of Islamic law. In the country's constitution, it is stated that Bahrain is an Arab Islamic State and *Shari'ah* is the main source of legislation. However, some differences with neighboring countries can be observed; for example, the country has a Ja'afari majority, but is governed by a Maliki minority. In addition, both secular and *Shari'ah* courts exist, the latter being divided in Sunni and Shi'a departments. Three levels of *Shari'ah* courts are found: junior and senior *Shari'ah* courts and the High *Shari'ah* Court of Appeal.

Qatar has a predominantly **Wahhabi** population but has strong British influences in the judicial system. It is an Islamic country with *Shari'ah* as the fundamental source of legislation. No permanent constitution exists; however, basic regulations define the status of executive and judiciary. The court system is also two-pronged with civil and religious *Shari'ah* courts, the latter being restricted to family law and some criminal matters. Judges at the two levels of *Shari'ah* courts (First Instance and Appeal) apply Hanbali law.

The **United Arab Emirates** adopted a permanent constitution in 1996 with Islam as the official state religion and *Shari'ah* as a primary source of legislation. The majority of the Emiratis are Sunnis, whereas a large minority are Shi'a. Most of the people in the country, however, are foreign nationals. The legal system of the seven emirates remains mostly uncodified with very few national regulations and many local exceptions. Only **Abu Dhabi** and **Sharjah** have some type of regulations for the otherwise independent *Shari'ah* courts.

After its independence in 1970, **Oman** issued limited codes on commercial, criminal, and tax law, but not in the personal status. A Basic Law similar to a constitution adopted in 1996 claims that Islam is the official state religion and the *Shari'ah* is the basis for legislation. The majority of the population follows the **Ibadi** branch of *Kharajism* with only small minorities of Sunnis and Shi'as. The judiciary is comprised of three levels of courts: *Shari'ah* courts, Magistrate Courts, and Specialized Courts. The highest level and court of appeal is the Complaints Committee. *Shari'ah* courts in general are increasingly limited in handling family law and a few criminal cases. The 1996 Basic Law introduced a new additional legal system comprising primary courts, appeals courts, and the Supreme Court, affirming the independence of the country's judiciary.

See also **Madhhab**.

FURTHER READING

Amin, S.H. *Middle East Legal Systems*. Glasgow, Scotland: Royston, 1985.

Al-Ghadyan, Ahmed A. "The Judiciary in Saudi Arabia," *Arab Law Quarterly* 13, no. 3 (1998): 235–251.

Mallat, Chibli. *Introduction to Middle Eastern Law*. New York: Oxford University Press, 2007.

Al-Muhairi, Butti Sultan. "The Development of the UAE Legal System and Unification with the Judicial System," *Arab Law Quarterly* 11, no. 2 (1996): 116–160.

Redden, Kenneth. *Modern Legal Systems Encyclopedia. Middle East*. Buffalo, NY: W.S. Hein, 1984.

al-Suwaidi, Ahmed, "Developments of the Legal Systems of the Gulf Arab States,"*Arab Law Quarterly* 8, no. 4 (1993): 289–301.

Vogel, Frank. *Islamic Law and Legal System: Studies of Saudi Arabia*. Leiden, The Netherlands: Brill, 2000.